Aden & the Indian Ocean Trade

AND MUSLIM

NETWORKS

Carl W. Ernst and

Bruce B. Lawrence,

editors

Aden & the Indian Ocean Trade

150 Years in the Life of a Medieval Arabian Port

ROXANI ELENI MARGARITI

The University *of* North Carolina Press | Chapel Hill

Manufactured in the United States of America

Designed by Kimberly Bryant
Set in ITC Galliard
by Tseng Information Systems, Inc.

This book was published with the assistance of the William R. Kenan Jr. Fund of the University of North Carolina Press.

The paper in this book meets the guidelines for permanence and durability of the Committee on Production Guidelines for Book Longevity of the Council on Library Resources.

Library of Congress Cataloging-in-Publication Data
Margariti, Roxani Eleni, 1969–
Aden and the Indian Ocean trade : 150 years in the life of a medieval Arabian port / Roxani Eleni Margariti. — 1st ed.
p. cm. — (Islamic civilization and Muslim networks)
Includes bibliographical references and index.
ISBN-13: 978-0-8078-3076-5 (cloth : alk. paper)
1. Aden (Yemen)—Commerce—History. 2. Indian Ocean Region—Commerce—History. 3. Shipping—Yemen—Aden—History. I. Title.
DS247.A27M37 2007
382.095335—dc22 2006023439

11 10 09 08 07 5 4 3 2 1

THIS BOOK WAS DIGITALLY PRINTED.

Contents

Foreword by Carl W. Ernst & Bruce B. Lawrence ix

Acknowledgments xi

Introduction 1

PART I. The Physical Entrepôt

1 | The Environment 33

2 | Topography of the Harbor 68

3 | Topography of the Port City 86

PART II. The Commercial Entrepôt

4 | The Customshouse 109

5 | Ships and Shipping 141

6 | Mercantile and Legal Services 176

Conclusion 206

Notes 215

Bibliography 307

Index 331

Figures, Maps, and Tables

FIGURES

Judeo-Arabic document from the Cairo Geniza 14

Satellite image of Aden peninsula 45

Schematic map of caravan routes connecting Aden with the rest of Yemen 54

The Crater area 73

Bird's-eye view of the port of Aden 84

Schematic plan of the medieval city of Aden 93

MAPS

1 | The Indian Ocean and the Eastern Mediterranean: Seas, Regions, and Main Ports 4

2 | The Gulf of Aden and the Southern Red Sea: Main Ports 36

3 | The Hinterland of Aden, Including Archaeological Sites 60

4 | The South Arabian Coast: Ports and Archaeological Sites East of Aden 172

TABLES

1 | Ibn al-Mujāwir's List of Entry and Exit Tolls 127

2 | Aden Exit Tolls in Geniza Documents 129

3 | Aden Import Taxes in Geniza Documents 130

Foreword

Aden and the Indian Ocean Trade: 150 Years in the Life of a Medieval Arabian Port is the sixth volume to be published in our series, Islamic Civilization and Muslim Networks.

Why make Islamic civilization and Muslim networks the theme of a new series? The study of Islam and Muslim societies is often marred by an overly fractured approach that frames Islam as the polar opposite of what "Westerners" are supposed to represent and advocate. Islam has been objectified as the obverse of the Euro-American societies that self-identify as "the West." Political and economic trends have reinforced a habit of localizing Islam in the "volatile" Middle Eastern region. Marked as dangerous foreigners, Muslims are also demonized as regressive outsiders who reject modernity. The negative accent in media headlines about Islam creates a common tendency to refer to Islam and Muslims as being somewhere "over there," in another space and another mind-set from the so-called rational, progressive, democratic West.

Ground-level facts tell another story. The social reality of Muslim cultures extends beyond the Middle East. It includes South and Southeast Asia, Africa, and China. It also includes the millennial presence of Islam in Europe and the increasingly significant American Muslim community. In different places and eras, it is Islam that has been the pioneer of reason, Muslims who have been the standard-bearers of progress. Muslims remain integral to "our" world; they are inseparable from the issues and conflicts of transregional, panoptic world history.

By itself, the concept of Islamic civilization serves as a useful counterweight to that of Western civilization, undermining the triumphalist framing of history that was reinforced first by colonial empires and then by the Cold War. Yet when the study of Islamic civilization is combined with that of Muslim networks, their very conjunction breaks the mold of both classical Orientalism and Cold War area studies. The combined rubric allows no discipline to stand by itself; all disciplines converge to make possible a refashioning of the Muslim past and a reimagining of the Muslim future. Islam escapes the timeless warp of textual norms; the additional perspectives of social sciences and modern technology forge a new hermeneutical strategy that marks ruptures as well as continuities, local influences as well as cosmopolitan accents. The twin goals of the publication series in which this volume appears are (1) to locate Islam in multiple pasts across several geo-linguistic, sociocultural frontiers, and (2) to open up a new kind of interaction between humanists and social scientists who engage contemporary Muslim societies. Networking between disciplines and breaking down discredited stereotypes will foster fresh interpretations of Islam that make possible research into uncharted subjects, including discrete regions, issues, and collectivities.

Because Muslim networks have been understudied, they have also been undervalued. Our accent is on the value to the study of Islamic civilization of understanding Muslim networks. Muslim networks inform the span of Islamic civilization, while Islamic civilization provides the frame that makes Muslim networks more than mere ethnic and linguistic subgroups of competing political and commercial empires. Through this broad-gauged book series, we propose to explore the dynamic past, but also to imagine an elusive future, both of them marked by Muslim networks. Muslim networks are like other networks: they count across time and place because they sustain all the mechanisms—economic and social, religious and political—that characterize civilization. Yet insofar as they are Muslim networks, they project and illumine the distinctive nature of Islamic civilization.

We want to make Muslim networks as visible as they are influential for the shaping and reshaping of Islamic civilization.

Carl W. Ernst & Bruce B. Lawrence, series editors

Acknowledgments

This project took off thanks to Abraham Udovitch and Mark Cohen, who exposed me to the wonderful world of the documentary Geniza and trained me in reading and analyzing Judeo-Arabic Geniza documents and in contextualizing the merchants' testimonies within a broader evidentiary and historiographic record. Their insights, patience, and encouragement over the years have been invaluable. In their expert curatorship of the S. D. Goitein Laboratory for Geniza Research at Princeton, they preserve and expand Goitein's formidable legacy and make of it an invaluable gift to future generations of scholars. I also owe a great deal to Molly Greene, a mentor, role model, and dear friend who has shaped my ideas about merchants, maritime trade, and mercantile culture; conversations with her about these topics have encouraged me to think comparatively and have kept me convinced of the relevance of my work on medieval Aden to the study of seaports and merchants across the seas and through the ages. Thomas Leisten read this work early on; his experience and insights into the material culture of Middle Eastern cities profoundly influenced my approach to the study of the medieval Arabian port.

Dan Varisco and Jere Bacharach read my manuscript patiently and repeatedly at different stages of preparation and offered invaluable and detailed advice. I am extremely grateful to both of them. Dan has been a great supporter of this project from the beginning and helped me enormously in fitting the study of Aden within the broader context of Yemeni historiography, which he knows so well. He exposed me to the newly emerging and marvelous world of Rasulid documents and supplied me not only with many references but also with volumes from Yemeni bookstores to which I would not have had access in the States.

I have also benefited immensely from conversations about port cities and coastal sites with architectural historian Nancy Um and archaeologist Axelle Rougeulle. I have been following their respective work on 18th-century al-Mukhā and the Hadrami ports with great interest, and I am grateful to both of them for contacting me and initiating fruitful and ongoing discussions of the questions that occupy us in common. The expert and incisive comments of G. Rex Smith and McGuire Gibson on Aden's topography challenged me to partly rethink my presentation of the harbor's reconstruction and generally kept me on my toes. Finally, I am grateful to a number of colleagues and friends in Atlanta; Princeton; and Athens, Greece, who read and commented on the text or otherwise offered their expertise in solving problems in the manuscript, including Orit Bashkin, Noa David, Tamer al-Leithy, Yossi Rapoport, Marina Rustow, Asma Sayeed, Petra Sijpesteijn, Lennart Sundelin, and Samer Trabulsi. Danae Stasinopoulou generously applied her design wizardry in producing the schematic topographic plan of the port.

While I am grateful to all the members of Emory University's Department of Middle Eastern and South Asian Studies for their sustained support and encouragement, I owe special thanks to Kristen Brustad, Shalom Goldman, and Devin Stewart. All three have been excellent advisers on the intricacies of the publication process and have helped me stay on track. In addition to generous encouragement and unflagging support, Kristen has also proofread and commented on large segments of the manuscript, often on short notice and always with remarkable insight, enthusiasm, and sensitivity.

Elaine Maisner at the University of North Carolina Press has guided this project to publication from my first contacts with the press to the final stages of manuscript preparation. I cannot imagine a more discerning, efficient, and encouraging guide, and I consider myself extremely fortunate to have had her support and advice. I am also grateful to Paula Wald for her guidance and especially to Ellen Goldlust-Gingrich for her patient and meticulous copyediting.

Finally, I am grateful to the deans of Emory College and the Graduate School at Emory for their generous publication support, to the Cambridge University Library Genizah Unit for providing a beautiful illustration of a famous Judeo-Arabic document, and to the American Institute for Yemeni Studies for sponsoring presentations of my work.

The completion of my work would have been impossible without the love and understanding of my family over many years and across long distances. I dedicate this book to them.

Aden & the Indian Ocean Trade

Introduction

Khurūj al-insān min al-baḥr ka-khurūjihi min al-qabr wa-al-furḍa ka-al-maḥshar fīhi al-munāqasha wa-al-muḥāsaba wa-al-wazn wa-al-ʿadad.

[A man's return from the sea is like his rise from the grave, and the port is like the place of congregation on the Day of Judgment: there is questioning, and settlement of accounts, and weighing, and counting.]

IBN AL-MUJĀWIR, *Ta'rīkh al-mustabṣir*

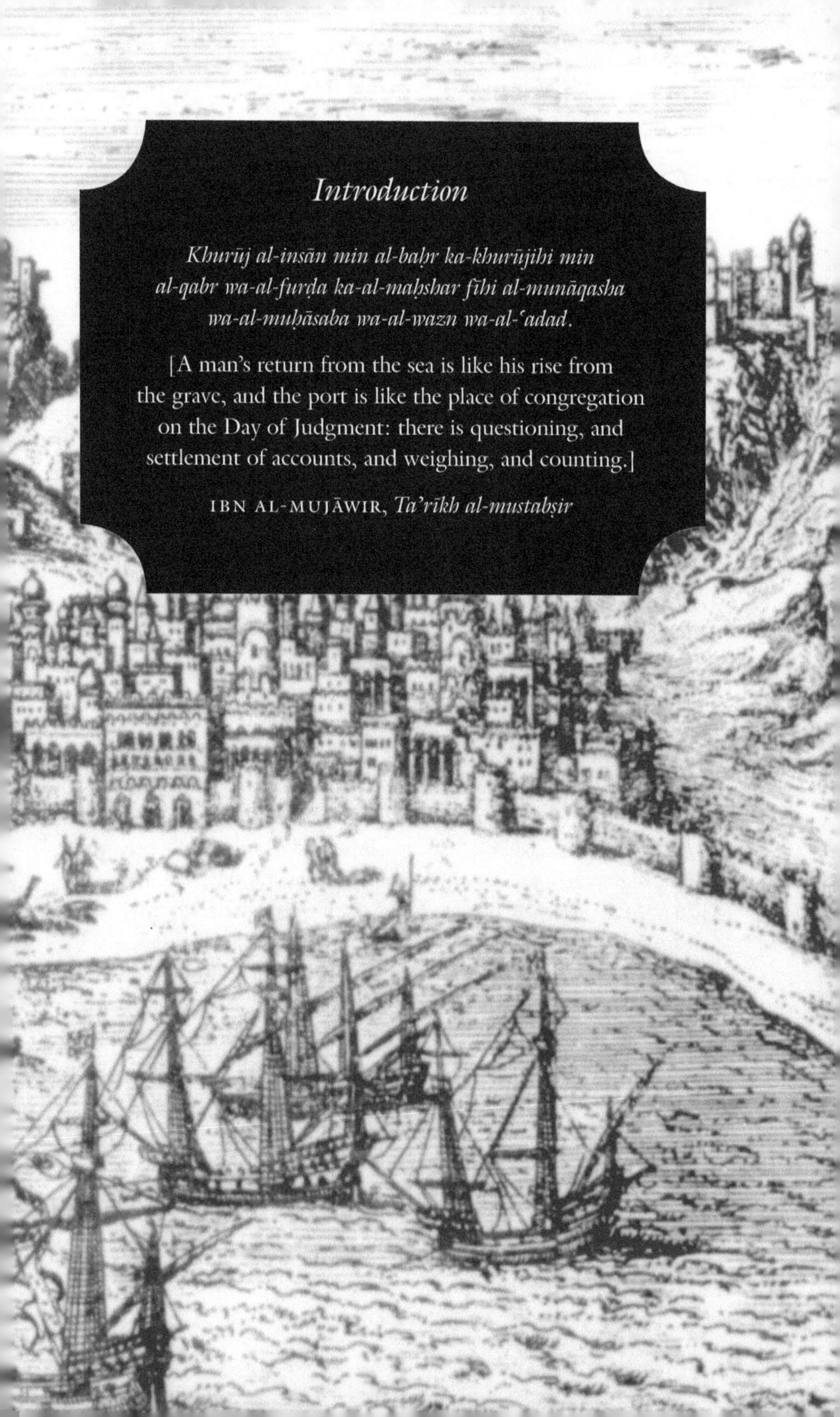

Standing at the margins of intersecting worlds, the port city of Aden occupied the center of western Indian Ocean commercial networks in medieval times. Reflecting on his detailed description of Aden, well-traveled 7th/13th-century author Ibn al-Mujāwir invented the eerie eschatological simile that so aptly conveys the simultaneous centrality and liminality of cities standing on the shores of seas. Located on Yemeni soil at the southwestern corner of the Arabian peninsula, Aden flourished as a safe haven, a place where maritime and market risks could be managed, profits maximized, and losses mitigated. From the 4th/10th century onward, Aden served as a major entrepôt on the main axis of the trade system that linked the Indian Ocean with the Mediterranean, the "India trade."[1] In an era of slow and precarious communications, trade on such global scale would have been impossible without the infrastructures that maritime cities such as Aden provided. This book offers a portrait of the city that Ibn al-Mujāwir saw, traces its development under the Zurayid and the Ayyubid dynasties in the 150 years prior to his visit, and reveals the parameters of its centrality to medieval trade networks.

This book takes as its overarching theme the development and deployment of physical space and institutions for the sake of transoceanic trade, emphasizing the urban stage and its actors, who looked constantly seaward. I highlight the city's dramatic and strategic landscape, the land and sea routes leading to it, its harbor, its walls, its bustling commercial buildings, its ships, and its traders. By privileging geography, local ecology, commercial institutions, and the merchants' use of urban and maritime space over political history and religious dynamics, I argue that trade, not religion or politics, functioned as the main force behind urban development in this Arabian entrepôt.

The two parts of the book reflect two separate yet interrelated areas of inquiry: one focuses on the city's physical world, while the other examines commercial institutions. Part 1, "The Physical Entrepôt," brings to life the shapes and forms of the maritime city. Chapter 1 explores Aden's geography and ecology. The impact of the sea and its seasons on the character and annual rhythms of port-city life is discussed first. The topography of the Aden peninsula, its anchorages, and rocky terrain come next, followed by a discussion of water resources and water supply. This close look at the environment and the character of the land exposes both the advantages and the disadvantages in the development of a major entrepôt at that particular corner of Arabia. The rest of this chapter traces the contours of the city's hinterland in terms of resources, accessibility, and settlement hierarchy; a picture emerges that shows Aden as a "central place" at the head of a web of important routes and commanding several satellite sites.[2]

After examining Aden's environment and environs, the focus shifts to the physical realities of the port itself. The next two chapters are therefore devoted to harbor and city topography, respectively. By focusing on deliberate interventions in the urban and maritime landscape, such as the building and subsequent renovations and expansions of fortifications and the construction of a protective breakwater across the harbor entrance, I set the stage for the processes and institutions to be examined in part 2 and highlight the dynamic ways in which state and merchants both responded to and exploited the opportunities offered by large-scale maritime commerce.

Part 2, "The Commercial Entrepôt," discusses trade-related urban institutions that the city's merchants and government officials fashioned and ran and to which they were subject in the interest of trade and profit. I isolate those institutions that were central to the city's role as a major Indian Ocean entrepôt and investigate their structures and development. Chapter 4 is dedicated to the customshouse, the main state-run instrument for exploiting the immense revenue-yielding potential of transit commerce. Through mechanisms designed for efficiency of surveillance and collection, the customshouse became the city's supreme moneymaker. Yet the burden of taxation did not stem the volume of vital sea traffic, partly, I argue, because taxes were heavy but not crippling and because their imposition occurred within a fairly predictable framework.

The secret behind the Adeni governments' great success in squeezing high revenues out of transit trade lies not in some capacity to

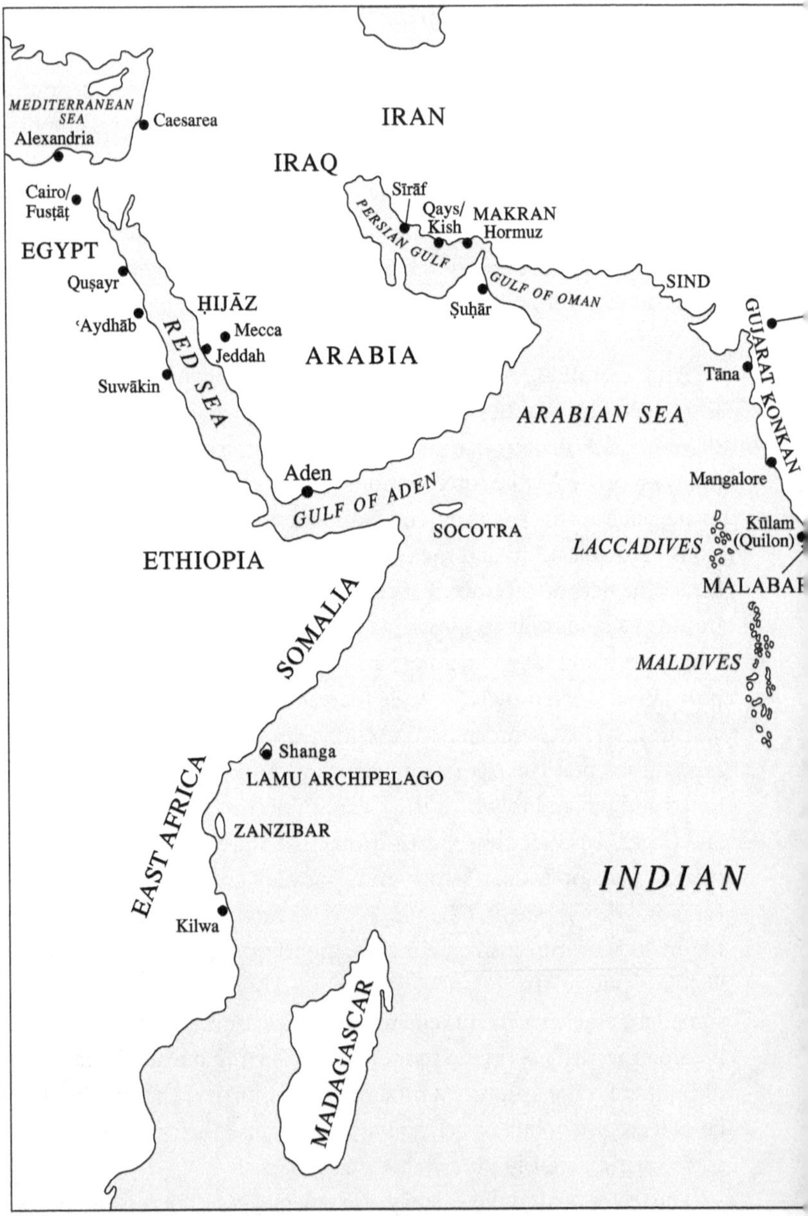

Map 1. The Indian Ocean and the Eastern Mediterranean: Seas, Regions, and Main Ports

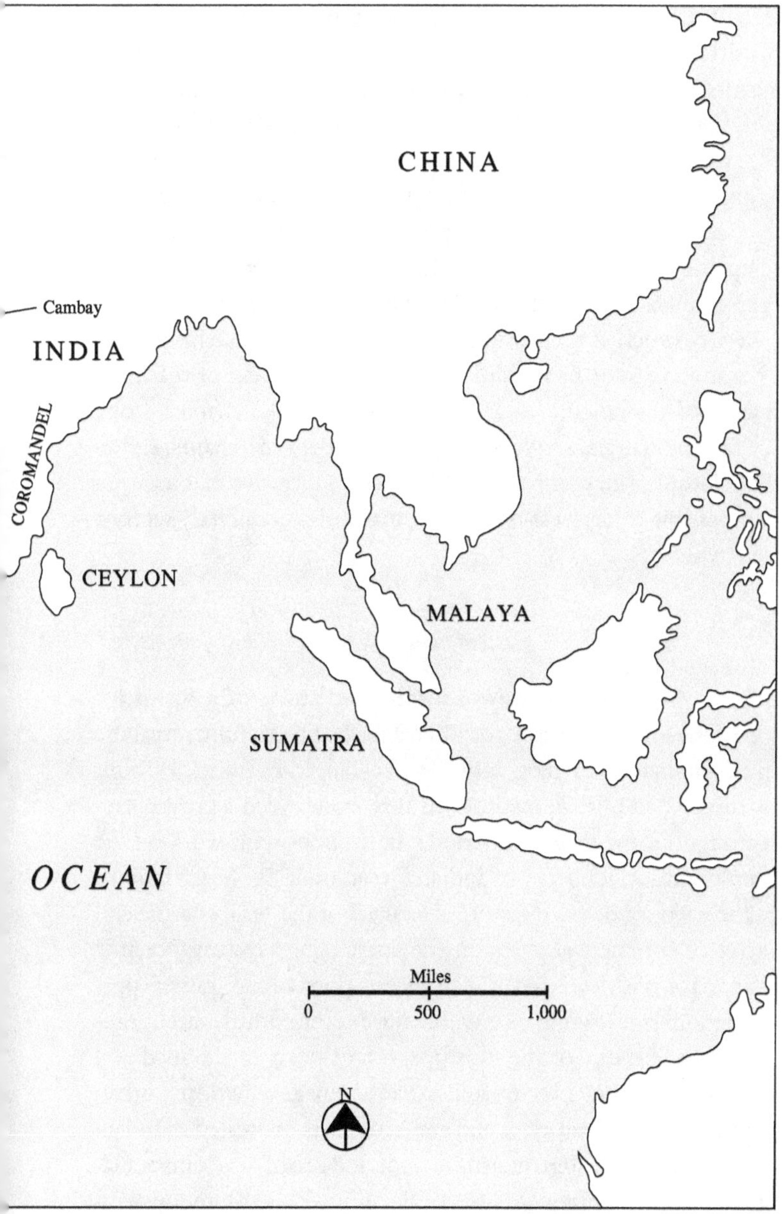
CHINA
Cambay
INDIA
COROMANDEL
CEYLON
MALAYA
SUMATRA
OCEAN
Miles
0
500
1,000
N

direct traffic through the city and extract taxes by force but in the services that the city offered to traders and in the ways in which its merchants became major entrepreneurs on the Indian Ocean scene. The last two chapters detail the unique commercial structures that made Aden particularly attractive to foreign businessmen and through which the local merchant population participated actively in the lucrative overseas trade. In chapter 5, I deal with the port's shipbuilding and shipping industries, which catered to local and foreign businesses alike. I outline the evidence for Aden's centrality to shipping networks across the western Indian Ocean and describe its role as a headquarters for boatbuilding and repair, policing of maritime avenues, and rescue and salvage operations. Finally, chapter 6 discusses the commercial services rendered by Adeni merchants, showing how local business expertise and the city's lucrative market were made accessible to overseas merchants, many of whom rarely set foot in the city itself.

Historiography

This is the first comprehensive source-based study of a formative period in the medieval history of Aden and the first to fully reveal the unique combination of geographical and ecological advantages, built infrastructure, and urban institutions that made Aden a great entrepôt throughout the medieval period.[3] In his important work on the economic and social history of Indian Ocean trade, K. N. Chaudhuri notes the need for detailed historical analysis of the "exact nature and character of commercial cities on the coast of the Indian Ocean."[4] Scholars have not neglected Indian Ocean ports alone; rather, port cities of the Islamic world as a whole have received little attention.[5] Even Alexandria, one of the most important ports of the medieval Mediterranean, is nowhere treated exhaustively as a maritime urban center.[6] To this day, historians and archaeologists interested in Indian Ocean and Middle Eastern maritime trade and urban development lament the paucity of pertinent historical studies. This volume answers that persistent call.

Most present-day knowledge of western Indian Ocean ports of the medieval period comes from the work of archaeologists. By 1985, when Chaudhuri published his work, surveys and excavations had already taken place in a number of western Indian Ocean ports, and investigators had published the results in preliminary reports and monographs. Sīrāf, on the Iranian side of the Persian/Arabian Gulf; Julfār, in the Arab Emirate of Ra's al-Khayma; the Omani port of Ṣuḥār, on the Arabian Sea; and the East African ports of Kilwa and Manda began to emerge into the historical limelight.[7] Several other coastal sites soon followed, such as the port of Shanga in the Lamu Archipelago, Ayla/Aqaba at the head of the homonymous gulf, and the Red Sea port of Quṣayr al-Qadīm, an impressive site still under intensive study.[8] Closer to Aden, the Yemeni ports of the Tihāma and the Ḥaḍramawt have become much more than uncertain dots on the historical map.[9]

To supplement and elucidate the unearthed fragments of these old ports and to gain some understanding of the social and economic lives of their inhabitants, archaeologists and other researchers shift through texts by travelers and geographers and juxtapose this textual evidence with the material data. The results of these efforts provide invaluable comparative material for this volume even as they highlight the unevenness of the sources. On the one hand, travel accounts, geographies, histories, and chronicles usually give little more than impressionistic accounts of trade and traders. On the other, administrative or personal documents that would flesh out port lives and institutions have generally not been preserved. The fortunate coincidence of substantial material remains and voluminous written documentation that characterizes Middle Eastern imperial cities such as Samarra and Cairo and European maritime centers such as Genoa and Venice does not generally obtain for Middle Eastern ports.

Aden offers one of the few exceptions to this rule, with a wealth of evidence paralleled in only a handful of other western Indian Ocean ports. While pre-19th-century material remains of the city are comparatively limited, literary and unparalleled documentary sources allow for precisely the kind of historical study that illuminates the functions of the port and the lives of its inhabitants. Here is an opportunity to trace the nexuses among trade, built space, and commercial institutions in a maritime city par excellence, a city that was neither an imperial center nor a provincial backwater and as such offers an alternative model for the study of urban development in the region.

What place would such an alternative urban model occupy in the already century-old field of Middle Eastern urban studies? In the past three decades or so, scholars have engaged in a spirited debate over the shapes and forms of the "Islamic city" and its use as an analytical category.[10] This debate has slowly blurred the outlines of the impossibly neat blueprint of the "Muslim town" offered more than half a century ago by Gustave von Grunebaum, in which Islam was the defining principle and the mosque provided the ultimate focus of urban topography and city life.[11] Most scholars today consider this frame too simplistic and narrow to fit all the complexity and variety of urban forms in the Middle East. Perhaps the greatest lesson of the Islamic city debate lies in its ultimate inability to replace that old model with a single new definition. A multitude of case studies undertaken in the process clearly demonstrates the futility of looking for a single model.[12] In addition, the contest for definition through a variety of disciplinary lenses highlights the multiplicity of forces that shape cities in the Middle East as well as those everywhere else in the world.

Largely missing from this healthy plurality of inquiry are studies of port cities. Because of their social complexity and fluidity, their simultaneous connection to hinterlands and forelands, and their general borderland character, ports defy categorization even more than do other urban centers. Their study can thus dramatically illustrate the futility of monolithic models and can serve toward the construction of new, flexible interpretive schemes that highlight confluences of forces behind urban development and map the particularities of natural ecologies, local and regional geographies, social and institutional realities, and unique historical trajectories onto analyses of regional unity and diversity of urban forms.

This study of medieval Aden is informed by a broad consideration of several other ports in the western Indian Ocean and particularly of three parameters of their urban existence: the environment, links to maritime forelands and rural hinterlands, and institutions that developed through participation in global trade. The emphasis on the environment reveals the diverse ecological, geographical, and topographical forces that govern the shape and form of all Arabian and Indian Ocean cities. The configuration and significance of Aden's marine topography can best be understood in the comparison with the similarly well-protected deepwater harbor at Manda, the harborless anchorage of Sīrāf, the seasonally sheltered and distant roads in the bay of al-Mukhā, and the combination of inlet moorings and open roadstead at Ṣuḥār.[13] The scarcity of water resources in Aden's arid environment was countered by the deployment of a technical and administrative apparatus that refers to the shared and unique features of other Arabian and western Indian Ocean ports: the wells, cisterns, and extensive irrigation conduits at Ṣuḥār and Sīrāf; the cisterns at Manda; and the wells and catchment basins at Sharma.[14]

Links to markets in the maritime foreland and to resources in the immediate and distant hinterland constitute another avenue for studying Indian Ocean ports. This book shows that for Adeni merchants, the Indian coasts constituted the locus of alliances, coalitions, collaborations, and partnerships that characterized the cosmopolitan world of trade described by Janet Abu Lughod as an "archipelago of world cities";[15] indeed, the world of Indian Ocean trade was a constellation of urban centers where merchandise and ideas were exchanged. At the same time, this world was not entirely free of competition, and the construction of seawalls and other fortifications hints at the role of conflict and warfare in the life of medieval cities of the Indian Ocean, a topic scholars have generally ignored.

The relationship between the port and its environs emerges as the connections between an urban center and its satellites: industrial activity, agricultural production, and some of the disorder of transience were relegated to places apart yet within reach. Earlier studies of Indian Ocean ports have clearly illustrated the implications of controlling a productive hinterland: in Sīrāf and Ṣuḥār, city refuse was used to fertilize fields miles away, providing an archaeological record of the association between the city and cultivable land in its environs, while pottery and iron production appear to have connected the port of Shanga with the African mainland.[16] Aden also had links further afield to the Yemeni highlands, in the Zurayid period only through loose economic ties and on the terms of a recently gained political independence and later as a part of a larger territorial state controlling most of the country. Other Indian Ocean ports too had discreet orbits: Ṣuḥār's position at the head of Wadi Jizzi rendered the city the hub of communications between the coast and the interior of Oman;[17] on the African coast, the relationships between Shanga, Manda, and Kilwa and the African mainland in all its economic, social, and political implications have been the subject of debate.

Owing their existence to trade, ports of the western Indian Ocean were shaped both physically and institutionally for commerce. While the fragments of its built structures are lamentably few, Aden's historical record preserves a wealth of information about its customs-house, shipping industry, and legal and commercial services, which emerge as characteristic of and central to the port's economic life. The resulting picture can serve as a template against which to interpret other ports, such as the newly discovered South Arabian harbors, where warehouses, shops, manufactories, and dwellings survive yet the preserved testimonies of merchants and travelers do not flesh out the rhythms and structures of commercial life quite so vividly. Conversely, Aden's commercial institutions are illuminated by templates emerging from studies of the configuration and deployment of urban space at other ports. The port of Sīrāf, for one, provides the example of an undifferentiated and mixed urban layout governed primarily by the concern with looking seaward; it also offers a clear view of tall merchants' houses standing not very far from the seashore.[18] Similarly 18th-century al-Mukhā engenders an apt explanatory model for what the sources attest about medieval Aden: at the Red Sea port that eventually replaced Aden, wealthy merchants conducted their business at home so that the "actual practices of urban merchants collapsed any fixed and rigid understanding of form and function, and the needs of a flourishing trade blurred a firm boundary between the public and private realms."[19]

Methods and Sources

In the quest to understand how people lived in a far-removed moment in time, seemingly mundane and uninspiring fragments of texts and artifacts can fire up the historical imagination and provide startling glimpses of past life. As the historical lens shifts away from the exalted and the historically self-conscious, simple documents of daily life—letters, accounts, contracts, potsherds, fragments of walls, and pieces of shipwrecked boats and cargoes—open what one eloquent student of the past has called "a trapdoor into a vast network of foxholes where real life continues uninterrupted."[20] By juxtaposing all surviving fragments of medieval Aden with formal historical texts and by using the interpretative techniques of archaeology, philology, and textual analysis, I seek to access these historiographical foxholes and offer insights into the real life of a great port city.

Fernand Braudel's formidable historical achievement in his influential *La Mediterranée* inspired me to follow this line of inquiry into Aden's medieval history. The debt consists of the impetus to consider geography and environmental structures (Braudel's "*longue durée*") alongside period-specific institutions such as trade and commercial culture (Braudel's "*conjonctures*") and short-term historical events (Braudel's "*événements*"). I also follow the example of attempting an *histoire totale* that utilizes all available sources to their fullest. My debt extends to the work of K. N. Chaudhuri, who was the first to look at the Indian Ocean in "Braudelian" terms.[21] Chaudhuri gave a broad and perhaps overly ambitious view of long-, middle-, and short-range structures over a daunting 1,000 years of history across the Indian Ocean world. Starting from that endeavor but also in contrast to it, I examine a 150-year period and the limited geographical region of Aden and its surroundings, focusing narrowly on the city's commercial history.

The variety of sources that make up the historical record of Zurayid and Ayyubid Aden offers a tremendous opportunity even as it poses a serious methodological challenge. The opportunity for social history lies in the combination of literary, documentary, and material vestiges of Aden's medieval past and the complementary insights they offer. The challenge, however, lies in the chronological, quantitative, and qualitative unevenness of these sources. One problem is that no one written source evenly covers more than one period. To avoid the risk of weaving disparate, discontinuous, and highly idiosyncratic records into a superficial, impressionistic, and ahistorical account of the past, I have chosen to rely primarily on written sources that date from the 150 years under investigation. I use later sources to flesh out aspects of the city's historical *longue durée* and to observe changes and continuities in urban institutions and by extension in the life of the port as a whole.

Also related to the general challenge that diverse sources pose is the issue of complementarity of material and written sources. Because archaeologists have contributed most decisively to the study of Indian Ocean ports and because my background in archaeology commands it, I place particular emphasis on the findings of past and recent archaeological work in Aden itself, in its environs, and in its further hinterland. This record is even more fragmentary and uneven than the written corpus. The surviving fragments of Aden's pre-Islamic past are few and can only serve to emphasize how little is retrievable from that long period.[22] Later occupation has largely obliterated even medieval layers. What survives can be understood only in light of written sources; this juxtaposition leads to important conclusions concerning the city's harbor works and water supply, both vital aspects of port city development and serviceability.[23] In addition, archaeology has contributed decisively in drawing the outlines of Aden's hinterland.[24] Reading the material record of this hinterland against the testimony of the written sources provides crucial insights into commercial and urban organization and development.

A final issue concerns the positionality of the written sources. A perusal of my discussion of these sources will reveal that most prominent among them is a corpus of Judeo-Arabic documents preserved in the Cairo Geniza that comprises letters, lists, accounts, and legal documents, many of which were written by or for Adeni Jewish merchants as well as other Jewish participants in the India trade. In the paradoxically dichotomous world of today as well as in view of the importance of ethnic and religious affiliation in the Middle Ages, one question immediately arises: If the focus of this study is medieval Aden, a city of the Islamic world, how can a record of evidence dominated by Jewish documentary material represent the physical and institutional realities of the city as a whole? Answering this question and fully grasping the relevance of the Cairo Geniza documents to the study of medieval Middle Eastern and Islamic history requires a review of the position of Jewish communities in Arabian and Middle Eastern medieval society.

Like their Christian counterparts, Jewish communities formed an integral part of the Islamic states they inhabited. Their status as *ahl al-dhimma* (people of the pact) granted them protection under Islamic law, which stipulated their communal right to legal self-regulation and self-government. In an important work of comparative history, Mark Cohen uses the concepts of hierarchy, marginality, and ethnic diversity to explain how and why the *dhimmī* system embedded non-Muslim groups in Muslim-ruled societies and rendered them organic parts of the whole.[25]

Embeddedness meant much more than toleration; it also engendered shared language, shared culture, and shared history.[26] The Geniza documents' Judeo-Arabic, a medieval Arabic vernacular spoken by the Jews of the Arab world and written primarily in the Hebrew script, perfectly mirrors the common cultural ground. In addition to the common language, Jewish and Muslim communities shared the practice of *geniza*, the preservation and ritual disposal of written material; one of the most spectacular "Islamic *genizas*" to have been preserved is the collection discovered in the roof of the Great Mosque in Sanaa.[27] In terms of economic life, moreover, Jews and Muslims had similar and in several instances interchangeable business and even legal practices. Finally, in places as far apart as Spain and Aden, Jewish notables and elites wielded significant political clout,

Judeo-Arabic document from the Cairo Geniza, the last letter sent by India trader David b. Maymūn (David Maimonides) to his famous brother, Moses Maimonides. David perished at sea shortly after sending this letter in 1169 or 1170. (Or. 1081 J1, recto; courtesy of the Syndics of Cambridge University Library and the Taylor-Schechter Genizah Research Unit)

maintained close ties with the top Muslim state officials, and even occupied offices of political import.[28]

Thus, as Cohen puts it, the "geniza is not just for Judaicists."[29] These documents are invaluable for Arabists, Islamicists, and scholars of the Middle East in general. The relative paucity of documentary sources for the Middle East before the mid-7th/13th century heightens their historical value for all medievalists. The work of Werner Diem, for example, amply demonstrates the inextricable link between the study of Arabic papyrology and that of Judeo-Arabic.[30] Important studies of social, economic, and legal Islamic history by Abraham Udovitch, Hassanein Rabie, Eliahu Ashtor, Remie Constable, and Hassan Khalilieh, among others, have set the precedent of writing general Middle Eastern and Islamic history by relying heavily on the documents of the Cairo Geniza.[31] Scholars working in the Arab world, such as Egyptian historian Hassanein Rabie and Kuwaiti historian of medieval Yemen Nayef ʿAbdallāh al-Shamrookh, also use this "Jewish" source to write "Islamic" history, no small token of the historians' willingness to recognize the common ground.[32] Finally, "Indian Oceanists" too have caught on to the importance of the documents for the region's history: the work of Amitav Gosh on the life of Bamma, a Hindu slave who passed through medieval Aden, and of Ranabir Chakravarti on maritime traders of India and Arabia speaks volumes to the broader relevance of the Cairo Geniza and the interconnectedness of the world that produced those documents.[33]

The story of the Jews of Yemen illustrates these historical and historiographical arguments for embeddedness. First, the political and spiritual leaders of the Jews of the Islamic world regarded the Yemeni Jewish communities as a distinct group.[34] The presence of Jewish communities in Yemen is traceable to the 4th century, but Yemeni Jewish tradition in general and Adeni Jewish lore in particular claim a much longer connection with the land, placing the arrival of the first Jews in Yemen in biblical times, before the destruction of the Solomonic temple.[35] Beyond the modern debate about the historicity of these claims and the origins of the South Arabian Jewish community,[36] these traditions convey the community's sense of rootedness in

Yemen. The flourishing of intellectual life in medieval times also exemplifies the engagement with the dominant Arabo-Islamic milieu; Jewish intellectuals in Yemen not only wrote both in Hebrew and in Arabic but also engaged the same literature as the Muslim majority.[37]

With the exception of Aden, very little is known about the social and economic life of the medieval Jewish communities of Yemen. In an early document showing an exchange between a Muslim ruler and a Yemeni Jewish population, the first Zaydi imam, al-Hādī, imposed limitations and a special tax on land held by the Jews and Christians of Najrān. Is this evidence of economic discrimination and disempowerment? Prominent historian of Yemeni Jews Yosef Tobi argues that this late 3rd/9th-century document in fact reveals that Jews were important landowners and were allowed to continue owning and purchasing land.[38] He thus contests the received wisdom of Jewish historiography that Jews of the Islamic world were barred from landownership and thus excluded from an important aspect of economic life.[39] In the following century, letters from the Babylonian *gaon*, the head of one of the two yeshivot in Iraq, to a number of Yemeni communities offer a fleeting glimpse of the distribution of Jews in the Sanaa area and in the south, including Aden.[40] In the mid 5th/11th century, Jews from a number of communities in the Yemeni highlands, including Sanaa, appear to have been attracted to the Sulayhid capital of Dhū Jibla; a tradition that the city was originally named after a Jewish man again demonstrates the community's rootedness.[41] Scholars have often cited the forced conversion of Jews throughout Yemen and simultaneous imposition of harsh taxes on traders under the short reign of eccentric Ayyubid ruler Muʿizz al-Dīn Ismāʿīl (593–98/1197–1202) as evidence of deteriorating conditions for Jews in Yemen and elsewhere.[42] While clearly a crisis for the Jewish community, this episode was as exceptional as the discriminatory measures were temporary, and the restoration of order was met with relief but did not come as a surprise. Geniza documents from Aden demonstrate that even at the height of the crisis, business and trade continued.[43]

The uniquely well-documented medieval Jewish community of Aden is indeed the paradigm of a flourishing group that participated fully in the port's vibrant economic life. The example of Maḍmūn b. Japheth, a figure who will appear throughout this book, is instructive. Maḍmūn belonged to the Bundār family, an important line of Jewish traders that may have originated in Iran but was firmly entrenched in Aden.[44] Possibly starting with Maḍmūn's grandfather, Bundār, several members of this family served as leaders of the local Jewish community. Moreover, their authority was sometimes said to have extended over all the Jews of Yemen and even India; indeed, Aden stood at the center of the Yemeni Jewish diaspora.[45] The careers of these men illustrate two major themes in their communal history: first, the symbolic prominence of Adeni Jews within the Indian Ocean Jewish diaspora, and second, the political power and agency that Jewish traders could exercise within the city of Aden. The latter theme is starkly prevalent in Maḍmūn's life; as chapters 4 and 6 will show, he occupied an important position in the administration of Aden's customshouse and was close to the city's Zurayid governor, Bilāl b. Jarīr: the two men sustained a protracted business partnership. The latest datable Geniza document relating to Aden comes from between 622/1226 and 625/1228; significantly perhaps, it relates a story of oppression of Jews and is addressed by a mother to a son who appears to have immigrated to Cairo.[46] Yet the community did not disappear, and its absence from the record does not necessarily bespeak its contraction or economic decline.[47]

I do not intend to diminish the historical specificities of a minority population living under the rule of a different confessional group or to ignore Jewish history and Judaic studies as fruitful historiographical frames for the study of medieval Jewish communities of Aden and Yemen. While recognizing the merits of these other lenses and remaining mindful of the minority status of Jews under Islamic rule, I choose to read the Jewish merchants of the Geniza documents as representative members of a diverse commercial world and as valid witnesses of life in a diverse commercial city.[48]

The Cairo Geniza and S. D. Goitein's India Book

The story of the repository of medieval documents known as the Cairo Geniza is as remarkable as the startling window it opens into the past. In the Judaic context, the term *geniza* evokes a variously observed custom according to which anything written in the Hebrew script and/or containing the divine name is treated with respect even after the end of its useful life.[49] Torn and tattered pages of books, letters, and old documents of every description, public and private, literary and mundane, are periodically transferred to the local synagogue and placed in a special chamber, or *geniza*, until they can be removed and disposed of in an appropriate manner, such as burial in a cemetery.

Thanks to circumstances of history and preservation, one such depository survived with all its textual wealth and was rediscovered in modern times. The synagogue of the Palestinians, Ben Ezra Synagogue, in Fusṭāṭ (Old Cairo) never emptied its *geniza*. A mixed paper trail accumulated at variable rates from the late 3rd/9th to the early 19th century, but only in the mid-1800s did traveling antiquarians begin to recognize the significance of the corpus and to acquire small batches of papers as collectibles. Modest sampling eventually turned into full-fledged mining, and by the beginning of the 20th century, the *geniza* of the Ben Ezra Synagogue had been emptied and its contents dispersed around the world's university and research libraries, museums, and private collections.[50]

Dazzled by the "new world" of past literary production that the opening of the Cairo Geniza put before them, scholars did not immediately recognize the value of the documentary material, which in any case comprised only a small fraction of the entire corpus, about 15,000 of the staggering total of more than 750,000 fragments.[51] The nonliterary fragments were written mostly in Judeo-Arabic, the medieval Arabic vernacular spoken by the Jews of the Arab world and recorded in the Hebrew script, and comprised the lettered stuff of everyday life: correspondence, lists, accounts, contracts. Initially ignored, these mundane fragments of the now dispersed corpus soon found a most enthusiastic champion. From the late 1940s until his death in 1985, Shlomo Dov Goitein spent a remarkable lifetime of scholarship reading, transcribing, editing, glossing, and analyzing thousands of Geniza documents and spreading word about this invaluable historical resource through the pages of some six hundred articles and several monographs.[52] His single-most-influential achievement was the writing of *Mediterranean Society*, a five-volume social and economic history of the medieval Mediterranean based overwhelmingly on Geniza documents.

The Indian Ocean world plays an important role in this multifaceted story of Mediterranean society and economy, and Yemen forms the crucial link between the two oceanic spheres.[53] Goitein's interest in Yemeni Jews and the world of Indian Ocean trade began in the very early stages of his academic career at the then newly founded Hebrew University of Jerusalem, when he engaged primarily in ethnographic work on Yemeni Jews living in Israel.[54] Geniza documents relevant to the trade between the Mediterranean and the Indian Ocean first caught his attention in the early 1950s, when Goitein was working on Islamic and Jewish legal history from rabbinical court records found in the Geniza and came across a series of papers detailing the protracted legal suit between Joseph al-Lebdī and Jekuthiel Abū Yaʿqūb al-Ḥakīm, Jewish merchants and India trade business associates who will appear several times in this volume.[55] Any documentary traces of Indian Ocean medieval history were significant because, as Goitein put it in a later assessment, until that time "no letters or documents . . . had been known to exist on either the Arabian or the eastern shores of the Indian Ocean."[56]

By 1954, Goitein had published his first two articles that dealt with the world of the India trade through the testimony of Geniza documents. One of these works focused on two documents describing the dramatic maritime siege of the city of Aden by a naval force from the Persian Gulf, an event otherwise known only through the account of Ibn al-Mujāwir.[57] These fortuitously preserved accounts of a momentous but otherwise little-known episode in the city's history offered an impressive example of how Geniza documents might contribute to the study of the maritime world of the medieval Indian Ocean. The story they told also specifically highlighted Aden's paramount role in the region.

Ironically, in 1954 Goitein viewed the study of the India trade corpus as a self-contained and finite endeavor, a potential pilot project of Geniza documentary research and analysis to be completed before delving into the mass of Geniza material available for the Mediterranean world.[58] He quickly realized, however, that the Geniza materials included many more Indian Ocean trade documents than he had initially expected—a total of about four hundred. More importantly, the Jewish mercantile networks in the Indian Ocean between the late 5th/11th and early 7th/13th centuries were so inextricably connected with the Mediterranean scene that they could not be properly studied before understanding and describing the Mediterranean communities. Diverted to the much larger proposition that ultimately led to the publication of his *Mediterranean Society*, Goitein never finished the monograph on the Indian Ocean trade that he had envisioned. Yet he worked on the Indian Ocean material to the day he died, leaving behind an invaluable archive of chapter drafts, research notes, extensive indexes, transcriptions, translations, and copies of the relevant Geniza documents, collectively known as the India Book.[59]

The India Book constitutes an incomparable resource for any scholar working on Indian Ocean life and society and has served as the indispensable foundation for my analysis of Geniza documents that pertain to the study of medieval Aden. However, despite their great value as direct testimonies to life and trade at the Yemeni port, preserved letters and legal documents from the Cairo Geniza provide only partial coverage of the subject. Only a tiny sample of all the documents produced in the course of Jewish participation in the India trade ended up in the Ben Ezra Synagogue; many of these documents were already damaged, and after deposition, few intact specimens survived the ravages of time. More importantly, the Cairo Geniza provides only a small glimpse of Aden from a decidedly Cairene perspective.

Thus, of the valuable but uneven assemblage of India trade documents preserved in the Cairo Geniza, I have chosen to use all documents that refer to Aden as well as those written by people who lived there permanently or passed through repeatedly and had close ties to the city. This means that a few characters will appear again and again in the analysis of the intersection of the urban environment, commerce, and its institutions. Archives kept by local merchants in Aden itself and in other Indian Ocean communities must have remained there, to be disposed of appropriately after they fell out of use. Only one such assemblage is known to have survived; it comprises documents written in Arabic dating to the first half of the 7th/13th century and belonging to a Muslim merchant at the Red Sea port of Quṣayr al-Qadīm.[60]

Comparison of the Cairo Geniza documents with the Quṣayr material is instructive, shedding light both on the mechanics of commercial record keeping and on the linguistic specificities of merchants' writings. Chapter 6 will discuss the former issue as it relates to the question of business practices. That the Judeo-Arabic documents examined here have a lot in common in content and form with the Arabic texts from Quṣayr is not surprising. Like some of their Quṣayr equivalents, most of these Judeo-Arabic documents speak in a language that "shows a high degree of literary formalism" yet "betrays a great deal of deviations from the norms of Classical Arabic (CA), under the influence of Middle Arabic (MA)."[61] The extensive studies of Judeo-Arabic as a variety of Middle Arabic anticipate the similarities between the India trade Geniza papers and their Quṣayr equivalents: some formal Classical Arabic elements of syntax and style, mixed with nonclassical features such as the omission of case endings, the nonstandard conjugations of verbs, the lack of agreement between subject and verb, and colloquial usages and vocabulary that classical dictionaries often cannot elucidate.[62]

Beyond language, other shared features of Arabic and Judeo-Arabic commercial texts include script-related peculiarities such as logograms or monograms, especially for the formal opening invocation (*basmala*); letter numerals, obviously using Hebrew letters in the Judeo-Arabic for numerical notations; and abbreviations.[63] Some differences also exist: Judeo-Arabic documents often use Hebrew for interjected invocations and honorifics as well as relatively long blessings and other quotations; Aramaic also appears, especially for legal material. Some of the invocations, honorifics, and blessings are abbreviated, and while some abbreviations are marked by strokes or dots, others are left unmarked. Conversely, the Judeo-Arabic script, with its distinct unconnected letters, is generally far simpler to read than cursive Arabic writing. Thus, reading the Jewish merchants' letters requires a good grasp of the Hebrew alphabet, a degree of patience with variant spellings of proper names and other words, and a facility with the forms of the Arabic language that would have been used by Ibn al-Mujāwir, the 7th/13th-century traveler to Aden to whom I now turn.

Travel and History Writing

Of all those who wrote about Aden, Ibn al-Mujāwir (fl. ca. 626/1228) and Abū Muḥammad al-Ṭayyib b. ʿAbdallāh Abū Makhrama (870–947/1465–1540) are the two keenest witnesses of city topography and urban lore.[64] Ibn al-Mujāwir was a traveler from Central Asia and author of a valuable and at places delightful account of Arabia in the early 7th/13th century, *Taʾrīkh al-mustabṣir*. This work's description of Aden and its history, buildings, and commercial life is so detailed as to suggest not only that he spent a memorable time there but also that he was a merchant who saw the city through a merchant's eyes.[65] Abū Makhrama, conversely, was a native of Aden, belonged to a family of scholarly renown, and lived and taught in the city.[66] His unfinished *Taʾrīkh thaghr ʿadan* is the only extant medieval monograph exclusively dedicated to the port city and its luminaries. The significance of the *Taʾrīkh al-mustabṣir* is evidenced by the fact that the native son of the "well-guarded port" incorporated into his account of his hometown the traveler's observations and testimony.

Because he visited Aden at the end of the period under consideration here, Ibn al-Mujāwir's account provides an appropriate contemporary backdrop to the voices of the Geniza documents. Thanks to his keen interest in commercial space and port administration, moreover, he recorded information often elided in the business and family letters and the commercial documents of the Geniza traders, who naturally took for granted the details of commercial space and procedure and usually wrote about them only in passing, without extensive explanations or elaborate descriptions. Thus, without Ibn al-Mujāwir's physical descriptions and historical sketches, little would be known about the walls that rendered the port truly "well-guarded." Although a fairly detailed picture of customs administration and taxes emerges from the Geniza corpus alone, much would have remained in the dark without Ibn al-Mujāwir's vivid depiction of procedures for ships, merchants, and merchandise arriving at port. Beyond providing entirely new glimpses of port city topography and commercial urban life, Ibn al-Mujāwir's work often corroborates or clarifies items alluded to in the traders' documents, and vice versa.

When Ibn al-Mujāwir visited, Aden was in the early stages of its heyday; days of even greater commercial boom lay ahead under the Rasulids. Abū Makhrama's account adds the depth of time to this early eyewitness history. When the Adeni historian wrote, the sea before Aden had become the arena of a confrontation between outsiders, the Ottomans and Portuguese, both of whom were intensely interested in capturing Aden. Some of the places lay in ruins, either as a direct result of the geopolitical ambitions of the two newcomers or because of the earlier onset of administrative decline in the last days of the Rasulid dynasty. But the city was decidedly denser than it had been in Ibn al-Mujāwir's days, and its physical and institutional spaces were layered with the intervening Rasulid developments. Quoting Ibn al-Mujāwir's topographical notes, Abū Makhrama testifies both to the expansion of the city in Rasulid times and to the general contraction of the city's hinterland during his days.

Rasulid Documents

Further supplementing, contextualizing, and historicizing the testimony on Aden that Geniza documents and Ibn al-Mujāwir's account offer on the Zurayid and Ayyubid periods requires a consideration of the richly documented subsequent era. Succeeding the Ayyubids, whom they had followed to Yemen, the Turkoman Rasulids (626–858/1228–1454) continued their predecessors' systematization of government and fiscal administration. The new rulers not only benefited from revenues from the ever-flourishing transit trade but often were merchants in their own right, taking meticulous interest in all things commercial.[67] Aden was of paramount importance to them, and a number of texts produced under their auspices reflect this interest. In spite of belonging to a later period, three of these texts are used here because they directly illuminate the history of mercantile structures dealt with in this book.

The earliest of the three texts presents a remarkable compilation of administrative and fiscal archives from the time of the greatest and longest-reigning Rasulid Sultan, al-Malik al-Muẓaffar Yūsuf b. ʿUmar b. ʿAlī b. Rasūl (647–94/1249–95). Known as al-Daftar al-Muẓaffarī and by the title *Nūr al-maʿārif*, under which it was recently published, this corpus of administrative and fiscal documents was compiled by a number of different authors.[68] Its contents can be divided into thematic units: prices and modes of manufacture as well as services, especially transportation; port regulation, especially at Aden; and agricultural revenues, laws and regulations, and remittances.[69] As the editor notes, this is not an exhaustive treatment of economic administration but instead an assemblage of archives.[70] But because it showcases trade, merchants, merchandise, and the administration of Yemen's lively commerce through Aden, this text is crucial for contextualizing the data from the earlier period under investigation here. Written in the same period by al-Muẓaffar's son and successor, the scholarly al-Malik al-Ashraf ʿUmar b. Yūsuf (d. 696/1296), the second Rasulid text to which I will refer here is a yearbook or almanac that forms part of a larger astronomical treatise.[71] The almanac is the oldest such text for medieval Yemen, and its meticulous description of the cycles of economic and social life shows Aden as the paramount reference point for topics of navigation and commerce.[72] The last text of immediate interest is an early-15th-century document that resembles in scope and interest the Muẓaffar register but is in fact an administrative treatise known by the shorthand title *Mulakhkhaṣ al-fiṭan*.[73] Its author, al-Ḥasan b. ʿAlī al-Sharīf al-Ḥusaynī, lived around 815/1412. Al-Ḥusaynī devotes a long section to the administration of the port of Aden, providing valuable data on taxation, commercial procedures at the port, and hierarchies in the port's administrative structure.[74]

Periodization and Chronology

Any venture into "premodern" "non-Western" history must confront terminologies and periodizations that stem from Eurocentric perspectives and that consequently fit poorly subjects with distinct historical and historiographical trajectories.[75] While the application of the term "medieval" to Yemeni and Middle Eastern history has been rightly challenged, no workable alternatives have been proposed so far.[76] I therefore use the designations "medieval" and "Middle Ages" conventionally to refer to the era between the end of the formative or classical Islamic Age in the 4th/10th century and the arrival of Ottomans and Portuguese on the Indian Ocean scene around the turn of the 10th/16th century. Although from its inception the concept of the medieval has carried various obscuring connotations of middleness,[77] here the term should be read as nothing more than a necessary shorthand that corresponds to widely practiced periodizations of Middle Eastern history[78] and roughly situates the history under investigation between two chronological borders significant both for Adeni and Indian Ocean history: on the one hand, the end of the unified Islamic caliphate signaled the rise of Cairo as a natural partner for Aden in the intensified trade between the Indian Ocean and the Mediterranean; on the other hand, the beginning of the age of gunpowder empires introduced new players into the Indian Ocean and brought both the Portuguese and the Ottomans before Aden's magnificent walls.

Firmly situated within the Middle Ages, then, the specific time span in the life of Aden covered by this study begins in the late 5th/11th century and ends in the early decades of the 7th/13th century. The choice of this time frame is based on two methodological considerations. First, the available sources dictate it. Geniza documents referring to Aden are plentiful between 1080 and 1160, then slowly peter out between 1160 and 1240;[79] Ibn al-Mujāwir's narrative dates to the first quarter of the 7th/13th century. By the second half of the 7th/13th century, the unique combination of sources examined here gives way to a new set of voluminous material, invaluable to historical research but different in nature, scope, and coverage. In addition, this century and a half saw the rise of two different political regimes in the city; the period therefore lends itself to observation and analysis of the impact of political change on trade policies. Such analysis prepares the ground for better understanding the changing patterns of trade that may partly account for Jewish traders' disappearance from the historical record.

A broader historiographical reason also exists for focusing on this era in the port's development. This period immediately precedes the full-blown integration of European, Mediterranean, and Indian Ocean economies into what Abu Lughod describes as the "world system of the thirteenth century." Aden formed a crucial link in the chain of cities that the system engendered, but by the time of the system's full development—the one hundred years between 1250 and 1350 C.E. treated by Abu Lughod—the port was no longer an independent city-state but part of a larger Yemeni state ruled by the Rasulid dynasty.[80] An investigation of Aden's earlier status as an autonomous principality under the Zurayids and of its transformation into the main port of a larger state under the Ayyubids expands and in part modifies Abu Lughod's compelling account of the parameters of the medieval world system's integration. Most strikingly, Aden's story suggests that within the Indian Ocean "system of laissez-faire and multiethnic shipping,"[81] individual participants' interests and ambitions at times produced regional tensions and even open conflict.

A Brief History of Aden to 626/1228

The earliest recognized mention of Aden as a port dates to the first century C.E. and appears in a maritime merchant's manual with the Greek title *Periplous tês Erythras Thalassês*. The anonymous author of this invaluable early guide to trading and seafaring in the Indian Ocean states that in his time, Eudaimôn Arabia was simply a "village" (*komê*) with suitable harbors; he adds, however, that it had once been a "full-fledged city" (*polis*) and the final terminal of merchants both from India and Egypt.[82] The downturn in the port's fortunes may not have lasted long. Later tradition counts Aden as one of the thirteen fabled pre-Islamic markets of the Arabs (*aswāq al-ʿarab*) and preserves the memory of Persian jurisdiction over the port and its trade in prized incense on the eve of Islam.[83] In sum, contemporary and later writings on Aden's pre-Islamic period as well as material fragments that evoke the classical past add up to little more than tantalizing glimpses of a place that must have been of some importance.

Only in the 3rd/9th and 4th/10th centuries did a city of Aden emerge as a major emporium: the writings of Muslim geographers and historians leave no doubt that by that time, Aden was perceived as an important urban commercial center.[84] The shift of focus of Islamic power from Iraq to Egypt in the Fatimid period meant that the Red Sea received a greater share of the overall volume of trade than had previously been the case. A well-plied Red Sea route linking the Indian Ocean and the Mediterranean had enormous implications for Aden. Al-Muqaddasī conveyed the sense of crossroads when he described the port as "the anteroom of China, entrepôt of Yemen, treasury of the West, and mother lode of trade wares." In the same breath, he hinted at Aden's urban character by the formulaic characterization of the city as one "of many castles, and offering blessings to those who visit it, and excitement to those who inhabit it."[85]

The period covered by the relevant Cairo Geniza material and Ibn al-Mujāwir's thorough account coincides with two discreet eras of city politics; in the first segment, from circa 476/1083 to 569/1173, Aden was ruled by the Zurayids, a locally based dynasty that had been appointed by and initially paid allegiance to their Sulayhid overlords. In 569/1173, Tūrānshāh, brother of Saladin, invaded the country and captured key cities, including Aden. Still at the precarious beginnings of their domination in Egypt, the Ayyubids had many reasons to turn to Yemen, which had already fallen within the Egyptian sphere of influence under the Fatimids. Perhaps the most powerful incentive was Yemen's significance in the collection of revenue from the India trade.[86]

According to Yemeni writer and poet Najm al-Dīn ʿUmāra al-Ḥakamī (d. 569/1174),[87] before the Zurayids, Aden had been ruled by the Banū Maʿn, whom the Sulayhids had subjugated but left to administer the city and pay a hefty tribute, presumably from port revenues; in fact, al-Ṣulayḥī had bestowed the city on his daughter-in-law, later Queen Arwā, at the time of her wedding to his son, al-Mukarram Aḥmad. Al-Mukarram eventually expelled the insubordinate Banū Maʿn from the city and installed in their place the brothers al-ʿAbbās and Masʿūd, sons of al-Mukarram b. al-Dhi'b. Each man controlled half of the city from a fort: al-ʿAbbās controlled the only land access to the city from fort al-Taʿkar, and from fort al-Khaḍrā' Masʿūd had charge of the maritime side. The dual rule generated tensions down the line, however, eventually breaking down in 532/1137 or 533/1138, when open conflict between the two rulers resulted in the defeat of the descendants of Masʿūd, ʿAlī b. Abī al-Ghārāt and his family, and the death of ʿAlī. The victor, Saba' b. Abī al-Suʿūd, took total control of the city and its environs.[88]

The Zurayid rulers initially honored their obligations to their Sulayhid overlords, but when Arwā's husband, al-Mukarram, died and she became sole sovereign, the situation shifted. Before long, the Adeni dynasty first halved and then completely withheld her agreed share of the port revenues. In addition to estrangement manifest in fiscal relations, the two regimes drifted apart in matters of faith and foreign policy. Both contemporary and later sources suggest that the Zurayid dynasty took on the Fatimid mission by aligning itself with the prevailing contestant for the Egyptian Fatimid leadership, al-Ḥāfiẓ; the Sulayhids maintained allegiance to a defeated pretender to the imamate, al-Ṭayyib.[89] Aden's rulers' decision to side with the winning Egyptian faction is instructive regarding the city's ties and best interests: maintaining a commercially crucial alignment with the foreland now engendered an additional, ideological separation from Aden's erstwhile overlords in the hinterland. Not long thereafter, the same dynamic obtained in a different but symmetrical context. In a conflict between the head of the Jews in Cairo and the spiritual Jewish leadership in Iraq, local Jewish leaders in Aden threw their weight behind the Egypt-based faction.[90]

After conquering Yemen in 569/1173, the Ayyubids chose Aden as one of their main bases and as the natural maritime center in the Indian Ocean. The city was no longer autonomous, but it had certainly become one of the most important centers of Ayyubid power in Yemen. In the early Ayyubid period (that is, during the reigns of the conqueror, Tūrānshāh, and his brother, Ṭughtakīn), Aden was the only town in the Ayyubid Yemeni dominion to mint gold coins.[91] The advent of the Ayyubids marked a period of renewal and expansion of important commercial infrastructure and of establishment of new institutions, which the Rasulids inherited and expanded after they took over in 626/1228. Chief among these developments were the rebuilding of the city's fortifications and the launching of coastal maritime patrols.

PART I

The Physical Entrepôt

1 | *The Environment*

At the Gate of the Orient, sentinel stands
Aden Majestic, o'er Araby's sands.

TROOPER BLUEGUM, "The Home-Sick Anzac"

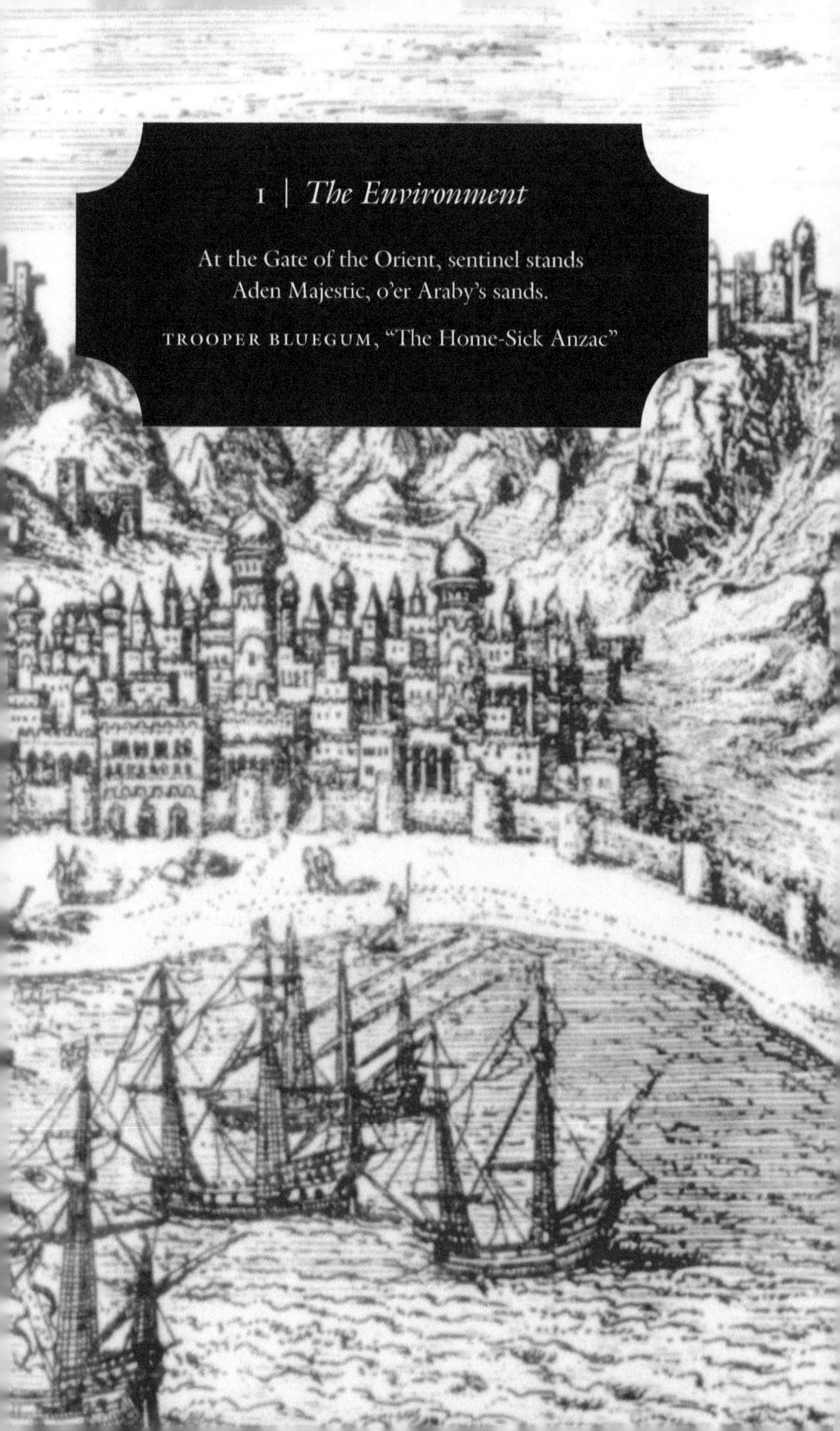

Sentinel to the East or the West—depending on one's direction and point of view—Aden occupies a doubly strategic location: it stands in close proximity to the Bāb al-Mandab, the straits that command the flow of sea traffic between the Indian Ocean and the Red Sea, and straddles a most important juncture of north-south and east-west Indian Ocean trade routes. Yet even as it calls like a Siren to the commercially minded, the rocky peninsula on which Aden stands is far from idyllic. In the early 7th/13th century, Ibn al-Mujāwir, author of the most valuable account of the city in medieval times, pronounced the climate of Aden "stifling," adding that "it turns wine sour within ten days."[1] In the 1880s and despite such modern amenities as automatic ventilation, a clearly disillusioned Arthur Rimbaud described Aden in his letters as "a horrible rock, without a single blade of grass or a drop of fresh water. . . . The heat is extreme, especially in June and September, which are the dog days here!"[2]

Even allowing a grain of salt for literary exaggeration and poetic idiosyncrasy, these reports hardly stray far from the truth: Aden's rugged terrain, lack of fresh water, and notoriously harsh summer months, when even night temperatures rarely drop below eighty-five degrees Fahrenheit, are facts mentioned again and again in the literature on Aden, both ancient and modern.[3] Such geographic "handicaps" would seem to undermine the place's usefulness as a commercial entrepôt and even its suitability for the development of any urban center worthy of the name.

While different historical trajectories led to the flourishing of trade and society on Aden's barren rocks in three different time periods, the three distinct cities—the ancient, the medieval, and the modern—were partly shaped by a common geography and climate. Moreover, the cities that flowered in these different historical moments share their geographic and climatic attributes with their shadowy forerunners and their obscure remnants. All of these settlements stood on the same rugged peninsula, were buffeted by the same set of winds, and were surrounded by the same luminous and beckoning sea.[4] What are the characteristics of this constant, and how do local and regional geography and climate intersect with the historical processes and events in medieval Aden? To put it in Braudelian terms, this chapter examines the elements that define the *longue durée* of Aden's history and highlights the ways in which these elements underlie the middle-range structures of Aden's mercantile society and short-range events that took place in the city during the century and a half under consideration in this volume.

In the first three sections of this chapter, I discuss the three defining elements of Aden's physical world—the sea, the "insular peninsula," and water. I then analyze the relationship between the city and its immediate and farther hinterland. Individual settlements in Aden's environs emerge as functional satellites to the port, while the less visible and perhaps more tenuous connection to the fertile Yemeni highlands proves to have been important for the subsistence of the maritime center's nonagrarian population.

The Sea

In telling the story of a city surrounded by sea, it is appropriate to start with precisely that sea, even as Braudel in telling the story of "*une mer entre les terres*" starts with the mountains, the plateaus, and the plains. The sea that washes the Aden peninsula also laps at the Horn of Africa (Cape Asir or Cape Guardafui) and at the gates of the Red Sea. It is the northwesternmost stretch of open Indian Ocean waters, and it is naturally named after Aden, its most important port. Like the Gulf of Oman, the Gulf of Aden resembles a funnel, narrowing westward toward the Bāb al-Mandab and opening widely eastward onto the Arabian Sea—so widely, in fact, that the dividing line between the two seas, which lies abreast of the Horn, where the Gulf of Aden is about two hundred miles wide, appears to be arbitrary.[5]

In terms of sea traffic and its control, the configuration of the Gulf of Aden means that the flow of ships converges—and is therefore easier to supervise or prey on—at its western end, in the general area of the Bāb al-Mandab. If proximity to the straits were the pivotal factor in harnessing the sea traffic, a site directly adjacent to the Bāb al-Mandab would have wrested the privilege from a place fur-

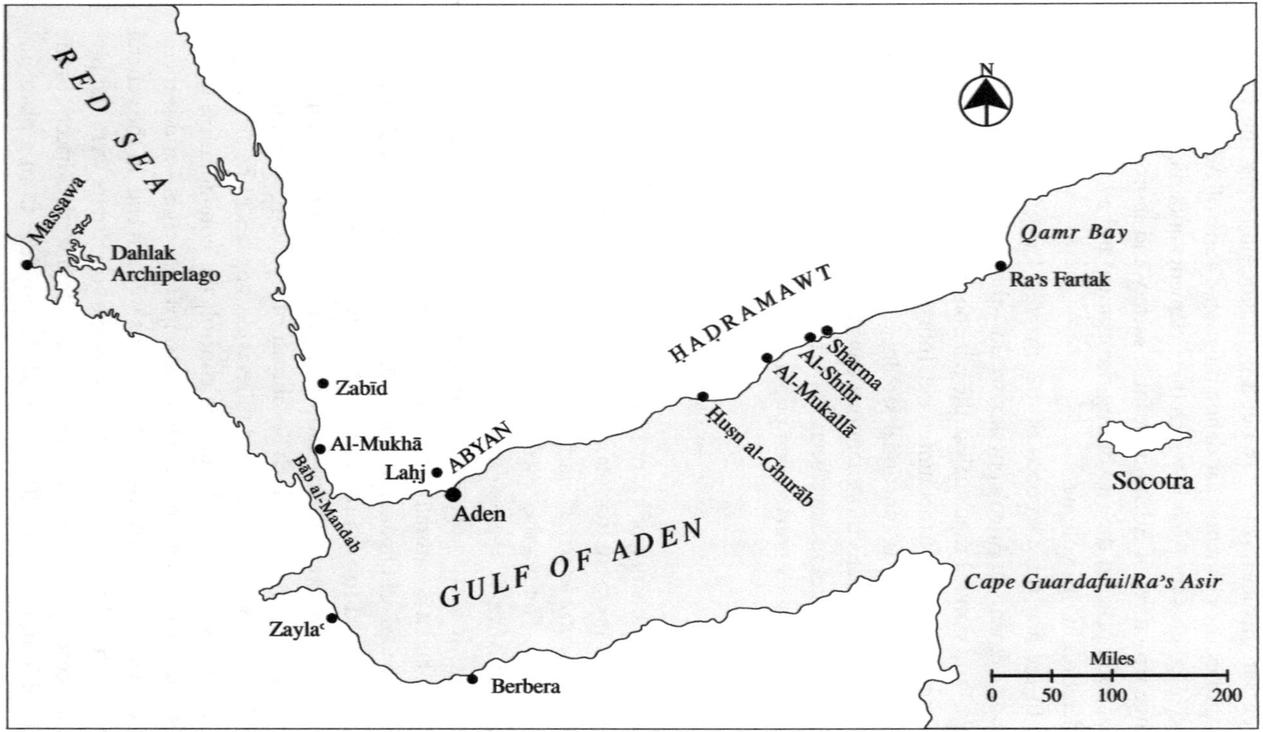

Map 2. The Gulf of Aden and the Southern Red Sea: Main Ports

ther away such as Aden. While not close enough to physically control traffic through the straits, however, the Aden peninsula lies advantageously near the mouth of the funnel, so that a maritime force, state, or group based there could exercise adequate command over regional waters. In addition, the spatially limited environment of the Gulf of Aden lends itself more readily to thorough navigational mastery by local mariners.

Both documentary and literary sources from the medieval period testify to the city's vested interest in the safe conduct of merchants, merchandise, and the ships that carried them. In their efforts to manage risk and mitigate damages, city officials and merchants took active measures to safeguard shipping against piracy and the elements; their efforts will be discussed in detail in part 2 of this book. Proximity to the city emerges as a critical factor in the implementation of such measures. Maritime patrols appear to have operated exclusively within the manageable maritime vicinity of Aden, while escort ships must have been most effective within the same maritime space. Furthermore, among all the instances of Indian Ocean shipwreck, the one documented case of a relatively successful marine salvage operation in the medieval period was sent forth from Aden and took place in the well-plied if treacherous waters near the Bāb al-Mandab.[6]

A watery realm easily within the city's physical control played an important role in the success of maritime endeavors originating in the city. Maritime morphology and climate also contributed. Modern sailing directions for the area make special note of the absence of underwater hazards, reassuring mariners that "the Gulf of Aden is so clear of dangers that its safe and expeditious navigation depends mainly on a knowledge of the prevailing winds and currents."[7] Although local winds and currents were not to be overlooked, local knowledge and experienced seamanship could easily have handled these perils.[8] Overall, the absence of treacherous shoals, shallows, and reefs in Aden's immediate maritime foreland and the manageable local winds and currents meant that merchants operating from and through the city had fewer reasons to worry when expecting or sending forth a ship. In other words, by virtue of location alone, the port of Aden conferred a small measure of confidence on the generally unsafe business of shipping during the age of sail.

A comparison with the port of Alexandria, the great maritime port at the Mediterranean end of the India trade, demonstrates the true importance of the relative safety of Aden's sea approaches. S. D. Goitein has shown that the most treacherous part of the voyage when shipping through Alexandria was in fact braving the coastal waves; the Geniza documents bear witness to several disasters occurring in the shadow of the Pharos.[9] The great port of Jeddah on the Red Sea also suffers from very treacherous approaches, primarily as a result of offshore reefs and coral-encrusted coastal shallows. Even the accurate charts, gyroscopic compasses, radar, and depth sounders of modern times cannot always prevent disaster, as the visible relics of modern shipwrecks at the edges of the navigable channels of Jeddah Harbor testify.

If the sea was an open road to and from Aden, sailors had to reckon with the weather before any journey could begin. With its regular and marked seasonality, the monsoon system of winds and precipitation that prevails across the Indian Ocean significantly affects local and regional sailing patterns. Studies of seafaring practices in the medieval Mediterranean set in high relief the ways in which maritime seasons acted as the clock for littoral communities.[10] Similarly, the Indian Ocean had a distinct maritime calendar based on the seasonal wind patterns, the winter northeastern and summer southwestern monsoons.[11] In the Gulf of Aden, the local manifestations of the general monsoon system of the broader Indian Ocean region have important implications for the rhythms of port life.

Yemeni almanacs of the Rasulid period reflect the nexus of wind patterns and life in Aden by offering a remarkably intricate schedule for sailing to and from the city, defining seventeen discrete sailing periods through optimal times for travel between different harbors of the western Indian Ocean and the port of Aden.[12] Such port-specific sailing seasons (*mawāsim*) also constitute a key concept in the technical Arabic literature on navigation that flourished in the

9th/15th and 10th/16th centuries.[13] This concept, moreover, informs a discreet branch of navigational science, as exemplified by renowned Arab navigator Ibn Mājid, who devoted lengthy chapters to the tabulation and explication of optimal arrival and departure periods for each of the principal ports of the Indian Ocean, including Aden.[14]

The Cairo Geniza documents of merchants living and sailing these seas from the 5th/11th to the 7th/13th centuries reveal that neither the Yemeni almanacs nor the later navigational treatises were purely prescriptive or schematic in their summary of actual sailing practice. The authors of the Geniza letters allude to a season of shipping, as they often refer to the end or the beginning of sailing. In one example dating to 529/1134–35, Maḍmūn b. Japheth, a prominent Adeni merchant and communal leader who will appear repeatedly in this volume, writes to a business associate and friend in India that the market for pepper in Aden was slow a week before the time of sailing but picked up closer to the day before the sellers' appointed time of traveling, when buyers who had been hitherto detained arrived at the port.[15] Here "traveling" or "sailing" (*al-safar*) refers to a fixed time by which the merchants who had brought pepper and other merchandise from India were to leave the city and head homeward—that is, east to India.[16] In a letter to the same recipient written about twenty-five years later, another Adeni deals with the fact that business has to be delayed until "after the departure of the ships."[17] He thus makes it clear that maritime travel from Aden happened all at once, with all ships' itineraries presumably scheduled to approximately the same timetable to fit within the optimal sailing season.

Sailing outside of the *mawāsim* was to be avoided. Operating sailing vessels on the high seas with minimal navigational aids and no weather forecasts is by definition risky business. A tradition shared by Arabs and Jews describes the frailty of seagoing vessels and the precariousness of human existence on the high seas as being like "a worm clinging on a log."[18] Shippers and mariners were naturally averse to taking extra risks and generally avoided sailing in the period of predictably unfavorable weather: at those times, sea routes were "closed." In the Mediterranean, most sailing took place primarily between late

May and early September; the entire sea was considered closed for the winter.[19] The Indian Ocean sources, however, give a more detailed calendar of opening and closing of particular sailing routes. While sailing year-round was not impossible in this region, little sailing took place during June and July, the middle months of the summer southwestern monsoon, when winds were particularly strong and unpredictable.[20] Under such conditions, sailing eastward toward a lee shore such as the western coast of India was clearly a bad idea.

When was it safe and therefore customary to sail to and from Aden? The Rasulid almanacs, Ibn Mājid, the much earlier *Periplus of the Erythraean Sea*, and modern sailing manuals generally agree on the timing of Aden-centered seasons. Late August and early September, the period at the tail end of the southwesterly summer winds, was a good time to leave Aden for India.[21] In late July and early August, ships sailed down the Red Sea; pushed by the locally prevailing northwesterly out of the Bāb al-Mandab, they would thus arrive at Aden just in time for the departure of the India-bound ships.[22] With the benevolent northeasterly blowing steadily all winter, the return trip from India could be undertaken any time from late October onward for ships coming from Gujarat in northern India and a little later as a result of heavy rains in southern India if coming from Malabar. The cutoff date for the return is the middle of April. Sailing from Aden westward, particularly up the Red Sea, was good from October until April, at which time the northeastern winter monsoon (*azyab*) was deflected near the Bāb al-Mandab and turned into Red Sea southerlies that pushed vessels northward.[23] As ships returned from India, goods that cleared through Aden could be forwarded to the northwest, up the Red Sea and from there to the ports of the Mediterranean.

Even the briefest comparison of this schedule with the timetable of Mediterranean seafaring reveals that Aden stood at an important intersection of the time and space continuum between the two seas. As Mediterranean boats were putting into their home ports at the onset of the fall and being dragged up on shore for repairs, Indian Ocean traffic was picking up. Western merchandise could arrive in Aden in late summer and make it to India by the fall. Red Sea merchants who carried that merchandise to Aden would presumably then have stayed on, bound by weather and the anticipation of the arrival of Indian goods. By late winter at the latest, they could pick up Indian goods arriving in Aden and sail back up the Red Sea with the local southerly winds. These goods would make it to the Mediterranean ports in good time for the beginning of the sailing season there. As for the voyage eastward, Aden-based merchants arguably had an advantage over their India-based counterparts: if the latter chose to sail west during the prescribed window after October, they would have to wait in Aden for a minimum of four months before sailing back to India.

The codification of knowledge about optimal sailing times under the rubric of *mawāsim* as well as the documentary and literary references or allusions to sailing specific routes within specific narrow windows of time thus suggest that wind patterns dictated not only when to sail but also to some extent who did the sailing of the different segments of the maritime routes and at what times. In terms of city life, this must have meant periods of intense activity from late August on, followed by somewhat of a lull starting in May, when apart from building up stocks of locally available trade commodities and assessing gathered information, people sat waiting for the sea to "open" and the ship traffic to resume. According to Ibn al-Mujāwir, at such times lookouts were posted on the peninsula's highest peak and a whole chain of heralds stood by to convey the news to the town.[24] The whole city turned seaward in anticipation.

In addition to constituting the broad avenue whereby the commercial fortunes of the entrepôt ebbed and flowed, the waters of the gulf and of the Arabian Sea further afield provided the city with much of its nourishment. The bounty of these warm waters ensured that once established, a community could survive here regardless of the viability of trade routes. Local fishermen lived dangerous and laborious lives, as the best catches could be ensured only by fishing during the stormy summer months, when dense schools of large fish passed by the immediate vicinity of the Aden shores; however, the yields were prodigious, and local populations could subsist on a variety of ocean fish.[25] Archaeological investigations in other seaports of the western Indian Ocean have shown that in addition to fish, local diets included dugong, a sea mammal native to these tropical waters, and that whales were caught and processed for blubber, a fatty substance used in the preservation of wooden boat hulls.[26] Furthermore, tiny fish caught in large quantities may have served as fodder and fertilizer, as Ibn al-Mujāwir attests for al-Manṣūra, further east on the Arabian coast, and as is the current practice in traditional maritime economies all along the Arabian littoral.[27]

To this inexhaustible source of food, the Gulf of Aden added two more valuable resources: salt and ambergris. In a delightful rags-to-riches story from the 4th/10th century about an Adeni man named Saʿīd al-Faqīr (Saʿīd the Pauper), a small batch of salt sent by the protagonist to India as his only tradable asset leads to great fortune in the form of a gigantic pearl hiding in a salted fish's belly.[28] More soberly, Ibn al-Mujāwir speaks of the production of salt at a place outside of Aden bearing the suggestive name al-Mimlāḥ (saltworks). The salt flats apparently had previously been open to exploitation by private individuals but in the author's time had been brought under the jurisdiction of the state. The Ayyubid governor retained part of the production and farmed out the rights to the rest.[29] It is very likely that locally produced salt was used in the preservation of fish, probably destined both for local consumption and for export.[30] The medieval salt flats must have stood on the mainland opposite Aden. Their exact location remains a matter of conjecture, as the written sources are rather vague.[31] It is tempting, however, to identify them with the saltworks that in British colonial times were located in the vicinity of the mainland village of Shaykh ʿUthmān, a short distance northwest of Aden.[32] In the early 20th century, the exploitation of these flats brought considerable profits to the local populace, so that the industry's decline in the 1950s and 1960s dealt a blow to the local economy.[33]

As for ambergris (*ʿanbar*), a marine product that consists of solidified whale secretions and washes up on seashores around the western Indian Ocean, the written sources testify to its trade both in medieval and modern times. Used by druggists in the concoction of perfumes and aromatics and sent forth from Aden both westward and eastward in the Geniza period and even earlier, the substance was probably collected from the nearby shores. It may also have been brought into Aden from Socotra, which appears to have been one of the most important sources (according to Ibn Mājid the only source).[34] Thus, if Ibn al-Mujāwir's account is accurate, ambergris was readily available in the waters between Aden and the Bāb al-Mandab, even if not in chunks of such prodigious size as to fund the entire building of a mosque, as he claims.[35]

The Insular Peninsula

The modern city of Aden has grown in the buildable pockets of a rugged peninsula surrounded almost completely by the sea. The western and northwestern edges of this peninsula look onto a large protected bay and a headland beyond it known since British colonial times as Little Aden. Its southern and eastern shores are more exposed, opening directly onto the ocean. The Aden peninsula connects to the mainland by a narrow strip of land. In the early days of the British protectorate, this isthmus was partially covered by the sea at high tide, and not until a causeway was built in the second half of the 19th century could the land bridge be traversed at all times.[36] Ibn al-Mujāwir, however, testifies to the existence of a similar causeway or bridge (*qanṭara*) since early medieval times but also preserves the memory of a time when the low isthmus was submerged and the Aden peninsula was a veritable island surrounded on all sides by water. He further envisions a still earlier era of even higher sea levels that left only three peaks—presumably the peninsula's highest—above water.[37]

As with other major works in Aden and elsewhere, Ibn al-Mujāwir attributes the initial construction of a bridge to the Persians (*al-aʿājim*), who first dug a canal to cut off the peninsula from the mainland and later built up the isthmus to provide easier access for beasts of burden.[38] Regardless of its pedigree, the bridge was known during the period under study here as al-Mazaff or al-Maksar. The latter appellation seems to have also applied, as it has through British times to this day, to the district on the mainland side of the isthmus.[39] Sea erosion must have necessitated occasional maintenance, which the rulers of Aden were all too eager to perform given the land bridge's significance for communications with the hinterland. Ibn al-Mujāwir speaks of such a renovation of the bridge by ʿAbdallāh b. Yūsuf al-Tilimsānī (probably an Ayyubid official), who apparently funded the project with some of the city's agricultural tax revenues.[40]

On the peninsula itself, adjoining the isthmus to the west, was the small town of al-Mabāh, which seems to have stood guard on the land access to the peninsula as a whole and to the town of Aden itself.[41] Both as an island and as a peninsula, the rocky massif was easily defensible; its relative isolation and the configuration of the isthmus meant that defenders could fully monitor approaches by land and could block potential invaders. Abū Makhrama relates that in 922/1516, when the Turks arrived in Zabīd, the Adenis, faced with the threat of an invasion, stationed one force at the harbor and one at al-Mabāh, thus fortifying both the seaward and landward approaches.[42] Centuries later, the British built defensive lines across the isthmus and chose to garrison the same spots, the harbor and the crossing to the mainland.[43]

Aden boasts a dramatic landscape. Volcanic in origin and strikingly barren, the rocks of Aden rise from the sea to form precipitous peaks, the highest of which were known in the Middle Ages as Jabal ʿUrr, Jabal Ḥiṣn al-Taʿkar, and Jabal al-Akhḍar.[44] These peaks belong to a mountain range that is, in fact, the remnants of a defunct volcano. Part of the ancient crater encloses an area of rather flat ground, located east of the high peaks and surrounded by them on all but the eastern side, where it opens onto the sea. The medieval town and its harbor occupied this space—a beach surrounded by mountains, as al-Hamdānī describes it.[45] In British colonial times, the Crater, as this area was unofficially named at the time and has subsequently been called, became one section, the "old town," of a city that came to in-

Satellite image of Aden peninsula. (Courtesy of Google Earth)

clude separate districts on reclaimed land in the western and northern parts of the peninsula.[46]

In both ancient and medieval times, the Crater was the natural choice for settlement on the peninsula. It offered the only substantial stretch of naturally flat ground as well as a sense of security and defensible isolation. The only way into the city by land was through a single gap in the surrounding mountains. Located to northwest of the town, this opening was known in British times as the Main Pass. Ibn al-Mujāwir refers to it as *al-bāb* (the gate), giving the impression that as the sole access to the city by land the pass was considered the main city gate.[47] The dramatic aspect of the narrow opening obviously gave rise to the medieval legend, related by Ibn al-Mujāwir, that Shaddād b. ʿĀd, the legendary builder of the Iram Columns, had dug the volcanic wall and opened this passage into the city.[48] In more practical terms, the pass played a strategic role in the control of traffic, commercial and otherwise, in and out of the city, and, as al-Muqaddasī testifies in the 4th/10th century, it was built up and guarded like a proper gate.[49]

Accessing Aden by sea was a different matter altogether. Despite its ominous aspect, the rocky outline of the peninsula is dotted with small bays that provide excellent anchorages for small craft. A feature so conducive to shipping does not fail to attract the attention of seasoned sailors, such as the author or informants of the *Periplus* and its modern counterparts.[50] While the numerous bays around the peninsula can provide temporary or short-term shelter to smaller craft such as fishing boats and small cargo carriers, the long-term shelter required for commercial shipping is available in two wider anchorages on the eastern side of the peninsula: Ṣīra Bay (Front Bay), immediately facing the old town, and Ḥuqqāt Bay (Holkat Bay). In addition, Back Bay, the large shelter on the western side of the peninsula, has served as Aden's main port since the beginning of the British colonial era.

The Geniza documents and the medieval chronicles, geographies, and travel accounts leave no doubt that Ṣīra Bay served as the city's main harbor before the modern era.[51] This fact may appear as somewhat of a puzzle: Ṣīra Bay is not as fully protected from the winds as is Back Bay, which is also more spacious. Ships that anchor in front of the old town can find shelter from southerly winds on the lee of the small but steep islet of Ṣīra, which stands very close to the shore. Anchorage in front of the old town also lends protection against westerlies, thanks to the peninsula's mass. The site, however, is exposed to the winds of the *azyab*.[52] This presented a real problem and eventually forced medieval Adeni authorities to devise a solution, which I will discuss in chapter 2.

Despite its nautical disadvantage, the eastern anchorage served as the main harbor in what proves to have been the natural and perhaps the only choice given the exigencies of Aden's premodern settlement. Not only was the Crater the sole large segment of flat ground on the peninsula where an urban/residential settlement could grow without extensive land reclamation, but it was also the most easily defensible spot on the peninsula. Located directly east of the Crater, Ṣīra Bay afforded direct and easy access between the city and its port and ensured tighter control and defense of the harbor and its traffic. Not until the 19th century did the center of commercial gravity shift to the excellent western anchorage. Back Bay was then transformed into a major maritime port by the dredging of its shallow and silty bottom, the building of quays and piers, and the growth of the modern districts of al-Tawāhī and al-Maʿalla' along its shores.[53]

This combination of defensibility and excellent sea approaches constituted indisputable assets for the insular peninsula on which substantial cities sprung up in ancient, medieval, and modern times and that was otherwise devoid of natural attractions. The place was painfully arid; the only thing present in great abundance and variety was stone.[54] Ibn al-Mujāwir hints that some local stone served the needs of building construction in the city, and Abū Makhrama elaborates on the story. Stone for building the city's more prominent structures was imported from the area of Abyan, but at some point in Zurayid times, Abū al-Ḥasan ʿAlī b. al-Daḥḥāk al-Kūfī, a newcomer to Aden, came up with the obvious idea of quarrying closer to home. Others followed his example, and the individual quarries (*al-miqlāʿ*) acquired the names of the persons who worked them, their rights of usufruct eventually transformed into full ownership.[55]

These accounts of local quarrying raise questions about individual private and state access to the resource, investment, labor, and technology. Abū al-Ḥasan, for example, is said to have used slave labor to quarry the stone, which was then transported to the town on pack animals. The widespread utilization of stone in building construction also had a significant impact on the topography and character of the urban space, and local availability of stone may have allowed a greater number of inhabitants to build durable and more sophisticated residences. Systematic exploitation of local and readily available sources of building materials ultimately affected the ways the city functioned, looked, and felt.

Water

Long before Rimbaud bemoaned the aridity of Aden, others had noted the complete absence of greenery from the landscape; like al-

Muqaddasī in the 4th/10th century and Ibn Baṭṭūṭa in the early 700s/1300s, most visitors must have noticed a paradox in the existence of a city large and important yet lacking in crops, trees, and fresh water.[56] While tiny plants manage a short-lived growth in the nooks and crannies of the rocks during the somewhat cooler winter months, the long months of intense heat and the extremely low annual levels of rainfall—as low as two inches total—combine to inhibit the growth of any substantial vegetation.[57] Abū Makhrama paints a vivid picture of largely empty, preurban Aden replete with thorny trees and not much else.[58]

Water, in fact, constitutes the site's most acute problem (*mushkilat al-mashākil*), as a present-day Yemeni historian confirms.[59] This is not to say that Aden had no water at all, however. Medieval sources confirm that several wells lay within the Crater area and in the immediate vicinity. Yet, with inadequate rainfall and the general dryness of the climate, locally available well water alone could not have covered the town's drinking, washing, industrial, and provisioning needs. As Aden grew into the region's great maritime entrepôt, residents combined several methods to meet the constant and ever-growing thirst of the city and its port.[60]

Ibn al-Mujāwir devotes a long section of his work to Aden's wells, providing an impressive list. His discussion can be divided into four headings—freshwater wells within the city (*al-ābār al-ʿadhba'*), brackish-water wells (*al-ābār al-māliḥa*), seawater wells (*ābār mā'uhā baḥr ʿadan*), and finally sweet-water wells on Aden's outskirts (*al-ābār al-ḥulwa bi-ẓāhir ʿadan*). Interwoven into this list of wells is a digression on cisterns and springs at various locations on the peninsula.[61] The account reveals that most wells were identified with private individuals. Specific wells are referenced as the "well of so-and-so" (for example, *bi'r ʿAlī b. Abī al-Barakāt b. al-Kātib*) or even the "well belonging to so-and-so" (for example, *bi'r li-ʿAlī b. al-Ḥusayn al-Azraq*).[62] In one such case, the person named is Dā'ūd b. Maḍmūn al-Yahūdī (*ābār thalāth li-Dā'ūd b. Maḍmūn al-Yahūdī*), a Jew and very likely a member of the Bundār family, which appears to have maintained an enduring partiality for though probably not monopoly over the name "Maḍmūn."[63]

The formulation by which the medieval authors refer to wells suggests that at least in some cases, wells, like quarries, were administered and practically owned by private individuals. Ownership of a well must have represented an asset of paramount importance, particularly for those involved in the shipping business; timely, dependable water was a vital prerogative for the smooth running of shipping schedules. Because water was such a precious commodity in medieval Aden, the question of rights of access and exploitation of water sources within the city must have given rise to many disputes. Not surprisingly, riots could break out over water (and firewood).[64]

Also noteworthy is the inclusion of brackish- and seawater wells in Ibn al-Mujāwir's long list. Nonpotable water wells obviously were not useless. Brackish water was probably adequate for a variety of domestic uses, such as washing clothes and surfaces, watering animals, and perhaps even irrigating small urban gardens. Both brackish water and seawater could also have been used in industrial production, such as potteries, glassworks, and tanneries.

Local wells alone ultimately did not suffice. Ibn al-Mujāwir makes it clear that wells on the mainland provided a crucial supplement to the city's water supply, just as was the case in the colonial era.[65] Laḥj and in earlier times a vaguely defined area known as al-Ḥayq are mentioned as places where the Adenis fetched part of their water.[66] In addition, Ibn al-Mujāwir claims that in the era of the Persian settlers, water was shipped to Aden from the port of Zaylaʿ on the African coast.[67] This is not surprising, as "water boats" were common along the less accessible parts of the South Arabian coast until the proliferation of desalinization plants in recent decades. Bringing in water from afar, however, was always not only cumbersome but also precarious. Especially on land, the supply line was vulnerable to attacks from hostile tribesmen. Ibn Baṭṭūṭa relates that in his time, the city dwellers had to bribe "the Arabs" with money and clothing to guarantee some continuity in the procurement of the vital resource, and it seems reasonable to conclude that a similar situation may have prevailed earlier on.[68] Thus, while Adenis remained dependent on remote water sources, they never ceased to look for ways to maximize and secure their water supply.

The unique Adeni solution to water management takes the form of a system known collectively and somewhat misleadingly as "*ṣahārīj*," "*ḥiyāḍ*," "tanks," or "cisterns." To explain the impetus behind the development of these impressive public waterworks, Ibn al-Mujāwir claims that dependence on remote water sources—in particular, shipping water from Zaylaʿ—had become too cumbersome and necessitated a new solution. Indeed, this impressive system of interconnected water drainage channels and basins hints, by its extent and complexity, at the magnitude of the water problem and at the multifaceted expertise employed to solve it. As Adeni preservationist and historian Abdallāh Aḥmad Muḥayriz notes in his detailed study of the *ṣahārīj*, heavy-handed Victorian restorations have all but obliterated the original features of the intricate hydraulic system.[69] A critical reassessment of the 19th-century intervention coupled with recent surveys of the structures has provided a better understanding both of what the medieval accounts describe and of the overall system of canals and tanks that ultimately brought water from the wadis around the Crater area to the city.

That original system was complex and sophisticated: a series of canals and dikes built or hewn into the sides of wadis surrounding the Crater channeled floodwater from higher ground to the wadi floors, and from there it eventually reached the city cisterns, the *ṣahārīj* of the early travel accounts. A levee or bank in the lower part of the wadi floor was designed to filter the water from rocks and silt so that it could reach the lower basins relatively clear of impurities. In the period following Aden's medieval heyday, the higher–ground channels fell into disrepair, and the free flow of water into the wadi eventually silted up the wadi floor. The British engineers who undertook the restoration of the substantial remains in the Wadi Ṭawīla, which runs west-east toward the Crater area and constitutes a crucial component of the overall system, did so without a clear understanding of the original system. They overlooked the canals and dikes and focused on the basins; they turned some of the canals and dikes into storage tanks and built barrage walls across the wadi floors, presumably to contain occasional flash floods.[70] The Ṭawīla remains were thus converted into veritable water depots, and their original function of collecting every drop of rainwater and directing it to the town was irreparably reversed.[71]

The original network of course included tanks whose primary function was water storage. These "urban" tanks, which al-Muqaddasī calls *ḥiyāḍ* and Ibn al-Mujāwir and Ibn Baṭṭūṭa dub *ṣahārīj*, lay at the end of the chains of channels and feeder basins near or in the Crater area. The Rasulid texts mention *maṭarāt*, which may be another reference to these tanks.[72] In addition to receiving the torrential runoff that even a slight rainfall would cause to flow down the steep, rocky ground of the hills around town,[73] the cisterns in the Crater area also stored water imported from elsewhere. Ibn Baṭṭūṭa notes that Aden's cisterns were filled with "water on the rainy days of the year, for water was far away from the town," but he also testifies to the transport of water from the faraway out-of-town sources.[74] Indeed, the practice of storing water transported from elsewhere in urban cisterns made sense at other Arabian ports with water difficulties, such as the Red Sea port of Jeddah, where cisterns were in use at least as early as the 4th/10th century and through the period examined in this volume.[75]

Who built the *ṣahārīj* at Aden? The lining of the basins and canals, which one early Victorian account correctly describes as "a fine coat of fine stucco, which externally bears a strong resemblance to marble," appears to point to an indigenous tradition of hydraulic architecture.[76] Ibn al-Mujāwir perhaps refers to this type of lining when he claims that the initial building of the *ṣahārīj* required the transfer of clay (*ṭīn*) from either Abyan or Zaylaʿ.[77] It is not unlikely that the cisterns were in fact lined with *quḍaḍ*, a waterproofing and lining compound used in traditional Yemeni architecture to this day and found in ancient hydraulic works in the country, most notably at Ma'rib.[78] Ibn al-Mujāwir attributes the original construction to the "people of

Sīrāf,"[79] yet given the use of traditional Yemeni materials and techniques, an alternative but equally plausible explanation for their origin links the Adeni structures to the impressive water installations of Sabaean-Himyarite times.[80]

If these various solutions to Aden's water problem ensured a more or less adequate supply, how did ships in the harbor receive their water? Anyone who has sailed small boats on seas washing arid coasts and islands and has anxiously waited for the water truck to arrive and fill the port depot knows that the question is of utmost concern both to sailors, who want to ensure their supply, and to port authorities, whose reputation and that of their port depends on providing regular service. In Rasulid times, three special officials were in charge of "sweet water," and two others were responsible for the *maṭarāt*.[81] Thus, while the provision of water to ships in the harbor appears to have been institutionalized by the 8th/14th century, it is unclear whether a special office was in place in earlier times. Abū Makhrama mentions water supply for ships only once, in connection to Rubāk, a village west of Aden where "ships sometimes stopped for water."[82] I have located only one relevant passage in the Geniza documents: in a letter from Maḍmūn b. Japheth to Ben Yijū in India, the list of expenses charged to Ben Yijū's account includes an entry for water and shipboard equipment for his slave/agent Bamma, who was about to sail back to India after a sojourn in Aden.[83] The amount charged was one dinar, but there is no way of knowing how much of that was spent on water.

Despite its laconic brevity, the reference to water in Maḍmūn's letter illustrates that water was a commodity and came at a price and suggests that each passenger was responsible for bringing on board a personal water supply. The question of source and access or distribution remains unanswered. Some arrangement may well have existed for keeping water permanently at the port, perhaps in a cistern built for this purpose. In times of drought, shipowners would likely have become anxious and crews and passengers would have become frustrated. If the ship schedules followed closely the timetable of sea and weather and if foreign vessels continued using the port, the city's administrators and local merchants must have worked hard to ensure that the water supply did not fail at the critical times of the boats' departure or arrival.

Aden's Hinterland: Access and Itineraries

Water was only one of the resources for which Aden had to turn toward its immediate and further hinterland. In spite of its strong seaward orientation, Aden was never completely cut off from the land behind it. To be sure, access to the other side of the Aden peninsula was limited, and the passage over the rough terrain arduous and slow. In fact, the precipitous peaks that surround the area of the Crater have counted since antiquity as part of Aden's hinterland rather than of Aden itself.[84] Once Adenis and visitors left the port and crossed al-Maksar, they found themselves off the urban stage and in a dramatically different setting. Yet a handful of small settlements in the city's immediate vicinity buffered the transition from insular Aden to the largely empty open spaces of the coastal plain. These settlements accommodated industries and services that did not fit, either physically or socially, into the fabric of the port city. Knowledge about them has survived mostly because they served as way stations on the routes that connected Aden with the rest of Yemen.

Ibn al-Mujāwir's narrative is, in fact, framed by a series of itineraries that attest to the concatenation of towns, villages, and wells that made possible connections between Aden and the rest of Yemen. Some of the places on the itinerary lists are described only summarily, while others are just mentioned by name; not all of them can be securely identified on the ground.[85] Still, these chains of place-names and distances inscribe settlement patterns and density onto maps that would otherwise appear largely empty of human habitation. A geography of water also emerges, as itineraries were sometimes drawn up—and no doubt frequently imagined—as chains of wells. Ibn al-Mujāwir offers lists of named wells, distinguishing between those close to and connected with specific way stations and those located between settlements.[86]

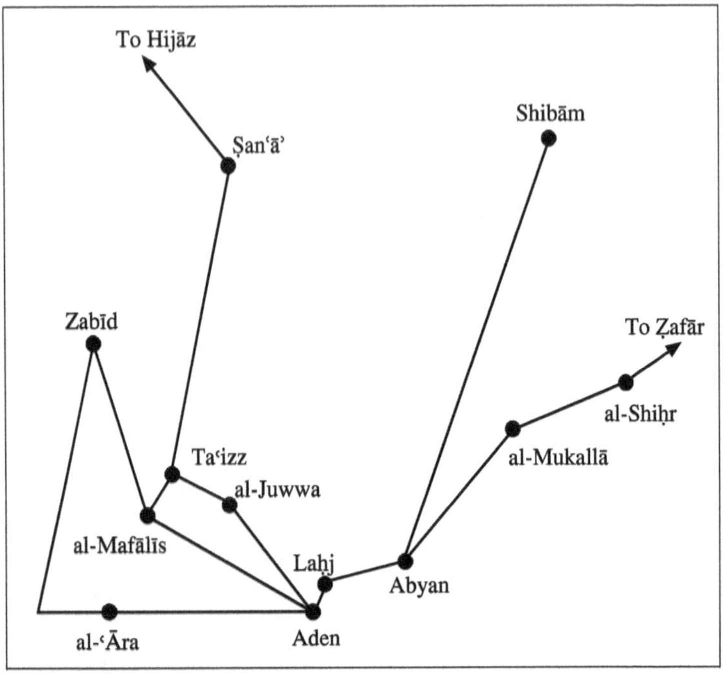

Schematic map of caravan routes connecting Aden with the rest of Yemen.

Plotting the 7th/13th-century traveler's itineraries involving Aden results in a map of lines radiating out of the port city in five main directions. A coast-hugging route runs through al-ʿĀra, travels around the Bāb al-Mandab to the Tihāma, and ultimately connects Aden with Zabīd.[87] A second westward route runs inland through the stronghold of al-Mafālīs, a fortified place built along the mountain path from which journeys to either the Tihāma coast or north to Taʿizz and other inland cities were possible.[88] To the east of the al-Mafālīs road, another route connects Aden more directly with the town of al-Juwwa, near Taʿizz. In the other direction, an inland route runs northeast to Shibām, in the Wadi Ḥaḍramawt, while closer to due east lies the coastal route that leads to the Hadrami and ultimately the Dhofari ports.[89]

These internal Yemeni land routes of course connect with greater roads that led to the rest of the Arabian Peninsula and beyond. In the descriptions of these latter roads, the usual geographic referent is access to Mecca. Indeed, the two coast-hugging routes—to the Tihāma and to the Ḥaḍramawt and Oman—clearly coincide with an extended route that took travelers all the way between Oman and Mecca.[90] The inland routes to al-Juwwa and to al-Mafālīs also could lead to Taʿizz, Sanaa, and ultimately to the holy city, either along the interior Najd road or along the better-known coastal route.[91] Keeping the routes open was thus both a matter of immense economic importance and a question of prestige. Rasulid sultans built and maintained routes, water facilities, and travelers' accommodations; led expeditions against highway robbers; and promoted traffic by establishing settlements and markets in remote areas. Centuries earlier, al-Ḥusayn b. Salāma, a regent of the Ziyadid dynasty, is said to have established mosques all the way from Ḥaḍramawt to Mecca.[92]

The comparison with a colonial map of caravan routes radiating out of Aden is eloquently instructive about the difference between roads and routes. Some roads appear to have remained in use (or of interest to the administration at Aden) during the British colonial era: the route to Mafālīs appears to be identical with its medieval counterpart, and a second inland road running further east and to the north may coincide with the Juwwa route. Conversely, the westbound coastal route represents a striking absence from the colonial map, and the eastward routes appear abandoned in favor of a much shorter haul to the port of Shuqrā, where goods were exported to al-Mukallā and al-Shiḥr by boat.[93] By contrast, the significance of pilgrimage land routes and complex settlement connections of the medieval period inscribed the coastal routes into the map of Aden's heyday. All of these connections between the city and its inland and coastal hinterland filtered through the city's environs. A number of place-names that can only have been situated in Aden's immediate vicinity recur in the itinerary lists; these places were inextricably tied to the city's fortunes.

Al-Mabāh

On Ibn al-Mujāwir's itineraries, the first stop after leaving the city or the last one before entering it (and thus presumably the closest locale to Aden) was al-Mabāh, a small village that the sources appear to locate on the peninsula itself, close to al-Maksar and to the city.[94] The medieval place-name has gone largely unnoticed by modern scholars, but if Ibn al-Mujāwir's and Abū Makhrama's accounts are mapped onto the present-day topography of the peninsula, it becomes clear that al-Mabāh must have stood at the site of present-day al-Maʿalla' on the northwestern shore of the Aden peninsula.[95] In the early part of the 19th century, al-Maʿalla' was a small fishing village and caravan terminal, separate from Aden; only later did it become a district of the modern town.[96]

Abū Makhrama provides a relatively detailed account of al-Mabāh, which in his days had been reduced to ruins, doubtless as a result of the conflicts that the Portuguese and Ottoman presence in the region entailed. In earlier times, Abū Makhrama recounts, the inhabitants of al-Mabāh were mostly fishermen, and they produced *nūra* and *ḥuṭum*, two compounds apparently produced by burning.[97] The increasingly busy and commercial waterfront of Aden proper may no longer have been able to accommodate the local fishermen with their little boats, jumbles of nets, and other fishing equipment; al-Mabāh then would have grown out of their displacement from the city proper.[98] The sources mention fishermen (*ṣayyādīn*) at Aden proper only in connection with its ancient past and never again thereafter.[99] The absence of references to "urban" fishermen probably does not result merely from a bias in the record against the city's invisible workers but may indicate that fishing activities had moved to al-Mabāh.

As for the industries that Abū Makhrama associates with the place, the local production of *nūra*, a lime-and-fat compound used to preserve ship timbers, is connected with fishermen's cultures in the region to this day.[100] The medieval fishermen of al-Mabāh probably mixed the compound and used it to maintain their boats. It is also likely that they specialized in the maintenance and repair of ships in general and that the village was Aden's boatbuilding center. The location of al-Mabāh on the western shore of the Aden peninsula means that the local beach is better sheltered than the Crater beach on Front Bay and is therefore ideal for boatbuilding. In fact, it was being used for that purpose when the British arrived.[101]

Both Ibn al-Mujāwir and the Muẓaffar register connect *ḥuṭum* production with soap making and with the Zabīd area.[102] The Adeni substance may be related to the homonymous compound manufactured in the 19th century from the *ʿasal* plant and possibly to the potash made by burning "Aden balsam" and exported to colonial India as a cleaning agent.[103] *Ḥuṭum* appears to have shared with the manufacture of *nūra* a process that involved burning and possibly noxious gases. Lime kilns, in which lime for building construction was produced by heating up and then quenching lumps of local coral, operated in al-Maʿalla' in the 19th century, and the potash sent from Aden to India was also produced outside of the city.[104] Similarly, in medieval times, polluting industrial activity appears to have been relegated to al-Mabāh, a location beyond the urban limits of the port city.

Finally, Abū Makhrama locates a *miḥlāja* (cotton gin) at al-Mabāh.[105] The existence of a thriving textile industry in medieval Yemen is well known, and Rasulid sources not only offer a wealth of new information about organization and production but also testify to a lively trade in imported textiles and raw materials.[106] That Aden was a center of textile manufacture throughout the medieval period seems clear. Medieval authors occasionally apply the designation "Adeni" to cloths and clothing.[107] Moreover, Geniza documents, Ibn al-Mujāwir, and Rasulid sources testify to the imports at Aden of dyeing materials potentially destined for local use.[108] Finally, Rasulid sources also mention large-scale production of cotton in nearby Laḥj and Abyan.[109]

An inventory preserved in the Geniza and dating to around 527/1133 includes "a red *burd* cloak of local manufacture" among the possessions of an Egyptian merchant who died in Aden.[110] Adeni cloth does not feature prominently in the records of the Jewish traders, and the imports of textiles and garments from India and Egypt may indicate that local Yemeni cloth was at this time no match for the more fashionable Indian and Egyptian products.[111] However, ready access to abundant raw materials, both local and imported, as well as to a cosmopolitan market of buyers must have helped the factory at al-Mabāh, and the local product may have filled a special niche in the market. Such was the case with locally produced glass, as will be discussed later in this chapter.

The presence of a *miḥlāja* in al-Mabāh hints at a deliberate ordering of urban and extraurban space, with the relegation of industry to the environs of Aden proper. The term "*miḥlāja*" implies processing of the vegetal material and production of thread; such an industry entailed a complex organization, which a simpler sartorial operation relying on imported thread or cloth did not. That the facilities, regardless of their nature, were located at al-Mabāh made good sense: they took up no space in the city yet stood within easy reach of the center of commercial activity.

In addition to hosting the manufacture of cloth, boats, and building construction materials, al-Mabāh was also a terminal on the great caravan road network connecting the Yemeni highlands with the Indian Ocean coasts of Arabia. Abū Makhrama quite explicitly describes the functions of a caravan stop so close to the city: those intending to travel from Aden to the hinterland gathered at al-Mabāh, where they waited for a caravan to fill out in numbers and depart; those entering the city by land took advantage of this stop to cleanse themselves and get dressed—presumably, to shed their travel garb and put on city clothes. In other words, Al-Mabāh not only stood sentinel for Aden but also performed the important function of keeping the disorder of animals and road-worn travelers outside the city.

Rubāk

On the mainland beyond al-Maksar but not far from al-Mabāh stood a village known as Rubāk that appears to have been the next-closest settlement to the city. Ibn al-Mujāwir places Rubāk at the tail end of the itinerary from Zabīd to Aden along the coastal route—that is, decidedly to the west of Aden—and at a distance of one *farsakh* from al-Maksar. He describes Rubāk as a place of wells and pools (*ābār* and *birak*) where governors and prominent inhabitants of Aden planted trees and created entire gardens (*basātīn*).[112] Abū Makhrama adds that westward-bound ships stopped at Rubāk to replenish their water supplies from the village's plentiful sweet-water wells.[113] The distance of one *farsakh* from the isthmus (which itself is said to be one *farsakh* from Aden), the seaside or near-coastal location west of Aden, and the sweet-water wells match the characteristics of a location that appears on the first comprehensive archaeological survey map as Bi'r Rubāk.[114] Nothing is known about the archaeological assemblage there except for the fact of the site's existence.[115]

Both Ibn al-Mujāwir and Abū Makhrama treat Rubāk as a place that had seen better days; Abū Makhrama, in fact, describes its last days during the advent of the Ottomans in the region. Archaeology might help clarify the site's chronology, but the extant evidence alone effectively suggests that the place's fortunes were inextricably connected with the fate of Aden itself. Rubāk seems to have fulfilled the same role for the medieval port as the modern village of Shaykh ʿUthmān fulfilled for British colonial Aden: a garden resort and a source of water. During these two periods, Aden's notable and wealthy residents maintained gardens and pleasure houses beyond the peninsula in Rubāk and Shaykh ʿUthmān, respectively, while common folk from Aden, from Laḥj, from Abyan, and from their surrounding villages visited once a month, presumably to fetch water, buy garden produce, and enjoy the oasis-like surroundings.[116] During the medieval period, westbound ships stopped at Rubāk to replenish their water supplies; in British colonial times, Shaykh ʿUthmān was the terminus and source for an aqueduct that brought water to the port city.[117]

In addition to being a garden city, medieval Rubāk may also have supplied Aden's boatbuilding industry with timber for use in ship construction. According to Abū Makhrama, in 625/1227, a shipowner, ʿUmar al-Āmidī, planted a tree in Rubāk that can be iden-

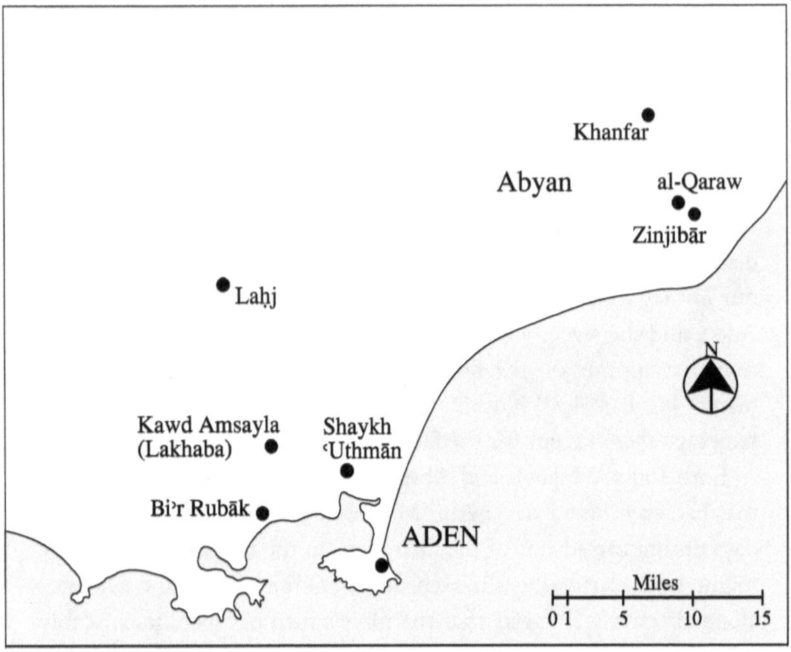

Map 3. The Hinterland of Aden, Including Archaeological Sites

tified with the jackfruit trees (*Artocarpus integrifolia* or *Artocarpus heterophyllus*) used in traditional Arabian boatbuilding to this day.[118] While the date the Adeni chronicler provides lies at the tail end of the period under consideration here, it is not unlikely that the cultivation of this tree at Rubāk went back to earlier times.

Lakhaba

Slightly further inland, about ten kilometers from Aden, lay the village of Lakhaba. Lakhaba appears in all of the primary sources used in this study, including the archaeological record, but still does not make it into regional and general geographies and histories. Among the earlier of these works, even Yemeni specialist al-Hamdānī seems unaware of its existence, which suggests that this place, too, grew along with the fortunes of Aden. Ibn al-Mujāwir states that the town was founded by Abū ʿAmr ʿUthmān b. ʿAlī al-Zanjabīlī, the governor installed by the Ayyubids toward the end of the 6th/12th century; the author also credits this man with the construction of new city walls and the customshouse.[119] Abū Makhrama, who describes the place as a formerly populous but now mostly abandoned village, repeats Ibn al-Mujāwir's foundation date.[120] Geniza letters dating from the first half of the 6th/12th century, however, mention both Lakhaba and its products, thus proving that the place was of considerable significance and size before the Ayyubid period.[121]

Both the literary and the documentary sources agree that Lakhaba was a glass-manufacturing center. Ibn al-Mujāwir and Abū Makhrama explicitly state that it was a source of glass for Aden,[122] and Geniza documents speak of Lakhabī glass exported from Aden to India.[123] Moreover, the manufacture of glass in Aden's hinterland emerges clearly from archaeological surveys and excavation in the Aden and Abyan regions. Of the various sites identified so far, one in particular seems to fit the specifications of medieval Lakhaba. Kawd Amsayla lies about nine kilometers from Aden, a distance that roughly corresponds to Abū Makhrama's 1.75 *farsakh*. More significantly, the glass shards, wasters, and slag that litter this area as well as the widespread ashy deposits indicate extensive glass-making activities and leave little doubt that this place was indeed the origin of Aden's glass exports.[124]

In addition to glass, Lakhaba is said to have supplied Aden with baked bricks (*al-ājurr*),[125] undoubtedly used in general building construction. Abū Makhrama also speaks of presses (*maʿāṣir*), perhaps the traditional type used in Yemen to this day for extracting sesame seed oil.[126] But far from being simply an industrial site, Lakhaba was also a way station, as it was conveniently located both on the northward Mafālīs route and on the track that led from Aden and al-Mabāh to Laḥj and the highlands as well as on the route east to the nearby district of Abyan and further to the Ḥaḍramawt and Dhofar. With several wells in the town itself or in its immediate vicinity, Lakhaba made an ideal caravan stop. Ibn al-Mujāwir describes these wells in some detail, noting the watering capacity of each one.[127] To serve the caravan traffic and the needs of merchants, however transient, the town must have featured some commercial facilities. Abū Makhrama speaks of stores or shops (*dakākīn*),[128] and some negotiations between the people of the coast and the itinerants of the highlands presumably took place there.

Although Lakhaba was a fairly large and settled village with its own mosque, several houses, a score of industrial workshops, and shops and stores serving commercial traffic and transactions, the town remained a roadstead and as a transitional place accommodated venues and behaviors that may have been unacceptable in the city. The evidence that Lakhaba had more than meets the eye in the literary sources is hidden in a postscript penned by a novice India merchant writing to his patron and boss in Egypt.[129] ʿAllān b. Hassūn had arrived at Aden from Egypt, apparently with instructions from ʿArūs b. Joseph to connect with a local cousin, Joseph, before proceeding to India. The two young men clearly did not get along, and ʿAllān makes their differences clear in a letter to ʿArūs b. Joseph, writing plaintively, "Do not ask what Joseph did to me."[130] The cousin had apparently tried to deter ʿAllān from traveling and had then taken money and goods from him for undeclared and, the reader is forced to conclude, suspect purposes. ʿAllān clearly was upset and could not resist insinuating the worst about the cousin. At the end of the letter, after extending final greetings, ʿAllān writes, "Joseph is now sitting in Lakhaba with the *zonot*, fellow revelers, and a beardless youth who ser[ves them drink]."[131]

Why would one have to go all the way to Lakhaba to find fellow revelers, wine bearers, and prostitutes, here cryptically referred to by the Hebrew "*zonot*"?[132] Lakhaba apparently offered not only the establishments where such company could be joined but also, and perhaps more importantly, sufficient distance from Aden's restrictive social space. This is not to say that no revelry occurred in Aden itself, and three Geniza documents offer fleeting but striking glimpses of drinking in town; that one of these occasions ended up in terrible trouble for the participants, however, indicates the potential risks.[133] The taverns of a full-fledged caravan town such as Lakhaba must have thus attracted not only travelers and other transients but also upstanding Adenis who apparently saw the town as a temporary refuge, conveniently accessible within less than a day from Aden but far enough removed from the city's proprieties.

Laḥj

Further inland to the north of Lakhaba, one night's journey away from Aden, according to Ibn al-Mujāwir, was the town of Laḥj.[134] Unlike the small places discussed so far, Laḥj appears in the sources as early as the 3rd/9th century.[135] It apparently formed part of the territories of Aden and at least from Zurayid times onward was governed by the port's rulers.[136] Yet few archaeological remains of any significance have been assigned to the medieval period in Laḥj itself; medieval layers may have been obliterated by periods of intense occupation and agriculture.[137] Moreover, the Geniza documents make no mention of Laḥj, and Ibn al-Mujāwir refers to it mostly in passing: twice he simply places it in relation to the sites around it, and only once does he give it lengthier consideration, speaking of its wells and telling the apocryphal story of their excavation by the mythical Shaddād b. ʿĀd and adding that Adenis in his day got their water from the same wells.[138]

The silence of the Geniza documents is somewhat perplexing, especially in view of the connections between the Adeni Jewish merchants and the Jewish communities in the Yemeni highlands that will be discussed shortly. Laḥj was located on the great roads connecting Aden and the coast around it with the mountains in the north and with the eastern regions of the Ḥaḍramawt and Dhofar.[139] Thanks to its wells and fertile surroundings and to its convenient location a night's journey away from Aden, the town constituted a good stopping point both for travelers heading anywhere through the mountains and for traffic approaching the port. Thus, it is unlikely that Jewish merchants did not, like everyone else, stop at Laḥj. Rather, their silence may indicate that their sojourns in town were brief, without any specific local business interest that might warrant a mention in their correspondence. This lacuna may indicate that the Jewish traders did not usually deal in foodstuffs, the most likely exports from Laḥj to Aden.

Indeed, food supply must have constituted an important link between the two settlements. The town was and remains surrounded by fertile land and, given its abundant wells, must have provided Aden with agricultural products that covered part of the city's victual needs. Rasulid texts note the cultivation of sorghum and millet at Laḥj as well as taxes levied on local date palms.[140] More significantly for Aden, Abū Makhrama states that ʿAbdallāh b. Yūsuf al-Tilimsānī earmarked for his renovation of the isthmus bridge "crop revenues from the cultivable lands in Laḥj."[141] Abū Makhrama's account thus suggests that a significant quantity of agricultural produce grown at Laḥj not only fed Aden but also fell under the direct control of the city's administration.

Abyan

Produce and raw material also came from the area of Abyan, the last place in Aden's immediate hinterland to be discussed here. The place-name refers to both the territory northeast of Aden, at about eighteen kilometers from the port, and to its main town.[142] This fertile land has supported considerable settlement since early times, and recent archaeological surveys and excavations have been mapping and describing these settlements. In addition to yielding significant evidence of local agricultural and industrial production, the material record of these settlements also includes imported ceramics, thereby confirming the connection between the district and the world of Indian Ocean trade, probably through Aden.[143]

That a regular connection existed between Aden and Abyan is clear from travel itineraries that mention Abyan as a station on the road leading from the southwestern coast of Yemen to the Ḥaḍramawt and linking Aden with Shibām as well as on the route from

Aden to the region of Dhofar.[144] Two archaeological sites, al-Qaraw/Zinjibār and Khanfar, have yielded substantial medieval material in the district of Abyan, and archaeological opinion leans toward identifying the former with the main settlement in the area during the period under study here. A large site, al-Qaraw, has yielded both a significant assemblage of Chinese ceramics and signs of local industrial activity, most notably pottery and glassmaking.[145] Ibn al-Mujāwir claims that clay used in the building of the cisterns of Aden and that stone for the building of the first finer houses in Zurayid times were transferred to the port from the territories of Abyan.[146] Taken together, the medieval traveler's account and archaeological data suggest the existence of clay sources and stone quarries in the Abyan area as well as the infrastructure for their exploitation on a regional scale.

Given the district's considerable advantages, it may appear strange that the region's globally connected port was at Aden rather than Abyan. Ibn al-Mujāwir, in fact, claims that Aden's population grew and its port rose to prominence only when the *port* of Abyan (*furḍat Abyan*) fell into ruins; in a separate geographical work, Abū Makhrama speaks of Abyan towns and villages that had been ruined and were in his time uninhabited.[147] The combination of Abyan's favorable natural ecology and strategic geographical location on roughly the same major land and sea routes as Aden would make for an excellent entrepôt. Yet Abyan lacks Aden's impregnable defensibility. The insularity of Aden's peninsula perhaps constituted the key factor sustaining its independent and dominant position as the leading maritime entrepôt in the region in medieval times. Abyan, conversely, remained an agricultural and industrial center, privileged environmentally by the surrounding oasis and closely connected to Aden, which far outshone Abyan as an urban center, exploited its resources and location, and probably was the immediate source of all finer things there, such as the Chinese pottery discovered by the archaeologists.

Further Hinterland

A few other names of settlements in the vicinity of Aden appear in the sources. Most of the sites along the caravan routes appear only by name, and it is therefore impossible to evaluate their significance in regional economic, social, and political patterns. But even if they are counted as small villages with little importance beyond their location on the trade and pilgrim routes, they still alter the overall picture of Aden's immediate hinterland, which thus emerges as more populous and settled than has previously been imagined.

A systematic study of subsistence patterns along the southern coast of Yemen in medieval times would contribute enormously in understanding Aden's relationship with its hinterland and dependence on it for food. How much of Aden's food was imported from overseas, and how much was transported there from its hinterland? Of the Yemeni production, how much of what ended up feeding the population of Aden came from the port's immediate hinterland, and what percentage was brought in from further afield, the fertile terraces of the Yemeni highlands? The sources offer glimpses of imports of highland products, such as sesame and the dye plant madder, from the mountains into the city.[148] And while the amount or percentage of grain from the highlands entering Aden is elusive, the city appears to have depended on its hinterland as much as on its foreland for nourishment.

A Geniza letter from Aden dating from the first half of the 6th/12th century highlights the fact that the Yemeni hinterland contributed significantly to the city's food stores in Zurayid times. Khalaf b. Isaac informs his correspondent and business associate, Ḥalfon b. Nathanel, about a drought that is plaguing the entire country and has caused prices to skyrocket.[149] To emphasize the gravity of the situation, he quotes the price of millet (*dhukhn*) and wheat (*burr*) as one dinar or more for three measures (*makāyyal*) of grain, adding that all foodstuffs sell at exorbitant prices.[150] Khalaf also tells of the political turmoil that ended the dual rule of Zurayid Aden; in his narrative, the power struggle appears to have followed at the heels of and perhaps been fueled by the food crisis.[151] Even before imagining the social and political ramifications of this food crisis, it seems justifiable to argue that the dramatic effect of local drought and crop failure on the economy of the city proves beyond doubt the dependence of that economy on local agriculture.

Basic staples were also imported from abroad, at least by the time of Ibn al-Mujāwir's visit: prominent on his list of merchandise that did not incur import taxes at Aden's customshouse are grain imports, particularly wheat (*ḥinṭa*) and flour (*daqīq*) from Egypt and rice from Egypt and India.[152] The list also includes other victuals such as oils and sugar. The silence of Jewish traders concerning large-scale grain imports may simply reflect their noninvolvement in the grain trade as a whole. Alternatively, imports from overseas and reliance on nondomestically grown grain and other victuals may have intensified by the time the Geniza letters petered out.

Finally, Aden's economic relationship with its immediate hinterland and with the Yemeni highlands beyond it was of course at least partially reciprocal. Not all of the port's transit trade moved by sea. An indeterminate quantity of goods that passed through the city and originated either in the Indian Ocean or in the Mediterranean worlds found its way to inland Yemen. Archaeology and the Geniza documents provide occasional clues that simply spotlight a few of the endless possibilities for the types of merchandise involved. Scatters of Far Eastern ceramic wares at sites in Aden's immediate hinterland such as Kawd Amsayla and the settlements in the Abyan area are most likely to have transited through Aden and represent a ubiquitously desirable India trade good. A letter from Aden's Maḍmūn b. Japheth to his good friend and business partner in India, Ben Yijū, highlights the case of a third merchant, Abū al-Khayr, who had just left Aden for the highlands with a consignment of Egyptian linen.[153] There is little reason to doubt that pepper and other spices, dyeing materials, and iron reached the same inland destinations as linen and pottery.

2 | *Topography of the Harbor*

Nature supplied a mountain city on the sea, a fair port on a harsh coast.

STEPHEN EPSTEIN, *Genoa and the Genoese*

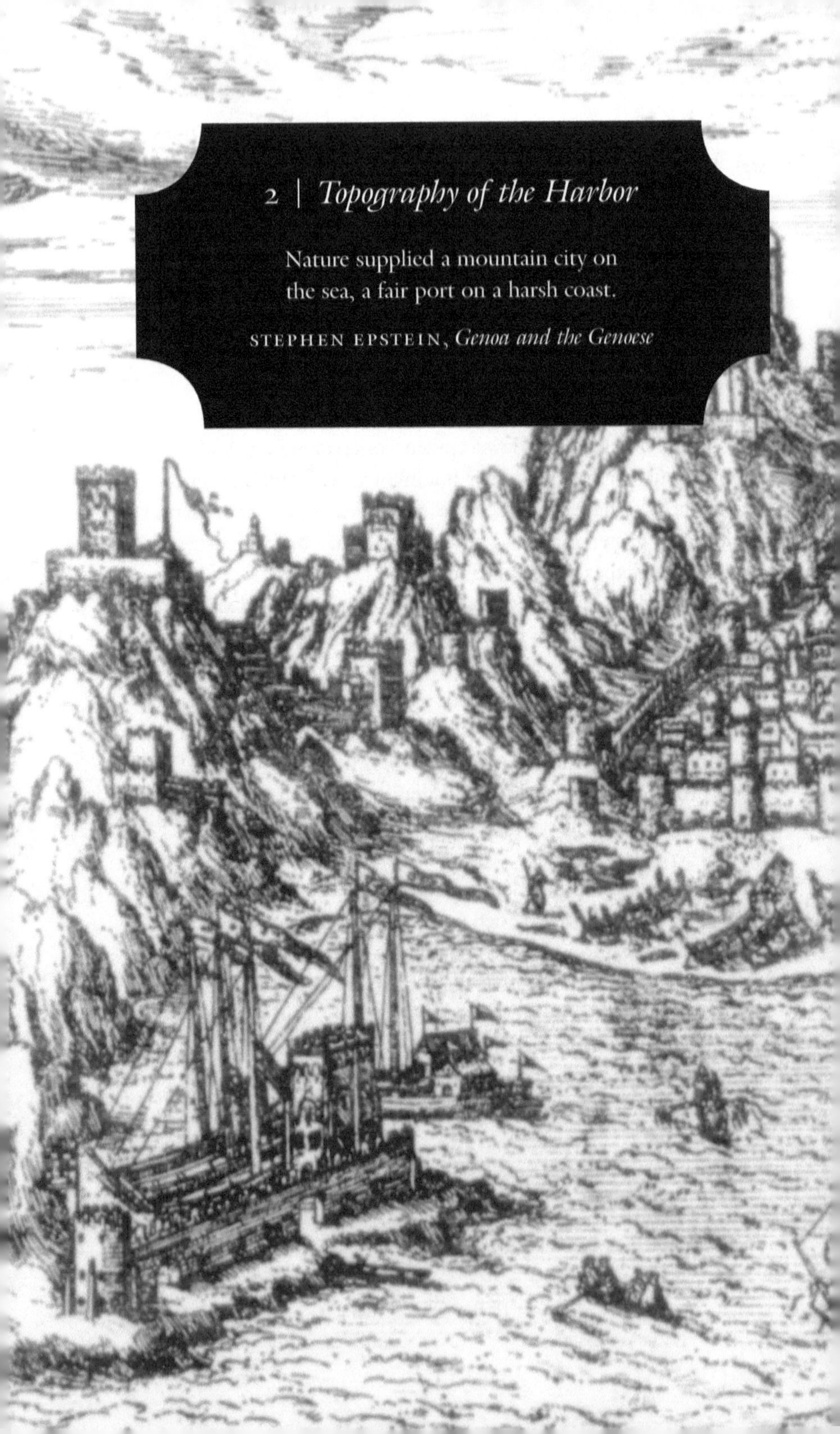

The Quest for Harbor Topographies

Marine topography is one of Aden's greatest geographical assets: "a fair port on a harsh coast" is as apt a description of the Arabian entrepôt as of Genoa in the Mediterranean. From the humblest fishing village to the busiest international port, all maritime settlements can be said to include watery extensions of the inhabited urban space. Beyond the basic distinctions of protected and unprotected anchorages and natural and artificial harbors, anchorage and harbor types and typologies are as varied as the landscapes, climates, and cultures of the littoral. In this chapter I offer a reconstruction of the layout of Aden's main harbor, with the aim of elucidating the procedures associated with it and the events enacted in its space. This investigation also sheds light on the effort required to maintain the harbor for the purposes of long-distance trade. Finally, the study of Aden's harbor speaks to the emerging typology of western Indian Ocean ports, a topic to which I shall return in the concluding chapter.

The building and maintenance of harbor works has rightly been considered an indicator of the technological, administrative, economic, and social complexity and sophistication of a coastal community.[1] It is important, however, not to fall into the interpretative blind spot that equates lack of built maritime infrastructure with lesser degrees of maritime and urban development. In fact, the absence of formal harbor works often entails alternative efficient and often ingenious solutions to issues of port layout and function, such as anchorage, berthing, lighterage, and loading and unloading. Thus, my discussion of built harbor infrastructure rests on the premise that harbor works simply constitute one window—a tangible, easily accessible, and therefore welcome kind of testimony—on the complexities and peculiarities of administering a maritime entrepôt.

While classical archaeologists and other scholars of the premodern Mediterranean have made important contributions to harbor studies,[2] until recently little scholarly attention was paid to harbors of the Islamic world and less still to their physical components.[3] The received wisdom concerning the configuration of ports of the southern and eastern Mediterranean emphasizes the decline in early Islamic times of the sophisticated inner harbors of the Greco-Roman period and the Muslim states' failure to muster the technological know-how and organization required for harbor restoration and revitalization.[4] That some of the Greco-Roman harbors slowly declined and fell into ruins in Late Antiquity is an indisputable fact,[5] but recent studies of the harbors built after the Arab conquests are beginning to flesh out an interesting and complex historical picture that can hardly be dismissed as a story of decline.[6] One example is the port of Clysma/Kulzum at the head of the Gulf of Suez; the takeover by the Muslim conquerors spurred new development there, including the construction of harbor works.[7]

As for Indian Ocean ports, the prevailing view is that they generally lacked formal built features, partly because in contrast to the Mediterranean world, the Indian Ocean was perceived as relatively free of naval warfare until the 16th century.[8] Again, individual studies of western Indian Ocean ports reveal that this generalization obscures the variety of solutions to anchorage challenges that maritime people of the region devised. In some areas, coral growth and rapidly deposited alluvial silt create shallows that are nonnavigable for even medium-draft ships. Building any kind of harbor works in such terrain would require an enormous input of labor and resources, and solutions other than built harbor works indeed prevailed. Ships anchored at roadsteads, at some distance from shore, changed station according to the prevailing winds, and unloaded their wares onto small lighters that could safely carry cargo over the shallows. While archaeology and written sources show that this scheme applied at important medieval ports of the Indian Ocean such as Ṣuḥār and Sīrāf,[9] it should not be considered "typical" of the Indian Ocean. Other places such as Manda in the Lamu Archipelago,[10] Kish/Qays in the Persian Gulf,[11] and Aden itself exhibit a number of different, tellingly adaptive anchorage arrangements.

The City's Seaward Orientation

If Aden were a theater, its harbor would be the main stage. Portuguese, German, and Dutch engravings and drawings as well as photographs from the British colonial era show that in times of wealth and expansion, the city filled the narrow plain of the Crater and spread amphitheatrically away from the sea to the higher ground of the surrounding foothills.[12] The sea views from the edges of town must have been spectacular and the sense of theater heightened when approaching ships appeared on the horizon or when departing vessels made for the open sea. In the 10th/16th century, Abū Makhrama describes how "in the old days" the populace gathered at an elevated open plaza (*faḍā*) overlooking the harbor and sat there admiring such views. This must have been the state of affairs in Zurayid and Ayyubid times. At a later time, the Adeni historian informs us, Tahirid ruler ʿAbd al-Wahhāb b. Dāwūd ordered the construction on that spot of the Dār al-Bandar, a formal two-story structure designed specifically as a convenient observatory for ship traffic, a place where the people of Aden could stroll and rejoice in the maritime vistas.[13]

The reasonable assumption that Adenis must have delighted in the nautical spectacle is thus neatly supported by the textual evidence in what is a rare glimpse of the pleasure that the common folk of a medieval maritime city took in waterfront views.[14] Even without such explicit confirmation from the sources, however, it is easy to imagine that all of the city's commercial eyes would turn when ships and their precious cargoes entered the harbor to drop anchor and unload or, newly laden with the city's fortunes, made for the open sea. In the days when overseas market conditions were largely unforeseeable and the whims of the weather could make or break any commercial enterprise, the sight of ships coming or going would stir some combination of joy, expectation, and anxiety in the hearts of those urban spectators who made their livings through trade.

Despite the prominence of the harbor in urban life, however, the local merchants, as far as their personal correspondence preserved in the Cairo Geniza indicates, seldom made more than fleeting references to the topography of the anchorage facing the town. A good example of such casual remarks appears in a letter from Joseph al-Lebdī to Ḥasan b. Bundār. The author, an India trader whose protracted lawsuit in Egypt produced a valuable series of surviving documents, remembers how the addressee, a member of the prominent Jewish-Adeni Bundār family, had come to the waterfront to bid him farewell when he was departing from Aden: "You graciously came down and saw me off at the sea."[15] While the letter makes only this vague allusion to the harbor, Ḥasan clearly bid his friend farewell on the beach as the latter prepared to catch a ride on a lighter and head out to board a ship anchored offshore. Alternatively, Ḥasan may have taken a lighter out to the ship: passengers commonly boarded ships the night before departure.[16]

Precisely where in the harbor a ship was anchored may have briefly concerned crew, boatmen, porters, merchants, passengers, and their friends staying on shore, but such information understandably never appears in routine mercantile correspondence. In view of this general silence on topographical details, it is all the more exciting to find the odd reference to place and topography in letters written by Jewish traders. In one such case, extraordinary historical circumstances, keenly observing and avidly corresponding eyewitnesses, and the fortunate accident of preservation have produced two surviving accounts full of allusions to the layout of Aden's harbor.[17] In addition to these two documents, passages from Ibn al-Mujāwir and Abū Makhrama and the results of recent archaeological investigations in the area of the Crater contribute to a tentative reconstruction of medieval Aden's main anchorage.

Two adjacent bays are associated with the site of the Crater. They are separated by the steep and narrow island of Ṣīra, which stretches like a curved arm roughly perpendicular to the shoreline. The bay di-

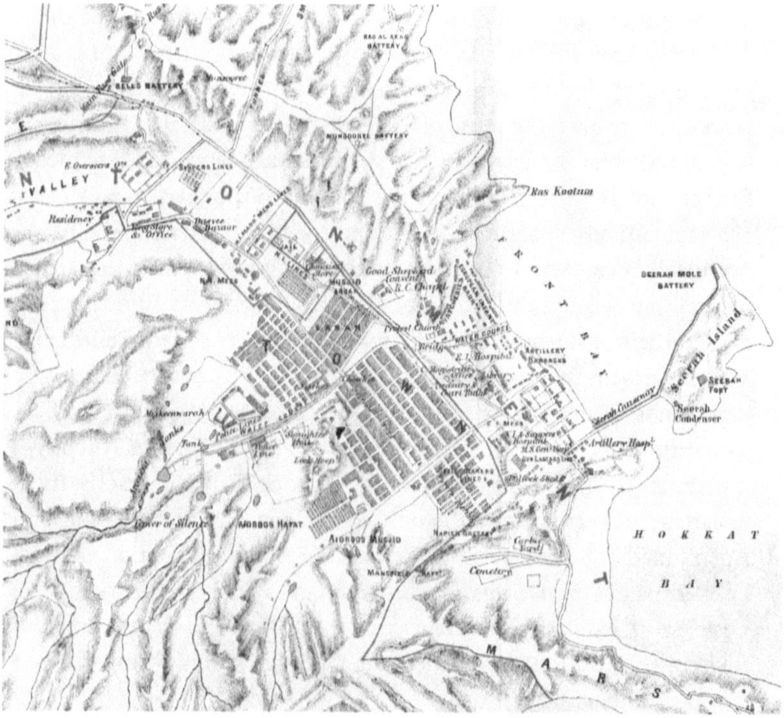

The Crater area, part of a topographical map of the Aden peninsula. (From Frederick Mercer Hunter, *An Account of the British Settlement of Aden in Arabia* [London: Trübner, 1877])

rectly in front of the Crater, north of and partly embraced by Ṣīra Island, is Ṣīra Bay, also known since the British colonial era as Front Bay. A causeway has been built to connect Ṣīra Island to the peninsula, but in Ibn al-Mujāwir's time a deep channel, known as al-Maʿjalayn, separated islet and peninsula.[18] Immediately to the south, on the other side of Ṣīra, is Ibn al-Mujāwir's Ḥuqqāt, modern Holkat Bay, which served as an occasional anchorage but lacked the immediacy of access to the city that Ṣīra Bay offered.

Ṣīra Bay thus served as Aden's main harbor.[19] With its limited space, shallow waters, and extensive mud flats (*sabkha*), which become exposed at low tide, Ṣīra Bay today may appear to be an unlikely candidate for the main anchorage of an important entrepôt, hosting thirty or more ships simultaneously.[20] Here geoarchaeological research helps make sense of a largely altered landscape: sondages have shown that the bay was once significantly deeper and extended further into the flat ground of the Crater than it does today. The bay's unnaturally straight shoreline and the lack of boats in the harbor are eloquent signs of the land reclamation and gradual silting that have all but deleted the old harbor's contours.[21] An additional witness to the transformation of the shoreline between medieval times and the present may be the position of a pre-19th-century structure that stands in the Crater at some distance back from the sea. The structure is known as the Aden minaret, but it is unclear whether it ever served as a tower attached to a mosque. Edward Prados, the researcher who conducted the only serious physical investigation of Aden's medieval harbor, proposes that the structure functioned as a light- or signal house. Signs of erosion and remains of marine deposits at its base suggest that it once stood closer to the water and thus constitute additional evidence that the bay extended much further inland than it does today.[22]

Deeper and broader, the Ṣīra Bay of medieval times was therefore better suited for hosting seagoing ships than its present shape would suggest. Mud flats must have existed even then, but with enough space to anchor the ships within the bay at some distance from shore, shallow-drafted lighters could easily transport people and merchandise over the final short distances from anchorage to shore. While the geomorphology of the bay did not, after all, detract significantly from its desirability as an anchorage, its exposure to waves caused by the prevailing winds of the winter monsoon constituted a real handicap. Indeed, this factor would have rendered Ṣīra Bay less desirable than the western bay had the peninsula's geography differed. Modern sailing manuals mention the eastern side of the peninsula as a possible haven and commend the sheltered waters at the lee of Ṣīra Island in the summer months but caution that heavy swells set in during the northeastern monsoons of winter.[23] How was the potentially nagging problem of a seasonally exposed anchorage managed when this bay served as Aden's main harbor?

One possible answer is that during the busy months of the northeastern monsoons, when mild weather and steady winds allowed the heaviest sea traffic, most ships left Aden for western India, where they remained for weeks or even months, collecting merchandise. The vessels returned only at the end of the winter season, just in time to run homeward before the last of the northeasterlies. The emphasis on travel while the weather held meant that during the winter, ships rarely stayed at port to face the nuisance of winter swells.[24] By the time the trading season ended and ships returned from their missions, the calendar had already turned to late spring. When the summer southwesterlies set in, rendering shipping unsafe and confining ships to their home ports, Ṣīra Bay offered the necessary shelter for long-term anchorage.

But even if seasonal traffic patterns meant briefer sojourns in Aden's harbor at the time of year when it was most exposed to the weather, the inconvenience of alternative temporary anchorage and protracted lightering during this period must have driven the authorities of the port and the city to a more decisive solution. This solution appears to have entailed the building of a breakwater or mole, known from Abū Makhrama's account as *al-shiṣna*. The late medieval historian tells us that the *shiṣna* was of sturdy construction and occupied a spot at the far end of the harbor (*al-bandar*), behind the anchorage (*marsā al-marākib*), on the seaward side.[25] He attributes its building to the ancients (*al-awwalūn*) and unequivocally states that its purpose was to protect the harbor from heavy swells that set in during the season of the *azyab*, the northeast winter monsoon.[26] In Tahirid times, some of the structure was dismantled, and the stones were reused for the building of the Dār al-Bandar; the ensuing gap allowed the waves to rush into the harbor and destroy a great many ships at anchor. Alarmed by the disaster, the Adenis immediately used stones and dirt to repair the breakwater well enough to fulfill its role as a barrier but apparently did not reconstruct the original well-appointed form.

What evidence corroborates Abū Makhrama's testimony? Neither a description of the structure nor even the term "*shiṣna*" as such appear in any other written record. However, early modern pictorial renderings of the port show a structure at one end of Ṣīra Island that appears to be a mole.[27] Moreover, the recent archaeological survey of the port by Prados and his team located a segment of a breakwater, visible "at the extreme end of the harbor on the northern side of Ṣīra Island." They then traced a built feature extending from the above-water remains.[28] While Prados does not mention Abū Makhrama's *shiṣna*, his find must be identified with the medieval structure. The location and identification of the breakwater is of great importance because, as Prados notes, it indicates the builders' capacity for underwater construction. Moreover, its existence elucidates the configuration of the medieval harbor as a whole, supplementing the testimony of Ibn al-Mujāwir and the two remarkable Geniza letters.

Accounts of a Naval Blockade

In addition to riveting narratives of dramatic action, contemporary accounts of naval sieges offer maritime historians and archaeologists some of the most valuable and detailed data on ancient and medieval harbor topography.[29] Neither Ibn al-Mujāwir nor the two Adeni authors of the relevant Geniza letters set out to describe the topography of Aden's harbor but simply sought to tell the exciting story of the naval siege of Aden by a force from the island Kish/Qays. This was a unique occurrence in the city's history to that date, and the attempt to divert or usurp the port's commercial fortunes provided prime material not only for the account of the city's keenly observing visitor but also for the correspondence of its business-oriented residents; if nothing else, the disruption of the tempo of commercial life affected both the Adenis and their business partners and friends abroad. While the authors of the two letters may have expected their correspondents to know the harbor well, and while Ibn al-Mujāwir shows no special concern for his readers' grasp of the local topography, the descriptions of movements and clashes that unfolded before the city's waterfront yield several invaluable topographical clues.

Kish/Qays was the island port that replaced Sīrāf as the main entrepôt in the Arabian Gulf from the 5th/11th century onward.[30] Geographers and travelers in the 6th/12th and 7th/13th centuries describe Kish/Qays as an affluent port with a lively market, a cosmopolitan community of traders, and rulers whose power depended primarily on shipping.[31] Given its maritime aspirations, the government at Kish/Qays must have seen Aden as a formidable competitor. Obviously interested and informed, the ruler of the island chose a moment of strife within Aden's leadership to attack the Indian Ocean port in hopes of adding its tremendous trade revenues to those of his dominion.[32] Ibn al-Mujāwir gives no specific date for the event but associates it with the time of the Zurayid cousins Muḥammad b. Abī al-Ghārāt and Saba' b. Abī al-Suʿūd, who ruled the city and its territories jointly from their forts al-Khaḍrā', at the seafront, and al-Taʿkar, at the inland entrance to the town, respectively.[33] Later rivalry between Saba' and Muḥammad's brother and successor, ʿAlī b. Abī al-Ghārāt, escalated into open hostilities and ultimately resulted in the defeat and death of ʿAlī in 533/1138; ironically, the victor died later that year.[34] The naval siege of Aden apparently took place sometime before the eventful year that witnessed the dramatic power struggle and deaths of the two rulers, and Goitein has shown that the two letters contain sufficient evidence to fix the events in 529/1134–35.[35]

How do the authors of the two Geniza letters describe the siege, and how do their eyewitness reports compare with the account of Ibn al-Mujāwir? In a long letter to his India-based business partner and friend, Ben Yijū, Maḍmūn b. Japheth devotes no more than thirteen lines to the events. He starts by briefly mentioning claims by the ruler of Kish/Qays over a piece of Aden (*qiṭʿa min ʿadan*), then enumerates the force launched when these demands were summarily dismissed. Fifteen enemy ships and seven hundred men in all arrived in Aden and waited in ambush for incoming ships at the *mukallā ʿadan* (Aden's station for ships).[36] *Al-mukallā* thus appears to have been the routine anchorage for oceangoing ships in Aden's harbor.[37]

To offer adequate berths for fifteen vessels, an anchorage in the harbor must have been at some distance from shore, clear of the coastal shallows of Ṣīra Bay. In addition, the anchorage must have offered some protection from the weather: the expectation of incoming ships and the voyage of the enemy vessels from Kish/Qays point to a time during the winter months, not only the sailing season but also the period when Aden was exposed to the winds of the northeast monsoon that drive heavy swells against the harbor. Maḍmūn explicitly states that the attack by the force from Kish/Qays came "this year at the beginning of [the seafaring] season."[38] The prescribed and customary navigational schedules suggest a time between early November and mid-December: in the late 9th/15th century, Ibn Mājid advises that the best time for westbound ships to leave the Arabian Gulf is at the end of October,[39] while in the late 7th/13th century, the almanac of al-Malik al-Ashraf specifically notes that the earliest arrival of ships from Kish/Qays at Aden occurs in early November.[40] Following sailing custom, the naval expedition must have reached Aden sometime in early November, when the northeasterly winter monsoon had set in. If the vessels stationed inside Aden's harbor, then some protection against the prevailing winds must have been available there. Here, then, is supporting evidence for the existence of a breakwater—Abū Makhrama's *al-shiṣna* and the structure that Prados appears to have located at the northeastern end of Ṣīra Island.

Maḍmūn relates that the enemy did not enter the town (*al-balad*) but that the mere presence of the seven-hundred-strong force in the anchorage (*al-mukallā*) caused great panic among Aden's inhabitants. Defenders and attackers clearly stood facing each other, presumably the former from behind some kind of city waterfront defenses and the latter somewhere in the far (that is, seaward) side of the harbor. Although the physical distance between the opponents appears to have been generally maintained throughout the siege, Maḍmūn's report suggests that a melee took place at some point: in addition to enemy lives lost to thirst and starvation (a clear indication of physical isolation and lack of supplies), he speaks of the killing of enemy troops and the damage inflicted on enemy ships by spears.[41]

Despite suffering hardship and losses, the enemy apparently persisted, and the situation was resolved only when two friendly ships broke the blockade and brought reinforcements to the city. According to Maḍmūn, the first vessels to reach the besieged city were two ships belonging to Rāmisht, an important personality on Aden's shipping scene.[42] The enemy engaged the two vessels but failed to overpower them. Breaking through the enemy ranks, Rāmisht's ships then "entered the harbor, took on a great number of troops, and [the enemy] were expelled from the harbor and left to roam in the open sea." In both instances translated here as "harbor," Maḍmūn uses the term "*al-bandar*."[43]

Maḍmūn's *al-bandar* clearly differed from *al-mukallā*: in his account, the former term denotes the wider harbor space extending from the beach, where the troops boarded the newly arrived boats, to the seaward end, where the ships first entered. Beyond *al-bandar* is the open sea (*al-baḥr*), where the enemy forces roamed for a while after being expelled from their besieging position in the harbor. *Al-mukallā*, conversely, appears only in connection with the station of the enemy ships and presumably of any ships that anchored in the harbor; it constituted but a part of the harbor, a protected place where seagoing ships could anchor. Its distance from shore and its apparent proximity to the harbor's entrance place it at harbor's outer, seaward, end. *Al-mukallā* was probably created out of the building of the mole or breakwater, *al-shiṣna*. The anchorage thus comprised the waters between the line of the mole and Ṣīra Island.[44]

The second letter, sent by Maḍmūn's relative, Khalaf b. Isaac, to Cairo and to associates who had previously been in Aden, runs to more than twenty-six lines of text and gives a significantly more detailed account of the events of the siege, or, as he puts it, "what befell us after your departure."[45] He specifies that the blockade lasted two months, not only lending perspective to Maḍmūn's assertion that some enemy troops died of hunger and thirst but also casting new light on the absence of ships from the harbor throughout the siege and until the arrival of Rāmisht's ships. While it was not unusual for the harbor to remain largely empty for several weeks after the sailing season had started, that two months passed without a single arrival indicates that news of the blockade kept prospective visitors away from the port.

Khalaf also more explicitly describes the adversaries' positioning: the defenders were on land and had fled from their houses to the city's forts (*al-ḥuṣūn*), while the attackers were at sea at *al-mukallā*.[46] This information suggests that whatever wall screened the town along the waterfront did not inspire sufficient confidence; otherwise, large numbers of the inhabitants would not have fled their houses. However, the city seems to have been configured so that the enemy did not dare take the offensive. A light wall, perhaps made of perishable materials, or a continuous facade of waterfront houses must have shielded the goings-on inside the town from outside view and discouraged the Qaysi troops from any attempt to disembark on the stretch of beach in front of the city.[47] Locked in a tense standoff, neither side could make a move; even when a thousand men arrived to reinforce Aden's five hundred defenders, the deadlock continued.

Before coming to the final episode of the siege, Khalaf provides one more clue about the spatial relationships among town, Ṣīra, anchorage (*al-mukallā*), and breakwater (*al-shiṣna*). The enemy, Khalaf relates, had disembarked on Ṣīra Island and remained there "day and night."[48] Divine providence, however, intervened with bad weather, stranding the enemy troops on Ṣīra. The defenders seized on the opportunity to attack, heads rolled, and the enemy camp was thoroughly looted.[49] This attack probably explains the casualties and damage of which Maḍmūn writes.

What does the Ṣīra incident reveal about the location where it took place? First and foremost, it indicates the proximity between *al-mukallā* and some part of Ṣīra Island, where it made sense for the enemy troops to disembark. Second, it shows that although *al-mukallā* provided reasonably safe berths for ships, particularly strong weather from the northeast could still pose a threat to vessels steering close to Ṣīra's lee shore: heavy swells meant that ships could not near the shore and pick up the stranded troops. Finally, it suggests that the landward side of the island had not fallen under enemy control, so that when the opportunity presented itself, the Adeni forces crossed safely from the mainland and decimated their foes.

According to Khalaf's recension, the weather—in particular, the monsoon-driven waves—helped end the siege. As Rāmisht's ships made a go for the town, a strong wind drove the pursuing enemy "left and right" and gave the friendly ships the opportunity to enter the harbor unharmed.[50] His description makes perfect sense in light of the location of the harbor entrance, the effects of the prevailing winds, and the exigencies of sailing with the lateen sails that all ships in this incident must have been carrying. In the prevailing northeasterly, ships entering the harbor would be running before the wind or would have been pushed to shore by the waves. Ships exiting the harbor to block the way of the incoming ships, conversely, would have had to struggle against wind and waves and to change direction by wearing around—Khalaf's "sailing right and left"—several times.[51]

To Maḍmūn's report of the siege's outcome, Khalaf adds that when the enemy lost the maritime advantage over the defenders, the attackers had to flee "*khalfa al-jabal*" (behind the mountain) until the weather turned favorable for their sailing homeward.[52] Khalaf's "mountain" must be either Ṣīra Island—dubbed "Jabal Ṣīra" (Mount Ṣīra) as a result of its precipitous terrain[53]—or the mountainous peninsula itself. If the *jabal* intended is indeed Ṣīra, then the enemy forces, when driven from their station on the harbor side of the island, found refuge at its far, or southern, side.[54] If, on the contrary, the phrase refers to the central massif of the Aden peninsula, then the ships of Qays/Kish sailed with the prevailing wind to the western bay, well clear of the city and the harbor, and waited in its protected waters until the weather allowed them to sail home.

How does Ibn al-Mujāwir's narrative complement these eyewitness reports? After all, had it not been for the extraordinary preservation of the relevant Geniza documents, his would have been the only surviving testimony of the event. Ibn al-Mujāwir wrote several decades after the siege. In addition, his main interest in the political ramifications of the events, coupled with his tendency toward literary embellishment and inflation, detracts from his account's overall reliability. In his version, the most important event was the massacre of the enemy troops at Ṣīra, which he attributes not to bad weather but to a ruse devised by one of Aden's two governors. As Goitein notes, the details of the stratagem are reminiscent of several topoi in Arabic literature, and the inclusion of lines of poetry does little to increase the sense of the account's accuracy. Still, the actual events lie close to the embellished surface of Ibn al-Mujāwir's story, which must be based to some extent on vivid impressions preserved in the city's historical memory; thus, his version provides glimpses of local topography and a sense of place that constitute a valuable addition to the historical record.[55]

Ibn al-Mujāwir is most helpful when he explicitly reports that the ships anchored "*taḥt jabal ṣīra*" and elsewhere, referring to the same moment that the sailors weighed anchor at "*marsā ʿadan*."[56] The first coordinate he provides clinches the argument that the anchorage (the Geniza merchants' *al-mukallā*) lay directly adjacent to Ṣīra Island. The second reference to the anchorage simply indicates that by Ibn al-Mujāwir's time, *al-mukallā* had become known as *al-marsā*, as was clearly the case later on, when Abū Makhrama described the position of *al-shiṣna* "at the far end of *al-bandar* behind *marsā al-marākib*."[57] Elsewhere in his work, moreover, Ibn al-Mujāwir seems to be using the term "*al-marsā*" to denote the part of the harbor where seagoing ships anchored to load and unload passengers and merchandise. Ibn al-Mujāwir's description of the events and procedures related to the arrival of ships at Aden recounts that port officials sailed out to the approaching ships on lighters; when the initial inspection and documentation of passengers and merchandise was over, ships proceeded to *al-marsā*, where they dropped anchor and the passengers disembarked.[58] In other words, the initial reception of the incoming ships took place after they had rounded Ṣīra and were entering the harbor, and the final station, Ibn al-Mujāwir's *al-marsā*, refers specifically to the anchorage.

When the invaders disembarked, encouraged according to Ibn al-Mujāwir by the treacherously servile and submissive attitude of the commander of the seaward fort, al-Khaḍrā', they did so at *al-sawāḥil*, a vague description of location that nevertheless makes sense in light of the eyewitness reports. The phrase likely refers precisely to the shores of Ṣīra, where, Ibn al-Mujāwir writes earlier, the ships were anchored.[59] The author presumably imagines the enemy troops as having camped at that same spot where they disembarked. He does not report any change of position when the scheming governor sent them provisions and wine from his fort, al-Khadrā'; when they took to feasting, heedless of the warnings of their own commander; or when the soldiers defending the city under the leadership of the commander of al-Taʿkar, who had taken charge of both forts, attacked and decimated them the next morning.

The massacre resulted in a heap of heads (a detail confirmed by Khalaf's report) and was reflected in the toponym "Jamājim" (Skulls).[60] While no other mention of this place-name occurs elsewhere and it is unclear whether it was indeed used locally or is simply a literary device that Ibn al-Mujāwir chooses to embellish his narrative, the extant information on the invaders' anchorage and movements indicates that the site of the massacre was located on the northwestern shore of Ṣīra Island, on the side of the town.

Harbor Panorama

In conclusion, how does Aden's harbor, also known as Front Bay or Ṣīra Bay, emerge from archaeological and topographical surveys, the accounts of Ibn al-Mujāwir and Abū Makhrama, and the testimony of the two 6th/12th-century eyewitnesses? Ṣīra Island protected the harbor's southern side, with the shores of the peninsula wrapped around the island's southwest, west, and northwest edges. Embraced between Ṣīra and the town, the harbor waters were exposed only to the waves produced by the *azyab*, the wind that set in during the navigable winter monsoon. To alleviate the potential nuisance that heavy swells entailed for anchored or approaching ships and their handlers, a breakwater was constructed. The above- and below-water remains of the feature located by Prados strengthen the evidence culled from the written sources that the mole extended from the northeasterly

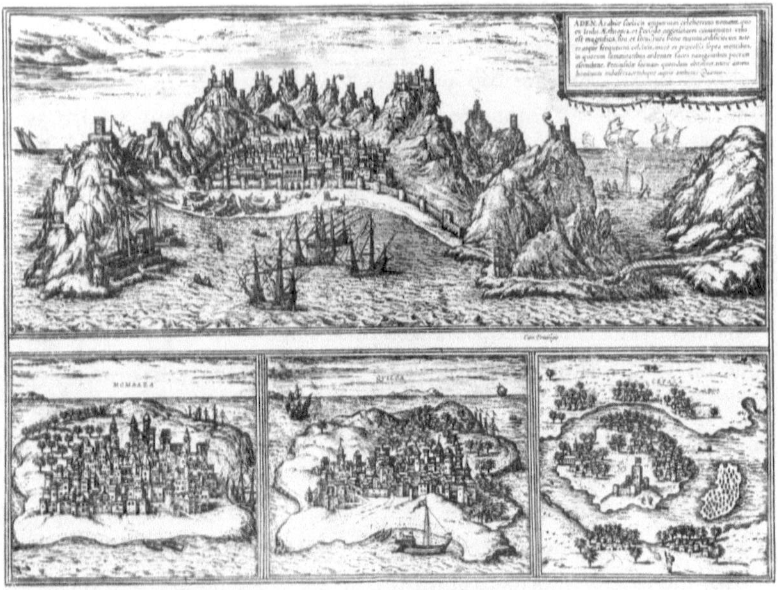

Bird's-eye view of the port of Aden, juxtaposed with representations of the East African ports of Mombasa, Kilwa, and Sofala, in the celebrated work by engraver Franz Hogenberg and editor Georg Braun, *Civitates orbis terrarum*, the first volume of which appeared in 1572. (From Georg Braun and Franz Hogenberg, *Civitates orbis terrarum*, 1:53, Rare Books Division, Department of Rare Books and Special Collections, Princeton University Library; courtesy of the Princeton University Library)

point of Ṣīra Island northwest across the seaward edge of Ṣīra Bay. Construction took place a long time before Abū Makhrama wrote the sole contemporary description of the feature in the 10th/16th century. Abū Makhrama's attribution of the construction of *al-shiṣna* to the "ancients" (*al-awwalūn*) as well as the existence and attributes of *al-mukallā* or *al-marsā*, the anchorage mentioned casually in the sources, lead me to believe that the breakwater was in place at least by the beginning of the 6th/12th century.

With this composite picture in mind, a look at the European engravings depicting the harbor and the town behind it raises a host of questions concerning both the art history of the works themselves and the historical topography of the town. The most accomplished of these images, the 1572 engraving in Georg Braun and Franz Hogenberg's city atlas, *Civitates orbis terrarum*, bears eloquent witness to both the limitations of artistic representation as historical document and the delightful aid that such representations can lend to urban reconstructions.[61] Based on secondhand accounts and drawings and like many cityscapes of the same vintage, this view of Aden is highly stylized. Still, after imagining the harbor through nonpictorial sources, one is struck both by the overall aspect and by many of the particular details in the images, which are clearly based on strands of real topography. In showing the town and Ṣīra Island bordering the harbor, the mountains towering over town and water, and the bay carving a crescent curve out of the shoreline, the engravings agree perfectly with all of the other sources. The precipitous aspect of Ṣīra and the jagged peaks of the peninsula are but some of the details that confer individuality and a sense of place to images that may otherwise have seemed generic. These renderings bespeak the impression that Aden's dramatic and unique landscape made on its beholders in the early modern period and suggest a similar effect on viewers centuries earlier.

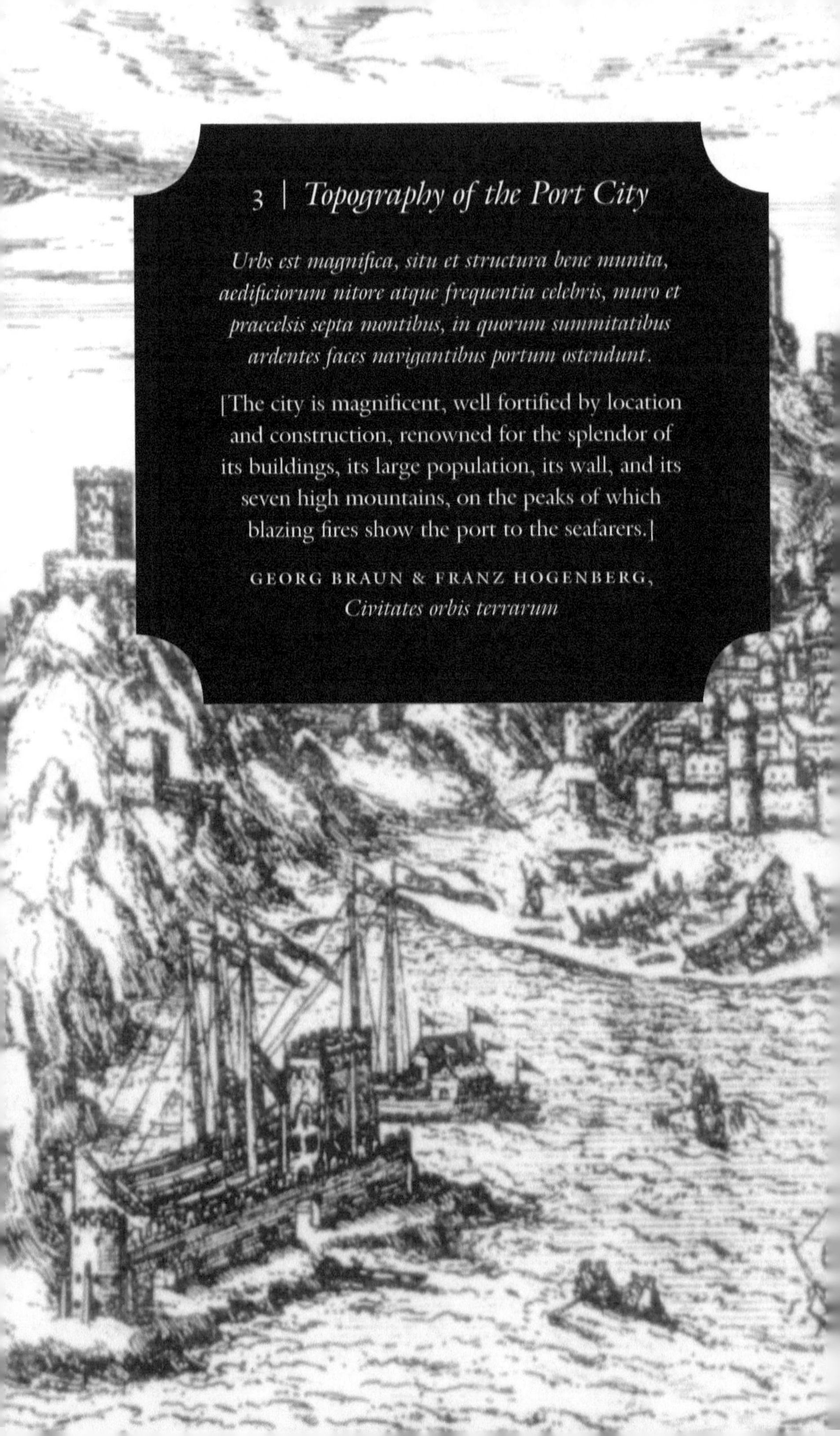

3 | *Topography of the Port City*

Urbs est magnifica, situ et structura bene munita, aedificiorum nitore atque frequentia celebris, muro et praecelsis septa montibus, in quorum summitatibus ardentes faces navigantibus portum ostendunt.

[The city is magnificent, well fortified by location and construction, renowned for the splendor of its buildings, its large population, its wall, and its seven high mountains, on the peaks of which blazing fires show the port to the seafarers.]

GEORG BRAUN & FRANZ HOGENBERG,
Civitates orbis terrarum

Fortifications

Franz Hogenberg's evocative sea- and cityscape draws the eye beyond Aden's marine space onto terra firma and the outline of city buildings. Most prominently depicted and most clearly discernible out of the variegated city mass are crenellated circuit walls and outlying fortification towers. To Ludovico di Varthema, the "Roman" whose description of Aden informed and inspired the late-sixteenth-century representation, these walls may have represented the formidable odds against which his captivity at Aden eventually ended. To the Portuguese, who never made it into town, the walls not only constituted the most visible elements of Aden's architecture but also symbolized the port's impregnability and thus provided a tangible explanation for the fruitlessness of their efforts and their ultimate defeat.

Aden's fortifications also feature prominently in what appears to be a local tradition concerning the seawall's initial construction. The story fixes the original erection of the wall in the time of the Zurayids.[1] The narrative begins with the nighttime arrival of a foreign ship at Aden and its anchoring in the harbor. The ship's master (*nākhūdha*)[2] disembarked, wandered around town, and ended up knocking on the door of a striking, towering house illuminated by candles and scented by incense.[3] The master of the house received the visitor, who politely but without hesitation requested permission and space to hide some of his ship's cargo "out of fear of the *dāʿī*,"[4] he explained, presumably alluding to excessive customs dues on imported goods imposed by the local ruler.[5]

His request was graciously granted, and after having one-third of his cargo unloaded and transferred to a designated location, the man returned to spend the night on board his ship. The next morning, however, he awoke to a nasty surprise: his host of the night before turned out to be the *dāʿī* himself. Embarrassed and bewildered by his bad luck, the man exclaimed, "I feared the rain, so I stood under the gutter."[6] Yet his panic proved unjustified: instead of punishing him for trying to evade customs dues on his merchandise, the *dāʿī* rewarded the foreigner by exempting his merchandise from duty and offering him a thousand dinars and the house he had used for storage. When the baffled trespasser asked the reason for the undeserved royal treatment, the *dāʿī* replied that the man had earned it with his middle-of-the-night visit.[7] Immediately thereafter, Ibn al-Mujāwir tells us, the ruler built the waterfront wall.

Ibn al-Mujāwir's point is clear: the *dāʿī* was grateful to the hapless man for unwittingly revealing the Achilles heel of the port's system of monitoring commercial traffic and collecting customs' dues. The revelation was worth many times the thousand dinars, house, and exemption from taxes granted; without physical defenses against the smuggling of merchandise, the city was steadily losing revenues to merchants and seamen operating as the foreigner had but going undetected. Looking beyond the dramatic and dramatized details, the specific tale offers a reminder that the Zurayid period, in which it is set, witnessed increasingly heavy trade passing through Aden, with the tax revenues to match.[8] The stakes were being raised, and the precious sources of revenue had to be more zealously and systematically guarded. In other words, the story reflects a period of changes made necessary by the boom in international trade and by the city's intensified participation in it.

Were the Zurayids indeed the first to build a wall along the shoreline, in effect shielding the coveted market within and tightly controlling the flow of merchandise to it? It seems unlikely that previous administrations of the city had not taken some measures to protect their turf from commercial and military intruders, and an earlier reporter, al-Muqaddasī, speaks of a 4th/10th-century wall "stretching along the sea from mountain to mountain, with five gates."[9] Ibn al-Mujāwir's story, however, hints at a contemporary awareness that the Zurayid period saw the intensification of Aden's participation in overseas trade and a concomitant structuring of urban space and institutions. In that story, the wall serves as a palpable symbol of the devices by which the city harnessed the booming trade from the Zurayid period onward.

Later governments also took a keen interest in the city wall, and various rulers' building campaigns transformed it into a structure conveying the impression of solidity and impregnability, an impression reflected in the European engravings. Before examining other evidence on the history of the structure, however, it is necessary to consider the role of the two forts, al-Khaḍrā' and al-Taʿkar.[10] Ibn al-Mujāwir states that the two forts served as the seats of Aden's first two Zurayid governors appointed by the Sulayhid overlords[11] and specifies that the Zurayids' "first" wall extended from "*al-ḥiṣn al-akhḍar*," clearly already in existence, to Jabal Ḥuqqāt.[12] Al-Khaḍrā', also appearing as Ḥiṣn al-Khaḍrā' and al-Ḥiṣn al-Akhḍar, was located near the sea, overlooking the harbor,[13] and Jabal Ḥuqqāt is the hill opposite Ṣīra Island and separated from it by the sea channel al-Maʿjalayn. If the wall extended along the shoreline between them—protecting the city from the seaward side was the whole point of Ibn Mujāwir's story—and Jabal Ḥuqqāt on the southeastern edge of the city formed the wall's southern end, then the only possible location for al-Khaḍrā' was the northern edge of town and its beach.

The two sister forts, al-Khaḍrā' and al-Taʿkar, thus formed integral parts of Aden's fortifications; in Zurayid times, these forts also corresponded to the eventually ill-fated administrative division of the city between the two governors. The forts' positioning was connected to these governors' control of separate aspects of Aden's transit trade and the discreet revenues they entailed. Al-Khadrā' monitored the shore and the ships, while al-Taʿkar commanded the "land and the gate."[14] At a time when city wall did not extend inland, the designation "the gate" with reference to a place looking toward the mainland can only refer to the single opening in Aden's ring of mountains, which gave access to the land bridge and the mainland beyond it—in other words, what later came to be known as the Main Pass. That al-Taʿkar was indeed a fort within the city and should not be confused with the inland Yemeni stronghold is clear from, among other evidence, ʿUmāra's statement that Saba' b. Abī al-Suʿūd "was buried at the foot of al-Taʿkar, inside the city."[15]

The division of power and revenue was as uneasy as the corresponding spatial arrangement appears unwieldy. Given the lucrative nature of the maritime trade, the master of al-Khaḍrā' had the better deal. Ibn al-Mujāwir's famous passage describing the arrival of ships at port further emphasizes the fort's connection to the harbor and its supervision: the lookouts, whose job was to spot arriving ships in the distance, are said to have been positioned exactly on Jabal al-Akhḍar where the fort stood.[16] That one of the two joint rulers had such unilateral control over the city's most important asset boded trouble, and it is no surprise that the underlying tension over access to transit trade revenues eventually manifested itself in the conflict between Saba' b. Abī al-Suʿūd and ʿAlī b. Abī al-Ghārāt, the two Zurayid governors of the city in the early 6th/12th century. Both Ibn al-Mujāwir and a letter from the Geniza written by Khalaf b. Isaac b. Bundār to Ḥalfon b. Nathanel describe the events that led to ʿAlī's downfall and, according to the eyewitness account of the letter, the destruction of al-Khaḍrā'.

Ibn al-Mujāwir reports that each governor had a deputy responsible for collecting his share of tax revenues and that ʿAlī's deputy and cronies were extorting far beyond what they were entitled to in their maritime dominion, even trespassing on Saba''s interests and authority on land. Saba' and his newly appointed deputy, Bilāl b. Jarīr, staged a two-pronged attack on the offenders and their allies, subduing the enemy both in the city and in the hinterland and capturing his administrative seat, the fort of al-Khaḍrā'.[17] The portrayal of ʿAlī as a villain is reflected in the intriguing fragments of Khalaf's letter, which also speaks of severe drought and crop failure across Yemen.[18] Having reported the food crisis, Khalaf speaks of the political turmoil, which thus appears to have been partly connected to and perhaps inflamed by the shortage of food and the soaring prices resulting from the drought. He writes that the people feared sultan ʿAlī b. Abī al-Ghārāt, that Saba' took him on militarily, and that his victory involved the destruction of al-Khaḍrā'.[19]

Both reports suggest that ʿAlī had become too powerful and greedy in his supervision of incoming trade; that regulating the maritime trade economy—and in his case, abusing that power—could only have been effectively performed from a base such as the fort, al-Khaḍrā'; and finally that eliminating him and taking full control of the city meant appropriating that base. There is little doubt that Ibn al-Mujāwir believed that power and control of port traffic and revenues were inextricably linked if not synonymous. Khalaf's letter reveals that the city's political leadership and the urban population at large, especially the merchant community, shared this perception.

Ibn al-Mujāwir relates that the wall's seashore location as well as its weak construction led to its slow dismantling and eventually to its complete ruin.[20] Its replacement was a light, temporary structure consisting of some sort of reed latticework or palisade.[21] Such a structure was presumably enough both to control traffic and to play, occasionally at least, a defensive role. Despite the projected image of the medieval Indian Ocean as a largely conflict-free world of trade, evidence has already shown that a lucrative market such as Aden could—and at least once did—attract the predatory interest of another state. During the naval siege of the city by the forces of Qays/Kish, the invaders never dared a direct approach on the city shore even as the inhabitants felt more secure in the city's forts than in their houses. Partial screening and separation of the city from the beach left the enemy feeling far too unsure and vulnerable to attempt an attack.

Finally, the Zurayid walls must have offered the city's waterfront buildings some protection against waves and sea spray driven by the prevailing northeasterlies during the winter months. Seawalls designed specifically to protect a coastal settlement from wave erosion appear in earlier western Indian Ocean port sites. The most prominent examples are Sīrāf on the Arabian Gulf and Manda in the Lamu Archipelago, both of which feature extensive remnants of seawalls meticulously recorded by archaeological investigators.[22] Although less exposed than Sīrāf, Aden was certainly vulnerable enough to benefit from the presence of some kind of waterfront barrier. If the disintegration of the initial wall was caused in part by pounding waves, then the need for protection becomes all the more intelligible.

Not until the Ayyubids took over the city did a major reorganization of the fortifications take place. Abū ʿAmr ʿUthmān b. ʿAlī al-Zanjabīlī, the Ayyubid governor credited with founding the town of Lakhaba, is said to have rebuilt the waterfront wall, to have erected new walls, and to have added a new series of gates that served elaborate access patterns and traffic control.[23] If Aden was already easily defended, the Ayyubid works rendered it practically impregnable. Like its predecessors, the Ayyubid edifice also aimed at regulating the flow of people and merchandise to and from the market and the city, as the number of gates and the assignment of each to a different kind of traffic indicates. In addition, however, its several distinct parts were integrated into a structure of unmistakably defensive character.

The sources thus speak of fortifications that comprised three distinct walls: one stretching between Jabal al-Manẓar and the edge of Jabal al-ʿUrr, another extending from al-Khaḍrāʾ (presumably restored after its destruction by the forces of Sabaʾ) to al-Taʿkar along the mountaintops, and a third running the length of the waterfront from somewhere on the northern end of the beach. The third structure is clearly the reincarnation of the old seafront wall, as Abū Makhrama specifies that it stretched from the foot of the Jabal al-Khadrāʾ to Jabal Ḥuqqāt.[24] The other two walls were the land extensions of this main segment. The Jabal al-Manẓar/Jabal al-ʿUrr section stretched inland on the southern end of the seafront wall, while at its northern end the al-Khadrāʾ/al-Taʿkar segment extended northwest. Jabal al-Manẓar stood at the southeastern end of town, in close proximity to the Jabal Ḥuqqāt and directly opposite the islet of Ṣīra.[25] Its single gate suggests a relatively short wall built to block access into town from the alternative anchorage in the Bay of Ḥuqqāt. Ḥiṣn al-Taʿkar guarded the Main Pass (*al-bāb*); therefore, the wall extending from there to al-Khadrāʾ was built in relation to the main land access to the city. In summary, the Ayyubids gave the initial waterfront wall landward extensions at its northern and southern ends, preventing trespassers or other foes from sneaking into or storming the town by outflanking the fortifications.

The two forts, al-Khaḍrāʾ and al-Taʿkar, remained in use after the Ayyubid takeover but lost their role as fortified rulers' seats. For their official residence, the new lords of the city appear to have chosen a new or renovated structure, known in the sources as Dār al-Manẓar or simply al-Manẓar. Ibn al-Mujāwir attributes the building to the Ayyubids, while Abū Makhrama claims that it was originally built by

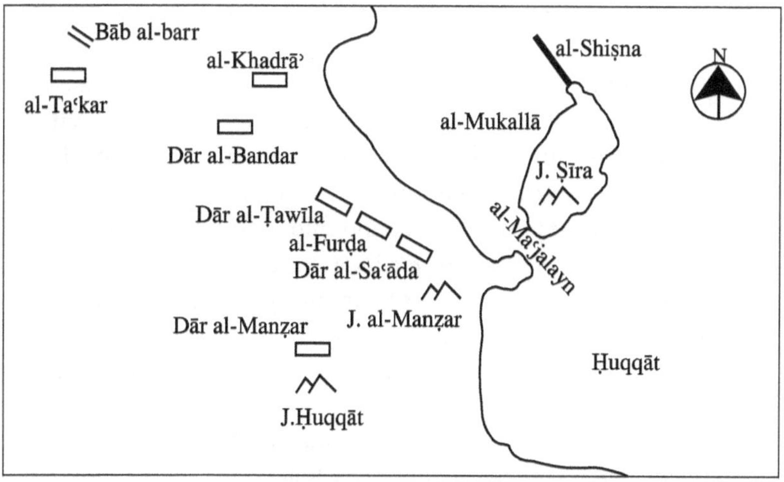

Schematic plan of the medieval city of Aden, including major buildings identified in the topographical analysis.

the Zurayids and perhaps only renovated by Ayyubid governor al-Muʿizz Ismāʿīl, son of Ṭughtekīn, who resided there during his short and eventful rule.[26] In any case, a Geniza letter dating to 594/1198 confirms that al-Manẓar indeed served as al-Muʿizz Ismāʿīl's seat and testifies that it became the stage of the dramatic (if temporary) forced conversion of local Jews. Self-styled caliph al-Muʿizz summoned all foreigners at Aden, as well as "the *shaykh* Maḍmūn," great-grandson of Maḍmūn b. Japheth and leader of the Jewish community, and forced him to convert on the spot to avoid shedding the blood of his people.[27]

The exact location of al-Manẓar is unclear; it shares its name with one hill, Jabal al-Manẓar, but appears to be built on another, Jabal Ḥuqqāt. Moreover, further confusion arises from Ibn al-Mujāwir's single reference to a Qaṣr al-Manẓar that he locates on Jabal Ṣīra.[28] What is clear, given its confirmed general location at the southern end of Aden's beach, is the Ayyubids' intentions: while they incorporated the Zurayid forts in the overhauled fortifications, they shifted the seat of power to a new location, equally strategic in terms of monitoring harbor traffic and thus both supplementing and supplanting al-Khadrā'.

Enveloped thus by its brand-new walls, the Ayyubid city and its successors offered a secure marketplace to all while reaping the benefits of closely monitored and efficiently taxed mercantile traffic. The revamped walls were part and parcel of a system designed to harness more efficiently the tremendous opportunities for revenues that transit trade had to offer. With the fortifications came a taxation scheme that included an elaborate set of tariffs and a closely monitored sequence of customs-clearing procedures that all merchants and merchandise arriving at Aden were required to follow. These institutional structures will be discussed in chapter 4, but their physical accoutrements deserve attention here inasmuch as they relate to the walls and the built environment of the port as a whole.

The Customshouse

Of all the trade-related buildings mentioned in the sources, the most prominent and important structures are those located on or in close proximity to the waterfront. The role of the al-Khaḍrā' fort in the supervision of seaborne trade has already been discussed, as has Dār al-Manẓar's assumption of that role in the Ayyubid period. From their elevated position overlooking the harbor, these two structures served as watchtowers and symbols of control. The actual processing of people and merchandise took place in the harbor and on the waterfront, and central to the operations involved in clearing traffic in and out of the city was the customshouse, which the sources describe as al-Furḍa.

The term "*furḍa*" appears in classical Arabic geographies with the meaning of "harbor," "seaport," or "port" in the general sense of port of entry and perhaps even in the more specific sense of clearinghouse.[29] When al-Muqaddasī describes Aden as "*furḍat al-yaman*," he could be referring simply to the fact that Aden was the most important southern Arabian port, Yemen's main port, but he may also be alluding to its role as a clearinghouse for Asian goods traded westward and Mediterranean merchandise traveling eastward.[30] By the beginning of the 6th/12th century, however, the term "*al-furḍa*" had three distinct if interrelated meanings in connection to Aden. Its general meaning, which applied to the city as a whole and described its function as an entrepôt and clearinghouse in the system of trade that connected the Mediterranean and Indian Ocean worlds, appears to have remained current, at least among outsiders.[31] But in the city itself, the term had come to denote a specific building within the port as well as the fiscal institution housed by that building.

Clearing customs in Aden meant that after a preliminary shipboard investigation by port officials, commercial goods were unloaded from the ships to the shore, unpacked, counted, and weighed to assess the appropriate customs dues and then released for sale in the city and often for reexportation. These procedures were in place in the Ayyubid period, when Ibn al-Mujāwir described them in some detail, but probably go back to the Zurayid times, as the Geniza documents indicate. In any case, it appears that during both periods, the central part of the process—that is, the assessment of taxes—took place inside the customshouse. Ibn al-Mujāwir speaks of unloaded cargos taken straight to al-Furḍa, where bales and packages were taken apart and goods counted, presumably to assess customs dues.[32] One Geniza letter speaks explicitly about weighing a taxable consignment of cardamom at al-Furḍa, and another alludes to merchandise residing there, presumably because processing had stalled.[33]

While several Geniza documents use the term in reference to the institution of customs, the clear reference in these two letters to al-Furḍa as a space is significant. Ibn al-Mujāwir suggests that the building was founded only in the Ayyubid period, by Abū ʿAmr ʿUthmān b. ʿAlī al-Zanjabīlī, the same Ayyubid governor credited with the construction of new walls and the foundation of Lakhaba.[34] Just as Lakhaba had existed before the Ayyubids, however, Geniza documents provide strong evidence that a physical space designated as the customshouse already existed in the first half of the 6th/12th century.

Thus, what Ibn al-Mujāwir presents as an Ayyubid foundation was most likely a renovation or expansion of a preexisting Zurayid building that took place as part of al-Zanjabīlī's public works program.

Since newly arrived taxable merchandise was taken directly from the boat to the customshouse, the building must have occupied a convenient and prominent position on the waterfront. Ibn al-Mujāwir's account of the Ayyubid wall indicates that the "*bāb al-furḍa*," which he describes as the door through which merchandise entered and left the city, was one of the central gates of the seafront wall.[35] The customshouse building, then, must have been located in the immediate vicinity of this gate, safely inside the city's wall. An instructive parallel from a later period highlights the logic of this spatial arrangement: the customshouse at al-Mukhā not only was known by the same term as its Adeni counterpart, al-Furḍa, but also stood near a "sea gate" within easy access from that port's jetty and the sea.[36]

The builders of Aden's al-Furḍa apparently gave the structure two doors to facilitate the flow of taxable merchandise from the boats to the building and, after assessment of dues, from the building to the city. Thus, one door opened onto the beach or, more accurately, onto the waterfront wall and its "Furḍa Gate," while the other door gave access to the city.[37] After merchandise had been assessed for taxes, merchants could choose to sell or store their goods, and the city offered a variety of spaces for either or both purposes. Indeed, according to the testimony of both Ibn al-Mujāwir and Abū Makhrama, al-Furḍa stood sandwiched between two buildings, the Dār al-Saʿāda and the Dār al-Ṭawīla, that appear to have served these important commercial functions.

Markets and Storerooms

The Dār al-Saʿāda and the Dār al-Ṭawīla may well have received a significant portion of the merchandise transiting through the city. The Dār al-Saʿāda is the more enigmatic of the two. Ibn al-Mujāwir ascribes its foundation to Ṭughtakīn and notes its location next to the customshouse. He suggests that the common people (presumably the local inhabitants) used that building's name as a byname for the city itself but offers no clues as to its function or any other aspect of its place in the urban landscape.[38] Abū Makhrama adds that the structure was located on the hill of Ḥuqqāt—that is, on the southern side of al-Furḍa. He quotes Ibn al-Mujāwir concerning the building's Ayyubid foundation but also provides two alternative traditions.[39]

The first story ascribes the building of the edifice to the fifth Rasulid sultan, al-Mujāhid al-Ghassānī (d. 764/1363). Heeding or evading a prophecy that he was to die "at sea" or "looking over the sea,"[40] he built this "House of Happiness" near the water. He indeed escaped death at sea and eventually died in that house by the water. The neat symmetry between the sultan's happy end and the building's name does little to dispel the apocryphal hue of this tale. Abū Makhrama's second story perhaps lies closer to the truth, ascribing the building to a shadowy group of merchants known as the Banū Khaṭaba or Khaṭba and said to have originated in Egypt. Abū Makhrama notes that some members of this group served as superintendents of the port during the reign of Rasulid sultan al-Ashraf b. al-Afḍal (778–803/1377–1400) but clearly envisions that their arrival and the building of the Dār al-Saʿāda took place long before the Rasulid period.[41]

While the connection to merchants of Egyptian origin may refer to the Geniza Jewish traders and their strong Egyptian ties, the proximity of the Dār al-Saʿāda to the Furḍa and to the Dār al-Ṭawīla, a commercial structure (*matjar*), constitutes firmer evidence of a commercial function. A business letter addressed to Maḍmūn b. Japheth confirms this. In the salient passage, the writer asks the recipient to arrange to have a certain consignment sold in *al-dār al-saʿīda*.[42] In a different letter, Maḍmūn speaks of weighing and selling a consignment of cardamom at "the house" (*al-dār*).[43] This casual remark could refer either to his own house or to a place that everyone knew, such as the "House of Prosperity" (*dār al-saʿāda*).[44] Thus, the Geniza partially validates the Adeni tradition linking the edifice to Egyptian merchants: even if not literally founded by them, the House of Prosperity emerges as important in the lives of the Jewish traders of Aden, whose strong Egyptian ties pass them as Egyptian even in modern historiography.

The Dār al-Saʿāda thus clearly existed before the Ayyubid period and, more importantly, functioned as a wholesale market for imports. Having cleared customs, newly arrived consignments of Indian goods and presumably other commodities from East and West were taken there to be sold on the spot, either in bulk or in smaller batches, for reexport or for local retail. The much-better-documented usage of the designation "*dār*" in connection with commercial buildings in Egypt suggests that a number of other commercial activities may well have taken place at the Adeni establishment. Although Egypt had no Dār al-Saʿāda, close parallels in style of designation include the Dār al-Baraka (House of Blessings), a place for financial transactions such as money exchange,[45] and Alexandria's Dār al-Mubāraka, which served as a wholesale market.[46] Other such establishments in the Egyptian capital were designated by a specific commodity, including the Dār al-Aruzz (House of Rice) and the Dār al-Zaʿfarān (House of Saffron).[47] Their primary function was the payment of tolls or customs on imports into the city or goods in transit there, but they also served as markets and storehouses and as a business address for money changers and other merchants.[48] At Aden, the system worked differently: al-Furḍa was the only locus of customs collection. Moreover, even though it is not entirely unlikely that the Dār al-Saʿāda, like the Cairene "houses," afforded storage and general business services, such services may in fact have been rendered at merchants' houses, as the following section will discuss.

The spatial and symbolic centrality of the Dār al-Saʿāda, the building that gave a nickname to the whole town, suggests that it may have been the central market, at least for wholesale transactions. Other places of sale existed, however. Ibn al-Mujāwir speaks of an old *qayṣāriyya* and a new *qayṣāriyya*, both founded by the Ayyubids and comprising stores built specifically for druggists, with lock and key. He also refers to markets (*aswāq*) and shops (*dakākīn*).[49] The term "*qayṣārīya*" refers specifically to a secure place for the sale and storage of valuable commodities, but the building type described by it is known to have housed various commercial functions at different places and times in Middle Eastern history.[50] Ibn al-Mujāwir's reference, however, gives the impression that Aden's *qayṣāriyya* conformed more strictly to what the term implies—that is, sale, retail or wholesale, of valuable commodities, goods that had to be kept under lock and key. As for "markets and shops," the phrase most likely refers to retail establishments. Thus, the Dār al-Saʿāda remains the only known locus of general wholesale transactions involving imported merchandise, with specialized and small-scale retail taking place at different marketplaces across the city.

On the opposite side of al-Furḍa from the Dār al-Saʿāda was an additional commercial building, which the chronicles refer to as the Dār al-Ṭawīla. Its date of construction is uncertain. The only indication that the place may have been already in use during the Ayyubid period or earlier is Abū Makhrama's claim that it was eventually replaced by a structure built in Rasulid times.[51] Located in close proximity to al-Furḍa,[52] this was also a commercial establishment, and Abū Makhrama describes it as a *matjar al-mulūk*, a very general term that may denote a trading place devoted exclusively to business carried out by or on behalf of the political elite.[53] The Adeni author adds that two covered benches on either side of its gates served as seats for al-Furḍa's scribes.[54] Thus, in addition to standing adjacent to each other, the two buildings were connected in the process of importation of trade goods in a way symmetrical to the relationship between the customshouse and the Dār al-Saʿāda. Goods clearing customs went either to the Dār al-Saʿāda or to the Dār al-Ṭawīla, depending, perhaps, on whether they belonged to ordinary merchants or were somehow connected with the city's rulers.

Aden's waterfront thus emerges from the sources as a nucleus of commercial structures. At the center stood the triad of the customshouse and the two wholesale markets. The *qayṣāriyya*s, smaller markets, and single shops may have stood further back, integrated within the downtown fabric of the port, or may have stretched north along the waterfront in an arrangement similar to that at the Arabian Gulf port of Sīrāf in earlier Islamic times.[55] If a tannery did indeed occupy the northern end of Aden's beach, that too would find a parallel at Sīrāf, where industrial sites have been excavated near the water.[56] Finally, the evidence for the configuration of the city walls both in Zurayid and in Ayyubid times suggest that Aden's commercial waterfront was shielded against weather and military threats, again in symmetry with the arrangement at Sīrāf.

Storerooms, where the merchants kept their merchandise before or after sale, for the long or the short term, also cannot have been far from the commercial waterfront. Letters written by Jewish merchants sometimes mention specific storerooms, identifying them not by coordinates of location but by owners' names. Storage may well have taken place in merchants' residences. According to the story of the foundation of Aden's seafront wall, the place where the aspiring smuggler hid his merchandise was a "house," a *dār* in the residential sense of the word.[57] Geniza documents confirm the practice of storing merchandise in merchants' houses. In a letter to Ben Yijū informing him of the fate of his shipwrecked merchandise, Khalaf b. Isaac notes that salvaged iron belonging to his correspondent had just passed through customs and was being carried to the "house of the illustrious *shaykh* Maḍmūn."[58] Is this the same place as the one Maḍmūn casually refers to as *al-dār* where he weighed and sold a batch of cardamom? In this and other ways that will be detailed later, it appears that a wealthy merchant's residence could have served as his business address and center of commercial activity. Finally, Khalaf b. Isaac's report that "houses were burnt and storerooms were looted"[59] during the days of famine and political strife in the 530s/1130s evokes the closeness of space in which medieval Adenis lived their private and commercial lives.

Merchants' Residences and Transient Accommodations

To complete the study of the layout of Aden's medieval port requires at least a brief discussion of precisely those residential quarters where native merchants lived and worked and of the accommodations available to transient traders. The evidence is admittedly very slight. No traces of the medieval urban fabric remain—they faded during the period of abandonment and decay prior to the 19th century and were obliterated by the British colonial urban development that followed.[60] Only mere glimpses of medieval Aden can be seen, and they are primarily of the houses of wealthy merchants and the political elite. Most evocative is the image of the stately house where the hero of the wall foundation story sought refuge: a tall stone house, well lit and perfumed with incense, featuring reception rooms accessible via an internal staircase, was apparently worthy of the commercial elite as much as the rulers. Indeed, the foreigner in the tale mistook it for "some merchant's residence."[61]

Multistoried houses were not atypical of Yemen or of Indian Ocean ports. Speaking of Yemen in general, Ibn al-Mujāwir describes two-story houses with storerooms on the lower level and living quarters on top.[62] Moreover, archaeological surveys and excavations at the Gulf port of Sīrāf confirm geographer al-Iṣṭakhrī's testimony that the port featured multistoried merchants' houses.[63] The thick, mortared rubble walls, floors of stone or mortar, and flat roofs spanned by imported wooden logs that archaeologists found at 4th/10th- and early-5th/11th-century Sīrāf would make perfect sense in Aden from the late 5th/11th century onward.[64] This is, after all, the time of the first local stone quarrying and the concomitant proliferation of stonemasonry in the city according to the authors of the sources discussed here. Of the materials involved in building houses like the archaeologically attested buildings of Sīrāf, only the wood would have had to be imported, but both the mangrove of eastern Africa and the teak of India were well within Aden's commercial reach.

Public and private space collided in the houses of Aden's commercial elite. Definitive evidence has already shown that goods could be stored at merchants' houses, and indications are that assessment and sale of merchandise may have also taken place in such quarters. In addition, foreign merchants at times may have stayed with local businessmen and performed transactions that required witnessing in that same space.[65] Local merchants presumably kept business records in their houses. Thus, instead of resembling Cairo, where commercial activity was for the most part relegated to specialized public structures, the use of space in medieval Aden appears to have had more in common with the spatial practices at the 18th-century Red Sea port of al-Mukhā. According to Nancy Um's insightful study of that city, the customshouse was the only public edifice where one aspect of the business of the overseas trade routinely took place; otherwise, negotiations, transactions, and commercial life as a whole unfolded in the residences of wealthy merchants.[66]

Not far from the well-appointed stone houses of merchants and the ruling elite, humbler dwellings served the housing needs of those porters, boatmen, lookouts, packers, and tanners who lived in the Crater and labored at the port and at the few industries not delegated to Aden's satellite settlements. Regional vernacular architecture, current to this day and historically attested for the days before the establishment of stone quarries on the Aden peninsula, when only few could build in stone, provides a sense of the construction of these shelters.[67] "Most houses were built of palm fronds," is how Abū Makhrama imagines early (pre-Zurayid) Aden.[68]

In fact, according to Ibn al-Mujāwir, the first to build palm-frond huts in Aden were early African immigrants; such huts still filled an entire section of town in his day.[69] Whatever his sources, in the 7th/15th century, Ibn Khaldūn claims that "most of [Aden's] buildings are made of reeds, and for that reason fires frequently break out often."[70] Ibn al-Mujāwir says that the original hut builders had occupied "the wadi," perhaps a reference to the area along the inland edges of the Crater, near the Main Pass, which remained filled with huts in his time. This brief comment constitutes the best clue about the city's residential topography: the best houses stood closer to the waterfront, perhaps on the northern and southern sides of the town, near the walls, where they could catch the sea breezes, enjoy maritime views, and participate fully in commercial and social life. Humbler dwellings were relegated to the enclosed, arid, and hot western end of the Crater, to the "valleys."

In addition to permanent residences, some kind of transient accommodation must have been available in Aden. The duration of stay as well as the means and status of the individual merchants must have determined the nature of accommodations required and provided. A merchant's stay in Aden might be as short as a few days or as long as several months.[71] The fact that the Geniza documents and the accounts of Ibn al-Mujāwir and Abū Makhrama contain not a single mention of a *funduq*, *khan*, or caravansary may be coincidental, a blind spot in the extant record. It seems more likely, however, that this silence has real significance and perhaps indicates a difference in the organization of transient residence between the Mediterranean and the Indian Ocean. Again, the parallel with the 18th-century port of al-Mukhā may be instructive: there, only the underclass of travelers, not international traders, used the single caravansary. Businessmen lodged in local merchants' residences, which, in conjunction with their function as business centers, offered accommodation to out-of-town business friends and acquaintances.[72] In medieval Aden, prominent and well-connected merchants may well have stayed with Adeni friends or rented houses; both practices are known from the Mediterranean in the same period.[73] Although no direct evidence of house rentals has survived in Aden, a record for such arrangements does exist for the inland capital city of Dhū Jibla.[74] The house that Ben Yijū rented there came complete with a mill or press, indicating that the tenant may have been involved in the production of flour or oil while in town.[75] When Ben Yijū left with the intention of coming back, the house was not returned to its owner but sealed to await the casual tenant's return.

Indirect evidence of residential rentals in Aden itself is gleaned from Geniza letters and accounts mentioning living expenses of merchants or mercantile agents. In one case, the living expenses in town of a mercantile agent, Abū al-Barakāt b. Joseph al-Lebdī, include, in addition to sustenance and the rent for a warehouse, the hiring of a *bilīj*.[76] The term, Malayan for "cabin," "shipboard space," or "bungalow," appears only in Geniza documents relating to the Indian Ocean and, with the exception of the case at hand, refers exclusively to an individual rented space or cabin on board a ship.

How can we make sense of a "cabin" on shore? Because Abū al-Barakāt's other expenses in the specific entry concern his stay in Aden, the *bilīj* may denote a bungalow or reed hut where the man spent his nights while in town. The structure would have been of the same type as the modest dwellings of perishable materials discussed earlier and would have provided adequate and economical accommodation for a short stay. Abū al-Barakāt was doing business for partners in Egypt. Most of the capital he handled in his dealings apparently came from such established merchants, and he seems to have been an agent rather than a capitalist in his own right. Younger and junior in the profession, such a man was presumably the type to put up with *bilīj* living.

The other alternative is that Abū al-Barakāt's *bilīj* was of the usual shipboard variety, a makeshift screen or portable shelter, and that he bought it in town with the prospect of making his stay on board his ship of passage more comfortable. Indeed, instead of renting a place in town, he may have slept on board throughout his stay. Merchants usually embarked the day before they were scheduled to leave: that final night at port was known as *laylat al-mabīt* or *laylat mabītī fī al-baḥr*.[77] While the total absence of references to a *funduq* does not necessarily indicate that Aden completely lacked this type of accommodation, junior and less connected merchants and agents may have commonly spent more than one night on board their ships of passage, along with the crew.[78]

One final possible question arises: Where are the baths, mosques, and other ritual spaces of a cosmopolitan Islamic city? These institutions undoubtedly played a pivotal role in the town's social life. They lie outside the scope of this investigation, which focuses exclusively on things commercial; in partial vindication of that choice of emphasis, both written sources and the archaeological record preserve only little concrete information about either such institutions or the buildings that housed them. Al-Muqaddasī's and Ibn al-Mujāwir's descriptions of a congregational mosque that stood far from the market and on the edge of the city contrast sharply with the topography of Sīrāf, where the equivalent sacred space had its qibla wall facing the sea and was "virtually surrounded by the bazaar."[79] But even if Aden's Friday mosque stood at the edge of the city, its foundation story beautifully illustrates the intersections among spiritual life, its physical manifestations in the urban context, and maritime commerce.

According to Ibn al-Mujāwir, Persians built the original mosque at Aden. These early immigrants found a large piece of good-quality ambergris, presumably washed up on the seashore.[80] They took it to the ruler of the town, who asked them to sell it and to dedicate the profits to building the mosque, "for no money is more legitimate than this money, and no cause is more righteous than this cause."[81] Money from sea trade built the emblematic edifices of the urban landscape as much as merchants' houses and commercial buildings; the only requirement was that the transactions generating the funds be straightforward and transparent, that the code of righteousness and trustworthiness guide the commercial process. The ambergris was sold off, and the congregational mosque was built with the proceeds.

PART II

The Commercial Entrepôt

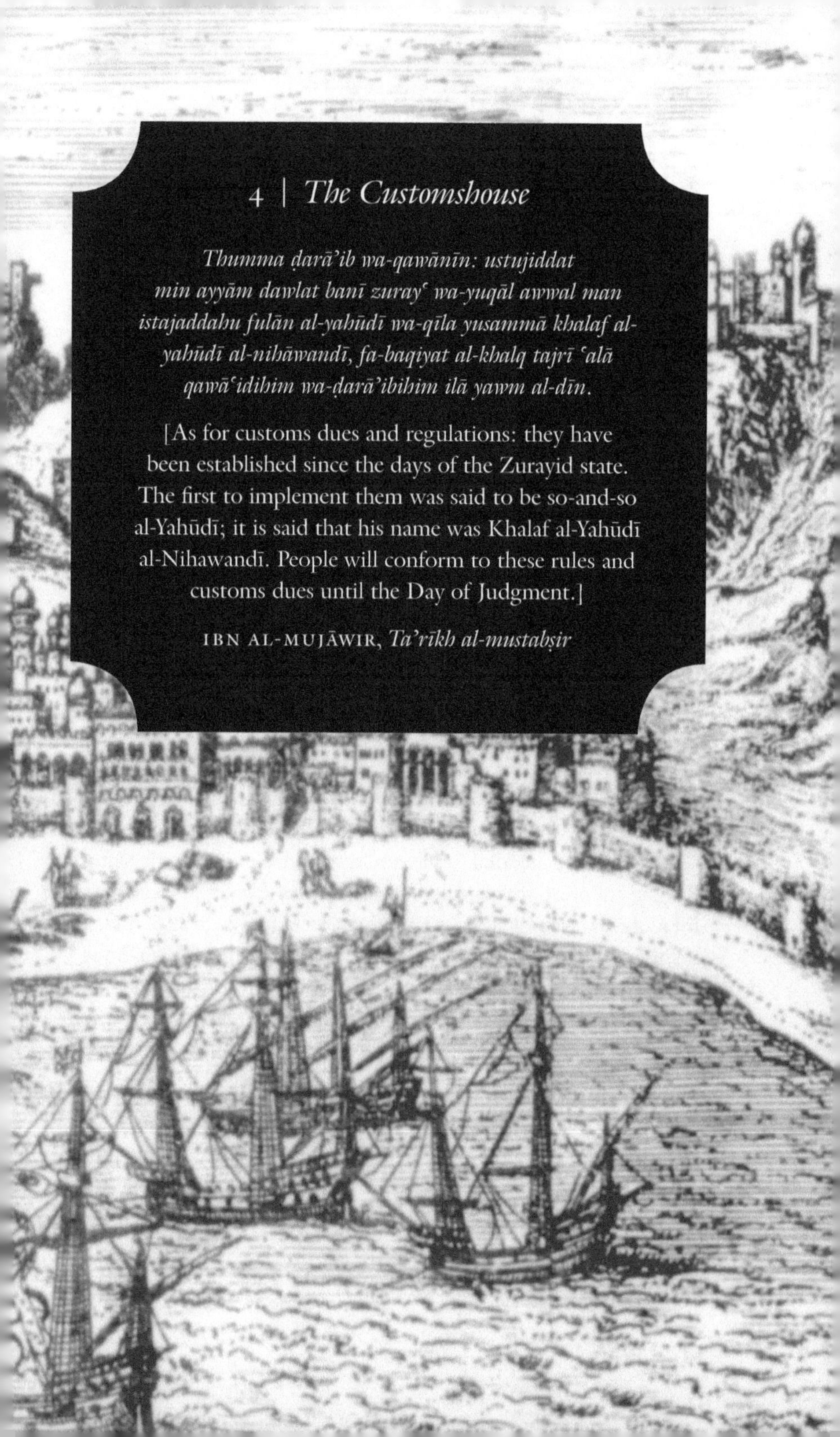

4 | *The Customshouse*

Thumma ḍarā'ib wa-qawānīn: ustujiddat min ayyām dawlat banī zurayʿ wa-yuqāl awwal man istajaddahu fulān al-yahūdī wa-qīla yusammā khalaf al-yahūdī al-nihāwandī, fa-baqiyat al-khalq tajrī ʿalā qawāʿidihim wa-ḍarā'ibihim ilā yawm al-dīn.

[As for customs dues and regulations: they have been established since the days of the Zurayid state. The first to implement them was said to be so-and-so al-Yahūdī; it is said that his name was Khalaf al-Yahūdī al-Nihawandī. People will conform to these rules and customs dues until the Day of Judgment.]

IBN AL-MUJĀWIR, *Ta'rīkh al-mustabṣir*

Sources

According to a story related by ʿUmāra, a historian of Yemen, early in the Zurayid dynasty's administration, governors paid stiff tributes to their Sulayhid patrons and overlords. The city's yearly contribution to the coffers of queen Arwā reportedly amounted to one hundred thousand dinars.[1] The number quoted may be formulaic, but it clearly spells out the notion that Aden was an affluent city and that its rulers had a great deal to gain from shaking off the Sulayhid hegemony, which they eventually did. International trade—more specifically, its regulation and taxation through the port's customshouse—brought in this wealth and provided the upstart dynasty with both the incentive and the capacity to act autonomously. After the city had freed itself of Sulayhid domination, control of the customshouse became central to the division of power between the two Zurayid rulers as well as to the power struggle this division eventually spawned.

If Ibn al-Mujāwir is to be believed, during the following period, tribute money was sent from Aden to the seat of the Ayyubid administration in Taʿizz in four different coffers (*khazāʾin*), each of which held 150,000 dinars. The designation of each coffer is probably meant to refer to the provenance of its funds: coffer of the arrival of ships from India, coffer of the importation of madder in Aden, coffer of the export of horses to India, and coffer of the departure of ships to India.[2] The total sum is not unreasonable: a 9th/15th century Rasulid administrative manual, *Mulakhkhaṣ al-fiṭan*, registers a grand total of 2,320,500 dinars from all ports, including Jeddah, Zabīd, al-Shiḥr, and Ẓafar; of that total, 1,470,000 dinars came from Aden.[3] Thus, while Ibn al-Mujāwir's numbers remain unverifiable, the point is again clear: the city's revenue and the corresponding contribution to the treasury of the sovereign power depended entirely on its capacity to levy taxes on international trade.

Aden's customshouse emerges as a vital part of the city's economy and the administration of commercial taxation as a major factor in the power relationships within the city and between the local government and larger centers of power. Thanks to the high visibility of the institution in the historical sources, it is possible to reconstruct its structure, mechanisms, procedures, and ultimate role in the life of medieval Aden. An important step in this direction and a springboard for my investigation is G. Rex Smith's study of Aden's customs administration through Ibn al-Mujāwir's account and the two official Rasulid documents, the Muẓaffar register and the *Mulakhkhaṣ al-fiṭan*; to his conclusions and those of his student, Nayef ʿAbdallāh al-Shamrookh, I add the testimony of the Cairo Geniza.[4]

Ibn al-Mujāwir devotes several paragraphs to the history of Aden's customshouse, the procedures associated with the importation of goods, and the taxes charged.[5] He provides a vivid account of clearing customs at Aden from a merchant's point of view. He describes the sequence of events that followed a ship's arrival at port and lists types and rates of taxes imposed on specific merchandise imported into the city. Yet given the literary nature of his work, his testimony is at times not to be taken at face value; it also does not provide a comprehensive record of Aden's customs procedure. His list of customs rates includes only thirty-four taxable items (table 1), which clearly does not cover the entire dazzling range of merchandise that the Rasulid documents show passed through Aden.[6] Moreover, the customs dues information Ibn al-Mujāwir provides relates almost exclusively to imports. Relying solely on his testimony might give the impression that the export taxes levied at Aden were relatively insignificant or applied only to very few commodities.

The two Rasulid texts, conversely, offer the fiscal perspective on commercial taxation as well as a wealth of information both on the merchandise traded in or through Aden and on the rates and methods of taxation.[7] Written by and addressed to civil servants in the late 7th/13th and the early 9th/15th centuries, respectively, these documents are invaluable for presenting the official face of the customshouse in the two centuries following the period under investigation here. In that later period, the control of the state in general and regulation of trade in particular had intensified just as mercantile traffic had increased. These texts provide crucial relevant comparative material but should not be taken a priori to speak for Zurayid and Ayyubid practices.

The testimony of Ibn al-Mujāwir and to some extent the data provided by the Rasulid administrative texts are here juxtaposed with the words of the Jewish merchants. Whether transients or local inhabitants, their involvement in overseas commerce rendered contact with the customshouse routine; their frequent references and allusions to customs procedures and tax payments help illuminate specific details of the bigger picture that emerges from the official sources. Moreover, while the matter-of-fact testimonies on clearing customs belong mostly to merchants, they also represent the point of view of at least one customs administrator, Maḍmūn b. Japheth, a prominent merchant and leader of the Jewish community.

For a broader picture of medieval customs practices that offers a general framework for the Adeni case, the better-documented Fatimid and Ayyubid taxation regime in Egyptian ports must be considered. Of particular relevance here is Claude Cahen's work on Egyptian administrative handbooks and S. D. Goitein's analysis of taxation through the testimony of Geniza documents.[8] Cahen dealt primarily with the fiscal treatise written in the first years of the Ayyubid period by Abū al-Ḥasan ʿAlī b. ʿUthman al-Qurayshī al-Makhzūmī, a legal expert and civil servant who supervised the administration of tax offices in late Fatimid and early Ayyubid Egypt. Despite its significant lacunae and partial publication and thanks to Cahen's painstaking treatment, the manuscript reveals much about the complexities of customs administration at the ports of Alexandria, Tinnis, and Damietta. As with the Rasulid texts, the vantage point is that of the state and its appointed tax officials. The merchants, however, see things differently. Their interest naturally lies outside the administrative details that are the bread and butter of bureaucrats and focuses sharply on the steps the merchants had to take to get their merchandise in and out of the port and on the taxes they had to pay. Without neglecting the official view, Goitein's analysis centers on the merchants' perception of customshouse realities.[9]

Comparing the findings of these two scholars brings to light important patterns of medieval customs administration. For one, it appears that in Cairo, Alexandria, and the lesser Egyptian ports, customs were charged both on imports and on exports, as was true in Byzantine and western medieval ports.[10] Al-Makhzūmī's treatise suggests that in principle, dues on certain products leaving Egypt were higher and were calculated on a different basis than dues on imports. The different treatment of exports leads Cahen to conclude that the Egyptian fiscal policy aimed at discouraging exports, especially if they were not linked with imports.[11] The Geniza papers, conversely, reveal that roughly similar rates applied to both exports and imports across the Mediterranean and that these rates never became excessively high.[12]

A second important point is that despite the injunction of normative Muslim law that non-Muslims pay twice as much as Muslims at customs, customs rates do not appear to distinguish between native subjects on the basis of their religion; in other words, Muslim, Jewish, and Christian merchants paid customs at equal rates during both Fatimid and Ayyubid times, with the exception of a brief period at the beginning of Ayyubid rule when crisis-induced militancy enforced the measure for a short time.[13] In the Mediterranean, however, foreigners were forced to pay a special toll when crossing the frontiers of the Islamic world.[14]

Finally, import tolls in Egypt apparently were calculated ad valorem rather than ad naturam: customs officials charged a standard rate on the current market value of imported goods and did not fix customs tariffs in advance according to the type and quantity of merchandise and without regard for the fluctuations of market values.[15] As one Jewish merchant puts it, "Prices are in the hands of God."[16] Given the significant fluctuation of prices typical of the medieval market, merchants would have suffered greatly from a fixed rate, which would have raised taxes to excessive levels when prices fell below normal.

In the same vein, the Egyptian sources also reveal that customs dues on both imports and exports were collected after the conclusion of all transactions, at the end of the merchants' stay at any given port.[17] This practice further facilitated merchants' conduct of business, eliminating both the need to raise significant sums of cash at the outset of their mercantile endeavor and the risk of carrying this money on their outbound voyage. The measure allowed them to pay only after the sale of their merchandise at their destination had rendered them solvent enough to do so.[18]

A comparison of the Zurayid and Ayyubid customs practices at Aden with the situation in the Mediterranean reveals that the great difference between the two systems lies in the rates charged on imports and exports: import dues levied at Aden appear to have been both excessively high when compared to Mediterranean imposts and disproportionately high with respect to exit tolls levied at Aden. Moreover, dues do not appear to have been calculated strictly on the basis of the fluctuating market value of goods but to have depended on both the nature of the taxed item and a standard market price assigned to that particular item. Conversely, as in the Mediterranean, customs practices at Aden appear to have made no distinction between Muslims and others and to have collected taxes after the completion of all business transactions, just before the merchants' departure from the port. Finally, export taxes in Aden were significantly lower than import taxes, a measure that alleviated the overall burden of taxation and attracted overseas traders who used the port as a market for merchandise from abroad.

Clearing Customs: Al-Furḍa

In addition to the common usage of the term "*al-furḍa*" to denote a place whence ships are launched (a harbor or port), residents of and visitors to medieval Aden routinely applied the term to the institution of mercantile taxation and to the building dedicated to the levying of such taxes.[19] The investigation of Aden's topography revealed that the customshouse stood just inside the waterfront walls, in immediate proximity to a city gate dedicated to the traffic in merchandise between the city and the sea. According to Ibn al-Mujāwir, merchandise was brought in and out of the city at the Furḍa Gate.[20] At this strategic location, the edifice fulfilled its function as a customshouse and hosted a number of activities that eventually channeled merchandise into the city markets.

Ibn al-Mujāwir's description of customs procedures at Aden starts much before the processing of the merchandise itself, with the spotting of approaching ships on the horizon. A chain of lookouts (*nāẓirūn*) linked the urban space with the upper reaches of the Jabal al-Akhḍar, the strategic location of the al-Khaḍrā' fort and clearly an excellent vantage point for the supervision of harbor goings-on. Through this chain of heralds, news of an arriving ship swiftly reached the city.[21] As fitting for a port city as this state of anticipation may seem, the arrival of ships from any given direction—India or the Red Sea or Africa—took place within a time schedule well defined by the clock of sea and winds. City officials knew roughly when to expect ships from overseas and therefore when to post lookouts on Jabal al-Akhḍar. In Ibn al-Mujāwir's days, these lookouts were employed and deployed by the customshouse and were paid from its coffers.[22] It is easy to see how this practice fit within the organization of the customs process: the efficient reception of a ship at port, the disembarkation of passengers, the unloading and processing of merchandise through customs, the assessment of taxes, and finally the transfer of the goods to the market depended on a timely mobilization of the customshouse officials.

Timing was very important indeed: Ibn al-Mujāwir states that after initial shipboard inspection and disembarkation of passengers, merchandise took three days to arrive on shore.[23] The lapse between disembarkation and unloading could not have been a deliberate policy; withholding merchandise from the market and risking its condition in the hot climate of the region and the damp conditions of a ship's hold went against everyone's interests. It is more likely that three days constituted the average waiting time during the sailing season, when numerous ships arrived at port. At least half of the seventy to eighty ships that Ibn al-Mujāwir states put into port each year are likely to have overlapped at Aden's rather narrow anchorage at any given time.[24] The Muẓaffar register specifies that ships were generally processed through customs on a first come, first served basis and that priority could be granted only in cases of ships needing urgent repairs, perhaps because leaking hulls could destroy cargoes and diminish customs revenues, or through the sultan's personal intervention.[25]

In addition to congestion at the port, delays in the customshouse itself may have occurred for a variety of reasons. A fragmentary letter from Adeni merchant Joseph b. Abraham to well-known India merchant Ben Yijū, who at the time had left India and had taken temporary refuge in Zabīd, informs the recipient that a consignment of iron, apparently belonging to him, had been held up (*muḥayyar*) in the customshouse.[26] The circumstances of the delay have not been preserved, but in the world of overseas trade, business by long-distance agency, and uncertain timing, such stalling must have irked both the merchants, who wanted to get their wares to the market quickly, and the customs officials, who must have been eager to clear goods as efficiently and profitably as possible.

The responsibility for spotting a ship as soon as it appeared on the horizon and promptly informing city officials and common people was thus an important task, and the *nāẓirūn* triggered a chain of events across town. Ibn al-Mujāwir makes this process come alive for his readers: he notes that visibility was best during sunrise and sundown, and he relates that the top lookout used a trick to verify that what he was seeing was indeed a ship and not a bird or an illusion. He held up a stick, aligned it with the object along the horizon, and watched the object move. If the object wavered left and right or over and under the extended stick, it was a bird. If it moved steadily along the line of the stick, then it had to be a ship heading straight to port. He then cried out "Boat," and the human chain carried the message to town.[27] It was important to verify first impressions; while bearers of accurate news received a reward of a local dinar per boat, false alarms earned the messengers ten blows with a stick.[28]

What happened after the news reached town? Ibn al-Mujāwir reports that the first to be informed was the city governor (*al-wālī*), followed by the customshouse officials (*mashā'ikh al-furḍa*). In later times, the governor became personally involved in the customs procedures, at least according to the testimony of the *Mulakhkhaṣ*: he not only kept the keys to the building but also was allegedly present at each ship's initial reception in the harbor.[29] Yet the same document's list of customshouse officials suggests a hierarchy in which the task of physically receiving the incoming ships at the harbor would have been delegated to the *wālī*'s subordinates.[30] The Geniza documents, moreover, make no mention of the involvement of the governor, and it seems improbable that he would have attended each and every arrival.[31] He may have been nominally in charge of customs operations, and he was undoubtedly kept informed of daily arrivals at port. Writing after the author of the *Mulakhkhaṣ*, Ludovico di Varthema testifies that the "officers of the Sultan" took charge of arriving ships on his behalf.[32] Thus, the governor wielded ultimate authority over the customshouse, while special customs officials (*mashā'ikh al-furḍa*) oversaw and directed the practical aspects of the reception of each ship.

Standing at the top of the customshouse hierarchy, the *mashā'ikh al-furḍa* oversaw the activities of a number of subordinate personnel whose roles emerge in some detail from Ibn al-Mujāwir's account.[33] In addition to the lookouts, one other category of customs clerk involved in the early stages of receiving a ship to port were the *mubashshirūn* (messengers). As the ship neared the harbor, these men jumped into small boats (*ṣanābīq*) and went out to meet the incoming vessel before it had reached its anchorage. After boarding and exchanging greetings, they conducted a preliminary interview with the new arrivals, asking the captain about the ship's provenance; answering his questions concerning the situation in town, the governor's name, and the prices of goods at the market; and relaying news of any passengers' acquaintances in town. Then followed the official part of the visit: the messengers' main task was to compile a list with the names of the captain and all the merchants on board and to obtain the ship's cargo list, a kind of bill of lading drawn in advance by the ship's scribe.[34]

This document, which Ibn al-Mujāwir refers to by the generic term "*ruqʿa*," appears both in Geniza documents and in the later Rasulid handbooks as "*satmī*," "*satmī al-markab*," and "*satmī al-rubbān*."[35] Merchandise was unloaded on shore and then meticulously inspected, counted, and weighed. Customs officials presumably based their assessment of taxes on the local record thus produced. Still, the bill of lading must have served as a rough draft for their final record. Moreover, once it was surrendered to customs and preceded the merchandise into the city, the list of incoming cargo became a valuable source of market information. Anticipating the types and quantities of merchandise, which, as mentioned earlier, took roughly three days to reach the customshouse and might be delayed even further, was probably important for the workings of a precarious, information-starved, and nervous market. That the city's customshouse took up market concerns is important for understanding the extensive intertwining of the entrepôt's institutions of trade regulation and mercantile services in both the Zurayid and Ayyubid periods.

After visiting the incoming ship, the messengers returned to town with the information they had obtained. According to Ibn al-Mujāwir's account, the lists went straight to the city's governor. After being relieved of their official duty, the messengers made the rounds of the city, bearing news to residents with relatives or acquaintances on board and receiving a reward for this service. At the same time, the ship proceeded to its berth in the port's anchorage and there received a second visit from customshouse officials—this time, male (*mufattish*) and female (*ʿajūz*) inspectors who examined the newcomers. Ibn al-Mujāwir gives a graphic description of the search, down to a full enumeration of body parts probed. The author's point is clear: customs procedures were obnoxiously thorough and thoroughly obnoxious.[36]

Rather strangely, the Geniza documents do not contain a single allusion to this process. If Ibn al-Mujāwir is not exaggerating or inventing his story, then the extensive search may have been an Ayyubid innovation, begun only toward the end of the period from which Geniza letters have been preserved. Such a change might have come as part of the intensification of port regulations and government control witnessed in the Ayyubid period. Like the massive walls screening the city and its market, so too the system of physical examination of all newcomers by sea showcases the authorities' determination to safeguard the sources of tax income and to ensure that every last drop of revenue had been squeezed from international trade.

After the shipboard inspection, the merchants were allowed to disembark. Their personal effects went with them, but their merchandise stayed behind. When the merchandise finally reached the shore, clearing customs started in earnest and took time. Ibn al-Mujāwir again dwells on the thoroughness of the process of inspection: goods such as clothes and textiles were unpacked bale by bale and counted piece by piece; goods in bulk were weighed on a scale.[37] Another group of customs employees, the scribes who Abū Makhrama reports spent the day on the two covered benches of the Dār al-Ṭawīla adjacent to the customshouse, recorded everything anew.[38]

This painstaking process must have served the purpose of assessing customs taxes on individual shipments. Ibn al-Mujāwir stops at this point to contemplate the magnitude of distress felt by the merchants as they passed through customs and, in their eyes, saw their wealth disappear into customshouse coffers. While he later resumes with a list of taxes, he provides few further details of the customs assessment process. Without the invaluable evidence of the Geniza documents, there would be no way to interpret his list of dues or to evaluate how taxes were assessed in practice. Before presenting the complexities of understanding taxes, however, it is important to say a few words about the men who were responsible for their collection.

*The Senior Officials (*Mashā'ikh al-Furḍa*): The Career of Maḍmūn b. Japheth*

According to Ibn al-Mujāwir, Aden owed the administrative structure of its customshouse to a Jewish man, reportedly named Khalaf and originating from the city of Nihāwand.[39] Easy as it is to dismiss this statement as a topos or a fantasy, records show that a Jewish merchant living in the early days of the Zurayid state indeed may have had charge of the Adeni customshouse. He was related to a man named Khalaf, but his name was Ḥasan b. Bundār. He belonged to Aden's famous Bundār family and was the father of Maḍmūn b. Japheth. While the Bundārs do not appear in the documents with the *nisba* linking them to the Jibāl city of Nihāwand, they apparently had Persian origins.[40] Ḥasan b. Bundār's name appears in a number of Geniza papers, mostly the legal documents and letters relating to the Lebdī affair in the last decade of the 5th/11th century—significantly, not long after the beginning of Zurayid rule.

The multifaceted lawsuit between Jekuthiel Abū Yaʿqūb al-Ḥakīm and Joseph b. al-Lebdī unfolded in Cairo but also affected Aden.[41] Joseph traveled extensively eastward to Aden and India and traded both for himself and for Jekuthiel, a well-established and sedentary Cairene merchant. Their dispute arose over settlement of accounts at the end of these voyages. Ḥasan b. Bundār was the Adeni contact who dealt with the partners' business in Aden and in India, and Joseph al-Lebdī later asked Ḥasan b. Bundār to testify concerning the details of each deal.

In one letter, Joseph asks Ḥasan to list all transactions executed in Aden on Joseph's behalf and to quote "what you have levied on each item in terms of taxes."[42] This does not necessarily signify that Ḥasan collected the taxes for the state; rather, as Joseph's representative, he might simply have undertaken the payment of these taxes on Joseph's behalf and then recorded them in his *daftar* (account book). But given al-Lebdī's turn of phrase, it is not at all unlikely that Ḥasan indeed determined the tax and paid it on Joseph's behalf. In other words, Ḥasan may well have been a customs official as well as a merchant, a mercantile representative, and an important enough personage in the Adeni community to merit the honorific "*sar ha-qehillot*" (prince of the congregations).[43] Not much later, one of his descendants with similar standing in the local community indeed filled all these roles.

While it is not clear that Ḥasan b. Bundār was the man behind the legend of the creation of Aden's enduring customs tariff system, less than fifty years after the establishment of the Zurayids in Aden, his son, Maḍmūn b. Ḥasan b. Bundār, served as a leader of the Jewish community, a respected merchant, a representative of merchants, and an official, perhaps the highest in rank, in the city's customshouse. His career as a merchant, mercantile representative, and city notable and his relationships in these capacities with foreign merchants stand as eloquent illustration of what made paying the hefty Aden taxes worthwhile.

The decisive evidence that Maḍmūn held office at the customshouse appears in a letter he wrote to his friend and business partner, Ben Yijū, in India, the same letter in which the author reported the dramatic naval siege of Aden in 529/1134–35.[44] In the passage that reveals the extent of his jurisdiction at the customshouse, Maḍmūn describes a slow pepper market toward the end of that same sailing season: "Mediocre news arrived from Egypt; the market [in Aden] was sluggish; there was no demand for pepper and no other item sold even for a *dirham* until just a week before the day of sailing [that is, the last day of departure for sailing ships]. Had I demanded the *ʿushūr* from the pepper merchants [when the market was still slow], they would have sold it [right away] for a dinar [instead of] twenty [?]. But I held off on the collection of the *ʿushūr* from them until the day of sailing; people then arrived from all over and the price of pepper reached 23 dinars a *bahār*."[45]

The main market for the Indian pepper transiting in Aden was of course Egypt, which at the time was experiencing a low. News of the situation had reached Aden, presumably before any Western merchants—the prospective buyers of pepper—had arrived in the city. Numerous pepper merchants came from Malabar to Aden, but the buyers from the West did not show up in time. The result was an oversupplied pepper market, with very low demand and correspondingly low prices. Given the general and perennial shortage of cash, customs must have been due after the goods were sold, as was the case in the Mediterranean; yet customshouse officials may have had discretion in demanding payment sooner rather than later, thus forcing sale. In this case, Maḍmūn apparently had decided to wait on the taxes, permitting the pepper merchants to hold onto their goods until the pace of the market picked up, presumably with the anticipated arrival of buyers.

In a general sense, customs officials' intervention in market affairs and influence on market prices is not without parallel. Goitein discusses Geniza evidence from Egypt that indicates that tollhouses in Cairo may have played a role in fixing market prices. But in those cases the desired effect was always to lower rather than boost prices, and the method involved withholding early arrivals until there was sufficient supply to ensure "reasonable" prices.[46] This is clearly very different from what Maḍmūn did for the *aṣḥāb al-filfil* in Aden. In the Egyptian case, the market presumably froze briefly, resuming business when all merchants and consumers could benefit; from the merchants' point of view, such measures removed the incentive and reward for arriving early but guaranteed even profits. In Aden, Maḍmūn's measure gave the merchants a break at a difficult moment and ensured the highest possible profits given the dire situation.

Maḍmūn's success in saving the pepper merchants from potential ruin illustrates both the structure of Aden's taxation regime and the extent of the man's influence and power. In addition to being the leader of the Adeni Jewish community of the time—or perhaps thanks in part to his capacity as such—Maḍmūn maintained close ties with the Muslim authorities. His correspondence contains several references to the powerful general and deputy of the Zurayid governor, Bilāl b. Jarīr, and the two apparently were personal friends and business partners.[47] That the city authorities and most likely Bilāl would have entrusted Maḍmūn with the important post of customs supervisor is therefore hardly surprising. The Jewish leader's extensive network could serve as an asset and a guarantee for those doing business with him and could ensure that he carried out his official duties with maximum efficiency.

The Burden of Taxation

In exaggerated language and somber tone, Ibn al-Mujāwir paints a grim picture of clearing customs at Aden: "Henceforth ill-fortune strikes the merchant, sadness all but kills him, and his fate takes an evil turn because of what [customs officials] do to drive away from him prosperity and happiness."[48] Arriving and disembarking at the port was an arduous process; the end result, Ibn al-Mujāwir suggests, was ruthless extortion that left the merchant exploited and bewildered. This negative description of the rapacious customs process is reminiscent of a report from the Mediterranean written in the late 6th/12th century. Ibn Jubayr presents a comparably grim picture of customs in Alexandria in 578/1183, lamenting the excesses of customs officials, which he asserts are directed indiscriminately against both Muslim and non-Muslim passengers on a Genoese ship.[49] Most merchants arriving in Aden or Alexandria, however, knew full well what to expect, either from previous visits or from the plentiful accounts that well-frequented ports must have generated. These merchants must have been financially and psychologically prepared to endure the procedures and pay the taxes imposed by the local administration. Even if taxation was excessive, the privilege of trading in the Indian Ocean port, as in Alexandria, was apparently still worth paying for.

It is thus noteworthy that the Geniza documents of the India trade contain virtually no complaints about excessive taxation or harsh treatment at the customshouse at Aden. The absence of complaints is all the more remarkable in the face of evidence of protest, harsh taxation, and irregularities at the customshouses of smaller Indian Ocean ports such as that of the island of Dahlak and the Persian coast town of al-Tīz. From Dahlak, one account describes a case in which a consignment of coral was slipped past customs and a boatload of Jewish and other traders slipped out of town, only to be chased by a naval force from the island.[50] In a letter to Egypt, an Adeni merchant and shipowner speaks of the injustice done by the ruler of the Persian port of al-Tīz to one of the addressee's fellow traders: while at al-Tīz, one-third of the man's merchandise had been taken from him without any compensation.[51] In yet a third letter, a trader complains about the variety and high cost of taxes in Red Sea ports on his way from Egypt to Aden.[52] That virtually no such complaints focus on Aden would seem to suggest that the merchants, while surely not happy to pay steep imposts, were nevertheless appeased by guarantees of relative order and security as well as the vibrant market that the great entrepôt offered.

The one clear reference to oppressive imposts comes from the brief period of turmoil in the city's history when the controversial Ayyubid ruler, al-Malik al-Muʿizz Ismāʿīl (593–98/1197–1202), arbitrarily assumed the title of caliph and proceeded to wreak havoc with the city's normal conduct of business.[53] A letter from this tumultuous period relates that al-Muʿizz forced Jews across Yemen to convert, persecuted and even punished by death any dissenters, and had all foreign merchants in Aden rounded up in his palace, al-Manẓar, with vague but grim intentions. A massacre was avoided, but excessive taxes were imposed on everyone: the transients were ordered to pay one-third of their poll taxes on the spot, regardless of whether they had already paid the taxes in their countries of residence. An extra 15 percent was imposed on all imported and exported merchandise, although the ruler apparently was persuaded to hold off on this new imposition until the following year.[54] It is not known whether the extortionate tax was ever in fact levied, but by the time the self-styled caliph was executed by government troops about three years later, the situation, including the conduct of business, appears already to have returned to normal.[55]

Thus, if the Geniza merchants had no bones to pick with customs collection in Aden for most of the 6th/12th century, does Ibn al-Mujāwir's later and persistently hostile treatment of the subject reflect a different era in tax collection in Aden? According to the same author, customs taxes had changed during his time. In his enumeration of the five specific taxes applicable in his day, Ibn al-Mujāwir distinguishes between the "old tax" (*ʿashūr qadīm*), which he explains as the customshouse revenue (*wa-huwa māl al-furḍa*) and which was clearly still applicable in his day, and four other taxes that appear to have been introduced by the Ayyubids: the *ʿashūr al-shawānī* (tax of the galleys), *dār al-wakāla* (mercantile representation money), *dār al-zakwa* (alms tax), and *al-dilāla* (brokerage tax).[56]

Ibn al-Mujāwir appears to be conflating dues charged in the marketplace with taxes levied at the customshouse: when he lists actual customs taxes on specific types of merchandise, he makes no reference to *zaka'a*, *wakāla*, or *dilāla* taxes and only occasionally quotes a *shawānī* impost.[57] Similarly, al-Makhzūmī's *Kitāb al-minhāj* discusses both customs taxes and taxes of the market (such as brokerage fees and market dues) under the same rubric. In al-Makhzūmī's world, a strict distinction between market taxes and customs dues was not of primary importance. Both kinds of imposts went to government coffers, because at least in theory the government controlled and taxed not only the movements of merchandise in and out of Alexandria and the lesser Egyptian ports but also their redistribution in the markets of those ports.[58] Perhaps the Ayyubid regime that Ibn al-Mujāwir encountered at Aden had consolidated customs and transaction costs and had centralized their collection under the jurisdiction of the customshouse. In their official documents, their successors, the Rasulids, routinely note both the *ʿushr* and *dilāla* taxes and, in certain cases, especially with goods coming from the East, a *shawānī* tax as well.[59]

If the standardization of such levies constituted part of the Ayyubid overhaul of port administration, did the situation in Zurayid Aden differ fundamentally? *Zaka'a* and *wakāla* taxes do not appear anywhere in the Geniza documents. *Dilāla* dues are only occasionally mentioned, and these references suggest that the *dallāl* was probably not a government employee but a free agent rendering services and remunerated individually.[60] The connection between brokerage fees and the customs tax, however, remains complex. If taxes were calculated on the basis of the market value of an item, ad valorem, the *dallāl* had a role to play in determining that market value. As a specialist in contemporary market prices, the *dallāl* could—and in the later periods did—serve as a consultant to the customshouse, certifying the prices on the basis of which taxes were calculated.[61] Even if the Zurayid tax officials used brokers in that capacity, the taxation regime in that earlier period of Aden's development may still have been less centralized and the dues levied lighter and less inclusive of additional costs.

Merchants whose active careers spanned both the Zurayid and Ayyubid periods may have noticed changes in their experience at Aden, and merchants in the later period may have felt the malaise expressed by Ibn al-Mujāwir and by Ibn Jubayr; that their complaints have not survived does not necessarily prove that no such complaints were ever voiced. In strictly economic terms, however, the result of mercantile taxation in its totality appears to have changed little. In both periods, merchants paid for the privilege of trading and passing through a commercial entrepôt. Moreover, as the next section will demonstrate, the sums on Ibn al-Mujāwir's list of taxes are not significantly higher than rates levied in the earlier years when the majority of the Geniza documents were written.

Import and Export Taxes

A closer reading of the relevant passage in Ibn al-Mujāwir's text reveals that all five taxes quoted apply to imports into Aden. All of the thirty-four goods and their taxes on his list carry an *ʿashūr* tax, and some also incur a *shawānī* tax.[62] For some of the items on the list, however, he quotes an extra sum payable upon departure from Aden, with formulations indicating that this was an export tax (table 1).[63] The Geniza documents, conversely, routinely mention two kinds of taxes. The merchants refer to exit tolls by the generic terms "*maks*" and "*kharj*" in various combinations (table 2), while they usually employ the common term "*ʿushūr*" (tithes) for the import tax (table 3).[64] Taken together with the solid documentation of import and export taxes in the Rasulid period,[65] the testimonies of Ibn al-Mujāwir and the Geniza documents attest to the consistent and diachronic application of both import and export dues at least since the Zurayid period.

On what basis were customs dues calculated? Ibn al-Mujāwir's list records customs dues for specific quantities of merchandise but does not indicate the value of these units; only in the special case of "imports" or sales of boats are customs said to have been collected on the basis of the boat's value, at a fixed 10 percent rate. This evidence may be interpreted in two ways. One possibility is that customs in Aden

TABLE 1: Ibn al-Mujāwir's List of Entry and Exit Tolls

Merchandise	ʿUshūr	Shawānī	Khurūj min al-furḍa
Pepper, 1 b.	8 d.	1 d.	2 d.
Indigo, 1 piece[a]		4 d. (?)	.25 d.
Assa gum, 1 b.	8 d.		
Perfumed cherry bark, 1 b.	3.5 d.		
Bamboo sugar, 1 b.	20.66 d.	1 d.	
Dafwā' wood, 1 stick	"half" of total		
Camphor, 1 far.	25.6 d.		
Cardamom, 1 b.	7 d.		
Cloves, 1 far.	10 d.	1 d.	
Saffron, 1 far.	3.66 d.		
Flax, 1 b.	7.5 d.		
Sale of a ship[b]	10 percent of sale value (payable by seller)		
Iron	"half" of total		
Lac	"one-third" or "one-quarter" of total + 2 d.		
Madder, 1 b.	12 d.[c]		
Tamarind, 1 b.	3 j.		
Maqāṭiʿ cloths, 10 pieces	2.5 d.		
ʿUqudāt cloths, 10 pieces	.75 j.		
Sheep, 1 head	.25 j.		
Horse, 1 head[d]	50 d.		70 d. (*fī khurūjihi ilā al-baḥr*)
Slave, 1	2 d.		.5 d. (*idhā kharaja min al-balad*)
Sindābūrī slave, 1[e]	8 d.	1 d.	.5 d. (*fī khurūj min al-bāb*)
Silk cloth of Zabīd, (?) pieces	1 j. + .5 d.		
Robe of Ẓafār, 1	1 j. + .25 d.		
White cloth, 1	.125 d.		
Sūsī cloth	4 q.		
Sūsī *fuṭas*, (?)	1 j. + .25 d.		
Maḥābis cloths, 1 khw.	4 d.		
Handwoven fabrics, 1 khw.	2.5 d.		
Loincloths, 1 khw.	2.5 d.		
Indian rough cotton robes, 1 khw.	2.5 d.		

TABLE 1: Continued

Merchandise	ʿUshūr	Shawānī	Khurūj min al-furḍa
Large Sūsī linen cloths, (?)	2 j. + 1 q.		
Small Sūsī linen cloths, (?)	2 j. + 1 f.		
Sorghum, 1 basket	.125 j. or .125 d.		

Source: Adapted from Smith, "Have You Anything to Declare?," 132–33, 136–37. I have added a column with Ibn al-Mujāwir's quotes of exit tolls; see Ibn al-Mujāwir, *Ta'rīkh al-mustabṣir*, 140–41. On the strength of Geniza evidence and Ibn al-Mujāwir's explanations of his tax quotes, the term "*ʿashur*" should be interpreted as import tax; it does not appear to apply to export dues. Divergences in specific quotations between the two tables result from different interpretation of the text and are accompanied by explanatory notes. Dues are given mostly in dinars (d.), *qīrāṭ* (q.), and in one case *fulūs* (f.). For several commodities, dues are incurred in kind, and the quantity owed is then quoted.

Note

b. = *bahār* or *buhār* (a measure of weight, about 300 *raṭl* [pounds], or 150 kilograms; see Löfgren, *Arabische Texte*, 2:24)

d. = *dīnār* (gold coin, dinar; for value and exchange rate in this period, see Goitein, *Mediterranean Society*, 1:359, 368–92)

f. = *fals* (copper coin; see Udovitch, "Fals")

far. = *farāsila* (a weight of about 20–35 *raṭl* [pounds]; see Löfgren, *Arabische Texte*, 2:49)

j. = *jā'iz* (eight fals, or half a dinar; see Löfgren, *Arabische Texte*, 2:27; Hinz, *Islamische Mässe und Gewichte*, 11–12)

khw. = *khawraja* (score, or eight pieces, an Indian term; see Löfgren, *Arabische Texte*, 2:56)

q. = *qīrāṭ* (1/24 dinar, a carat; see Goitein, *Mediterranean Society*, 1:359)

[a] Smith quotes the four-dinar tax as an *ʿashur* tax. The text states, however, "*wa-ʿalā qiṭʿat al-nīl arbaʿ danānīr shawānī wa-khurūjihi min al-furḍa rubʿ*."

[b] Smith skips this item for obvious reasons: rather than an import tax, it appears to be a sales tax. However, I believe that the text implies that a ship manufactured elsewhere is sold to a merchant in town. Technically this is an "import" into the city, even if the "imported item" does not physically pass through the customshouse.

[c] Smith notes that this rate was adjusted in the time of al-Muʿizz Ismaʿīl b. Ṭughtakin from the previous two or three dinars.

[d] Smith quotes both the fifty and the seventy dinars as *ʿashur* but notes that the former amount is charged for imports and the latter for exports.

[e] The difference between a *raqīq*, which must designate an "ordinary" slave, and an Indian slave, designated as *ʿawili al-sindabūrī*, is noteworthy.

TABLE 2: Aden Exit Tolls in Geniza Documents

Merchandise	*Exit Tolls*	*Destination*	*Source*
1. Fresh dates, aromatic wood, aromatic substances	*maks/maks ṣādir*	Cairo	Bodl. MS Heb. b3, f. 26/IB.193/VII.36, line 24, verso line 15 (ca. mid-490s/1100)
2. Lac (2 bales, 1,000 r., worth 113 d.)	*mūna*: 13 d. (probably includes both taxes and transport)	Egypt	Bodl. MS Heb. a3, f. 19/IB.32/II.32, line 9 (ca. mid-520s/1130)
3. Brazilwood (6 b., worth 100 d.), cinnamon (2 b., worth 29 d.), rhubarb (5 m., worth 15 d.); total value 144 d. (plus lac?)	*maks al-furḍa li'l-khurūj*: 16 d.	Egypt	Bodl. MS Heb. b11, f. 21/IB.20/I.33, line 24 (7 Shubat 1443/5 Rabiᶜ al-awwal 526/26 January 1132)
4. Red copper (1.5 b., cost 90 d. incl. exit toll)	*al-kharj min furḍa ᶜadan*	India	ULC Or1081J3/IB.61/II.26, lines 10–14 (ca. 528–29/1134)
5. *d-r-k-y* (1.5 b. of this mystery item)	*kharj* (included, with packing expenses, in cost of goods, 21.5 d.)	India	TS NS J241/IB.296/II.21, lines 4–5 (ca. 529–30/1135)
6. Lead (260 r., worth 17.33 d.)	*kharj al-furḍa*: .33 d.	India	TS NS J1/IB.199/II.24, line 3 (ca. 529–30/1135)
7. Copper (5 b., cost 415 d.)	*kharj al-furḍa*: 4.125 d.	India	TS24.66/IB.26/II.16, lines 45–46 (ca. mid-530s/1140s)
8. Merchandise (1 b. + 90 r., worth 126 d.)	*kharj* [. . .] *al-furḍa*: 1 d.	India	TS NS J285/IB.297/II.29, verso lines 4–5 (ca. mid-530s/1140s?)

Source: This table compiles data on exit tolls from Judeo-Arabic texts consulted and cited for each entry. In entries 1 and 4, the amount of the tax payment is either missing or lumped together with other payments, but the occurrence of the terms for exit tolls remains valuable.

Note

b. = *bahār* or *buhār* (a measure of weight, about 300 *raṭl* [pounds], or 150 kilograms; see Löfgren, *Arabische Texte*, 2:24)

d. = *dīnār* (gold coin, dinar; for value and exchange rate in this period, see Goitein, *Mediterranean Society*, 1:359, 368–92)

m. = *mann* (a two-pound weight; see Goitein, *Mediterranean Society*, 1:360)

r. = *raṭl* (pound, about 450 grams; see Goitein, *Mediterranean Society*, 1:360)

TABLE 3: Aden Import Taxes in Geniza Documents

Merchandise	*Import Taxes*	*Origin*	*Source*
1. Lac (four pieces, bought for 1,000 dir. in India)	*kharj al-maks*:[a] 80 *malikī* d.	Egypt	Bodl. MS Heb. b11, f. 21/IB.20/I.33, lines 2, 8 (7 Shubat 1443/5 Rabiᶜ al-awwal 526/26 January 1132)
2. Unbleached textiles (2 bales, 2 khw., bought for 1,200 dir. in India, fetched 330 *malikī* d. after customs)	*maks* (calculated in final revenue from sale of goods)	India	Bodl. MS Heb. b11, f. 21/IB.20/I.33, lines 4, 7 (7 Shubat 1443/5 Rabiᶜ al-awwal 526/26 January 1132)
3. Pepper (17 b., worth about 783 d. after *dilāla*)	*ᶜushūr* (plus baskets and porter): 159.25 d.	India	TS20.130/IB.28/II.20, lines 17–22 (ca. 527–28/1133)
4. Pepper (selling for 23 d. per b.)	*ᶜushūr* (not collected until last day)	India	TS20.137/IB.29/II.23, lines 25–28 (ca. 529–30/1135)
5. Pepper (22 b. + 60 r., worth 510.5 d. + 2 q.)	*ᶜushūr*: 155.5 d. + 2 q.	India	TS20.137/IB.29/II.23, lines 8, 28–30, 38–39 (ca. 529–30/1135)
6. Cardamom (2 sacks, 3 b. + 109 r., worth 172.5 d.)	*ᶜushūr*: 19.5 d.	India	TS20.137/IB.29/II.23, lines 31–41 (ca. 529–30/1135)
7. Clothes and textiles	*ᶜushūr wa-muwūn*	India	TS13J25, f. 13/IB.31/VI.27, line 23 (ca. 529–45/1135–50)
8. Merchandise	*ᶜushūr ᶜadan* (to be paid with extra betel nuts or pepper in baskets bought specifically for that purpose)	India	TS10J9, f. 24/IB.55/III.3, lines 12–13 (ca. 529–33/1135–38)
9. Merchandise (worth 48.66 d.)	*ᶜushūr furḍat ᶜadan*: 4 d.	India	TS24.37/IB.91/IV.12, margin (20 October 1137)
10. Iron (14 b. + 165 r., worth 247.5 d.)	*ᶜushūr*, *muwūn*, and porter: 27 d.	India	TS24.66/IB.26/II.16, lines 33–38 (ca. mid-530s/1140s)
11. Pepper (11 b. + 255 r., worth 402.83 d.)	*ᶜushūr*: 82.25 d. *ḥaqq al-qabḍ*: 4.16 d.	India	TS24.66/IB.26/II.16, lines 3–12
12. Iron pots	*mūna*	India	TS20.137v/IB.64/III.18, line 9 (ca. 533–44/1139–49)

TABLE 3: Continued

Merchandise	*Import Taxes*	*Origin*	*Source*
13. Pepper (6 b., worth 222 d., and 6 b. + 166 r., worth 236 d.)	*ʿushūr*: 96 d.	India	TS Box J1, f. 53/IB.81/ IV.1, lines 5–6, 18 (post-524/1130s?)
14. Cotton textiles (3 kinds, total value 519 d.)	*ʿushūr*: 64.75 d.	India	TS Box J1, f. 53/IB.81/ IV.1, lines 2–4, 19 (post-524/1130s?)
15. Musk (4 khm. + 10 m., worth ca. 23.25 d.)	*ʿushūr*: 2.33 d.	India	TS Box J1, f. 53/IB.81/ IV.1, lines 13–15, 20 (post-524/1130s?)
16. Musk (19 khm., price not listed)	*ʿushūr*: 4 d.	India	TS Box J1, f. 53/IB.81/ IV.1, lines 20–21 (post-524/1130s?)

Source: This table compiles data on import taxes from Judeo-Arabic texts consulted and cited for each entry. In entries 2, 4, 7, 8, and 12, the amount of the tax payment is either missing or lumped together with other payments, but the occurrence of the terms for import dues remains valuable.

Note

b. = *bahār* or *buhār* (a measure of weight, about 300 *raṭl* [pounds], or 150 kilograms; see Löfgren, *Arabische Texte*, 2:24)

d. = *dīnār* (gold coin, dinar; for value and exchange rate in this period, see Goitein, *Mediterranean Society*, 1:359, 368–92)

dir. = *dirham* (here Indian currency)

khm. = *khamāsiya*

khw. = *khawraja* (score, or eight pieces, an Indian term; see Löfgren, *Arabische Texte*, 2:56)

m. = *mann* (a two-pound weight; see Goitein, *Mediterranean Society*, 1:360)

q. = *qīrāṭ* (1//24 dinar, a carat; see Goitein, *Mediterranean Society*, 1:359)

r. = *raṭl* (pound, about 450 grams; see Goitein, *Mediterranean Society*, 1:360)

[a]Despite the fact that the writer uses here terms that usually describe exit tolls (*kharj* and *maks*), the tax on lac quoted must refer to import dues on the consignment. In the next example from the same letter, the term "*maks*" is indisputably meant to denote import dues, as the textiles that incurred the tax came from India and were sold in Aden. The lac was imported from India along with the textiles but was then reexported on behalf of the same merchant to Egypt. Whether it incurred exit tolls remains unclear, but a minimal exit toll on the lac consignment may be included in the exit toll quoted for items bought in Aden and sent along with the lac; see table 2, item 3.

were not calculated on the basis of the current market value (ad valorem), as was the case in Egypt, but entailed a fixed rate for each category of merchandise (ad naturam); this interpretation would have to regard the case of boats as an exception. Alternatively, some items on Ibn al-Mujāwir's list (those for which he gives customs dues as monetary sums) incurred taxes ad valorem but only on the basis of a value considered more or less stable and therefore without ad hoc calculations; other items (on Ibn al-Mujāwir's list those liable for payment of customs in kind) may be said to have incurred taxes according to kind, ad naturam rather than ad valorem. In accordance with Cahen's reasonable argument, the latter system (a combination of charges based on value and others based on type of merchandise) in fact appears to have been in place both in the time of Ibn al-Mujāwir and, based on the more comprehensive evidence of the Rasulid sources, in the later period.[66]

How can the Geniza documents contribute to deciphering the system of tax assessment in medieval Aden? Data sufficient for tabulating customs rates through time are unfortunately scarce in the India trade documentary material. The main problem is the size and range of the sample: most of the relevant documents date to the middle part of the 6th/12th century, and many of those items belong to the correspondence between Maḍmūn b. Japheth and Ben Yijū. Merchants often only briefly mention dues, the exact amounts of which have presumably been recorded elsewhere.[67] When specific references to customs dues appear in the Geniza letters and accounts, they often skip important detail, such as the weight, quantity, or market value of the goods taxed. In accountings of multiple transactions, merchants also tend to lump customs dues together with other expenses, often under the term "*al-mūna*," preventing an accurate estimation of the tax rate involved.[68]

Despite these difficulties, the extant data are invaluable in reconstructing customs rates at Aden, and a comparison with the somewhat richer and more varied evidence from the Mediterranean is instructive. As has already been noted, Goitein gives examples from 5th/11th- and 6th/12th-century Mediterranean documents, which reveal customs rates for both imports and exports of around 5 percent; he concludes that customs, like transport costs, do not appear to have been excessive.[69] The picture that emerges from the admittedly sparser data on customs charged at Aden is quite different.

On the one hand, imports appear to have been very highly taxed and often to have far exceeded even the nominal 10 percent that the term for import taxes (*ʿushr/ʿashūr*) suggests. On the other hand, no uniform tax rate appears to have been levied on all merchandise, and with the possible exception of pepper, it is not possible to determine any patterns in the rates charged for specific goods over the years. A letter from the 530s/1140s, for example, reported that a pepper consignment worth 402.8 dinars incurred 82.25 dinars—that is, approximately 20 percent of its total value—plus an additional charge designated as "*ḥaqq al-qabḍ*." In the same letter, iron incurs a tax of approximately 10 percent of its value.[70] The highest rate attested in the extant documents is charged on pepper around 529/1135: 22 *bahār* and 60 *raṭl* worth 510 dinars and 2 *qīrāṭ* incur a customs tax of 155.33 dinars and 2 *qīrāṭ*, 30 percent of the market value. Significantly, this is the same document that reveals a sluggish pepper market and, despite Maḍmūn's intervention and improvement of the situation, a comparatively low final price for pepper. In the same document, two sacks of cardamom weighed at the customshouse to 3 *bahār* and 109 *raṭl* and later sold for 172.5 dinars incurred 19.5 dinars in tax, approximately 12 percent.[71]

How do these numbers compare with Ibn al-Mujāwir's quotes? Ibn al-Mujāwir probably reported rates current at the time of his sojourn in Aden.[72] Like the quotes extracted from the Geniza documents, his rates bespeak customs dues levied on the basis of the type of merchandise but perhaps also on the basis of a more or less standard price that the specific item was expected to fetch in the market. A perusal of both Ibn al-Mujāwir's list and the Geniza evidence reveals that neither in the 6th/12th nor in the 7th/13th century were customs levied at a uniform rate; different rates applied to different types of goods.

A comparison of the different rates charged on pepper in the two sources may be instructive. If a *bahār* of pepper fetched an average price of about 35 dinars, Ibn al-Mujāwir's quote of 8 or 9 (including the *shawānī* tax) dinars per *bahār* would bespeak a tax of 22 percent of the value. This amount is only slightly higher than the rates charged on pepper in the second quarter of the 6th/12th century (table 3, items 3, 11, and 13), with the exception of the aberrant year of 1135 (table 3, items 4 and 5). Does this constitute a truly significant pattern? Only more documents can answer that question. These findings might show, however, that customs did not distinguish between merchants of different religious denominations. Not only do the sources lack any references to such a distinction, but the comparable rates on pepper given by the two main witness groups, Ibn al-Mujāwir representing Muslim merchants and the Jewish merchants of the Geniza, suggest that everyone was charged equally.

If Aden's customshouse taxed imports at much higher rates than did customshouses of the Mediterranean ports, export tolls charged in the Indian Ocean port were, by contrast, significantly lower, as is clear both from Ibn al-Mujāwir's list and from the very low quotes of export tolls in the Geniza. In two separate transactions in the second quarter of the 6th/12th century, lead and copper exported to India are charged with a mere 1 percent of their total value (table 2, items 6 and 7).[73] Significantly, the same regime of much lower export taxes emerges from the data in the Muẓaffar register.[74] Why did such a dramatic difference exist between taxes on imports and taxes on exports? The local authorities may have chosen to use low export taxes as a low-cost extra incentive for foreign merchants to buy merchandise in the city. These low export rates certainly went some way toward balancing the burden of excessive import dues.

Exemptions

Not every item that entered Aden incurred exorbitant taxes; in fact, some items appear to have been tax-free. Ibn al-Mujāwir dedicates a separate section to merchandise that did not incur taxes (*alladhī lam yu'khadh ʿalayhi ʿushūr*), and despite the obvious and extensive corruption of the text, it merits discussion. The author's list of nontaxable goods comprises only imports and is divided into imports from Egypt, imports from India, and a third category that may denote imports via the Ḥaḍramawt port of al-Shiḥr.[75] Predictably, the items include mostly foods (staples such as wheat, sugar, rice, and salted fish and delicacies such as sweetmeats, nuts, and honey), sundry necessities (such as soap), and animals (male and female goats). Miscellaneous items such as baskets, mats, sandals, and beads also appear on the list; the reason for their exemption from taxes is less obvious.

The state's interest in ensuring a regular supply of victuals and making them accessible both to the people and to the ruling elite is understandable;[76] tax exemption is an obvious measure aimed at promoting the flow of such merchandise. The same motive, however, may lie behind a different measure, taxation in kind. Ibn al-Mujāwir's list of taxable imports includes three items that incur taxes in kind (see table 1): lac, iron, and a type of wood (*dafwā'*). All three must have served important industrial uses in which the state may have had a vested interest. Lac was a dye fixative essential in the manufacture of textiles, and iron could have served a variety of purposes from the manufacture of tools and weapons to building construction.[77] Thus, Ibn al-Mujāwir's list gives the impression that foodstuffs and articles of everyday use were exempted from tax, while raw materials useful in manufacture were extracted in kind from consignments of international trade to secure adequate supplies for local industries.

The Geniza papers are practically silent on the issue of exemptions. Since the merchants who wrote them dealt primarily in the highly taxed spice trade, this is perhaps not surprising. The one possible exception, however, is instructive, as it suggests a different kind of exemption—that is, exemption from export taxes. It occurs in an accounting drafted by Abū al-Barakāt b. Joseph al-Lebdī for Isḥāq al-Nafūsī and dating to 526/1132.[78] While in India, Abū al-Barakāt had bought for Isḥāq lac, textiles, and a few other minor items, which Abū al-Barakāt then imported into Aden. He sold the textiles and noted the price they fetched after extraction of customs tax (the import tax) (table 3, item 2). He did not, however, sell the lac but simply reported a customs charge for it (table 3, item 1) and repacked it in eight bales, clearly with the intention of sending them on to Egypt.[79] After buying brazilwood, cinnamon, and rhubarb in Aden, he dispatched the lot to Egypt through the African ports of Baḍiʿ, Dahlak, Nizāla, Suwākin, and ʿAydhāb, where additional customs were charged on the entire shipment. The exit toll charged at Aden appears to have applied only to the three items bought there, and no exit toll is reported on the newly packed lac.

Two scenarios are possible: either Abū al-Barakāt implicitly included the exit toll on the lac in the one customs charge recorded, or the lac did not incur any exit toll because it had just been imported with the purpose of direct reexport. Given the relative informality of the merchants' accounts and their tendency to lump separate expenses under one charge, the former scenario may very well correspond to what actually happened. The latter explanation, however, finds some support in an enigmatic entry in Ibn al-Mujāwir's list of tax-free items. First among such imports from India he notes "everything sent by sea" (*kull mā yurāsalu fī al-baḥr*); Smith understands this phrase to mean "items for re-exportation."[80] Because the vast majority of merchandise came and went by sea and was imported only to be reexported and because both imports and exports incurred taxes, the only way this phrase could make sense is if Ibn al-Mujāwir uses it to refer specifically to merchandise imported but not sold or redistributed in Aden—that is, items for reexportation *by the same shipper*. Such merchandise still incurred the hefty import tax, presumably based on the going market price, but perhaps was exempt entirely from exit tolls.

Although it would account for Ibn al-Mujāwir's strange statement, the idea that strictly transiting consignments paid only import tolls raises questions. Why should the customshouse miss the opportunity to tax merchandise exiting the city, perhaps by doing so at a low rate? The idea may have been to promote business by giving merchants an additional modest break from the otherwise relentless regime of taxation. The other Geniza papers contain no definitive evidence for the practice, but it is perhaps telling that the references to exit tolls generally pertain to items that originated in India or Egypt but were in fact bought in Aden.

Extra Charges

Because the paucity of references to specific dues on goods of declared quantities and value render the determination of rates and ultimately the deciphering of the system of taxation difficult, the few instances where enigmatic terms and expressions appear in association with some aspect of the tax assessment process must be taken into account. "*Ḥaqq al-qabḍ*" is one such expression: it designates a payment made to customs in addition to the import tax on pepper.[81] Although it appears only once in this form, the action of obtaining the goods after they had cleared customs is often designated by the verb "*q-b-ḍ*," and this process may have incurred a routine payment. Supporting evidence comes in the form of an entry for a charge designated as "*tafrīj*" (release), presumably of goods in transit through customs, at the Mediterranean port of Tyre.[82]

Goitein translates "*ḥaqq al-qabḍ*" as "the right for obtaining the goods" and tentatively interprets it as a government tax.[83] If correct, this would agree with the evidence of the plethora of charges additional to the customs dues proper attested in the work of al-Makhzūmī. Why is there no mention of charge in other cases where "obtaining" of goods upon their arrival at port took place? Because the actual amount is fairly small, such charges might plausibly have been lumped together with other "expenses" or perhaps with the import taxes themselves. As Cahen points out, the merchants were ultimately concerned with the bottom line, whether in terms of profits or in terms of charges incurred.[84] Alternatively, the impost may have applied to large shipments only, as compensation for the extra time and effort required for processing.[85]

The Galley Tax

Ibn al-Mujāwir claims that Turānshāh was the first to bring galleys to Aden and that the Ayyubids instituted both the service of maritime patrols and the galley tax, a fee for the maritime protection provided by the warships. Ṭughtakīn b. Ayyūb, who served as the Ayyubid governor of Yemen, is said to have been questioned by "some men of reason" about how he intended to justify the extraction of taxes from merchants, to which he responded that he would do as the rulers before him had done. His advisers then pointed out that the previous regimes had ruled (and taxed) people by force but that he could do so by winning their gratitude.[86]

The way to accomplish this was simple: Ṭughtakīn's advisers pointed to the galleys (*shawānī*) lying idle on the beach since their arrival with the Ayyubid force and argued that he merely had to send them out to sea. These galleys would patrol the waters and protect commercial traffic from pirates, providing partial compensation for the steep taxes merchants paid at port. Ṭughtakīn enthusiastically recognized the wisdom of this idea and subsequently sent out galleys as far as India to monitor commercial traffic and ward off pirates.[87] Some higher officials in the court of the Ayyubid sultan Masʿūd later complained that sending out galleys cost the state treasury good money, arguing that the merchants would not mind paying for the privilege of protection. Given the size of their investments and the minimal rate of the galley tax, it is reasonable to assume that the merchants indeed did not object to paying the extra charge.

If Ibn al-Mujāwir's report of the establishment and development of maritime patrols in the Ayyubid period is accurate, does the same hold true for his statement that this was the first use of galleys in the city and that the Zurayids lacked galleys?[88] Would this suggest that the latter provided no protection for commercial shipping? Concrete evidence shows that the state built and maintained fleets in Rasulid times, but no official account exists of naval development in the Zurayid period.[89] The Geniza documents, however, provide some indication that the merchants were not entirely at the mercy of pirates and that some system of maritime protection already existed by the 6th/12th century.

The earliest instance of a possible reference to galleys occurs in Maḍmūn's description of the expedition of the ruler of Qays/Kish against Aden. Enumerating the besieging enemy's naval force, the author includes three vessels of a type that he describes by the term "*shaffāra*."[90] The word does not appear in any source outside the Indian Ocean Geniza material, and its etymology is unclear. Goitein proposed the Aramaic root "*shfr*," which would render the basic meaning of "covering" or "hull."[91] Another possible cognate, "*shabbāra*," appears to designate transport boats of the Euphrates in historical and geographical texts from the 4th/10th century on.[92] Alternatively, the term may derive from the Arabic "*shafra*" (large, sharp knife), an allusion to the ship's sleek, cutwater shape.[93]

It is tempting to see the naval function of the *shaffāra* in the episode of the siege as a confirmation of the latter etymology and its warship implications. Naval warfare, however, often relied on merchant ships recruited especially for the purpose of an expedition rather than on specially constructed warships. In fact, after their first dramatic appearance in the documents, *shaffāra* vessels occur only in commercial contexts. They carry merchandise[94] and accompany other, perhaps larger, boats in two-boat convoys.[95] The purpose of sailing in groups is clearly one of defense and risk management. A small ship, even if not galley-like in shape and propulsion, would have the extra advantage of speed and maneuverability in the case of a piratical attack or other emergency.[96] Yet such an escort, especially if oared, would have meant high operation costs, which begs the question of who could have launched and run them in 6th/12th-century Aden.

Given the fact that merchandise carried on a *shaffāra* did pay freight,[97] it is plausible that either the state or private individuals undertook the initial cost of the vessels' construction, launching, and operation. Higher freight charges, justifiable on account of the extra security and perhaps speed that these vessels offered, would have covered the initial investment, but it is hard to determine whether they would also have been sufficient to cover running costs. The evidence is slender, but no evidence indicates that any of the escort ships belonged to the state rather than to individual shipowners.[98] While it may seem puzzling that the state did not maintain a naval force, a look back at the accounts of the naval blockade of Aden shows how private vessels (the two ships of the *nākhudhā* Rāmisht, in that case) could be put to use for the state's purposes. If instead of state-orchestrated maritime protection, private shipowners provided their own protection and covered the cost by charging extra freight, an important similarity still exists between this service and the Ayyubid patrol boats; both practices constitute an important service through which the city both fostered and controlled overseas trade and justified the crushing customs taxes it imposed.

5 | *Ships and Shipping*

Markabāk muqbilān yajriyān ka-farasayn.

[Swift as horses, your two ships are drawing near.]

AL-JANADĪ IN LÖFGREN, *Texte*

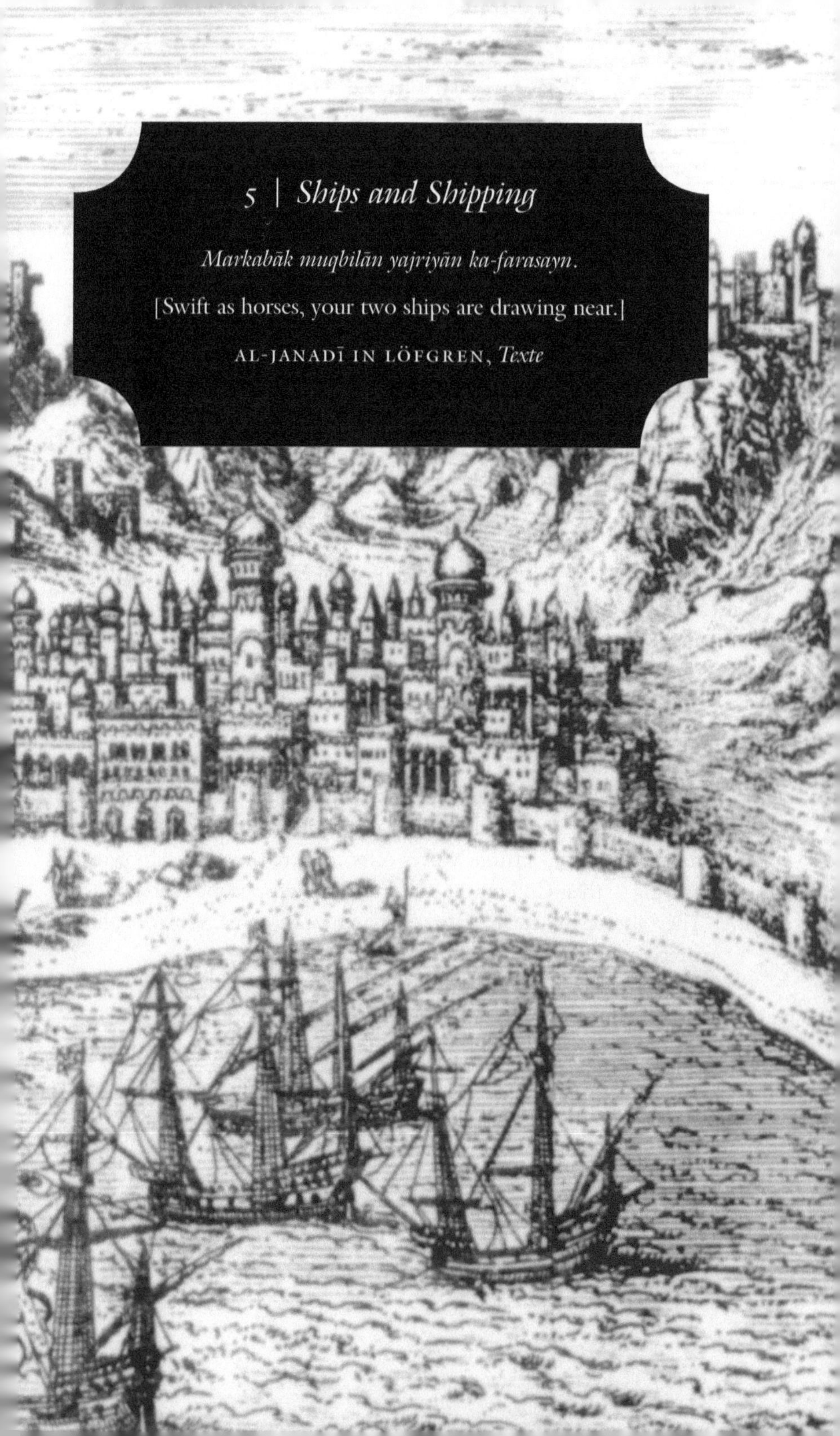

In the days of the Rasulid sultan al-Muẓaffar (647–694/1249–95), a ship is said to have arrived at Aden from India bringing bad news to a local shipowner named Kāfūr: on his way to Aden, the newly arrived shipmaster reported, he had spotted Kāfūr's ships engaged in fierce battle with pirates. The prospects were grim. Overcome by anxiety, the shipowner sought a certain *sharīf*, a guest whom the shipowner had encouraged to settle in Aden, and told him the news. After contemplating the matter, the *sharīf* reassured the worried Kāfūr that the pirates had been defeated and that his ships would safely reach port. "And it came to pass just as he had said."[1]

Part urban legend, part maritime lore, this tale appears in the biography of its clairvoyant hero, Abū al-Faḍl al-Sharīf al-ʿAbbāsī, who had emigrated to Aden from Syria.[2] It is no surprise that in a place such as Aden, the holy man would have been invited and inclined to perform a ship-related miracle. His inspired intervention consisted not of saving the ships but merely of "seeing" their deliverance from afar, long before any news of their fate could have reached the port. Like Kāfūr, other shipowners in town must have craved news of their ships. The magnitude of their investment and the extent and variety of risk involved would have perpetually unnerved even the most seasoned among them. From the era that ended only a few decades before the *sharīf*'s lifetime, Geniza documents provide a vivid albeit fragmentary record of city-based maritime enterprise and preserve the unmistakably anxious voices of both merchants and shipowners praying to their God for the safe arrival of ships, people, and goods.[3] They also testify to the frequency and catastrophic results of shipwreck, piracy, and other misfortunes on the high seas.

More than supplementing the services of a clairvoyant *sharīf*, the city provided shipowners with the necessary tools of risk management and damage control. It functioned as a terminal for information about overseas markets, crops, wars, and weather that could prove crucial for the success of trading ventures. It also provided a pool of materials and expertise for shipbuilding and ship repair as well as the capital and labor necessary to supply ships with victuals and to prepare them for travel, to police sea routes, to safeguard individual trading ventures, and to launch maritime salvage operations. As a result of its interconnectedness, the city provided the perfect environment for the development of a shipping industry. Shipping, in turn, shaped Aden's character and urban culture; together with market services and institutions, shipping and shipbuilding contributed to the port's multifunctionality, the characteristic that ultimately distinguished it as a unique urban environment and set it apart from other coastal settlements.[4]

During the sailing season, most of the participants in maritime services, including some of the shipowners, were highly mobile and spent a good part of their time in transit between port cities and under sail on the high seas. Even during those peripatetic times of the year, major entrepôts such as Aden functioned as focal points of order and organization. A 7th/13th-century document found at Quṣayr al-Qadīm preserves the desperate pleas of three men stranded in an insignificant harbor on the opposite Red Sea coast without basic supplies.[5] This situation could hardly have arisen in Aden, where the presence of supplies, services, and trading alliances ensured some relief in times of duress. This chapter examines the world of shipowners, captains, sailors, naval fighters, divers, porters, and harbor boatmen. It demonstrates that the city was indispensable to the business that literally moved the India trade and exposes the ways in which the people of the sea contributed to the port's urban identity.

Merchant Shipowners

References to ships, shipowners, captains, and crews abound in the written sources of the medieval Indian Ocean. One difficulty with this information is the fluid terminology used to designate people who ran and/or owned ships. Literally meaning "master of the ship," the variously spelled Persian word *nākhudhā* was current across the western Indian Ocean. It often but not always denotes a person owning a ship; it can also refer to the master of a ship on the high seas, the captain.[6] In the 10th/16th-century story of Kāfūr and the clairvoyant *sharīf*, both Kāfūr, a sedentary Adeni shipowner, and the bearer of alarming news, clearly a captain who had just brought a ship to port, receive the title "*nākhudhā*." The Judeo-Arabic Cairo Geniza documents contain both meanings: thus, there is mention of "*nākhudhā* Aḥmad the *nākhudha* of the ship of Fidiyār" (with variant spellings within a single line), clearly the captain of a ship belonging to a man named Fidiyār,[7] as well as of *nākhudhā* Maḍmūn, a prominent Jewish merchant who never left the city but is known to have owned ships.[8] To complicate matters further, writers of Geniza documents sometimes also used the designation "*rubbān*" to refer to a ship's captain.[9] And although they often identify a ship by its owner's name, sometimes they associate it with the name of its captain, a common practice across maritime cultures.[10]

While the current terms were used rather loosely and now appear fraught with ambiguity, several shipowners are distinguishable in the sources, and these references testify to the privileged position these men occupied in the maritime world of the medieval Indian Ocean. In an important study of Indian ship ownership, Ranabir Chakravarti reveals the commonalities in the social stature of such businessmen in the two interlocking worlds. The title "*nauvitakka*," a term symmetrical to the Persian *nākhudhā*, applied to men of considerable power and social capital in the maritime world of western India.[11] An illustrative equivalent from Arabic literature is the shipowner Rāmisht. According to historian Ibn al-Athīr (556–630/1160–1234), in 532/1137–38, "the cover of the Kaʿba was torn. . . . Rāmisht, the Persian merchant, took it upon himself to provide a new cover. He went all out in this, using the most exquisite cloths, so that the price of the cover amounted to eighteen thousand dinars. He was one of the merchants who traveled to India and had great wealth."[12] The restoration of the Kaʿba's cover (*kiswa*) was not the only pious dedication in Mecca by the man in question. According to Meccan chroniclers, Rāmisht also gave the city a golden waterspout and a *ribāṭ*.[13] He was also well known to the writers of India trade Geniza documents and their Indian Ocean seafaring world, primarily as a shipowner. Of all the ships that plied the waters between Aden and India, none appear more frequently in the Geniza documents than those of

Rāmisht. Ibn al-Athīr and most of the other literary sources describe Rāmisht as a merchant (*tājir*). His tombstone, however, agrees with the testimony of the Geniza merchants in hailing the benefactor of Mecca, who died in 534/1140, as a *nākhudhā*.[14]

Rāmisht was the archetypical *nākhudhā*, and his career illustrates an important aspect of the organization of Indian Ocean shipping in his days: at the high end of the trading world, wealthy businessmen ran both shipping and trading enterprises. Like him, other key players in western Indian Ocean commerce also owned one or more ships; conversely, all known shipowners bought and sold merchandise both for themselves and for others. The group included Maḍmūn b. Japheth, a prominent member of Aden's Jewish community, merchant, and chief customs official in the first half of the 6th/12th century, who invested in the business of building and running ships, often for specific, far-flung ventures; another Adeni, Maḥrūz b. Jacob, who was the brother-in-law of a prominent Cairo merchant, Abū Zikrī Judah ha-Kohen;[15] Joseph b. Abraham, a relative of Maḍmūn;[16] and ʿAlī al-Fawfalī, a resident of the South Indian coastal town of Fandarayna who is repeatedly referred to as a *nākhudhā* but who also acted as a merchants' agent and as a merchant in his own right.[17]

This pattern of ship ownership parallels the situation in the Mediterranean, where, according to S. D. Goitein, the "largest single group of shipowners were the merchants."[18] Conversely, persons connected with the government, including the sultan and members of the royal household, held the lion's share of Mediterranean shipping.[19] East of the Bāb al-Mandab, it is sometimes difficult to distinguish between investments in shipping by the political elite and private merchant enterprise. In Rasulid times, sultans participated actively in maritime trade and thus had an additional reason to foster and protect commercial institutions and Aden's booming market.[20] The stakes appear to have been similar for ruling elites in Aden and other ports of the western Indian Ocean seaboard in pre-Rasulid times. Judging by their names, three Indian Ocean shipowners appearing in the Geniza documents may have been government officials or at least communal functionaries: al-Fidiyār,[21] Fatan Swamī,[22] and Ibn al-Muqaddam.[23]

At least one account refers to a "ship of the sultan."[24] And ample evidence shows that Bilāl b. Jarīr, Aden's top government official, engaged in at least one ambitious shipbuilding and shipping enterprise in partnership with Maḍmūn b. Japheth.[25] But most other shipowners who appear in the India trade Geniza documents were merchants first and foremost.

It is important to compare the collaboration between Bilāl b. Jarīr and Maḍmūn b. Japheth, the two Adeni notables, with the association between two prominent Egyptian men, Nahray b. Nissīm and an unnamed *amīr*, who owned ships in Alexandria: the shipping component of the latter relationship was the exclusive domain of the government dignitary, with Nahray's participation restricted to the exchange of money and merchandise.[26] In the Adeni partnership, in contrast, both men participated in the outfitting of the vessel, and Maḍmūn appears to have been most intimately in charge of the shipyard aspects of the deal. Unlike the situation in the Mediterranean, many prominent Indian Ocean merchants had full control of the shipping component of their business.

One of the most striking results of the investigation into the identity of shipowners and captains involved in the India trade is the great ethnic and religious diversity of the participants. The late 5th/11th-century Geniza letters and documents relating to the case of Joseph al-Lebdī refer to the ships of two men with Persian names, Behzād and al-Qummī.[27] The more numerous documents from the 6th/12th century mention Rāmisht, al-Fidiyār, and Bakhtiyār, all apparently of Persian origin. In the same period, however, the merchants' papers also reveal the participation in the shipping networks of men whose names leave little doubt about their Indian identity, such as Tinbū, Buda, and Fatan Swamī.[28] One letter, moreover, mentions a Masʿūd al-Ḥabashī *al-rubbān*.[29] This captain's *nisba* securely identifies the man as an African, perhaps an immigrant to Aden or to India.

Aside from the obviously Persian and Indian names and the single African *nisba*, most of the Arabic given names, *kunya*s, patronyms, and *nisba*s can in themselves tell us very little about their bearers' ethnic and/or religious identity.[30] These names are shared by Jews,

Muslims, and Christians, and at least Jews and Muslims appear to have participated fully in Indian Ocean shipping, along with Hindus.[31] However, the context of the Cairo Geniza helps identify several of the participants in the shipping industry with the Jewish community that produced the documents. These items suggest, in fact, that most of the prominent Jewish India traders owned ships.[32] Jewish ship ownership in the Indian Ocean is remarkable for its sharp contrast with the situation in the Mediterranean, where little evidence attests to Jewish businessmen's direct participation in maritime services.

Finally, related to the identity of the Indian Ocean shipowners is the issue of their residence and mobility. The Geniza material reveals that some shipowners were sedentary capitalists, while others, perhaps the majority, traveled extensively. Despite his wide-ranging enterprises, Maḍmūn is never discussed leaving Aden, where his many and multifaceted responsibilities kept him fully occupied. And although the Geniza documents contain numerous references to Rāmisht's ships, not a single mention survives of Rāmisht either sailing the high seas or doing business at port. Conversely, the Geniza spotlight catches Joseph b. Abraham, Maḥrūz, ʿAlī al-Fawfalī, Ibn Abī al-Katā'ib, and his son, Abū ʿAbdallāh, as they shuttle between Aden and India.[33]

Traveling or sedentary, each shipowner almost certainly had a home base. With very few exceptions, the evidence for shippers and seamen of the India trade consists of fleeting and scattered glimpses of captains, owners, and/or their boats on their ocean crossings, a situation that makes it very difficult to determine the port of residence of any of these men. For most of them, all that can be said is that they operated on specific sea routes and moved between specific ports and coasts. A good example is Abū al-Ḥasan b. Abī al-Katā'ib, whose ships appear several times but whose place of residence, Aden or India, remains unclear. For some of these men, however, evidence permits the determination of a base or home port. Tinbū, for example, apparently was a permanent resident of the town of Tāna, north of modern Bombay.[34] ʿAlī al-Fawfalī also lived on the western coast of India, but further south, probably in Fandarayna, Ben Yijū's hometown.[35]

All the other Geniza-attested shipowners whose residence can be established with some degree of certainty resided in Aden. Maḍmūn b. Japheth heads the list and requires neither introduction nor proof of his Aden residence. His cousin, Joseph, also lived in Aden, as is confirmed by his several letters to Ben Yijū from there.[36] Maḥrūz b. Jacob received letters in Aden and returned there at the end of the sailing season.[37] More significantly, a letter from Aden to the son of Maḥrūz's brother-in-law, Abū Zikrī, proves that while Maḥrūz's sister had married in Cairo, his family remained in Aden even after his death.[38] Last but not least, Rāmisht also appears to have been an Aden resident despite his connections to Sīrāf and Mecca by birth and death, respectively. No other explanation exists for the enormous risk that his two ships took during the maritime siege of Aden by breaking through enemy lines into the besieged harbor. Moreover, one of his later biographers claims to have gotten his information from Rāmisht's son in Aden.[39] Residence in the city made sense for a businessman such as Rāmisht whose vessels appear so frequently on their way to and from the city and whose operations were so closely intertwined with those of the best-known Adeni Jewish traders. Even allowing for the bias of the Geniza record, Aden emerges as an important—perhaps *the* most important—base of the western Indian Ocean shipping industry. Multiple maritime shipping networks were centered on or wired through the city, offering invaluable opportunities for maritime connections as well as crucial services to ships and seamen.

Family Business: Shipowning Clans

As in many maritime societies to this day, the organization of medieval ship ownership in the western Indian Ocean appears to have relied first and foremost on the family unit. In a letter to Ben Yijū, Maḍmūn mentions three boats belonging to the extended Rāmisht family: merchandise had been dispatched "in the boat of Rāmisht, the boat of his two sons, and the boat of his two brothers-in-law."[40] Even though this constitutes the only Geniza reference to other members of the Rāmisht clan, it provides a succinct and compelling image of family business organization. Maḍmūn passed on his maritime business to his descendants. From an eerie description of a shipwreck in a report to the family of one of the many victims, we learn that Maḍmūn's son, Ḥalfon (Khalaf), had and lost a brand-new ship.[41]

Abū al-Ḥasan b. Abī al-Katā'ib and his son, Abū ʿAbdallāh, comprised another business based on familial ties. They appear in several letters addressed to Ben Yijū and in an account written in the latter's hand listing merchandise delivered for shipping and freight owed. The ships are usually referred to as belonging to the father, and he may have personally delivered one shipment of pepper to Maḍmūn.[42] On most known occasions, however, the son dealt directly with Ben Yijū and the Adeni merchants, delivering merchandise,[43] receiving payment for freight, and accepting cargo and payments on behalf of his father.[44] In addition, in 542/1147, he carried a letter from Khalaf b. Isaac to Ben Yijū on an apparently ill-fated ship; the letter never got to India, but extant evidence does not confirm that Abū ʿAbdallāh died in the incident.[45]

The careers of Ibn Abī al-Katā'ib father and son illustrate how family shipping businesses worked. Traveling was dangerous and physically demanding. While the father must have traveled extensively in his youth and was perhaps still traveling when the son joined the business, at some point the father retired from active service at sea and entrusted the running of the ships to his son. The payments that Abū ʿAbdallāh received on behalf of his father illustrate that fathers probably remained in charge throughout their lives, managing businesses from sedentary positions at home ports. In any case, the younger members of the family, no matter how established their clan, had to rise through the ranks. Collaboration between old and young in the family business ensured tight control of the operations and rigorous training for future heirs.

Using family ties as a major organizing principle for the conduct of business was clearly an effective and efficient practice that often brought great success and advancement to the family members involved. The Geniza documents provide some evidence for upward mobility within nautical families. In one of his letters to India, Maḍmūn mentions a dispatch of copper to India on one of Rāmisht's ships, in care of the "*nākhudhā* Aḥmad b. Bakhtiyār."[46] Whether Maḍmūn called Aḥmad a *nākhudhā* because he was a shipowner in his own right or because he was the captain of Rāmisht's ship is unclear; however, the Adeni merchant is more specific when mentioning a man named Bakhtiyār, who is referred to as *al-rubbān*.[47] In ethnographically and historically attested usage, the captain's titles "*nākhudhā*" and "*rubbān*" often connote different status, most frequently a distinction between small-time coastal pilots and accomplished masters of oceangoing ships.[48] These two letters give the impression that Maḍmūn indeed distinguished between the two titles and that *rubbān* is here inferior to *nākhudhā*.

Given the contemporary contexts and circles in which the two men appear and move, it is very likely that Bakhtiyār *al-rubbān* was Aḥmad's father; he may also have been known as "Bakhtiyār *ghulām* ʿAlī b. Jaʿfar," a slave/agent of an established Muslim merchant of India who appears in Aden around 533/1139 as a witness to a testimony involving his patron.[49] If Aḥmad was indeed a shipowner and the son of a slave/agent and captain, his and his father's success and upward trajectory illustrate how a person of few means and meager social standing could use his employment in the maritime component of the India trade to his and his descendants' advantage. The key lay in seizing the opportunities inherent in frequent travel to conduct informal small-scale trade and to create informal alliances with established merchants such as Maḍmūn, who were always seeking trustworthy carriers for their merchandise.

Home Port and Home Waters: The Segmentation of Shipping Lines

In addition to the family-based nature of their networks, another important characteristic of the shipping businesses that carried the bulk of the India trade was geographic segmentation. Such segmentation was manifest in the confinement of specific interests to specific routes. The Geniza documents indicate that merchants were involved in at least two distinct segments of shipping activity and that ships belonging to any one man or family plied the waters of only one of the two segments: they either sailed between Aden and India or between Aden and the Egyptian coast of the Red Sea. The fact that the Geniza materials contain few references to shipping east of India or down the African coast suggests that the routes between India and China and those between Aden and Africa constituted discreet segments of the maritime Indian Ocean world and that they lay largely outside the shipping reach of those traders whose letters ended up in the Cairo Geniza.

The ships owned by Rāmisht, Maḍmūn, Ibn Abī al-Katā'ib, and ʿAlī al-Fawfalī appear frequently in the letters and other documents of the India trade, although they do not appear at all in the waters west of Aden. Conversely, the sources contain far fewer references to individual shipowners and their ships plying the Red Sea. Yet numerous ships from the West put into Aden every year, bringing Western wares and taking on Eastern merchandise. The timing of the arrivals of these Western ships depended both on the seasonal winds and weather and on less predictable circumstances. Thus, one year Maḍmūn writes to his friend, Ben Yijū, in India that "this year no vessels [*jilāb*] arrived from Zabīd until the ships [*marākib*—that is, ships for India] had left."[50] In a different letter, Maḍmūn mentions with relief the arrival of light vessels from ʿAydhāb and their delivery of a message that four other boats bringing several merchants and goods from the Red Sea port would arrive in their wake.[51] Finally, as has already been discussed, on yet another occasion, Western ships were delayed but arrived just before the end of the sailing season, saving the oversupplied pepper market at Aden from certain ruin.[52] The silence surrounding the names and the owners or captains of the boats that put into Aden from Zabīd and other Red Sea ports bespeaks a separate network. The entire corpus contains the names of only two Red Sea shippers: ʿAlī al-Dibājī and "al-Sharīf." The vessels of both men served the route from ʿAydhāb to Aden, sometimes sailing in convoy. The ships might stop at the Sudanese port of Suwākin and at the island of Dahlak,[53] but neither man appears to have sent his vessels on the sea routes east of Aden.

There is an additional indication of the specificity of Red Sea shipping. While relatively limited, the Geniza record on shippers plying the Red Sea before the early 6th/13th century is remarkable for offering the earliest occurrence of the term "*kārim*." According to the standard definition of this etymologically enigmatic term, the *kārim* or *akārim* were a "group of Muslim merchants operating from the major centers of trade in the Ayyubid and Mamluk empires" and dealing primarily in spices.[54] It has become clear, however, that this definition depends primarily on data from later Ayyubid and especially Mamluk sources and is colored by the genealogy of the early scholarship on the *kārim* that developed before the Geniza references could be fully explored and digested. Instead of referring to a kind of loose federation of Muslim merchants, for most of the period under consideration here the term did not apply to a specific merchant group at all; rather, it designated convoys of ships traveling in the western Indian Ocean to and from Egyptian ports. These convoys transported merchants of a variety of confessional backgrounds; Jews and possibly even Christians were part of the *kārim*, along with Muslims. Goitein, who demonstrated most convincingly this earlier meaning of the term, originally appeared prepared to concede that the understanding of the *kārim* as exclusively Muslim might still hold for the post-Fatimid period; given additional data that he subsequently presented, however, it now appears that the notion of confessional exclusivity should probably be reconsidered.[55]

In eleven Geniza documents, Jewish merchants speak of the *kārim* in terms that leave no doubt of their stake in the institution:[56] they announce merchandise sent or to be sent by them in the *kārim* or included in the *kārim*;[57] inform or inquire about the contents of the *kārim* and whereabouts of business friends and relatives;[58] deplore the addressee's failure to return to Egypt with that season's *kārim*;[59] and in one exceptional case, express relief that the harsh customs regime imposed (temporarily) by al-Malik al-Muʿizz will not apply to "this *kārim*."[60] Three aspects of these references emerge as central to the debate about the nature of the *kārim* and the geographical extent of *kārim* activity. First, the range of usage exemplified by these few references indicates that in addition to denoting a fleet or convoy of ships, the term was expanded semantically to include the more abstract notion of the market engendered by such a convoy. Second, while most of the Geniza references belong to the earlier part of the 6th/12th century, at least two date to the end of that century and the beginning of the following one. In this light, even Goitein's concession about the possibility of change in the usage of the term in post-Fatimid times should be adjusted. Finally, in all of these cases, the *kārim*'s location is either explicitly declared or can be deduced to be either Aden or a Red Sea port.

Combined with the overwhelming later connection of the term "*kārim*" with Egypt, the Geniza testimony on *kārim* activity and the Aden–Red Sea route seems to suggest that the *kārim* were geographically focused on Egypt, that the ships involved were probably run primarily by Egyptian merchants, and that the destination port in the Indian Ocean was Aden.[61] The activities of the *kārim* as portrayed in the Cairo Geniza thus suggest both the segmentation of shipping routes and the terminus role that Aden played for Red Sea shipping in pre-Rasulid times. Rasulid sources, conversely, record the shipment of *kārimī* merchandise to India but also speak of *kārimī* merchants traveling all the way to China.[62] This evidence for the extension of previously truncated shipping lines as well as the appointment of *kārimī* merchants to important offices in Rasulid Aden[63] may be symptoms of the increased integration into the premodern world system envisioned by Janet Abu Lughod.[64]

In the formative period under investigation here, the segmentation of Indian Ocean shipping lines even beyond the Red Sea is most vividly expressed in a document's enumeration of the "ships from every sea" frequenting Aden's harbor, including "ships from India and its environs, ships from the land of Zanj and environs, ships from Berbera and Ḥabash and environs, ships from al-Ashḥār and al-Qamr and environs," clearly distinguishing the western coast of India, the coast of East Africa, the Gulf of Aden and the coast of Somalia and Ethiopia/Eritrea, and the southeastern coast of Arabia as different shipping centers. That these were not just circumstantial points of departure but actually ports of origin of the ships in question is confirmed in a different passage from the same letter that makes the distinction between Adeni, African, and other ships.[65]

Ethnographic and ethnoarchaeological evidence also exists for regional variety in boatbuilding styles of the different parts of the Indian Ocean; Red Sea boats are, to this day, distinguishable from their cousins of the Gulf, southern Arabia, eastern Africa, and India, which in turn form regional groups distinct from one another.[66] Ship nomenclature in the Geniza documents may hint at similar differences in boatbuilding styles in medieval times: the term "*jalba*" refers only to Red Sea boats and, to the best of my knowledge, appears only once in the context of the Aden-India route, in reference to a ship that carried armed men and sailed as an escort of a merchant vessel.[67] When referring to ships sailing between Aden and India, the Jewish merchants use almost exclusively the generic term "*markab*." Until the 8th/14th century, Arabic sources too apply the term "*jalba*" solely to Red Sea boats, and only in that century does the term appear as a designation of an Indian Ocean boat; if this later usage is not an arbitrary imposition of a term that was still not natively used, it may perhaps indicate the increasing integration of shipping lines and cultures.[68]

Given these ethnographic and linguistic clues, it is safe to assume that within the wider Indian Ocean boatbuilding tradition, local conditions and resources made for idiosyncrasies in the boats of each area. In a sense, these subdivisions parallel the segmentation of shipping lines; the reasons behind the divisions in both systems are to be sought in the climatic conditions that imposed complementary seasons of sailing, in the need for local navigation knowledge and expertise, and more importantly in the role of port cities as foci of local order and organization.

Beyond Family and Home Waters: Shipping and the Spirit of Intra- and Interdenominational Business Collaboration

From his investigations of Mediterranean shipping business, Goitein concluded that only rarely would a captain or sailor accompany or look after another merchant's goods on board his ship and then only when the goods to be transferred were few or of low value and volume.[69] In the Indian Ocean, the opposite seems to be the case: captains and even shipowners are the most frequently mentioned carriers of people's merchandise and correspondence. What were the terms of such informal collaboration? No specific or immediate reward is ever mentioned, but it stands to reason that even if informal and vague, the understanding between benefactor and beneficiary was that the favor would at some point be returned.[70]

A different kind of favor involved the exemption from freight charges (*nawl*) between shipowners. In one case, Maḍmūn reveals to Ben Yijū that his shipment of copper on board one of Rāmisht's ships and in the care of the *nākhudhā* Aḥmad b. Bakhtiyār was exempted from freight.[71] Perhaps Rāmisht or the captain of his vessel used his discretion to do a favor to a fellow shipowner. Alternatively, the favor may have been granted to the carrier of the consignment, Aḥmad, and relayed from him to Maḍmūn. Whatever the actual dynamic, the incident hints at the existence of systems of leverage between shipowners and seamen of different origins whose informal collaborations hinged on an exchange of mutual favors.

Beyond these informal relationships among captains, shipowners, and nonshipowning merchants, shipping and occasionally boatbuilding practices encouraged the formation of partnerships outside the circles of family and faith, as the partnership of Bilāl b. Jarīr and Maḍmūn excellently exemplifies. The two men joined forces to outfit and equip a ship of considerable size in Aden; to fill it with merchandise, perhaps exclusively owned by their partnership; and to launch an ambitious trading expedition to Ceylon while jointly sending a large quantity of lac to Egypt.[72]

The magnitude of their Ceylon venture investment can only be imagined. On a different occasion, Maḍmūn mentions the considerable (but apparently inadequate for the purpose) sum of two thousand dinars in connection with his outfitting of another ship.[73] The vessel that he was planning to launch in collaboration with Bilāl must have been a much larger affair. Moreover, a letter from Khalaf to Ben Yijū reveals that the two powerful Adenis were intent on a remarkably large cargo: for an entire year, Khalaf could not secure any of the locally produced glass items Ben Yijū had ordered because the Bilāl-Maḍmūn partnership had reserved the entire annual production.[74] Glass no doubt constituted only part of the cargo. The fact that a number of craftsmen, including three goldsmiths, were scheduled to travel on board this vessel provides an additional hint at the ambitious scope of the enterprise: Were these men freelancers, or did the partnership recruit them specifically to take advantage of local resources in India (where they would probably stop) and Sri Lanka, have them do the work there, and then return with finished objects, trading along the way?[75]

Whatever the specifics of this shipping venture, it brought together two of Aden's most powerful men, who in turn invested in it all that the city had to offer: materials, boatbuilding expertise, almost the entire local production of glassware, and doubtless other local products and Western imports. This incident constituted an exception to the rule of single proprietorship that prevailed in shipping practices of the southern Mediterranean and possibly the Indian Ocean[76] as well as an expedition that could not have been launched from a lesser entrepôt. Once again, comparing the Adeni partnership with that between Nahray b. Nissīm and the Alexandrian *amīr* is instructive. A. L. Udovitch has shown that the *amīr*, who controlled the shipping part of the collaboration, "used his political muscle to advance his financial interests."[77] While the economic roles are reversed in the case of Bilāl and Maḍmūn, the two partners relied on a similar combination of economic power and social and political capital. Their combined assets allowed them to put together the capital required to build, outfit, and man a large ship and to secure large quantities of merchandise, such as a year's worth of local glass production. And Bilāl's political status ensured that the partners had first bids on anything they cared to include in their venture; as a different note by Maḍmūn puts it, "No one may ask for something that master Bilāl has asked for."[78]

The alliance between Maḍmūn and Bilāl also illustrates the networking opportunities available within the city of Aden. Like other businessmen, however, shipowners contracted overseas partnerships and informal associations and did so perhaps with greater facility than ordinary merchants thanks to their privileged access to means of transportation and communication. The best example of such relationship is the case of the Indian *nākhudhā* Tinbū and the Jewish-Adeni *nākhudhā* Maḥrūz. The connection between the two men emerges in full historical light in a letter from Maḥrūz to his brother-in-law, Abū Zikrī ha-Kohen, written while both were in India.[79]

Abū Zikrī was somewhere along the Konkan coast when pirates attacked his ship; an escort vessel carrying a contingent of fighters fled the scene. The exact sequence of events is not known, but Abū Zikrī ended up at the port of Broach. Maḥrūz, who was in Mangalore at the time, initially wrote to his brother-in-law at Tāna, perhaps Abū Zikrī's original destination, then heard the news of the attack, and finally got word of his narrow escape.[80] In the salient letter, Maḥrūz urges Abū Zikrī to travel to Mangalore in time to take passage on one of Maḥrūz's ships back to Aden. He also encourages Abū Zikrī to contact Maḥrūz's friend Tinbū for money if needed: "Your servant thought that your honor my lord was in Tāna, and I had previously sent letters to the nākhodā Tinbū, advising him to pay my lord 21 mithqāls . . . or more. . . . If my lord, you need any gold, please take it on my account from the nākhodā Tinbū, for he is staying in Tāna, and between him and me there are bonds of inseparable friendship and brotherhood."[81] This remarkable passage requires little comment but speaks volumes about the level of collaboration and degree of trust between the two shipowners. Their close relationship, personal and financial, stands in marked contrast to the apparent polarization of partnerships and collaboration along denominational lines and their segregation within broad political boundaries in the Mediterranean in the same time period.[82] The letter also showcases the virtual proximity between Aden and the port towns of western India despite the oceanic divide. Maḥrūz sent Abū Zikrī an Arabic-script version of this letter, apparently so that he could present it to Tinbū and perhaps to other non-Jewish merchants as a means of introduction.[83] The dispatch of the Arabic letter reveals a linguistic layer of integration of shipowners and other businessmen irrespective of their religious and ethnic differences; by the 6th/12th century, Arabic clearly had become something of a lingua franca in the western Indian Ocean.

Boatbuilding in Aden

Of the maritime services available in the city, none was as central to the life and livelihood of the entrepôt as boatbuilding and boat repair. In his work on Genoa, Steven Epstein enumerates the characteristics of the commercially rising Italian maritime republics in medieval times: knowledge of overseas markets, sophisticated commercial contracts and a predictable legal environment, and a local shipping industry capable of producing seaworthy galleys and ships.[84] The sources reveal that Adeni merchants were intimately familiar with at least two sets of crucial overseas markets, in India and Egypt, and operated within a social and legal environment that was generally secure and predictable, if largely informal. Moreover, Adeni shipowners had access to and even control of a fully fledged shipbuilding industry, thereby placing them directly in charge of the means by which their business grew, challenged the competition, and protected itself from predators.

Very little is known about the organization of medieval boatbuilding in the Indian Ocean; the Geniza documents provide new and valuable insights into the state of the industry in Aden. It is hard to imagine an important maritime center without a boatyard, yet ethnographically and historically attested parallels suggest that complete dependency on an overseas source of ships was a possibility. Buying hulls built overseas or building them abroad and sailing them back to

Aden might have been an attractive solution to the dearth of locally available raw materials for boatbuilding in South Arabia.[85] Such a solution, however, would have rendered the city's shipping industry dependent and consequently vulnerable. The most compelling evidence that an important boatyard capable of producing a variety of substantial, oceangoing vessels operated in Aden emerges from documents relating to the affairs of Maḍmūn b. Japheth.

In his letters, Maḍmūn mentions the launching of at least two different ships, the ship used for the trading expedition to Ceylon in collaboration with Bilāl b. Jarīr[86] and a ship probably named *al-Mubārak*.[87] In one instance, Maḍmūn alludes to the building of ships, stressing how drawn-out such an enterprise could be: "My lord knows about my business with ships, and that is something that takes time."[88] The mildly impatient tone conjures up images of the busy man struggling to secure boatbuilding supplies in addition to his other responsibilities and rushing down to the shipyard to inspect the progress of construction.

In addition to building purely commercial vessels, moreover, Maḍmūn may also have had responsibility for building warships or naval troop transports. Broken phrases in a letter from Joseph b. Abraham b. Bundār to Abū Zikrī in Cairo reveal that Maḍmūn was directly involved in building or outfitting military transport ships (*jāshujiyāt*).[89] The exact differences between these transport vessels and ships launched for commercial purposes remain unclear, but their description as a distinct type with a specialized name emphasizes the diversity of the port city's boatbuilding capabilities. Finally, Aden's shipyard or shipyards must also have produced the lighters necessary for ferrying merchandise from the anchorage to the harbor front as well as the boats for fishing the waters of the Gulf of Aden and beyond. Ibn al-Mujāwir and Abū Makhrama describe lighters used in the days before the land bridge linked the peninsula with the mainland as *ṣanābīq* and *zawārīk*.[90] In the days of the Geniza merchants, as during Ibn al-Mujāwir's visit, such humble craft played an important role in the local economy. They carried people and merchandise between the ships and the customshouse, town, and market. Moreover, these vessels must have served as fishermen's boats, thus keeping the city stocked with fish, ambergris, and other marine products.

Beyond meeting the local demand for trading vessels, lighterage boats, and fishing craft, Aden emerges as a boatbuilding center for the entire region through the remarkable testimony of a letter sent by Maḍmūn b. Japheth to Ben Yijū.[91] In a postscript written in his own hand, Maḍmūn extends special greetings to four men in India; three names are readable and suggest that the group included Hindus and one Muslim. In addition to other orders for merchandise from Mangalore and from northern India, he asks for *qunbār*, the boatbuilding twine used to fasten hull planks together or the coconut husk for making this twine. The request for this indispensable boatbuilding material strongly indicates that boatbuilding activity occurred in Aden. Maḍmūn then adds, "If they go ahead with the outfitting of a ship in Aden and want me to be their partner, I will participate with them."[92]

It is at first surprising that a primarily Indian partnership would want to build a ship in Aden. Addressed from Adeni merchants to partners in India, requests for coconut husk twine, or *qunbār* (this letter), and timber (in a different letter from Maḍmūn)[93] hint at the well-known fact that raw materials for ship construction were abundant in India and were exported from there to Aden. While evidence from medieval times is scarce, little doubt exists that the maritime centers of the subcontinent also boasted the necessary boatbuilding expertise. Why then would the Indian businessmen elect not to build at home but to seek a partnership and stage their venture overseas, at a place where raw materials had to be imported? The answer lies in Aden's function as a boatbuilding hub as much as in the local availability of the capital necessary to fund big boatbuilding enterprises.

The development of a boatbuilding hub presupposes the concentration of craft expertise, a skilled labor force, and boatbuilding supplies. Adeni boatbuilders remain largely invisible in the historical record except through the indirect testimony of their products as they appear in the sources. In the German engraving showing Aden from the water, the beach in front of the town's walls is largely empty except for what appear to be three hulls drawn on the sand and propped up with shores; these must be local craft either under construction or under repair. Boatyards around Arabia often occupy beach space near or right in front of the inhabited part of a port town, and Aden's waterfront likely served that purpose. The boatbuilders must have included local craftsmen, especially inhabitants of Aden's satellite settlements such as al-Mabāh, where boatbuilding may also have taken place. Ethnographically attested models suggest, however, that craftsmen from other parts of the Indian Ocean may well have flocked to offer their services and expertise at a shipping hub as central as Aden.

For building new ships and for repairs, the boatbuilders required a steady supply of the necessary raw materials. What would these have been? The extant fragments of written and pictorial evidence agree that before the circumnavigation of Africa by the Portuguese, ships to the southeast of Suez were built in what is known as laced or sewn construction. The hallmark of this technology is the way in which ship timbers (external planking and internal strengthening member and fittings) are laced or sewn together with coconut husk twine rather than nailed in place or fitted with mortise-and-tenon joints.[94] Thus, materials for building ships in medieval Aden would have included strong and malleable timber in planks of sufficient length and width, *qunbār* (coir or coconut husk twine used to lace together ship timbers), and *nūra* (the lime-and-fat compound that served to coat ship hulls and protect them from *teredo* worm damage).

Nūra was produced locally, probably in the settlement of al-Mabāh.[95] Ibn al-Mujāwir lists perfumes and *qunbār* as the two main products that the inhabitants of the land sold for a living.[96] However impressionistic, his statement suggests that *qunbār* was a major trade item in Aden and that it may have been manufactured locally from imported material; Maḍmūn's request for the material in his note to his future Indian partners confirms the nature of the supply line from India. Securing and transporting supplies of timber must have been challenging but would not have been impossible, given the open lines of communication with the subcontinent. Every bit of wood counted: builders and businessmen must have tapped all possible sources and managed the available supply with extreme economy. High-quality material, such as planks of teak (*Tectona grandis*) or a similar timber known as *aini* had to be imported and went into building the ship's shell.[97] For internal structural elements such as frames and tackle, the boatbuilders had access to the shorter spans of lesser-quality wood that grew locally, such as the jackfruit tree (*Artocarpus heterophyllus* or *Artocarpus integrifolia*) that grew in Rubāk.[98]

Moreover, intriguing evidence suggests that ship timbers were recycled: in 546/1151, when a ship foundered four days' sail east of Aden, people collected surviving timbers that washed up on the shores of Abyan and al-Shiḥr and brought them back to the city.[99] In a region so poor in good timber, the readiness to surrender such a good harvest instead of using it in local buildings, boats, or even fires speaks volumes about the city's reach over its immediate hinterland as well as further afield, its role as the regional center, and the speed and efficiency of local information networks. Back in Aden, experts identified the timbers as brand-new and surmised that they came from a missing boat that belonged to Ḥalfon, son of Maḍmūn. They based this conclusion on the observation that of all the ships built in Aden that year, only Ḥalfon's ship had received all new fittings.[100] They could not have pointed more clearly to the practice of recycling older fittings and timbers in the construction of boats. Soon thereafter, local boatbuilders must have put the shipwrecked and salvaged boat parts to good use, either in the construction of new boats or in old vessels in need of repair.

Expertise and a reliable, steady supply of materials were vital prerequisites for the flourishing of a boatbuilding industry in Aden. Most importantly, however, the availability of capital provided the most powerful incentive for contracting the building of a ship in Aden. Maḍmūn's letter provides no indication of the terms of the prospective partnership between him and the Indian businessmen, but the Adeni notable may have been in a position to serve as the major capitalist. If the Indians were looking for a wealthy investor with a declared interest in shipping and shipbuilding, perhaps Aden was the natural place to start their search.

Safeguarding Trade and Revenues: Maritime Policing and Enforcement

The port of Aden hosted several shipping businesses, enabled multifaceted collaborations within the city and across the seas through which capital was pooled and major expeditions launched, and functioned as a major boatbuilding center for the western Indian Ocean. After maritime enterprises were under way, however, piratical ambushes and attacks as well as the occasional political upheaval threatened the participants, as did reefs, leaky boats, and bad weather. More than any other port in the Indian Ocean, Aden was equipped to confront these threats and to extend services that mitigated these risks facing mariners and shippers.

For the inhabitants of Aden and the foreign merchants who did business there, one of the most dramatic events in the 150 years of Zurayid and Ayyubid rule must have been the naval blockade of the port by the ruler of Kish/Qays.[101] The fact that no vessels called at Aden for two months suggests that news of the siege spread like wildfire and that foreign shippers were staying away.[102] The disruption of the usual pace of winter port life must have damaged the city's economy, and the change of itinerary must have been just as inconvenient for merchants and shippers. Gone were the opportunities to resupply, to unpack and air merchandise, and even to simply unload goods safely and turn back to the home port or move on to another destination. Yet this exceptional siege proves the rule of safety and stability that Aden guaranteed for those doing business within its fold. The failure of the attackers also attests to the city's physical impregnability, which under ordinary circumstances must have conferred a general sense of safety to locals and visitors alike. What does the incident tell us about "naval" ships, naval capability, and the participation of the city-state in the protection of its shipping?

According to the eyewitness account of Maḍmūn and to Ibn al-Mujāwir's text, the besiegers arrived with a fleet of two large round ships (*burmāt*), ten troop transports (*jāshujiyāt*), and three possible galleys (*shaffārāt* in the Judeo-Arabic account and *dawānīj* in Ibn al-

Mujāwir's narrative).[103] The available evidence does not allow for a clear picture of exactly how each type differed from the others, but the names suggest that main differences were hull shape and possibly propulsion: the first two types must have been large, sail-powered vessels designed to carry troops, supplies, and/or cargo, while the galleys were long and narrow, probably shallow-drafted boats powered primarily by oars and designed for speed and maneuverability.[104] This motley collection of round and long ships may well have been representative of the vessels available for war or peace to the Indian Ocean maritime states in the Middle Ages, before the arrival of Portuguese and Ottoman naval fleets. How did Aden's ships compare?

At the time of the siege, Aden's defenders had no ships at their disposal and therefore no means of attacking their enemies. It is doubtful that either of Rāmisht's ships that saved the day was a warship or even commercial galley, especially since the sources make no comment to that effect. Instead, the two vessels must have simply relied on their crew and on weapons carried as standard defensive armament and minimum precaution against trouble.[105] However the ships did it, they broke through enemy lines. When they made it to the beach, a significant force came on board and went back out to fight the enemy.

The need to defend the port itself arose very rarely. The main role of armament and maritime patrols launched from the city was the safeguarding of its merchantmen and occasionally of the legal framework within which merchants did business in the city. Protection against pirates was vital, for piracy shadowed trade in the Indian Ocean at least from the time of the *Periplus* and probably earlier.[106] As noted in the discussion of the galley tax (*ʿushūr al-shawānī*), the concomitant establishment of a maritime patrol squadron comprising oared galleys at least since Ayyubid times must have been a welcome measure and must have at least partially served its the purpose of protecting commercial shipping from piratical attacks. In the Zurayid period, a type of commercial galley called *shaffāra* like the Kish/Qays galleys formed part of the regular commercial fleet; carried merchandise, perhaps for extra freight charges; and served as an escort ship in commercial convoys, affording some degree of protection.[107]

As for the enforcement of justice against delinquent businessmen attempting to flee by sea, intriguing evidence comes from the report from Joseph b. Abraham b. Bundār to Abū Zikrī ha-Kohen in Cairo mentioned in the context of Maḍmūn's boatbuilding ventures. Despite its fragmentary condition, the relevant passage leaves little doubt that Maḍmūn was solely responsible for building and/or outfitting four troop transports (*jāshujiyāt*).[108] The letter then states explicitly that Maḍmūn had sent forth these ships to capture his former partner and friend, ʿAlī al-Fawfalī, who was apparently fleeing from debt or other responsibilities: "As for the illustrious *shaykh*, my lord Maḍmūn, [he sent forth] 4 *jāshujiyāt* to Zabīd and he charged their commander with the capture of al-Fawfalī, or the [confiscation?] of his *jalbas* and his bales, because he was bent on [fleeing to] Egypt.[109]

ʿAlī, himself a shipowner, had been Maḍmūn's right hand in India, and the Adeni notable had given ʿAlī full powers to deal with affairs in the subcontinent. Something must have gone terribly wrong, however, and Maḍmūn held ʿAlī accountable, either for mismanaging Maḍmūn's affairs or for some violation committed within Maḍmūn's jurisdiction as Adeni customs official and mercantile representative. It is a mystery why he dispatched as many as four ships on this mission, but perhaps it says something about the alliances al-Fawfalī may have been able to muster in a city such as Zabīd that lay beyond Aden's orbit. In any case, that Maḍmūn possessed the resources to take such extraordinary action against his erstwhile partner eloquently illustrates both his extensive powers within the city and the state's readiness to allow its merchants to enforce, at least at certain times, business rules and regulations.

How do these mechanisms of defending trade and shipping compare with the record of other entrepôts along the India route? Qays had a bad reputation as a rapacious state rather than as a stable legal environment where the rights of merchants were by and large upheld. Geniza evidence sheds light on an incident involving another maritime state, based on the southern Red Sea island of Dahlak, that reveals parallel motives and mode of state intervention on the high seas. The precise sequence of events is somewhat difficult to decipher, and two possibilities exist: either the little state acted on this occasion as a piratical entity, or it used its ships to enforce its rules for clearing customs and general business comportment at port.

Writing to Abū Zikrī in Cairo, Cairene merchant Samuel b. Abraham b. al-Majjānī in Aden gives a convoluted account of his travels from the Red Sea to Aden:

> I should inform your excellency, my master, about our people who took passage with ʿAlī al-Dibājī: Nahray, Ibn Nafīʿa, and Ibn al-Yatīm, the three of them in one *bilīj*, and al-Fāsī, and one other Jew whom I don't know ([*erased*:] apparently they are lingering in Dahlak and won't be joining us). They joined us the night before the eve of our departure for Aden. (I wrote that part of my letter the day before the eve of the departure and I was at the time planning on sailing to al-Qaṣṣ.) . . . I had hired space on board the *jalba* of al-Sharīf and sailed on it. When we reached the Bāb al-Mandab, the ruler of Dahlak sent his *jalba*s against us. He had imposed unreasonable demands on us and took some of our possessions, so we were fleeing from him. They fought with us a great battle, and they injured the *goyīm* and plundered the ship. They took the edge of the ship [boarded the ship?] and let us go, and took the bales of cloth that were in it.[110]

Samuel never really declares the meeting place and departure port, but it must have been Dahlak, for it seems unlikely that the merchants traveling on the ships of ʿAlī al-Dibājī would have gone as far south as the island and then returned to ʿAydhāb, only to head south again. "Lingering in Dahlak"[111] means perhaps that they were still debating whether to travel to Aden or simply stay on the island and do business there. Situated off the African coast, Dahlak was the southernmost port between ʿAydhāb and the Bāb al-Mandab. India traders stopped there quite frequently, not only to resupply their ships but also to peddle their goods. The city had a varied market[112] and even minted its own silver coins, which were used in international trade and had a documented exchange rate with Egyptian dinars.[113] Moreover, the island emerges as a base of rescue and salvage operations; a number of shipwrecked merchants who were considered dead reemerged there, some with part or all of their goods salvaged.[114] In other words, Dahlak was not just a maritime port of call but an important commercial entrepôt offering a variety of commercial services. The port must have served as a convenient terminal for merchants from the East who did not want to risk sailing further up the Red Sea as well as for Egyptian and other Western traders who preferred not to negotiate the treacherous straits of the Bāb al-Mandab.

Given such prominent role in the Red Sea route, Dahlak's customshouse not surprisingly extracted taxes from merchants who chose the privilege of trading or merely calling at port. It is perhaps significant that the first mention of clearing customs on the island, written half a century before the text discussed here, involves what is by all appearances a case of bribery.[115] Something equally irregular appears to have happened when Samuel was passing through. Writing in the margins as an afterthought, Samuel appears to be admitting having smuggled a consignment of coral belonging to Ibn al-Yatīm (one of the merchants who took passage on ʿAlī al-Dibājī's ships) as a favor.[116] Samuel's goods openly cleared customs and incurred only very low charges, perhaps as a result of further shady dealing. Such revelations lead to the question of whether the subsequent encounter on the high seas was somehow related to transgressions back at Dahlak.

Despite the obscurities of the text, the events can be reconstructed: Samuel and other Jewish traders arrived at Dahlak, some with the intention of traveling further. Samuel at first believed that his coreligionists were planning to stay on the island, presumably to do business there. He had not made up his mind about his destination and was considering taking passage on a ship to al-Qaṣṣ in India. On the evening before the day of the departure of eastbound ships, however, all of the other men decided to head to Aden, albeit in different ships. Samuel took passage on a ship owned by al-Sharīf, while his acquaintances boarded vessels owned by al-Dibājī, and the vessels set off in a convoy. Perhaps they left in haste, suspecting they were about to be pursued.

At this point, Samuel interjects comments about unreasonable demands and confiscation of possessions by Dahlak's ruler.[117] Samuel does not explicitly state whether these events occurred in Dahlak or on the high seas, but given the ensuing description of the battle, casualties, and final confiscation of a ship and bales of cloth, he seems to be recalling the stay in Dahlak to explain the pursuit. At Dahlak, the ruler probably asked for extra taxes or taxes that the traders considered unreasonable; the ruler subsequently took some of their goods. The merchants fled to avoid further confiscation and perhaps other repercussions for smuggling.

Samuel offers little explanation as to why during the naval encounter the *goyim* (that is, the Muslims in the convoy) suffered a worse fate than the Jewish traders.[118] The incident bespeaks transgressions and enforcement of the will of a maritime state. The Dahlak force clearly prevailed and presumably could have confiscated all of the cargo but elected not to do so. The reason may lie in a conscious or intuitive effort on the part of the island state and its ruler to strike a balance between force and legitimacy. Intercepting merchants on the high seas smacks of piracy, and being considered a pirate's lair would be bad for port business.

How would ʿAlī al-Fawfalī have considered his pursuit and interception at Zabīd by the Adeni force sent out by Maḍmūn b. Japheth? In a sense, the two episodes represent different sides of the same coin. In the case of the Adeni intervention, the involvement of a partner and coreligionist who was also a customs official and a friend and partner of the city's chief magistrate adds layers of complexity. From the point of view of the state at the ports whence the offensives were launched, these episodes constituted enforcement on the high seas of a known legal framework; the ruler of Dahlak took initiative, while Aden's magistrates clearly gave Maḍmūn their blessing.

For at least one of the victims, the incident was caused by the imposition of exorbitant taxes and confiscation of goods; whether Samuel considered the affair state-sanctioned piracy must remain uncertain, much like al-Fawfalī's reaction to his prosecution. Because of political instability and fragmentation and the limited jurisdiction and power of the states involved, the option of challenging such actions or lodging formal complaints does not appear to have existed as it did in the Mediterranean.[119] Order, based on mutual needs and understanding among merchants and between merchants and petty states, was naturally very precarious, efforts to maintain it when it broke down desultory, and results of conflict unpredictable and irreversible.

Shipwreck, Rescue, and Salvage

Two years after the sinking of a vessel belonging to Ḥalfon, the son of Maḍmūn b. Japheth, a document was drafted in Aden, dated Adar 1464 (Dhū al-Qaʿda 547/February 1153) and signed by eight notables from the local Jewish community. The document provides an extensive report of the events and aftermath of a shipwreck. Addressing the father-in-law of one of the victims, Egyptian India merchant Hiba b. Abī Saʿd, the authors explicitly promise to answer three questions that this man had clearly communicated from Cairo regarding the death of his son-in-law: What were the circumstances of Hiba's death and the death of his business partner and traveling companion? What would the Adeni notables advise concerning the status of this man's daughter, Hiba's wife? And what was the status of the unfortunate merchant's belongings? Perhaps the most dramatic section of the document is the reconstruction, from witnesses' reports, of the sequence of events that led to the loss of the ship in question:

> As for the circumstances of their perdition: they traveled together on the ship sailing from Aden to Kūlam. The ships departed, and this boat together with the boat heading to Barībatān proceeded in convoy for four days. On the evening of the fifth day, the passengers of the Barībatān ship heard clamoring coming from the people of the Kūlam ship, crying and yelling in the night. When the water had engulfed them [the people of

> the Kūlam ship] and daybreak came, the people of the Barībatān ship found no trace of the Kūlam ship. There was no news of this [in Aden] because the two ships had been sailing in convoy since they left Aden and did not part until the incident that befell the Kūlam ship. This happened just before they entered *al-maṣabb*. Ship timbers and ship fittings that looked brand-new later washed up on the coasts of Abyan and al-Shiḥr. They were brought from there to Aden. None of the new ships built in Aden that year, the year of the disaster, had all new equipment except the Kūlam ship.[120]

After narrating the events as reported by the passengers and crew of the companion vessel, the report shifts to the ensuing investigations. The timbers were examined, and some speculation was raised that they belonged perhaps not to the missing Adeni ship but to a different vessel. The possibility was ruled out, however, after interviews with travelers to Aden from all over the western Indian Ocean (*min kull baḥr*)[121] revealed that no other ship built of new timbers was missing; the interviews also determined that there were no signs of survivors or flotsam from the wreck. The effort and energy put into collecting information is palpable.

The report then details the opinions of the "experts" (*ahl al-khibra wa-al-maʿrifa*, literally "the people of experience and knowledge").[122] Sailing distances to Abyan and al-Shiḥr (where shipwreck debris was picked up) and to the spot known as *al-maṣabb* (where the ships were heading when the shipwreck took place) are quoted, as are the calculations of the location of the shipwreck and of the potential radius of the scatter of shipwreck remains. Could more survivors or further clues be expected? The experts concluded that the chances of survival for anyone lost at sea at that spot were minimal "because of the wildness of the sea, the coastal waves, and the multitude of fish."[123] The estimates and calculations as well as the final verdict offer a taste of the intimate knowledge of the sea that these experts in maritime matters peddled in the port city. This city-based information capital could be drawn on both in extraordinary situations, such as the one at hand, and in the everyday running of maritime business.

To the modern reader of this account, the exact location of the fateful event is much more of a mystery than it was for the people in Aden at the time. The two ships, one bound for the city of Kūlam (present day Quillon on the southern end of the Malabar coast) and the other for Barībatān (most likely Ballipattana on the southern Konkan coast)[124] must have been coasting from Aden to the spot where the Kūlam ship came to grief. The crux of the problem is in the meaning of "*al-maṣabb*," which the report indicates lay just ahead on the sea route when the disaster struck.[125] Geographical texts are of little help; they use the term in its literal meaning of "confluence," "river mouth," or "gulf"[126] and nowhere discuss it as a specific place-name. Perhaps *al-maṣabb* was just that, a confluence of routes or, rather, the spot where sea routes from Aden diverged and where the two ships would have parted ways so that the unfortunate vessel could have headed to southern India while its companion ship presumably sailed to somewhere further north on the Indian coast.

Regardless of the exact location of this veritable hotspot for travel and navigation, this document alone sketches the outlines of a multifaceted system of local knowledge that with Aden as its hub contributed to picking up the pieces after a shipwreck, both literally and figuratively. The city's information tentacles reached well beyond its immediate physical limits. When the timbers washed up in Abyan and al-Shiḥr, the local inhabitants brought them to Aden rather than scavenging them for their own purposes and perhaps received a salvager's fee. In Aden, shipwrecked material, travelers' accounts, and experts' opinions were mined in the writing of the report that settled a two-year case for the victim's relatives and dependents.

The experts played a particularly important role in this process. Their intimate knowledge of local maritime topography, weather, currents, and marine life was crucial in the interpretation of the shipwreck remains. Much like modern-day nautical archaeologists, they combined their knowledge of the structure of the ship that sank and

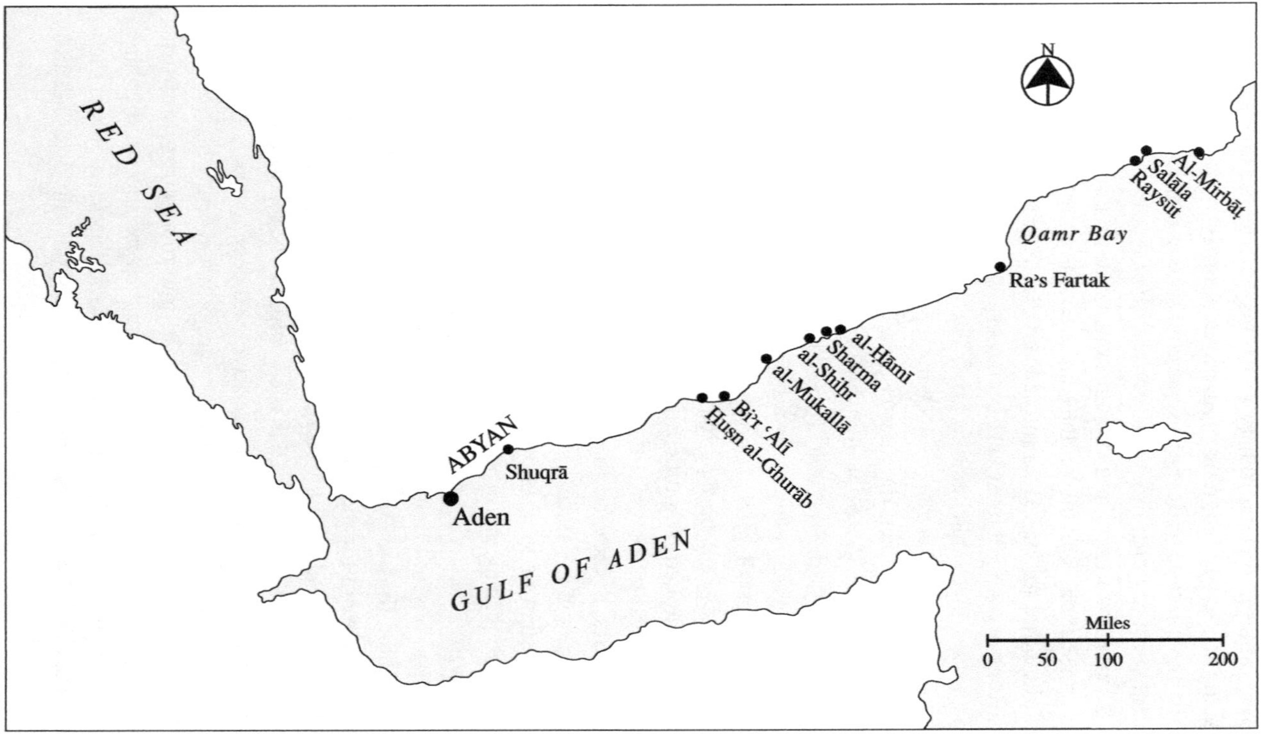

Map 4. The South Arabian Coast: Ports and Archaeological Sites East of Aden

data about its final voyage with their understanding of the local conditions that led flotsam to specific shores, thereby reconstructing the events pre- and postshipwreck. Such expertise must have come from years at sea; whether still active on the high seas or retired to a life in the city, the experts can only have been at some time captains, shipowners, or navigators—that is, seasoned seamen who had learned from their fathers and predecessors and had plied the waters of the western Indian Ocean countless times.[127] Not only were their services useful in identifying wreckage, as in the case that unravels in the account from Aden, but they also must have contributed to the success of salvage operations.

Salvage was routine in premodern seafaring, and the reasons become clearer in light of the idea that coasting as much as possible was the prevalent and preferred mode of sailing in premodern times. Coasting meant that shipwreck often occurred within sight of shore and within reach of salvage; news of an incident could reach a coastal center in time for a rescue and salvage mission to be launched or, as in the case just discussed, for shipwreck debris to be collected and recognized. The kind of intervention possible from Aden and the chances of success become evident in two different Geniza letters that document cases of shipwreck and salvage. In one case from the time of Maḍmūn b. Japheth, a ship went down so close to Aden that drowned bodies washed up on the peninsula's shores.[128] Not surprisingly, given the lookout system described by Ibn al-Mujāwir, this incident was spotted from Aden; divers went out to pick up what they could and salvaged enough of at least one man's property to lead to legal claims by his relatives back in Egypt.

In the same period, a letter from Khalaf to Ben Yijū in India testifies to what must have been a difficult salvage operation and to its relative success.[129] A ship carrying merchandise belonging to Ben Yijū and destined for Aden had for some reason reached the general vicinity of Berbera, an African port west of Aden, and had then been driven against the rocky shores of the Bāb al-Mandab, where it went down. Some of Ben Yijū's salvaged merchandise went through customs and was transferred to the "house" of Maḍmūn. How did the salvage operation take place? Khalaf explains that mariners (*baḥḥā-rīn*) were recruited and sent from Aden to dive on the wreck and retrieve the lost cargo. They brought back half of Ben Yijū's iron and perhaps other items from the wreck. These divers clearly possessed considerable expertise; the waters around Bāb al-Mandab were treacherous, and the salvaged material was heavy. A letter from the Mediterranean provides evidence for a salvage operation that lasted two days,[130] and the operation at the Bāb al-Mandab likely represents a similar expenditure of effort and time.

Khalaf does not mention any casualties from the disaster. Such silence might suggest either that those on board had the time to get into lifeboats or just the opposite—that is, that everyone on board drowned but that Khalaf, perhaps without relatives or acquaintances on board, avoids stating the obvious. He also does not tell us who brought news of the shipwreck to town and when or how soon thereafter people in the city responded by recruiting divers and sending them on the spot. However, it is known that the Bāb al-Mandab straits are about a day and a night's sail away from the port.[131] Even with the relatively favorable winds of the latter part of the winter monsoon, when this incident must have taken place, given the ship's provenance and destination, it is not certain that the operation relied entirely on wind. The need to act was urgent, as currents or scavengers could get to the merchandise before the salvagers. It is not unlikely, therefore, that the expedition used a fast vessel, a galley with both sail and oar capability, to ensure speed and efficiency.

It is unclear whether the state or private individuals launched such salvage operations. Khalaf's letter, however, reveals who paid for the service: "All expenses incurred for the diving and the transport will be deducted from whatever will be realized for that iron and the rest will be divided proportionally, each taking his proper share."[132] Regardless of how salvage was organized, the city provided both the expertise and resources necessary to launching such expeditions as well as a locus where the outcome could be negotiated and settled with some degree of predictability.

In conclusion, the welfare of shipping depended first and foremost on the city's role as an information hub. While naval patrols, escort vessels, and salvage operations went a long way toward mitigating the overall impact of human and natural menaces at sea, the most effective means by which merchants could protect their merchandise was the virtual shipping data bank encompassed within the port city of Aden. I refer not only to information about conditions along the well-plied sea routes and at overseas destinations but more importantly to local knowledge about ships and shipowners and to information on the reliability of shippers—that is, who sailed old, poorly built, or neglected vessels. The voices of traders in the Geniza documents ring loud and clear to this effect, as when Maḥrūz urges his brother-in-law, Abū Zikrī, to sail with Maḥrūz on his ship back to Aden rather than take passage on "other people's boats"[133] and when Ben Yijū urges Khalaf to send merchandise on ships "that have been proven safe in the past."[134] Such requests fully display the insight and knowledge that come with being part of the western Indian Ocean's most important crossroads of trade and information.

6 | *Mercantile and Legal Services*

Fa-qad ghamaranī baḥr ifḍālihā.

[I'm overwhelmed by the ocean
of your excellency's benevolence.]

BODL. MS HEB. a2, f. 16/IB.298/II.42

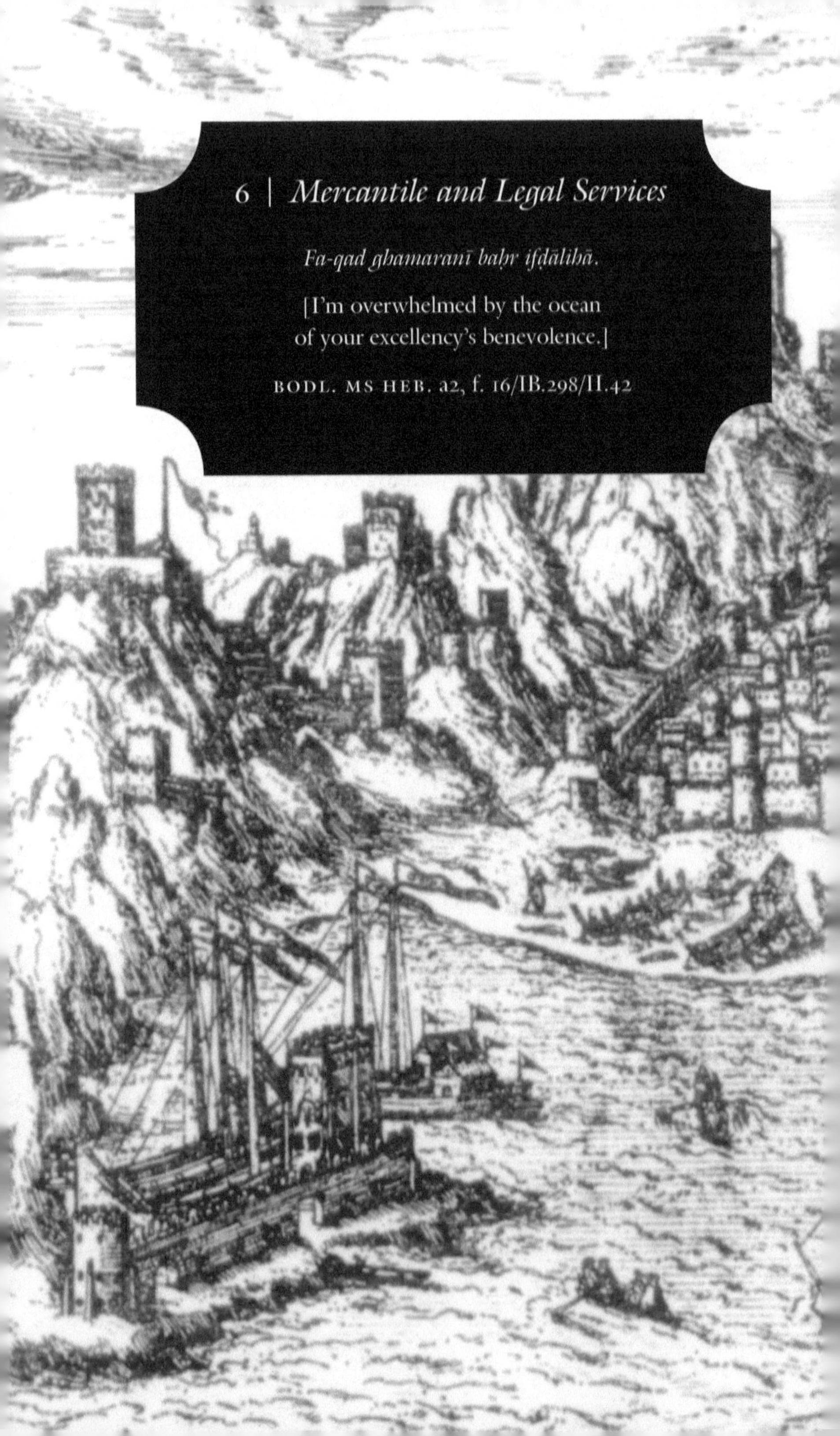

In the current era of giant container ships, GPS, and e-commerce, a single vessel can carry forty-eight hundred trailer-sized containers of merchandise from Bremen, Germany, to Elizabeth, New Jersey, in a single voyage.[1] The exact position of a ship is knowable at the push of a button and the blink of an eye, and one can place an order one minute and have confirmation of its receipt in the next. It is therefore difficult to grasp the medieval dimensions of distance and time. A respectably sized medieval Arab ship held the equivalent of about two trailer-sized containers.[2] At least two years, often more, were required for a round-trip voyage from Egypt to India.[3] An order for Western merchandise sent out from India to Aden in early spring would not be fulfilled until the following September at the earliest. And when a ship belonging to Ḥalfon, the son of Maḍmūn b. Japheth, mysteriously foundered off the South Arabian coast, four days' sail from Aden, news of its fate did not reach its home port until six months later. Adeni officials spent two years gathering information and testimonies before composing an official account of the events for the relatives of Alexandrian victims on board; that letter must have reached Alexandria about half a year after that.[4]

Vast geographical scope and limited, even precarious, means of transportation and communication compromised efficacy and safety in the conduct of overseas trade. The effects of distance and time somehow had to be mitigated. Moreover, even in a commercial culture based on the trust inherent in family relations and all-meaningful social bonds, all participants had to be held answerable for their actions, at least to some degree. By virtue of their geographical location and through formal and informal institutions, major entrepôts provided the organization and tools necessary to overcome the difficulties and risks of protracted travel and to track long-distance transactions.

Located at critical junctions of important trade routes, port cities allowed merchants to break up a physical journey into shorter, more manageable jaunts.[5] Services and organization within the entrepôt enabled both individuals and entire networks to divide what would have been single extenuated business ventures into safer, more circumscribed transactions. This chapter details how Aden fulfilled this role in the period of the Geniza merchants and what that meant for the merchants of the city and their overseas partners. Central to this discussion are (1) the institution that allowed local businessmen to represent the business interests of foreign or absentee merchants, and (2) the system of adjudication that ensured that disputes and claims from overseas parties could be adequately addressed.

Representing the Merchants: The Wakīl al-Tujjār

Once safely at port, a traveling merchant could gauge the local market, gather information about markets further afield, and decide what steps to take next. Depending on local and overseas conditions, the port might offer such merchant a number of options: he could sell all of his goods locally, buy more, then turn homeward; he could sell part of his consignment and then repack the rest along with new purchases and venture forward; if he had reason to hope that the market would pick up later in the season, he could choose to store some of his merchandise in town and defer sale until more lucrative times. Thanks to local businessmen working for no visible remuneration, all of these options were available not only to traveling merchants who accompanied their merchandise to Aden but also to overseas sedentary merchants whose merchandise arrived in town in the care of others.

The terms "*wakīl*," "*wakīl al-tujjār*," and the Hebrew equivalent, "*peqīd ha-soḥarīm*," translate to "trustee" or "representative of the merchants" and appear in a number of Cairo Geniza documents in connection with agents who handled other merchants' affairs. The first to discuss systematically the economic and social coordinates of these trustees was Shlomo Dov Goitein.[6] Basing his analysis on the copious Mediterranean material, he concluded that these titles designated individuals who served the interests of foreign merchants and who did so in an official or semi-official capacity. He discerned three interconnected functions of the *wakīl al-tujjār*: legal representation of foreign merchants in court, storage and marketing of merchandise, and arbitration in merchant partnerships.[7] The *dār (al-)wakāla*, a building that combined sale, storage, and sometimes residential facilities for foreign merchants, essentially served as a *wakīl*'s official place of business.[8]

Goitein placed considerable emphasis on the notion that these urban intermediaries performed their duties in an official or semi-official capacity, arguing that an established mechanism must have existed for officially confirming a *wakīl al-tujjār* to his office.[9] However, Goitein carefully noted that the *wakīl al-tujjār* was not the head of a merchants' guild but "a self-made, independent agent, in a society of independent merchants."[10] Subsequent scholars writing about trade in the medieval Muslim world have generally echoed Goitein's views.[11] Perhaps the most nuanced understanding of the issue appears in an article on the relationship between medieval commerce and the state by Abraham Udovitch, who believes that the ambiguity of the evidence and the fluidity of the institution point to "a movement from commerce to semi-officialdom."[12]

A careful reading of Goitein's analysis reveals that his argument about the official position of the merchants' representative relies on evidence from the careers of Maḍmūn b. Japheth and of a handful of other Jewish merchants and mercantile representatives who held government offices or who otherwise had close contact with the Muslim government of the realm.[13] He also connects the operation by some of these men of a *dār (al-)wakāla* with their official titles.[14] Without positive evidence of a formal connection between mercantile representation and the government in the pre-Mamluk period, however, such officials might merely have been running businesses independent of—even if benefiting from—their official standing. In other words, instead of acting as the appointee to a well-defined office, the *wakīl al-tujjār* might have rendered his services within a flexible framework of mercantile collaboration. The modes of operation varied according to political and social conditions and, as Goitein explicitly stated, according to the personal prestige of the individual acting as a representative of foreign or traveling merchants.[15]

Most of the evidence on the subject consists of fleeting, laconic references in letters and legal documents. References in Arabic literary or historical texts are few, elliptical, and as a rule come from later periods.[16] Administrative or fiscal treatises such as al-Makhzūmī's *Minhāj* do not discuss the issue of mercantile representation.[17] Turning to the evidence from Aden, Ibn al-Mujāwir mentions briefly a *dār al-wakāla* where a *wakāla* tax apparently was levied on imported merchandise but neither gives details about their function nor discusses the *wakīl* and his role in trade.[18] And while a broker or middleman (*dallāl*) and a brokerage fee (*dalāla*) appear frequently in the Rasulid economic texts, no mention is made of a *wakāla* tax or a building.[19]

That the city-based representative did not hold a formally appointed government office but rendered his services in a rubric that approximated the parameters of an informal partnership is also evident in the instances where a single overseas merchant relied on a number of different Adeni businessmen either at different times or simultaneously.[20] Several aspects of Maḍmūn b. Japheth's role as a mercantile representative emerge from his copious correspondence with Ben Yijū, who sent his friend consignments of pepper, cardamom, betel nut, and other India products to sell at the Adeni market; relied on the Adeni notable to supply bronze for his factory; and expected Maḍmūn to keep accounts of sales and purchases and to send balance sheets. Yet on different occasions, three other Adeni merchants—Maḍmūn's cousins Khalaf b. Isaac and Joseph b. Abraham as well as Joseph b. Meshullām—in addition to Yeshūʿā b. Jacob of the highland town of Jibla rendered similar services to Ben Yijū: they fielded his requests both from India and subsequently from Dhū Jibla and the Red Sea town of Zabīd and processed his merchandise in Aden.[21] Khalaf also tended to the affairs of other merchants,[22] as, it seems, did Joseph.[23] Florid expressions of gratitude fill the only two letters devoted entirely to thanking Adenis for commercial services rendered and graciousness shown: one went to Khalaf, the other to both Khalaf and Joseph.[24]

Finally, the language of the medieval traders casts additional doubt on the formality of the institution. The secondary literature often presents the term "*wakīl al-tujjār*" or its Hebrew equivalent, "*peqīd ha-soḥarim*," as a title conferred along with a formal office. Overall, however, the formula occurs infrequently in the Geniza period. With reference to Adeni merchants known to have taken care of the affairs of their non-Adeni colleagues,[25] only Ḥasan is hailed as a *wakīl* and only with reference to his involvement as an agent in specific transactions.[26] Thus, the evidence as a whole suggests that at the center of the institution of mercantile representation lay an organic relationship between foreign merchants and sedentary businessmen who represented their interests in the entrepôt city. The city offered opportunities for connections, and a representative's permanent urban residence and multiple local ties went hand in hand with his prestige, integrity, and dependability and guaranteed his answerability to the merchants he served. The informal nature of the institution is not a surprising phenomenon but rather fits the general picture of informality of trading mechanisms in the medieval Middle Eastern world.[27]

Men of Power:
Community Leadership and Mercantile Representation

There is little doubt that a successful *wakīl al-tujjār* first had to be a "successful merchant of means."[28] Breadth of experience in commercial transactions and business acumen rendered such a merchant capable of negotiating a variety of situations; in addition, success and long-term involvement in the trading world ensured that this person could rely on a wide range of business relations for information and favors. If indeed not an appointed official, the *wakīl al-tujjār* was also not a private business partner. The ability to represent absentee merchants without formal restrictions—to take possession of their merchandise, for example, and to dispose of it on the basis of informal understandings—and to mediate in mercantile disputes went above and beyond the limits of partnership. What were the sources of a *wakīl*'s discretionary power and the supports for this kind of authority?

Some observers have suggested that foreign origin was an important characteristic of the persons serving as merchants' representatives and that they generally belonged to foreign merchant groups living in diaspora.[29] Foreign origin and the connections it entailed may have been the decisive factor in an intermediary's career in other historical periods, but the opposite is true in the case of medieval Aden. The dominant merchant families were for the most part native Yemeni Jews or Jews who had emigrated as early as the 6th century from Mesopotamia and Iran and in all likelihood considered themselves rooted in Yemen. While Maḍmūn's Bundār clan may have originally hailed from Iran, the family was well settled in Aden by the Zurayid period and should be seen for all intents and purposes as native members of the local Adeni society.[30] That rootedness in fact constituted one of their greatest assets.

In the socially embedded economy of the Middle Ages, perhaps the most crucial factor for the career of someone whom people trusted with their livelihood was his status within the local community and his reputation beyond it—that is, the respect he commanded and the influence he exerted beyond the realm of commerce. Several of the known Mediterranean representatives were men of considerable status within their community. Goitein points to Muslim judges as well as Jewish physicians and other luminaries, including Jekuthiel Abu Yaʿqūb al-Ḥakīm, a powerful merchant and frequent benefactor of the poor who was the plaintiff in the protracted litigation against Joseph al-Lebdī that has already been discussed.[31] Another example of a powerful *wakīl tujjār* is Ḥisday b. Shaprūṭ, a leader of the Jewish community of Spain and a court physician who, in Goitein's words, "used the influence he gained" in the Spanish court "to establish himself as a great representative of the merchants." Ḥisday rightly boasts in a letter to the king of the Khazars that "all the business and all the affairs of the many merchants who come here from all the countries are being arranged through me."[32]

In Aden's compact and trade-oriented milieu, high communal status and the ability to render services to foreign transient or overseas merchants appear to have been inextricably connected. At least four of the known Jewish merchants' representatives were high-ranking community notables, with three of them—all related—known as *nagidim* ("heads of the Jews," or community leaders). Goitein states that "the trustee of the merchants served also as a head of the Jewish community in Southern Yemen"[33] and suggests that in a maritime city, the state would choose the merchants' trustee to serve as superintendent of the harbor and tax farmer at the customshouse.[34] The reverse would seem to be a slightly more accurate statement reflecting the realities of the careers of Maḍmūn and of the other sedentary Adeni merchants: anyone serving as head of the community and its judiciary and as a government official made a most appropriate merchant's representative.

The first Adeni mercantile representative to appear in the extant documents is Ḥasan b. Bundār, the father of Maḍmūn b. Japheth and apparently his predecessor in several social and economic functions. Ḥasan is sometimes referred to as "*sar ha-qehillot*," a title that distinguished some members of the Jewish upper class and implied a leading role in the community.[35] If Ḥasan and other male members of his immediate family were hailed as "princes of the congregations," his son, Maḍmūn, appears to have been the first to bear the title "*nagid ʿadan wa-al-hind*" (leader of the broader Jewish community of the Indian Ocean) as well as "trustee of the rulers of the sea and the deserts."[36] Maḍmūn's descendants, including his son, Ḥalfon/Khalaf; grandson, David; and great-grandson, Maḍmūn, are also styled *nagidim*.[37]

These were not empty honors but bespeak recognition of these men's real authority by the community on the one hand and by the Jewish ecumenical leadership on the other. These leaders included the head of the Palestinian yeshivot, based in Egypt at the time, and the leader of the Jewish diaspora (*rosh gola*), based in Babylon.[38] The titles appear in private letters addressing these men or indirectly referring to them as well as in legal documents produced in the courts of both Aden and Egypt. The first man to hold the title of *nagid* of Yemen was Maḍmūn, who became seriously embroiled with wider Jewish diaspora politics in the second quarter of the 6th/12th century. In a show of solidarity, Maḍmūn ordered that the name of Maṣliaḥ, the Palestinian *gaon* who had moved to Egypt in 521/1127, be read at synagogue after the established reading of the name of the *rosh gola*. The move provoked protest among some Egyptian merchants who opposed Maṣliaḥ's authority and were present in Aden at the time; furthermore, the arrival of a cousin of the Babylonian *rosh gola* in Yemen added fuel to the fire. While the position of Yemeni Jews indeed lay "between Babylon and the Mediterranean," this incident hints at the particular strength of Aden's ties with Egypt at a time when Jewish participation in the India trade had reached its zenith.[39]

In this context, the community leader's position was compatible with that of a representative of foreign transients or overseas merchants. Men such as Maḍmūn and his descendants not only represented the interests of a community that depended largely on trade but also were merchants. The combination of the aura of their communal standing with their social capital and commercial expertise fulfilled the requirements of trustworthiness and competence that must have been expected of a merchant's representative. This is not to say that the community leader's functions included by definition mercantile representation but rather that at the height of the India trade, the Aden's line of *nagidim* often played this role.

Limits existed on the powers of the merchants' representatives, even if they were *nagidim*, however. Whereas the *wakīl* generally seems to have had a kind of public sanction to perform routine tasks on behalf of others without documentation, at other times the same *wakīl* held a witnessed writ of *wakāla*.[40] In addition, when a dispute arose between merchants whose partnership he had served, a representative received official court notices or personal appeals from one of the two parties, provided notarized versions of his account books, and generally acted as an expert witness. To be valid evidence, the *wakīl*'s documents had to be notarized by a juridical assembly. In other words, mercantile representatives were readily available to the law and collaborated with one or more courts to solve disputes, as in one well-documented case.

In the protracted litigation between established Cairene merchant Jekuthiel Abū Yaʿqūb al-Ḥakīm and his partner, India trader Joseph al-Lebdī, the latter wrote to Ḥasan b. Bundār to request records of transactions performed on Joseph's behalf.[41] Acting as the partnership's agent in Aden, Ḥasan had stored merchandise belonging to Jekuthiel and Joseph and had followed instructions to sell the items separately.[42] He had entered the details of the various transactions in his ledger (*daftar*)[43] and had offered Joseph an advance of money against a consignment of pepper to be bought in Malabar.[44] In his letter of request for the records, al-Lebdī specified that in accordance with the demands of the court in Cairo, a copy of Ḥasan's *daftar* was not enough; the accounts had to be "written in court before the assembly of the elders and have their signatures in it."[45] In other words, the rabbinical court in Aden was responsible for ratifying Ḥasan's ledger. His function as a mercantile representative clearly did not give Ḥasan the prerogatives of an official, and his documents did not carry official validity; instead, he served as an expert witness, an informed and neutral party who provided pertinent information on the case at hand.

The processing of Ḥasan's records in the Lebdī affair also provides a clear image of the close collaboration between Adeni and Cairene courts, both of which played parts in a universal system of law that regulated or attempted to regulate Jewish affairs everywhere. Thus, while litigation took place in Egypt in this and other instances, the rabbinical court in Aden played an important role by producing, validating, and certifying operative documents. The final word on what a representative could and could not do rested with this ecumenical system, and he was answerable for his actions to the highest spiritual and political authorities of all Jews, who necessarily participated in this system and often functioned as judges. On one illustrative occasion, Ḥasan attempted to use his authority to effectively withhold the local assets of an Alexandrian merchant, Abū al-Faraj Nissīm, but this initiative was thwarted by an Egyptian *nagid*, Mevorakh.[46]

Nissīm passed through Aden on his way to India and apparently undertook to sell merchandise belonging to local Adeni merchants in the subcontinent's market with the understanding that he would send the proceeds back to the owners of the merchandise. When he failed to return as expected, the Adeni merchant community sounded the alarm. As a merchant's representative, Ḥasan possessed a consignment of camphor belonging to Nissīm and had been instructed to sell it and send the proceeds to Nissīm's family in Alexandria. The tension resulting from Nissīm's long absence led Ḥasan to the extraordinary measure of withholding the man's camphor or at least the proceeds from its sale as security against possible claims. The family members, who had been notified by Nissīm about the camphor and were expecting the proceeds from its sale, waited in vain.

A series of nine letters from the Cairo Geniza shed light on the negotiations that ensued. Despite Ḥasan's determination and his position as a representative of both the Egyptian man and the Adenis who had entrusted their goods to him, an intervention from the Egyptian *nagid*, Mevorakh, ended Ḥasan's action, forcing him to forward the money to the culprit's wife in Alexandria. The first letter by Nissīm's brother-in-law reveals that the most effective objection to Ḥasan's action was the legal prohibition against confiscation of one's property as security against possible (but not proven) transgressions and expected claims in the future; traders on their way to Yemen were to meet with Ḥasan to soften him as well as to warn him that sequestration was not permissible.[47] This incident highlights the real connections of the position of Jewish mercantile representative: his legal status and authority were tied primarily to the Jewish legal system and its internal hierarchies; he had little choice but to defer to the powerful Mevorakh and to comply with the injunction against unlawful and unjust seizure.[48]

A comparison of Ḥasan's retraction with the decisive pursuit and capture of the delinquent ʿAlī al-Fawfalī by Ḥasan's son, Maḍmūn, is instructive.[49] How did Maḍmūn have the power to outfit and deploy ships and troops against a single merchant who had not set foot in the city and whose flight appears to have been from his former colleagues—significantly, including Maḍmūn—rather than from the Muslim state? The state not only did not intervene but appears to have fully deferred to Maḍmūn's action. The extraordinary powers that Maḍmūn obviously wielded did not inhere in any commercial office that he or his father ever occupied; the extent to which he enforced his will testifies to his success as a businessman, to his authority as a community leader, and perhaps most of all to the significance of his liaison with the city's Muslim ruling elite, most notably general and governor deputy Bilāl b. Jarīr.

The distinction between the two capacities of *nagid* and representative of the merchants as well as the inherent complications in the combination of the two emerge from a case of complaint brought against Maḍmūn by three members of a Jewish community in the Yemeni highlands. The tensions that this case produced are apparent in the final verdict by the rabbinical court of Aden against the plaintiffs (three brothers from the city of Dhū Jibla) and in favor of the merchant and representative.[50] An earlier document, apparently written as a memo or summary for the Adeni court shortly before deliberations on the case at hand, details the events that led to the verdict.[51]

According to the plaintiffs, their father had placed a deposit with Maḍmūn's brother, Bundār. When Bundār died, the man from Dhū Jibla had "looked into his ledgers" (*dafātirihi*) and discovered the pending asset. Maḍmūn, who clearly had taken over his brother's affairs, wrote the man a witnessed receipt for the deposit, which he turned over to his sons. After the man's death, his sons tried to recover their property but succeeded only in infuriating Maḍmūn. According to the document, their heated correspondence with Maḍmūn contained "a lot of talk, which troubled his heart and angered him."[52] The affair ended when the Adeni court condemned the brothers for slander and fined them, providing Maḍmūn with a resounding vote of confidence from the elders of his community.[53]

Maḍmūn was standing trial in his capacity as a merchant, not as a community leader. Was this incident in any way related to challenges to his authority that arose at roughly the same time? It is difficult to assess the extent to which personal allegiance, sympathies, and politics played a role in the court's decision. Complaints against merchants' representatives who detained goods in their care or failed to settle accounts are not infrequent.[54] As discussed earlier, before the Jiblī brothers confronted Maḍmūn with his alleged failure properly to render accounts, his father, Ḥasan, had run into trouble in attempting to sequester Nissīm's goods. Still, the outcome of such complaints "depended on the specific circumstances of the persons concerned."[55]

Perhaps Ḥasan, who relented before the urgings of the Egyptian *nagid*, Mevorakh, had less clout than his son; it may be significant that nowhere is Ḥasan hailed as a *nagid*, although this lacuna may result more from the history of the title and institution in Yemen than from Ḥasan's position in the community. The circumstances and associations of the "victims" may also be important: when Ḥasan sequestered Nissīm's goods, the merchant's brother-in-law pleaded the case of the widow rather than that of the merchant himself, thus persuading the powerful Mevorakh to intervene and giving Ḥasan no choice but to defer to that authority. In Maḍmūn's case, the plaintiffs were relatively small fry from the mountains of Yemen moving against their own *nagid*, perhaps the most powerful man in the Jewish communities of the Indian Ocean world.

Business Routines

Focusing on the career and status of mercantile representatives in Maḍmūn's direct line runs the risk of ignoring the role of other men who were not *nagidim* but were simply well-respected local merchants performing the basic tasks of a *wakīl al-tujjār*. Two members of the Bundār clan, Khalaf b. Isaac and Joseph b. Abraham, as well as others of whom the sources provide only fleeting glimpses performed all the routine services associated with mercantile representation; they, too, played a significant role in the smooth operation of trading ventures. Their careers are, in fact, most illuminating for the study of mercantile representation in Aden, permitting the distinguishing of the functions of the institution from the added layer of communal and state involvement that Maḍmūn and his descendants brought into the picture.

What routine services could a merchant expect from any mercantile representative in Aden, whether that representative was Maḍmūn or his cousin, Khalaf? A document written by Khalaf and addressed to a well-known merchant and notable, Ḥalfon b. Nathanel, graphically reveals the many ways in which the Adeni merchant managed Ḥalfon's affairs in Aden while he traveled in India.[56] Khalaf's account (*ḥisāb*) maintained on Ḥalfon's behalf starts with credits for merchandise that Ḥalfon had sent to be sold in Aden, including various textiles, pepper, and musk, listing their value and a grand total in Ḥalfon's favor.[57] Khalaf then enumerated various deductions, including

- import taxes on some but not all of the merchandise[58] (indicating that Khalaf sold only part of the goods and paid taxes from the proceeds);
- cost of silver (vessels), gold coins, and coral[59] (Khalaf must have bought these on Ḥalfon's behalf, probably to send to him in India);
- rent for a storeroom and the cost of furnishing it with mats (*furush*)[60] (indicating that Khalaf stored some of the goods);
- the cost of airing and brushing (*sirqa*) two types of cloth included on the credits list but not on the tax deductions list[61] (items imported but not sold and therefore taxed but instead stored in the rented space; before storage, bales of clothes and fabrics that had traveled across the sea in a damp hold needed to be unwrapped and aired individually).

The final item on this list illustrates the importance of stopping at Aden to open, air, and sell, store, or repack and reexport merchandise that would be damaged by prolonged exposure to shipboard moisture. Packing and unpacking was a laborious and time-consuming task: "There was not enough time to unpack and repack," says Maḍmūn in a fragmentary note to Ben Yijū.[62] Yet doing so helped to prevent disasters, for even the relatively short voyage from India to Aden could ruin a wide variety of goods. Pepper, for example, spoils if kept in damp ship holds for long periods of time, a fact that centuries later tarnished somewhat the Portuguese triumph of circumnavigating Africa and circumventing Middle Eastern middlemen in the spice race. In one of his letters to Ben Yijū, Joseph b. Abraham in Aden notes with palpable disappointment, "As for the sack of lemons and the grapes, they arrived ruined, rotten; we threw them out."[63]

Apart from helping to preserve merchandise, opening and repacking large consignments into smaller batches was routine in a system that diffused risk by dividing goods among several ships. Merchants residing on either side of Aden along the geographic trajectory of the India trade relied on a representative in Aden to break up their goods into small parcels and judiciously place them on different ships. Maḍmūn, for example, oversaw the repacking of a large consignment of copper into three manageable packages, which he then sent to Ben Yijū in India on different ships.[64]

Packing itself was crucial to the success of a business venture.[65] In one sad letter from Aden, the hapless author laments that after a horrific trip from Egypt, he arrived at the Indian Ocean port to find that his rosewater had spilled out of its container and his glass items had been shattered.[66] Properly packed merchandise no doubt fared better, and some accounts drawn by Adeni representatives for overseas clients provide detailed entries for the costs of packing. Glass vessels were placed in baskets in a careful and orderly arrangement[67] or in "good" and "strong" crates.[68] Other goods were wrapped in skins[69] or rough cloth such as canvas.[70] These materials were charged to the recipient's account, along with the fee paid to the *muʿabī*, who did the packing.[71] The mercantile representative also concerned himself with proper labeling and finding a reliable escort, thereby ensuring that the shipment reached the appropriate party.[72]

All in all, it is hard to imagine the conduct of overseas trade without mercantile representatives. Even the simple task of transporting merchandise from the beach and the customshouse to the market required planning and local leverage. The same man whose rosewater spilled and whose glass was broken could not find a porter and had to carry his consignment of coral to the market by himself: most of the coral broke.[73]

Merchants residing overseas found it imperative to have an intermediary at Aden. Would Ben Yijū ever have managed to market the products of his bronze factory or to sell his pepper and procure the necessary raw metals from the West without Maḍmūn's mediation? Even with the help of his slave/agent Bamma, of the shipowners to whom he entrusted goods and money, and perhaps of other unnamed associates, Ben Yijū required the expertise and local knowledge not only of Maḍmūn b. Japheth but also of other Adeni contacts, including Khalaf b. Bundār, Joseph b. Abraham, and Joseph b. Meshullam. All of these men ran Ben Yijū's mercantile errands in the city and kept him informed of events in the Adeni and Cairene markets. Countless other merchants, only a fraction of whose names have survived, relied on the services of local businessmen when affairs took the merchants or their goods to and through Aden.

While other merchants traveled through Aden and sent their merchandise there from faraway places, their Adeni representatives usually stayed put. No evidence indicates that Maḍmūn ever traveled, and every glimpse of him has the city in the background. Maḍmūn's father, Ḥasan, may have ventured as far as India at least on one occasion, at least partly to purchase pepper for Jekuthiel Abū Yaʿqūb al-Ḥakīm.[74] However, traveling seems to have compromised the effectiveness of an Adeni merchant's mediation on behalf of absentee business associates. By definition, the services of a merchant's representative or of any middleman were most effective when rendered from within the confines of the city and its market. The familiar urban context empowered the *wakīl tujjār* simultaneously to negotiate the affairs of several merchants and to deal promptly and efficiently with crises.

Striking Deals

In addition to being in charge of absentee merchants' goods and performing routine tasks related to the safekeeping and processing of these items, merchants in Aden acted as mediators for foreign and local businessmen, witnessing and recording deals struck between merchants, receiving mail for foreigners, and generally facilitating the conduct of business in town. As a sedentary local merchant and as a businessman serving other merchants, the *wakīl al-tujjār* must have had a base or an office, a convenient space where he could fulfill his many duties. While the prevalent view is that this space should be associated with the *dār (al-)wakāla*, a term for a commercial building type and institution appearing in some medieval sources, an alternative hypothesis highlights the combination of commercial and residential functions in the houses of prominent merchants throughout the Middle East and perhaps especially in Indian Ocean ports.[75]

Several Geniza papers and other sources pertaining to commercial life in Cairo mention buildings by the designation "*dār (al-)wakāla*/*(al-)wakālāt*," variously translated as "agency house," "warehouse," or "caravansary." The functions of these establishments as documented by Goitein included sale, storage, and a variety of business services involving the *wakīl al-tujjār*. While little specific information has survived about who financed and ran the *dār (al-)wakāla* in pre-Mamluk times, references exist to a *ṣāḥib dār al-wakāla*, which perhaps indicates private ownership or at least management of some of these establishments.[76] The evidence for such spaces in Aden is slim. Ibn al-Mujāwir mentions briefly a *dār al-wakāla* where a special *wakāla* tax was paid; the payment of a tax perhaps designates this building as a government-run institution. Moreover, the Geniza documents contain not a single mention of a building by that name. It is not unlikely that some of the functions of the Cairene establishments took place at the *dār al-saʿāda/saʿīda*, the city's wholesale center.[77] Another possible business address for an Adeni mercantile representative was his residence.

Evidence that the mercantile representatives and other Adeni merchants conducted business at home may be extracted from the frequent references to Maḍmūn's *majlis* and *dār*. One letter writer speaks of a delivery of money that took place in Maḍmūn's "noble *majlis*" (*fī majlisihā al-karīm*). There, in the presence of the venerable Maḍmūn, one merchant gave another businessman two hundred local dinars.[78] In the Geniza papers, the word "*majlis*" (literally "seat") usually refers to a reception hall or social room in a residence.[79] Sometimes, however, a *majlis* is associated with high judges and decision making, and *nagidim* indeed used such rooms as audience halls.[80] It is thus unclear whether in this case Maḍmūn's role was that of a private businessman who acted as a witness to a transaction between colleagues in his own domestic reception hall or that of a communal legal official who presided over the exchange in his court of law.

That at least some business took place at Maḍmūn's house becomes clear from two Geniza references. In a long letter to Ben Yijū, Khalaf b. Isaac notes that merchandise salvaged from the shipwreck near the Bāb al-Mandab has already cleared customs and is being transported to the "house of the venerable *shaykh* my lord Maḍmūn" (*ilā dār al-shaykh al-ajall mawlā'ya Maḍmūn b. al-Ḥasan*).[81] Moreover, Maḍmūn speaks of weighing a consignment of cardamom at what may be the same house.[82] These admittedly fleeting but clearly significant references to a space identified unequivocally with Maḍmūn conjure the praising portrait painted by al-Jāḥiẓ of great and noble merchants officiating from home: "In their courtyard they are like kings on their thrones, with beggars calling on them and customers coming to see them."[83]

Did the business address of a representative, whether a *dār* (*al-*) *wakāla* or any other space of commerce, confer official validity to a transaction concluded there? Goitein argues in the affirmative on the basis of a document stating "that offers for the conclusion of a partnership were binding only when they were made in a *dār wakāla*, or merchants' warehouse, but not anywhere else."[84] The Geniza paper in question is a legal deposition by four merchants testifying about "the customary practices of merchants in Egypt in the formation of partnerships."[85] Indeed, the witnesses emphasize the value of concluding a partnership transaction in a *dār* (*al-*)*wakāla* as well as in a storehouse (*makhzan tujjār*).[86] This probably signifies that any space commonly recognized as a place of commercial business equally validated the transactions performed therein. In the case of Aden, this category would include the houses of people such as Maḍmūn. Furthermore, the deposition stresses that several traders should be present[87] and that the specifics of the partnership should be entered in the book of "the *wakīl* or the merchants."[88] The deponents further specify that a similar deal is invalid when struck in the middle of the street and later carried out by the person who proposed the partnership if no one is present.[89]

In other words, unilateral, unwitnessed action invalidated an agreement. But while neither the act of recording in a *wakīl*'s ledger nor location at a *dār* (*al-*)*wakāla* or other commonly recognized place of commercial business constituted absolute prerequisites for contracting legal and valid mutual obligation between two merchants, both space and record mattered. The city's topography was thus virtually marked by commercial activity, and space itself could contribute to the legal status of commercial transactions enacted in it.

Storage

This Cairene legal deposition highlights the role of storerooms as centers of commercial activity. It is easy to imagine the hustle and bustle of storage areas in a port city such as Aden: local and traveling merchants or their representatives would bring merchandise for safekeeping and would return to pick it up when the market was good or when a ship was ready to sail; prospective buyers would come to inspect stored goods that interested them; storage workers would air, unpack, and repack items, carry some off to the market, and rearrange the rest in the remaining space. This congregation of merchants and others turned storerooms into much more than depositories of merchandise; there, information was exchanged, deals struck, and acquaintances made. Storerooms annexed to prominent local merchants' residences thus intensified the public character of those residences.

Storage itself was crucial to the conduct of international trade and an important service for traveling and absentee merchants. Given the timing of Indian Ocean trade and the climatic conditions at many of its ports, waiting for markets to turn, prospective buyers to arrive, and ships to sail meant that merchandise had to remain in Aden for variable periods of time and had to be kept safe from thieves and the elements. The length of transit for merchandise must have varied greatly. The provenance of goods and their time of arrival at Aden, the vigor of the local market, and the circumstances affecting arrivals and departures of foreign buyers determined how long specific consignments remained in the city during any given year.

Under ideal conditions, turnover was swift, with westbound traders loading Eastern merchandise sometime before the end of the winter so that they could make their way up the Red Sea while the favorable winter southerlies prevailed.[90] Such smooth transit was not guaranteed, however, as unpredictable events could delay merchants at one end or the other or prevent them from reaching Aden. One letter, for example, reports that communications with Egypt had broken down for more than a year, and people in Aden remained uncertain whether anyone would arrive from Egypt as a result of an epidemic (*al-wabāʾ*).[91] Other circumstances could make the immediate sale of a particular consignment inadvisable.[92] Moreover, merchants coming from the West sometimes left unsold merchandise in Aden before proceeding to India, presumably with the understanding that their Adeni contacts would see to the sale or that the owners would later have ready access to the merchandise.[93]

Entries for cost of storage in the Jewish merchants' letters and accounts reveal that the merchandise rested on mats (*furush*) spread on the storeroom's dirt floor to keep the merchandise free of dust, mud, and moisture. When storing goods for an absentee merchant either in his own storeroom for which he charged rent or in a storeroom rented from a third party, a mercantile representative bought these mats from local market and charged his customer's account a separate fee for them. Khalaf b. Isaac, for example, charged Ḥalfon b. Nathanel 1.5 dinars for storeroom space plus .25 dinar for mats.[94]

The organization of storage space must have been somewhat of a challenge for local representatives who handled and stored goods for several merchants. Since the preserved documents contain few complaints about lost or misplaced merchandise, consignments belonging to different merchants apparently were generally well labeled and kept in discrete parts of the storeroom as much as possible. In at least one instance, clutter resulted when owners deemed unsold merchandise and remainders of large consignments worthless and abandoned them in storerooms.[95] Moreover, items at times became buried under other merchandise, making immediate retrieval impossible: Joseph al-Lebdī used this excuse when asked for the record of all transactions he had conducted on behalf of Jekuthiel, claiming that the document was buried under baskets of indigo, presumably in Jekuthiel's storeroom.[96] In addition to keeping track of transactions and the flow of goods in and out of his storerooms, the merchant's representative clearly had the added headache of maintaining some order in the storerooms.

Finally, keeping merchandise safe from humans was not always easy, even in the circumscribed milieu of well-guarded Aden. While the sources are virtually devoid of obvious references to ordinary thieves, looting of storerooms could and did take place during times of political instability and civil unrest. Describing the conflict between the city's two Zurayid rulers, Khalaf b. Isaac writes of the burning of houses and the looting of storerooms.[97]

Documentation: The Wakīl*'s Ledger*

The cases already examined demonstrate that both merchants and mercantile representatives kept records of their actions and transactions. Is it reasonable to assume that each merchant of some importance maintained a kind of personal archive and that mercantile representatives would have accrued the most voluminous such collections? Written documents were useful for keeping and setting records straight and could serve as evidence in courts of law. Indeed, the world of merchants represented in the Cairo Geniza has produced two types of trade-related records: unwitnessed accounts or ledgers and witnessed, legal documents of investment, partnership, acknowledgment of or release from debt, and empowerment.

Formal commercial legal documents are rarer. Neither Islamic nor Jewish law required written contracts, and Geniza scholarship has shown that informal arrangements were much more extensive and frequent than formal contracts.[98] Both the normative legal discussions of Muslim jurists and the Geniza material, however, confirm that documents were sometimes drawn to seal contractual relationships; such writs could serve as evidence at the dissolution of the contract, especially in case of difficulties such as the death of a partner or disagreements.[99] Surviving documents pertaining to the India trade also show that merchants, including those who often acted as mercantile representatives, sometimes officially appointed colleagues to take possession of merchandise and deal with it on their behalf.[100]

Conversely, numerous informal accounts, ledgers, and lists have survived, demonstrating that such documents could play an important role in both routine settlement of business and adjudication of disputes. The Lebdī affair provides ample evidence that at least Ḥasan b. Bundār kept a detailed account of transactions he participated in or brokered. Maḍmūn must also have kept extensive ledgers; his letters to Ben Yijū in India contain detailed accounts of the multifaceted transactions he performed on behalf of his friend and colleague. Despite meticulous documentation and close personal ties, however, the occasional wrinkle was unavoidable. One letter betrays Maḍmūn's annoyance with Ben Yijū's claim that he had not received a payment for pepper: "My lord's account is wrong, you only imagined it; I have the records."[101]

In the dispute between Maḍmūn and the family from Dhū Jibla, records again play a prominent role. When Maḍmūn's brother, Bundār, died, Yaʿqūb ha-Kohen, the father of the Jiblī family, went in person to Aden to lay claim on a deposit he had made with the deceased and had had recorded, presumably in Bundār's book. After searching Bundār's records and finding evidence of the deposit, Maḍmūn ostensibly gave the man a witnessed writ of the outstanding debt.[102] The man's sons brandished this document in their complaint against Maḍmūn. As Maḍmūn's irritation rose in the face of their complaints, he challenged them to come down to Aden and show him their piece of paper.[103] Documents obviously mattered; less clear is whether the eventual condemnation and fining of the three brothers means that they never produced the disputed document or that their writ carried less weight and validity than Maḍmūn's records.

Thus, it seems fair to expect that sedentary merchants' representatives and merchants in general must have had kept some sort of working archive.[104] The Geniza documents themselves provide indirect evidence: most striking are groups of preserved documents belonging to single merchants, such as Ibn ʿAwkal and Nahray b. Nissīm in the early and later parts of the 5th/11th century, respectively.[105] The sensational archaeological find of early 7th/13th-century mercantile papers in a building described by the excavator as the "Sheykh's house" in Quṣayr al-Qadīm provides a model of what the remains of such an archive might look like.[106] Indeed, excavations revealed a complex of apartments, storerooms, and two stairways leading either to a second story or to the roof in the Islamic segment of the site.[107] The owner of the structure has been identified with *shaykh* Abū Mufarrij on the basis of references in the documents; he appears to have been the head of a trading clan, and the complex may have housed at least two generations of his extended family.[108]

The Quṣayr collection comprises primarily economic texts. Could this really have been a family business archive similar to what Maḍmūn or his father, Ḥasan, would have kept for reference and future use? Li Guo originally described the find as "the only private archive known so far of a Muslim community" and later dubbed it "a private archive in the loose sense of the term."[109] The archaeological context of the thousands of scraps of paper that made up the 150 reconstructed documents is a little puzzling. The fragments were apparently scattered inside and outside the structure and were mixed in with pottery and other artifacts.[110] Moreover, they were reportedly shredded by hand into small pieces and possibly even "kneaded into a paper ball of sorts."[111] However, the structure was clearly a residential complex with storage capacity, a situation that fits nicely with the evidence from Aden and al-Mukhā for overlapping domestic and commercial functions of merchants' houses: a document depository would not have been out of place here.

The fragmentary state of the papers may suggest that at the time of abandonment, they were no longer in use and were not being kept in an orderly fashion for future reference. Were these writings kept as a *geniza*? On the one hand, the presence of ritual texts mixed in with economic material would seem to point to the religiously inflected custom of preserving the written word. On the other hand, if indeed deliberate, the shredding and kneading of the paper appears to suggest a different impulse. Unless the postdepositional history of the assemblage can be ascertained with any degree of certainty, the question will remain open. Whether an abandoned and forgotten archive or a *geniza* remnant of an archive, however, this important find allows a glimpse of a merchant's paperwork and testifies to the type of documents that the owner of a commercial establishment had once kept close at hand for ready reference.

Settlement of Estates, Jewish Courts, and the State

Legal mediation constituted a main component of a distinguished sedentary merchant's role as a trustee and an intermediary. In fact, Goitein considered the representative's legal duties to be his defining function.[112] As has already been discussed, Ḥasan b. Bundār provided expert testimony in disputes between merchants. In conjunction with the rabbinical court of Aden, Maḍmūn and other Adeni merchants who acted as representatives also took the necessary actions when the death of a merchant with active assets in the India trade necessitated the settlement of his estate. The extant documentation of such settlements reinforces the picture drawn thus far: local courts worked in close collaboration with Jewish courts in Cairo, with Aden's prominent merchants participating by facilitating the process of recovery, proper storage, and dispatch of salvaged goods to the appropriate parties.

Just as the Jewish courts in Egypt resorted to the testimony of Adeni mercantile representatives when disputes broke out in Egypt between two Egyptian India trade partners, so too Egyptian courts and families turned to Aden when an Egyptian merchant died on the India route and the settlement of his estate was pending. It is significant that none of the various Adeni merchants who at times acted as mercantile representatives for absentee merchants ever appears in the documents as dealing with cases of estate settlement after shipwreck. The parties involved in every case of such settlement are the courts of Egypt and Aden and those members of the Bundār family who were not only mercantile representatives but also *nagidim*. The dramatic episodes that unfold in the pages of legal documents and letters clearly show that these men had authority to take possession and dispose appropriately of merchandise belonging to deceased merchants.

Property that became the object of negotiation could comprise salvaged goods belonging to a sedentary merchant, salvaged goods belonging to a merchant lost in a shipwreck, or live assets tied up in transactions along the India route at the time of their rightful owner's death. The Geniza documents offer examples of all three scenarios. When Fatan Swamī's bigger vessel foundered on its way from Fandayrana to Aden, Khalaf b. Isaac wrote to Ben Yijū to report what had been lost and what had been saved of the India merchant's consignments traveling on the ill-fated vessel.[113] Remarkably, despite the losses incurred, Ben Yijū's consignment still went through the customshouse, with taxes presumably paid. Also noteworthy is the readiness of the system in place, with the iron going directly to the storehouse of Maḍmūn, who represented Ben Yijū in that business affair.

Affairs involving shipwreck rarely ended so simply, with a swiftly deployed and relatively successful salvage operation and a quick paragraph in a single letter. More often than not, both the mercantile representative and the courts in Aden and in Cairo became fully involved in the identification and management of outstanding assets and goods, the fulfillment of pending obligations, the settlement of estates, and the notification of interested parties overseas, whether the merchants or their families. Two documents, also examined earlier in the context of shipwreck and salvage, and three others relating to two more maritime incidents span the careers of three successive and related Adeni agents and *nagidim*, adequately explaining the process by which justice and information were dispensed.

The first case unfolds in a remarkable letter sent by the Egyptian court to Maḍmūn b. Japheth and concerning the estate of Ḥalfon

b. Shemarya Ibn Jamāhir, who died at sea and whose corpse washed up on the port city's shores.[114] Maḍmūn had taken possession of the unlucky trader's salvaged goods and had recognized the body with the help of an Egyptian merchant passing through town at the time. The eerie description of the corpse's identifiable profile precedes the report on the appointment of a trustee who would travel to Aden and to whom Maḍmūn was to deliver the salvaged goods and other assets. Recognizing Maḍmūn's position as a merchant's representative, the Egyptian court in effect notified him of the appointment of the trustee over the drowned merchant's estate. Egyptian authorities clearly deemed it important to follow this procedure of appointing an attorney for the settlement of the estate rather than having Maḍmūn simply send the material to Egypt.

The second case involves the mysterious wreck in which an entire ship belonging to Maḍmūn's son, Ḥalfon, disappeared within earshot of its sister vessel on the way to India. As has already been discussed, in 547/1153, the rabbinical court in Aden addressed a letter to the father-in-law of one of the victims, Hiba b. Abī Saʿd.[115] This document reveals that in addition to being a merchant and shipowner, Ḥalfon had his father's title and presumably his corresponding authority of *nagid* and continued his father's service of foreign and absentee merchants. Importantly, however, two years passed and many interviews were conducted before the court could compose its report.[116]

A marginal note on the verso of the letter provides information about the settlement of the man's estate. Goitein reads the relevant phrases as denoting that the man's property was sequestered in full by the ruler. The writing is unclear at that point, but I would suggest a different reading: "As for [his] estate, the court [*bet din*] has taken possession of the entirety of his property."[117] I find this reading more likely because no other Zurayid period evidence indicates that local rulers ever confiscated salvaged goods. Moreover, Ḥalfon b. Maḍmūn ultimately took custody of the estate until a rightful claimant arrived from Egypt; an undated subsequent legal document reveals that the widow of Hiba b. Abī Saʿd received a sum from her husband's estate.[118] If interpreted correctly, these events suggest a well-established and orderly system of dealing with potentially disputed property. Such a system would have added to the port's attraction for foreign merchants; instead of seeing the place as a rapacious exploiter, foreign merchants could expect that their property rights would normally be upheld.

The third case of shipwreck, salvage, and estate settlement to be discussed here appears in a document of release or acquittance (*barā'*) drafted by the rabbinical court in Fusṭāṭ for the *nagid* Maḍmūn b. David (that is, the great-grandson of Maḍmūn) for the estate of Petaḥya, a merchant who drowned near the Yemeni coast.[119] Maḍmūn II had apparently taken possession of the salvaged merchandise and had forwarded the equivalent sum to the victim's family in Alexandria in care of a Muslim *qāḍī*. This affair highlights the fact that his position did not absolve a *wakīl al-tujjār* from the kind of responsibility inherent in commercial relationships: by taking possession of someone's goods under any circumstances, a merchant's representative was held liable vis-à-vis the rightful owner or his heirs. Maḍmūn's liability ended when he restored the goods to the rightful heirs of the rightful owner, as the document of release marked.

The final case involves a package of pearls (presumably shipwrecked and salvaged). Both the court in Aden under Maḍmūn b. David and the court in Cairo under Abraham Maimonides take part in the litigation, and the witnesses commute between the two places of adjudication: thus, one of the parties involved, Abū al-Khayr al-Ḥalabī, testifies in Aden before the court (*fī majlis*) of Maḍmūn b. David about proceedings in Cairo before Abū al-Manā' (Abraham) Maimonides.[120] If indeed the term "*majlis*" is to be interpreted as a court of law, as this context suggests, this document sheds additional light on the potential conflict inherent in being both a merchant's representative, whose actions may be disputed by clients and who needs a record of release for his actions, and the head of the rabbinical court in Aden, who is supposed to solve the disputes and issue the documents. The efficient, relatively fast, and largely informal way in which Ben Yijū received notification of his losses at sea and of the safe handling of his salvaged merchandise compares favorably with the protracted, involved, and formal procedures followed when merchants from Egypt either lost merchandise at sea or perished in the Indian Ocean. The distance between Aden and Cairo or Alexandria was at least twice or three times as daunting as that between Aden and India, both in terms of traveling time and inherent risk. Mercantile representatives and courts in Aden, Egyptian courts, and an assortment of go-betweens had to apply themselves and collaborate to bring about closure to merchants who had suffered losses or families whose members had died at sea.

Beyond the Inner Circle: Commercial Disputes across Denominational Lines

The legal system that provided the framework for all the mercantile relations discussed here had no tangible means of enforcement. It relied instead on the authority it derived from communal bonds. People complied and conformed because of communal pressure and their leaders' prestige and influence; such influence stemmed from economic power as well as political clout derived from their relations with Muslim state dignitaries—that is, what Mark Cohen describes as an equivalent to the Muslim rulers' *hayba*.[121]

Some disputes between merchants remained unresolved despite the efforts of representatives and courts. The circumstances that led to a breakdown of the system must have varied, but the result was that one party would resort to an Islamic court of law and seek to obtain an Islamic legal document (*ḥujja*) in his favor. Two examples of such incidents in the India trade documents reveal that in Aden, such impasses could usually be overcome. On one occasion, Maḍmūn b. Ḥasan handled a lawsuit brought by the rather eccentric trader Makhlūf b. Mūsā al-Nafūsī against Ben Yijū. Makhlūf, whose profile emerges clearly from several pages devoted to him in Goitein's work, traveled to Aden and from there either threatened to obtain or obtained an Islamic writ against Ben Yijū in India.[122] Maḍmūn's intervention saved the day, if only by having Ben Yijū pay a hefty sum to get rid of the plaintiff.[123] In a different case from the days of Maḍmūn's grandson, David, one merchant took advantage of his adversary's absence and obtained an Islamic legal document absolving him from his debt. Again, further friction was avoided through the intervention of both "the elders"—presumably the members of the local rabbinical court—and "our *nagid* David."[124]

What happened when trouble arose between members of the Jewish traders' network and their non-Jewish India trade partners? Somewhat surprisingly, perhaps, the Geniza documents are almost silent about such disputes: the emerging picture generally shows harmonious collaboration across denominational lines rather than sectarian competition and confrontation. One significant exception, however, reveals a great deal about the limitations of both the merchants' representatives and the courts in mediating and solving mercantile disputes. The dispute in question arose between Ben Yijū and an unnamed partner who also had disagreements with Khalaf b. Isaac and Joseph b. Abraham, whose letters detail the affair.[125]

The man responsible for the trouble, at least from the Jewish traders' point of view, is referred to by the variously spelled designation "*kārdār*," which may apply to a port official[126] or to an "agent or middleman" who procured local products for overseas merchants.[127] His appearances in Geniza letters dating from the second quarter of the 6th/12th century suggest that this man came into repeated contact with Ben Yijū and through him with Khalaf and Joseph. The role of either port official or middleman could have brought the *kārdār* into frequent contact with those two men. The relationship was clearly both long and bumpy: writing in approximately 532/1138, Joseph b. Abraham is so incensed with the *kārdār*'s apparent callousness that he urges Ben Yijū to threaten the man with "excommunication" or "censure."[128] In another missive dating to about 541/1146, Khalaf openly curses the man for failing to deliver a consignment of cardamom for which he must have received payment; Khalaf asks Ben Yijū to deal with the *kārdār* and to spare Khalaf and Joseph the trouble of having to do so.[129]

The precise meaning of that early and clearly unfulfilled threat of "excommunication" is of particular interest because it illuminates the checks and balances in place for cases above and beyond both the influence of a *wakīl* and the power of the courts. Of course, excommunication could only be meaningfully directed against a person of the same religious community. Was the *kārdār* a Jew living in India? The extreme harshness of the curses used by both Khalaf and Joseph seemingly could not have been used against a member of the faith, and the absence of his name from their correspondence might also suggest that he lay outside the inner circle of family, ethnic, and religious affiliation—in short, that he was a despised outsider. The story is complicated, however, by evidence that the *kārdār* may have in fact been connected to Ben Yijū through his marriage in India; during his long stay there, Ben Yijū appears to have married a non-Jewish Indian woman.[130]

If the *kārdār* was not a member of the broader Jewish community, then, the expressions based on the root *sh-m-t* (to ban or excommunicate) should be understood in the metaphorical sense.[131] Khalaf and Joseph never discuss the possibility of taking the "accursed *kārdār*" to court or threaten legal action against his transgressions; the rabbinical court at Aden, which held jurisdiction over the "lands of Yemen and India" and more precisely over the Jewish communities of the Indian Ocean, had no power over this non-Jewish man, just as the community could not excommunicate him in the literal sense. However, the wronged Jewish traders could ostracize the transgressor, expelling him from their community of reputable merchants and fair play. A move to discredit the man in the eyes of other merchants might indeed constitute a serious threat and an effective weapon against arbitrary behavior in a trading world where all players were to some degree interdependent and where mutual favor, trust, and good reputation formed the cornerstones of business relationships.

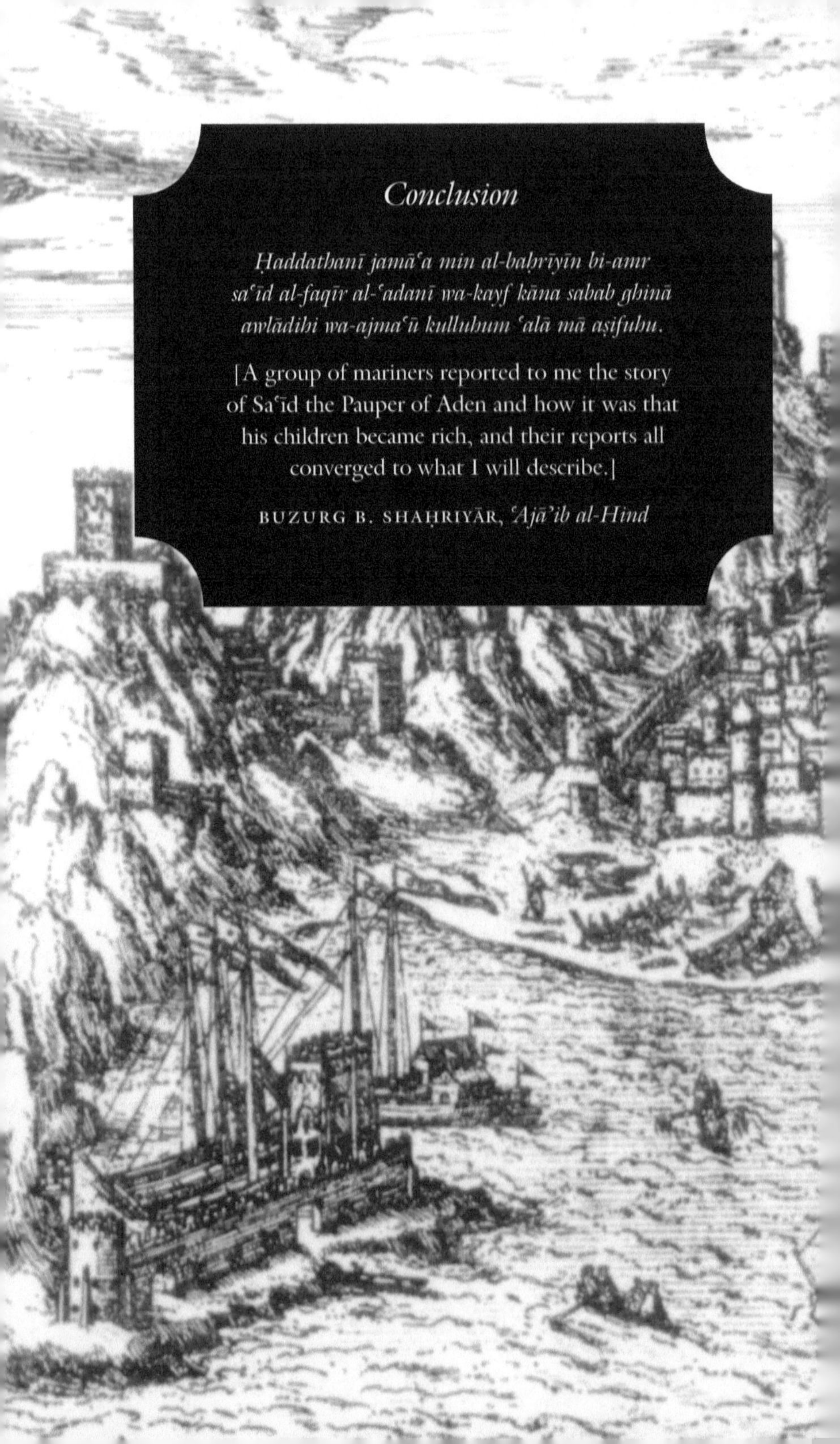

Conclusion

Ḥaddathanī jamāʿa min al-baḥrīyīn bi-amr saʿīd al-faqīr al-ʿadanī wa-kayf kāna sabab ghinā awlādihi wa-ajmaʿū kulluhum ʿalā mā aṣifuhu.

[A group of mariners reported to me the story of Saʿīd the Pauper of Aden and how it was that his children became rich, and their reports all converged to what I will describe.]

BUZURG B. SHAHRIYĀR, *ʿAjāʾib al-Hind*

In July 909/1503, Italian adventurer Ludovico di Varthema put into the port of Aden on a ship traveling east from the Red Sea. He saw Aden as "the strongest city that was ever seen on level ground," with "walls on two sides, and on the other sides . . . very large mountains." The city was "extremely beautiful" and "the capital of Arabia Felix." The bustling port appeared to be the "rendezvous for all ships which come from India Major and Minor, from Ethiopia and from Persia," and Ludovico conveyed a sense of crossroads by noting that "all ships bound for Mecca put in here." He was impressed by the strict supervision of port traffic by "officers of the Sultan" who meticulously recorded for each incoming ship "whence it comes, the nature of its cargo, when it left its own country and how many persons were on board." These officials then ensured that no ship left the harbor "without paying the dues to the Sultan." And he expressed relief that "the Sultan of this country never puts any one to death."[1]

This book has drawn a portrait of the medieval port of Aden in a much earlier, formative, and crucial yet hitherto understudied period of its commercial history. I have followed the city's historical trajectory from independent city-state to major maritime outlet of a larger Yemeni state and have traced the concomitant development of its urban form and commercial institutions. In the earlier of these two periods, from 480/1080 to 696/1174, the Zurayid dynasty and the merchants who made the city their base of operations laid the foundations of control and defense of the city's most valuable assets—its harbor, its customshouse, and its market. I have shown that Aden's seafront wall and two forts shielded the city from predators and transgressors of all kinds and that although it served a military defensive function, the fortification system primarily constituted a means of controlling mercantile traffic and ensuring that no goods escaped assessment by the city's customshouse.

The customshouse and the institution of commercial taxation emerge as important parameters of commercial organization in medieval Aden. The remarkable preservation of merchants' testimonies in the Cairo Geniza has enabled me to present and contextualize the earliest available evidence for customshouse procedures, customs personnel, and the port's taxation regime. My analysis of the Geniza documents has shown that the Zurayids presided over a customshouse that efficiently extracted substantial taxes from the lucrative Indian Ocean trade; that in administering that customshouse the rulers co-opted prominent Adeni merchants, as is illustrated by the case of Maḍmūn b. Japheth, a leading member of the local Jewish community in the first half of the 6th/12th century; and that although merchants paid dearly for the privilege of trading in or through Aden, the differential rates of high import taxes and low export taxes made the burden bearable and further encouraged traders to use the Adeni market as a terminus.

After the Ayyubid conquest of Yemen in 696/1174, the city's integration into a larger Yemeni state in no way diminished its status as a city or as an entrepôt, and the new rulers immediately grasped its immense revenue-yielding potential. They renewed urban buildings and defenses, bolstered and intensified control of commercial life, and further systematized the methods of taxation. Dating to the end of Ayyubid rule, Ibn al-Mujāwir's detailed account of customs procedures speaks to these developments. Also part of the systematization of government involvement in commerce was the Ayyubids' establishment of maritime patrols that ensured the safe conduct of ships at least within the city's maritime realm.

These trends continued into the subsequent era, when the members of the Rasulid dynasty inherited the Yemeni state from their Ayyubid patrons. The Aden that Ludovico di Varthema saw and admired under the relatively short-lived Tahirid dynasty (858–923/1454–1517) in fact constituted merely the fading successor of the bustling Rasulid city. Between the final years of the Ayyubid period and Ludovico's visit, the city under the Rasulids had grown, partly to accommodate increasing volume of trade, and had witnessed the unprecedented integration of Old World economies into what Janet Abu Lughod has described as the world system of 1300.[2] The official Rasulid texts mentioned here attest to the Rasulid state's intense commercial interests by providing voluminous and detailed entries on every aspect of maritime trade, with particular emphasis on Aden and the administration of its port. The dispatch to Rasulid Yemen of embassies from China, India, Iran, and Egypt, conversely, demonstrates the increasing interdependence of polities as well as economies in this period.[3] Many of these embassies passed through Aden, and both their visits and the gifts they bore constituted tokens of the more generalized and voluminous exchange between these different segments of the world system. The city sustained this increased trade and was sustained by it thanks to foundations that had been put in place in the period examined in this book.

If the politics of the commercial trends just outlined have been mentioned but not emphasized in the preceding pages of this book, it is partly because the extant written sources for the Zurayid and even the Ayyubid period are nonofficial texts, the testimonies of merchants and travelers rather than the writings of government functionaries. This emerging image of the port filtered through merchants' eyes offers significant advantages. First, these sources provide otherwise inaccessible insights into both daily commercial life and the ways in which commerce shaped the life of the city as a whole. By reading literary sources in the light of Cairo Geniza documents, material remains, and environmental data, I have reconstructed more of the commercial topography than has been possible hitherto and situated the diverse loci of commercial negotiation and economic life within and beyond the city. Within the city, I have shown that contrary to the prevailing wisdom on Mediterranean urban landscapes and more along the lines of the spatial practices revealed by the recent work on early modern al-Mukhā,[4] merchants' residences often housed business transactions and storage functions, thus transcending any ideological or social imperatives for separation of public and private space. Beyond the volcanic crater that cradled the medieval city, the surrounding settlements served as sites of manufacture, provided sources of raw material, constituted transit points to and from the city, and, as the testimony of one amazing set of Geniza documents reveals, offered entertainment that contravened the city's proprieties.

Second, merchants' voices reveal important aspects of commercial institutions that official, normative, and even literary sources might either overlook or deliberately obscure. One striking example emerges from the study of commercial taxation. The Geniza documents examined here detail the career of a prominent Jewish trader who held an important position at Aden's customshouse, thus not only contextualizing Ibn al-Mujāwir's claim about the Jewish authorship of Aden's original customs regulation but also illuminating the position of Jewish traders in the city. Moreover, by juxtaposing Ibn al-Mujāwir's testimony with data culled from Cairo Geniza documents, this study reveals that customs taxes were extracted equally from merchants regardless of their religious affiliations and that *dhimmī* and foreign merchants did not face discriminatory charges at the customshouse in spite of normative Islamic imperatives. Finally, Geniza documents reveal that the collection of taxes was rigorously enforced but that adjustments were made to accommodate the market's ups and downs.

Third, the focus on traders and trade contributes to a new understanding of merchants' participation and agency in shaping and running both trade and the city. In the Zurayid period, Maḍmūn b. Japheth not only served as an important customshouse functionary but also collaborated with the leading government official on a major trading expedition. Merchants too bore responsibility for both outfitting naval escorts and launching maritime salvage operations from the city. In the following Ayyubid period, the state assumed responsibility for maritime security, a trend that intensified during the Rasulid period, when al-Muẓaffar launched maritime expeditions and naval patrols.[5] At the same time, however, the collaboration with merchants continued, and Rasulid sources reveal that new players on the mercantile scene received important positions of power in the administration of Aden's port.[6]

Finally, the particular Geniza documents examined here provide new insights into the mechanics of overseas trade negotiations in the city, shedding new light on the institution of the *wakīl al-tujjār*. Using as a springboard A. L. Udovitch's work on formalism and informalism in the medieval economy, I have shown that the position of merchant's representative at Aden constituted neither a government appointment nor a circumstantial empowerment of agency but instead engendered the organic relationship between foreign merchants and a number of trustworthy sedentary businessmen who represented the former's interests at Aden. The representative's permanent urban residence and ties offered nonresident traders formidable access to services and information and guaranteed that these services would be rendered with integrity, dependability, and answerability.

A Working Typology of Indian Ocean Ports

One of the main themes examined in this book is Aden's connection to its maritime foreland in general and, to paraphrase a term coined by Abu Lughod, its prominent place in the archipelago of Indian Ocean ports in particular.[7] This perspective produces a typology of Indian Ocean ports based on precisely their interrelationships and their place in the broader Indian Ocean world. By the Zurayid period, Aden exemplified what I will term a first tier of ports. Good geographical location in the general area of convergence of many routes, excellent maritime topography, and defensibility were important factors of its prominence. More important, however, were the characteristics that developed through the agency of the port's rulers and merchants—perhaps most essentially, the creation of a safe and predictable environment of taxation and mercantile services. Also crucial was the grip on maritime technology and the direct access to shipbuilding resources and expertise. This volume has shown that during the Zurayid era, Adeni merchants took the lead in building ships and did so by forging remarkable overseas connections with Indian merchants that provided precious timber and other boatbuilding supplies. That Indian merchants not only sent timber to Aden but also invested in boatbuilding enterprises in Yemen constitutes a clear measure of the Adenis' success in both pooling resources and establishing an efficient shipyard in a largely timberless land.

A second tier of ports is exemplified by such maritime states as Dahlak and Qays/Kish. Although these ports both matched Aden's geographical and topographical advantages and in the case of Qays controlled significant boatbuilding capability, these sites were stifled by the competition of Aden and operated less through a stable and predictable customs organization and market environment and more through rapacious taxation and even piracy. The dramatic siege of Aden by the ruler of Kish/Qays as told by both Cairo Geniza letter writers and Ibn al-Mujāwir exemplifies one possible outcome of the interaction between ruling elites and merchants of different ports competing for the same routes, cargoes, and markets. During the Zurayid period, Yemeni traders frequented the Red Sea island entrepôt of Dahlak and at times ran into trouble with the assertive local authorities, who appear, however, to have avoided direct confrontation with Aden. By the Rasulid period, changing geopolitical relationships caused corresponding changes in the relationship between Dahlak and Aden, as is clear from the number of Dahlak embassies to visit the Rasulid court and from the fact that Dahlak's customs regime is recorded in the pages of the Rasulid administrative documents.[8]

Finally, a third tier of ports comprises coastal towns in the direct orbit of Aden. Al-Shiḥr and Abyan offer examples of places connected to Aden through regular coastal sea routes. The mid-6th/12th-century case of the collection of shipwreck flotsam in al-Shiḥr and Abyan and its transportation to Aden demonstrates that both places formed part of Aden's maritime hinterland, although the exact terms of the relationship will only be understood within the framework of further research into this period of Indian Ocean commercial history, especially through additional case studies of Arabian port cities. A number of recently excavated ports along the coast of the Ḥaḍramawt may also fall into this category of maritime satellites, but again, only further research and comparative study will reveal the geopolitical parameters of the connection. I hope, in fact, for a generalized comparative approach that will eventually map the ports of India and the East African coast in relationship to one another, will elucidate their roles and hierarchy, and in the process will expand the rudimentary schema of ports with nesting orbits of influence that I have attempted to draw here.

Aden and Indian Ocean Studies

This book has amply emphasized the notion that during the period under investigation here, Aden stood at a maritime gateway of East and West, North and South, serving as the conduit for an increasingly integrated global trade system that linked the worlds of the Mediterranean Sea and the Indian Ocean. In the past two decades or so, Indian Ocean studies have witnessed an explosion, and the connections of the two oceanic worlds have been much emphasized, most effectively for the medieval period by the 1989 publication of Abu Lughod's work of world history, *Before European Hegemony*. Inspired by this historiographical context and indebted to the bold work of scholars such as Abu Lughod, this volume speaks directly to the dynamics of medieval world trade and economy. Most striking in terms of these dynamics because it had previously remained hidden is the element of conflict and competition in the world of Indian Ocean trade. The adversarial relationship between Aden and Qays/Kish that resulted in outright warfare represents only one of several indications that underscore the hitherto neglected issue of conflict and competition among individual merchants and maritime states vying for control of markets, routes, and tax revenues. From this vantage point, it becomes clear that new research is necessary to adjust the widely held notion that the pre-Portuguese Indian Ocean world constituted a harmonious trading realm.

At the same time, this study of Aden through its trade and traders has highlighted a certain type of mercantile collaboration that transcended geographical, ethnic, and religious boundaries. Scholarship on the Mediterranean world of trade posits that medieval merchants' networks formed strictly along denominational lines. The notion of the Indian Ocean as a peaceful trading realm allows the recognition of a greater degree of collaboration across such lines than is possible in the Mediterranean, but the existing scholarship still focuses primarily on religious and ethnic affiliation as the main glue of the region's trading networks. Yet the Jewish Adeni traders whose lives unfold in the fragmented pages of their voluminous correspondence were true cosmopolitans. To be sure, they maintained close ties with their coreligionists in Egypt, India, and beyond and relied heavily on the bonds of family and religious community in conducting routine business, but perhaps their most crucial collaborations explored in this book —the connections that moved Indian Ocean trade between India, Arabia, and the Mediterranean world—were the alliances Adeni Jewish traders forged and the ties they maintained with their Muslim and Hindu counterparts at home and across the seas. A comparative study of networks in the Indian Ocean will reveal the parameters that formed and sustained those networks and will speak to the established views on the Mediterranean world as well. Port cities served as the anchors of these networks in both worlds, and port city societies potentially engendered and shaped some of the most resilient and efficient webs of long-distance commerce. Indeed, maritime trade and exchange in the 150 years under investigation here would have been very different without the magnificent city of Aden and its enterprising people.

Notes

Introduction

1 Heyd and Ferrand, who presented the relevant literary sources in their respective works, *Histoire du commerce* and *Relations de voyages*, referred to this commerce as "commerce des Indes." Goitein first used the term "India trade" with reference to the period covered by the Cairo Geniza (*Studies*, esp. 328) and speaks of "India traders" in his relevant chapter in *Letters*, esp. 175. Inalcik and Quataert similarly describe trade between the subcontinent and the Ottoman empire as the India trade (*Economic and Social History*, 315–63).

2 For a good discussion of central place theory and its limitations, see Cronon, *Nature's Metropolis*, 38–39.

3 Shihāb, *ʿAdan furḍat al-yaman*, and the works of Muḥayriz, an Adeni mathematician, educator, and historian, cited in subsequent notes cover the history of the port from ancient to modern times and provide excellent surveys of the medieval sources with the significant exception of the Cairo Geniza documents. I am grateful to Professor Daniel Varisco for introducing me to Muḥayriz's work. Among the many works on the colonial period, most useful are Hunter's 19th-century *Account of the British Settlement* and Gavin, *Aden under British Rule*, a modern study of the entire British colonial period.

4 Chaudhuri, *Trade and Civilization*, 175.

5 One notable exception to this rule is Petersen, *Towns of Palestine*, esp. 79–94.

6 Udovitch, "Medieval Alexandria," has laid the foundations for a study of medieval Alexandria. See also Udovitch, "Tale of Two Cities." Also important toward the social history of the medieval port city is Frenkel, "Jewish Community of Alexandria."

7 Studies on Sīrāf include Stein's seminal *Archaeological Reconnaissances* and six preliminary excavation reports by director David Whitehouse, "Excavations at Sīrāf." On Julfār, see Hansman, *Julfār*. On Ṣuḥār, see

Williamson, "Harvard Archaeological Survey"; Costa and Wilkinson, "Hinterland of Sohar"; Kervran, "Archaeological Research." On Kilwa, see Chittick, *Kilwa*. On Manda, see Chittick, *Manda*.

8 On Shanga, see Horton, *Shanga*. On Ayla/Aqaba, see Whitcomb, *Ayla*.

9 On the Hadrami ports, see Rougeulle, "Sharma Horizon"; Rougeulle, "Le Yémen entre Orient et Afrique"; Rougeulle, "Notes"; Hardy-Guilbert and Rougeulle, "Ports islamiques"; Hardy-Guilbert and Rougeulle, "Al-Shihr." See also Hardy-Guilbert, "Harbour"; Whitcomb, "Islamic Archaeology."

10 For an early effort to shift through definitions of Islamic cities proposed by scholars and to construct a meaningful model for the study of the cities of the Middle East, see Lapidus, "Traditional Muslim Cities." Abu Lughod, "Islamic City," gives a succinct summary of colonial and post-colonial scholarship on Islamic cities and lucidly disputes the monolithic concept of the "Islamic city." More recent discussions on the subject appear in Haneda and Miura, *Islamic Urban Studies*.

11 Von Grunebaum, "Structure." Von Grunebaum distilled the abstract and general "mosque-market-bath" paradigm of the "Muslim town" from specific case studies of mostly North African towns by Orientalist scholars such as Georges and William Marçais, Jean Sauvaget, and Louis Massignon. See Abu Lughod, "Islamic City," 157–58.

12 The usefulness of thorough case studies of individual cities becomes clear in Eickelman, "Is There an Islamic City?"

13 On the anchorages of Manda, see Chittick, *Manda*, 21, 36, 41; on Sīrāf, see Whitehouse, "Excavations at Sīrāf: First Interim Report," 3; on al-Mukhā, see Brouwer, *Al-Mukhā*, 121, 125–28; on Ṣuḥār, see Williamson, "Harvard Archaeological Survey," 82, 89–90.

14 On Ṣuḥār's water supply, see Costa and Wilkinson, "Hinterland of Sohar," 43–78. On Sīrāf, see Wilkinson, "Agricultural Decline," 127, 129; Whitehouse, "Excavations at Sīrāf: Fourth Interim Report," 9–10, 14. On Manda, see Chittick, *Manda*, 41. On Sharma, see Rougeulle, "Le Yémen entre Orient et Afrique," 213–14.

15 Abu Lughod, *Before European Hegemony*, 353, explores the concatenation of European, Mediterranean, and Indian Ocean markets.

16 On the agricultural hinterland of Ṣuḥār and Sīrāf, see Wilkinson, "Definition"; on Shanga's connections with the mainland, see Horton, *Shanga*, 416.

17 Williamson, "Harvard Archaeological Survey," 82.

18 Whitehouse, "Sīrāf," 143, 150.

19 Um, "Spatial Negotiations," 181. See also Um, "Red Sea Society."

20 Gosh, *In an Antique Land*, 15–16.

21 See Braudel, *Mediterranean and Mediterranean World*; Chaudhuri, *Trade and Civilization*, esp. 119–220.

22 The area of the Crater has yielded South Arabian inscriptions and fragments of four column capitals. In addition, fragments of buildings were located in the immediate vicinity of the Crater, under the Holkat Bay Road. See Prados, "Archaeological Investigation," 300; Playfair, *History of Arabia Felix*, 13.

23 Concerning the remains of medieval Aden itself, I will be referring to Edward Prados's coastal and underwater survey; see Prados, "Archaeological Investigation." The important remnants of Aden's water supply system are currently the focus of a UNESCO study and preservation project. The most thorough description and historical analysis on the so-called Ṭawīla tanks is the work of local Adeni historian Abdallāh Aḥmad Muḥayriz, *Ṣahārīj ʿAdan*. Regrettably, I was not able to obtain Norris and Penhey's much-cited work of the British colonial period, *Archaeological and Historical Survey*.

24 The two most useful and insightful syntheses of archaeological work on Aden's hinterland are Whitcomb, "Islamic Archaeology," and King and Tonghini, *Survey*. For references to post-1996 reports on archaeological work in the region, see Rougeulle, "Notes."

25 Cohen, *Under Crescent and Cross*, 107–9, 111–20.

26 Halkin, "Judeo-Islamic Age," esp. 215–33; Lewis, *Jews of Islam*, esp. 67–106.

27 See Cohen, "Geniza for Islamicists." See also Sadan, "Geniza and Geniza-Like Practices"; on a 21st-century manifestation of the custom among Muslims in Quetta, Pakistan, see Frantz, "Giving Proper Burial to Holy Books." Costa, "Moschea Grande," 505–6, discusses the discovery of masses of written material, including some of the earliest known copies of the Quran, during repairs in the roof of the Great Mosque in Sanaa; see also Von Bothmer, "Masterworks," 179; Von Bothmer, "Spätantike Voraussetzungen."

28 For other examples of influential Jews in Muslim political life, see the dated but still useful Fischel, *Jews*. Cf. Von Grunebaum, "Eastern Jewry," which claims that although in cultural terms Jews were part and parcel of Islamic societies, politically they were rendered irrelevant, a view that fails to explain the instances of political empowerment of Jewish elites.

29 Cohen, "Geniza for Islamicists." This article provides the clearest, most comprehensive, and most articulate exposition of the arguments for the Geniza material's importance to Islamic history.

30 Diem is declarative about this epistemological link and readily acknowledges his debt to Goitein, the doyen of Judeo-Arabic studies: "The linguistic value of Goitein's editions for the Arabist is shown by the fact that in my book *Arabische Privatbriefe auf Papyrus aus der Heidelberger Papyrus-Sammlung* . . . Goitein is by far the most cited scholar" (Diem and Radenberg, *Dictionary*, viii).

31 See Udovitch, *Partnership and Profit*; Rabie, *Financial System*; Ashtor, *Histoire*; Constable, *Trade and Traders*; Constable, *Housing the Stranger*; Khalilieh, *Islamic Maritime Law*.

32 In 1998, Nayef ʿAbdallāh al-Shamrookh visited Princeton and the S. D. Goitein Laboratory for Geniza Research to become acquainted with the Geniza material; see Cohen, "Geniza for Islamicists."

33 Gosh, "Slave of MS. H. 6." On the various spellings and proposed derivations of the slave's name, see Goitein, *Letters*, 191; Gosh, "Slave of MS. H. 6.," 171–85. See also Gosh, *In an Antique Land*; Chakravarti, "Nakhudas and Nauvittakas."

34 Tobi, *Jews of Yemen*, 41.

35 Lundin, "Jewish Communities in Yemen"; Tobi, *Jews of Yemen*, 3–4; Ahroni, *Jews of the British Crown Colony*, 10–11. See also Goitein, "Aden," which argues that Mediterranean Jews may already have reached Aden in Roman times and points to indications that eastern Jewish immigrants may have reached Aden during the time of Sasanian expansion in the 5th and 6th centuries.

36 For a succinct summary of this debate, see Ahroni, *Jews of the British Crown Colony*, 11–13.

37 Tobi, *Jews of Yemen*, 47.

38 Ibid., 11–33, esp. 22–25. The document dates to 284/897.

39 Ibid., 27–28. Tobi further argues that the laws of discrimination that applied to *dhimmī* communities elsewhere are not attested in Yemen until the 15th century, when such laws are "mentioned in the Zaydi law books." Even then, however, he insists that in the Zaydi Yemeni north, "the relations between Muslims and Jews preserved the spirit of al-Hādī's contract."

40 Goitein, *Yemenites*, 76–78; Tobi, *Jews of Yemen*, 5.

41 Goitein, *Yemenites*, 78, 203 n. 16. Goitein notes that the tradition about

the Jewish connection in the foundation of Dhū Jibla is related by both ʿUmāra and Yāqūt.

42 The crisis is usually associated with the famous "Epistle to Yemen" by Moses Maimonides, in which the great Jewish scholar simultaneously encourages and admonishes the Yemeni Jews in a time of external persecution and internal heresy. Maimonides' work and the crisis mentioned therein was initially dated to 567/1172 and associated with the renegade reign of ʿAbd al-Nabī and his successors, who were based in Zabīd and whose rule ended with the Ayyubid conquest. More recent scholarship, however, associates the event with the later Ayyubid ruler al-Muʿizz on the evidence of two Geniza letters from Aden that mention the forced conversion and the eventual assassination of al-Muʿizz. See Goitein, *Letters*, 212–20; Stillman, *Jews of Arab Lands*, 233, 234 n. 4, 240 n. 19; Ahroni, *Jews of the British Crown Colony*, 21. Cf. Tobi, *Jews of Yemen*, 41, which maintains the earlier position and dating. See also chapter 4 in this volume.

43 Goitein, *Letters*, 212.

44 On Maḍmūn and his family and for a family tree based on the evidence of the Geniza, see Goitein, *Yemenites*, 79–82. Goitein drew attention to the remarkable discovery of two tombstones that probably belong to members of the Bundār family: Abraham b. Bundār, who died in 1164 and was the uncle of Maḍmūn b. Japheth, and Maḍmūn b. Ḥalfon, who died in 1159 and was possibly the son of Ḥalfon b. Maḍmūn —that is, Maḍmūn's grandson; see Goitein, "Age of the Hebrew Tombstones," 82; see also Goitein's overview of scholarship on the tombstones, "Aden." Some of these tombstones were first published by Ben Zvi, "Jewish Tombstones." In 1959, Eli Subar presented thirteen more tombstones and their inscriptions; five of them apparently date to the late 6th/12th and first half of the 7th/13th century: "our prince Ḥalfon son of Maḍmūn" (d. 1172), "Maḍmūn son of the Honor of the Great Holiness, Rabbi Ḥalfon" (d. 1216), "Sach . . . Raya daughter of the Honorable Great Holiness Ḥalfon" (d. 1237), "our prince Ḥalfon son of the prince Maḍmūn" (d. 1247), "our Prince Yeshūʿā son of Maḍmūn" (d. 1249) ("Medieval Jewish Tombstones," 303–6).

45 Goitein, *Yemenites*, 80–82; Tobi, *Jews of Yemen*, 41.

46 Bodl. MS Heb. d66, f. 21/IB.177/VII.58. See Goitein, *Mediterranean Society*, 5:223, 516 n. 150, 566 n. 19. Goitein, *Studies*, 338, divides the chronological range of India-related Geniza documents into two

phases: a period of dense documentation between 1080 and 1160 and a period of a much sparser record between 1160 and 1240. It is not clear whether he meant this distinction in a general sense, but I can find no datable document relating directly to Aden after 1228.

47 The relationship of the Adeni Jewish community with that in the Mediterranean certainly persisted: see Assaf, *Texts and Studies*, 235, referring to Mediterranean women marrying in Aden as late as the 15th century.

48 The historiographical trend that focuses on persecution and humiliation as the main thread in Yemeni Jewish existence has numerous pitfalls. On the manifestations of this trend in the writing of Jewish history as a whole, see Cohen, *Under Crescent and Cross*, xv–16; on the same phenomenon in the study of the Jews of Yemen in particular, see Dallal, "On Muslim Curiosity," 78–79, 87. Dallal concludes that the "history of Jews under Islam is an integral part of the history of the Muslim world in which they lived. Upon close examination, even the sources that purport to portray Yemeni Jewish life end up reflecting, in many details, the lives of the Muslims of Yemen."

49 On the Cairo Geniza and the practice of *geniza* in general, see Cohen, "Geniza for Islamicists."

50 See Reif, *Jewish Archive from Old Cairo*, 14–17. Two now famous Scottish sisters with connections in Cambridge are responsible for the beginnings of the Cambridge collection, the largest and most significant of today's Geniza corpuses. Upon their return from a visit to Egypt, they presented a sample of Geniza material they had acquired there to Solomon Schechter, expert in rabbinic literature at Cambridge. Judaic scholars set the year of "discovery" of the Cairo Geniza in 1896, when Schechter, thrilled by the sample he had seen, traveled to Cairo to acquire additional documents. See, e.g., the catalog of the Israel Museum's 1997 exhibition, The Cairo Genizah: A Mosaic of Life, which according to its organizers commemorated the one hundredth anniversary of the discovery in Old Cairo of this treasure trove of Jewish history.

51 In a recent estimate, Cohen, *Poverty and Charity*, 9, gives a total of more than 210,000 shelf marks, with some shelf marks containing multiple leaves, or folios.

52 See Attal, *Bibliography*. Goitein's first encounter with the Geniza took place in 1948 in Budapest; see Cohen, "Goitein, the Geniza, and Muslim History." See also Reif, *Jewish Archive from Old Cairo*, 247; Udovitch, "Foreword," xi.

53 In his anthology of Geniza traders' documents, Goitein emphasizes the importance of the Indian Ocean world by devoting a separate chapter to letters of the India traders (*Letters*, 175–229).

54 In an autobiographical essay, Goitein emphasizes his early interest in the Yemenite Jewish community; see Attal, *Bibliography*, xxii–xxiii; Goitein, *Jemenica* (a work of ethnographic and linguistic research on Yemeni Jews); Goitein, *From the Land of Sheba* (an anthology of Yemenite stories); Goitein, *Yemenites* (a collection of articles published in 1983).

55 On the "discovery" of the Lebdī lawsuit papers, see Goitein, *Studies*, 330; Udovitch, "Foreword," xi–xii. About ten Geniza documents on the India trade had been published earlier in the 1930s and 1940s. In a pioneering 1954 article, Goitein noted that most of these ten documents were published only in Hebrew and that the editions needed revision ("From the Mediterranean to India," 184). E. N. Adler, collector and honoree of the eponymous collection now at the Jewish Theological Seminary in New York, was the first to publish an India-related Geniza document in his *Von Ghetto zu Ghetto*, 197–99. Other texts subsequently appeared in Strauss/Ashtor, "Voyage to India," 217–31; Strauss/Ashtor, "Documents"; Braslavsky, "Jewish Trade"; Assaf, *Texts and Studies*, 113–14, 149–51, 232–36.

56 Goitein, *Studies*, 329.

57 Goitein, "Two Eyewitness Reports." Goitein's other article published that year was "From the Mediterranean to India."

58 See Goitein, "From the Mediterranean to India," 183–84.

59 Goitein bequeathed his research archive, including the India Book, to the Jewish National and University Library in Jerusalem; a full copy of the India Book was also deposited at Princeton University in what is now known as the S. D. Goitein Laboratory for Geniza Research, where I conducted my research. Goitein rearranged the India Book chapters at least three times. His final scheme approximates the order in which he presented the contents of the corpus in the relevant chapter of his *Studies*, 336–38. In citing Geniza texts relating to Aden, I give each text's library shelf mark, along with the designations of Goitein's initial and final document arrangement. For example, a Geniza document in the Ethan Nathan Adler Collection of the Jewish Theological Seminary in New York is cited as ENA 1822, f. 75/IB.240/III.31. By adding the India Book designations, I indicate that I have examined the microfilms and photocopies of the original documents that Goitein collected

and that I have consulted his unpublished transcriptions and, in the case of the first two chapters in the final scheme, his translations and commentaries on these documents. The dating and identification of main persons and events in these texts are Goitein's unless I specifically state otherwise. The final version of the India Book has been painstakingly prepared by Goitein's student, Mordechai Friedman, professor of Talmud at Tel Aviv University, and will be published very soon; for the time being, see Friedman's enlightening article, "Abraham b. Yijū."

60 Guo, *Commerce, Culture, and Community*, 3–4 (on the documents' dating). See also Guo, "Arabic Documents, Part 1"; Guo, "Arabic Documents, Part 2."

61 Guo, *Commerce, Culture, and Community*, 117.

62 For the very similar deviations in the Quṣayr documents, see Guo, *Commerce, Culture, and Community*, 117.

63 Ibid., 111–14. Guo notes that the system of letter numerals is used relatively rarely in the Quṣayr documents; in the Geniza documents examined here, numerals are expressed exclusively with Hebrew letters.

64 Löfgren has jointly edited the two accounts in his two-volume *Arabische Texte*. The publication includes relevant excerpts from the texts by Rasulid official and *muḥtasib* of Aden Muḥammad b. Yaʿqūb al-Janadi (d. 732/1332) and 19th-century author ʿAbd al-Raḥmān b. Sulaymān al-Ahdal (d. 1250/1830), along with useful indexes and an invaluable glossary. For the complete edition of Ibn al-Mujāwir's text, see Ibn al-Mujāwir, *Ta'rīkh al-mustabṣir*. Professor G. Rex Smith, a great specialist on Ibn al-Mujāwir, has recently completed a long-awaited new translation of Ibn al-Mujāwir's difficult text. A new edition of the Arabic text by Muḥammad ʿAbd al-Raḥīm Jāzim is also forthcoming.

65 On the identity of the possibly Khurasanian Abū Bakr b. Muḥammad b. Masʿūd b. ʿAlī b. Aḥmad Ibn al-Mujāwir, see Smith, "Ibn al-Mujāwir's Ta'rīkh al-Mustabṣir." According to Smith, Ibn al-Mujāwir "would appear to write as a businessman, or at least he writes mainly in total sympathy with businessmen." See also Smith, "Ibn al-Mujāwir on Dhofar and Socotra," 79–80; Smith, "Ibn al-Mujāwir's 7th/13th Century Guide," 78–86.

66 Löfgren, "Makhrama." Löfgren, *Arabische Texte*, 1:12–14, reproduces a biography of Abū Makhrama by Ibn al-ʿAydarūs that appeared in a work titled *Sanā' al-bāhir*.

67 Al-Shamrookh comprehensively treats commercial history under the Rasulids in *Commerce and Trade*.

68 Muḥammad ʿAbd al-Raḥīm Jāzim prepared a painstaking edition of the entire manuscript that opens new vistas of research; see his two-volume *Nūr al-maʿārif*. See also Jāzim, "Nūr al-Dīn et al-Muẓaffar," on the two great Rasulid sultans of the 7th/13th century and the foundations of the state that produced the Muẓaffar register. Al-Shamrookh, *Commerce and Trade*, has already processed much of the data of the Muẓaffar register that relate to Aden.

69 Jāzim, *Nūr al-maʿārif*, v.

70 Ibid.

71 See the edition and extensive analysis of this work: Varisco, *Medieval Agriculture and Islamic Science*.

72 Ibid., 16–19.

73 G. Rex Smith has just completed an edition and translation of the *Mulakhkhaṣ al-fiṭan* that will appear shortly in the Hakluyt Society series. In the interim, see Smith, "Rasulid Administration." Cahen and Serjeant, "Fiscal Survey," announced the discovery of the *Mulakhkhaṣ* in 1957, and its contents received full attention in al-Shamrookh, *Commerce and Trade*. See also the extensive discussion of the *Mulakhkhaṣ* in Smith, "More on the Port Practices."

74 Two more Rasulid texts would be invaluable for writing the history of the port in the Rasulid period: one is a compendium of the Rasulid Sultan al-Afḍal (764–78/1363–77) that includes information on goods sent to the Rasulid court, tax records, and ship terms (Varisco and Smith, *Manuscript of al-Malik al-Afḍal*, esp. 8–23); the other is a newly discovered Rasulid manuscript dating from the time of the Rasulid Sultan al-Mu'ayyad (696–721/1296–1322) and now located at King Saud University in Riyadh. This manuscript also contains data on goods destined for the court and on taxation. I am obliged to Professor Dan Varisco for kindly alerting me to the existence of these valuable sources.

75 The terms "premodern" and "non-Western" obviously illustrate the predicament of perspective. I generally try to avoid them, although I occasionally use the term "premodern" in reference to issues of technology in preindustrial times.

76 Varisco notes the inherent incongruity in the Western imposition of the term "medieval" on Yemeni history just as in non-Western history in general but acknowledges the impasse in finding meaningful alternatives; see Varisco, "Study of 'Medieval Yemen,'" 10–11. See also Hodgson, *Venture of Islam*, 1:48–56.

77 I borrow the term from Freedman and Spiegel, who in turn quote Patterson on the discredited early view of the Middle Ages as the antithesis of the Renaissance, the Enlightenment, and ultimately modernity. On trends and debates in medieval historiography, on concepts of medieval alterity, and on both the "antimodern" and the "progressive" Middle Ages with specific reference to American academic discourse, see "Medievalisms Old and New," 677–79.

78 Hodgson uses the term "Middle Periods" to refer to this chronological frame and further distinguishes between an Earlier Middle Period (945–1250 C.E.) and a Later Middle Period (1250–1500 C.E.) (*Venture of Islam*, 2:3–4). Albert Hourani avoids the term "medieval" but considers the period between the 5th/11th and the 9th/15th centuries of the common era a distinct period of both unity and division of the Islamic world (*History of the Arab Peoples*, 81–82). See also, Humphreys, *Islamic History*, ix–x.

79 Goitein, *Studies*, 338. Indeed, India-related documents begin late in the 5th/11th century, almost a century later than the first floruit of medieval Jewish merchants emerges from the Mediterranean material.

80 Abu Lughod counts Aden as one of the premodern world system's small city-state ports, along with Venice, Palembang, and Malacca (*Before European Hegemony*, 355).

81 Ibid., 276.

82 *Periplus Maris Erythraei*, 26:8, 26–31; see Casson, *Periplus*, 64–65, 158–60. In his commentary, Casson discusses the identification of Eudaimôn Arabia (Roman Arabia Felix) with Aden, the changing fortunes of the entrepôt in the days of the Roman empire, and the evidence that the place-name "Aden" was already in use around the time when the *Periplus* was written in the first century C.E.

83 Ptolemy mentioned Aden as "Eudaimôn Arabia" in the 2nd century C.E.; ecclesiastical author Philostorgus wrote about "Adanê" in the 4th century C.E. (Casson, *Periplus*, 158–59). On the tradition of the Arabs' thirteen pre-Islamic markets, see al-Marzūqī, *Al-azmina wa'l-amkina*, 161–70, esp. 164 (on Aden). Al-Marzūqī conveys the tradition that Aden always came under the jurisdiction of Yemen's rulers, who imposed taxes on the visiting merchants; last to rule before the rise of Islam were the Iranian Abnā', who apparently took advantage of the Adeni perfume trade. On the Sasanian involvement in maritime commerce in the Indian Ocean, see Whitehouse and Williamson, "Sasanian Mari-

time Trade." On the Sasanian rule in Yemen, see Zettersteen, "Abnā'." On later Iranian migrations, see Aubin, "Ruine de Siraf."

84 Ibn Khurradādhbih, *Al-Masālik wa'l-mamālik*, 61; Ibn Ḥawqal, *Kitāb ṣurat al-arḍ*, 37; al-Muqaddasī, *Kitāb aḥsan al-taqāsīm fī maʿrifat al-aqālīm*, 67, 85, 111; al-Hamdānī, *Ṣifat jazīrat al-ʿarab*, 53.

85 Al-Muqaddasī, *Kitāb aḥsan al-taqāsīm fī maʿrifat al-aqālīm*, 85: *dihlīz al-ṣīn wa-furḍat al-yaman wa-khizānat al-maghrib wa-maʿdin al-tijārāt kathīr al-quṣūr mubārik ʿalā man dakhalahu muthīr li-man sakanahu.*

86 al-Shamrookh, *Commerce and Trade*, 45–51. Al-Shamrookh notes a tradition preserved by Ibn al-Athīr, according to which when Aden fell to his army, Turānshāh opted to preserve the city and appropriate its revenues rather than loot and destroy it.

87 For the first, classic edition of ʿUmāra's text, see Kay, *Yaman*. Details of the life of ʿUmāra, who wrote his *Ta'rīkh al-Yaman* for Fatimid government functionaries and later served as an adviser to the Ayyubid invasion of Yemen, only to be executed as a conspirator against the new regime, appear in Kay, *Yaman*, v–vii. ʿUmāra's biography appears in the biographical dictionary of Ibn Khallikān, *Wafayāt al-aʿyān*, 3:431–36. Kay includes Yemen-related excerpts from Ibn Khaldūn's general history and from the work of Rasulid official and author al-Janadī.

88 For ʿUmāra's account of the Zurayids, see Kay, *Yaman*, 64–80 (English), 48–59 (Arabic). The episode also appears in Ibn al-Mujāwir's account and is confirmed by a Geniza letter, as chapters 1 and 3 will show.

89 On how the two Yemeni factions drifted apart, see Bates, "Chapter."

90 Goitein, *Yemenites*, 80; see also chapter 6. Stronger ties with its "foreland" and weaker ties with its "hinterland" constitute a constant feature of Aden's history. In his recent monograph on Yemeni history, Dresch says of British colonial Aden, "The port itself is connected most immediately in Britain's maritime empire with Suez and India, London and Singapore" (*History*, 10).

91 Balog, *Coinage*, 34–35.

Chapter One

1 Ibn al-Mujāwir, *Ta'rīkh al-mustabṣir*, 130: *hawā'uhā karib . . . khalla al-khamr fī muddat ʿasharat ayyām.*

2 Rimbaud, *Complete Works*, 251. Rimbaud had fled Europe in search of the "Mythical East" and was for a while employed in Aden as a workers'

supervisor at a coffee trading firm (Taminian, "Rimbaud's House in Aden," 468–72).

3 In one case, a book summarizes the geographical disadvantage in its title: Lunt, *Barren Rocks*. Aden's summer heat is of legendary intensity. Sailing manuals, in fact, note that the annual mean of eighty-six degrees Fahrenheit, observed at various parts of the southern Red Sea and the Gulf of Aden, is "the highest known for the earth"; regional air temperatures over water are also the highest "known on any water surface except the Persian Gulf" (*Sailing Directions for the Red Sea* [1976], 22). The constant high temperatures and unrelenting sun are occasionally magnified by a dry northerly wind, locally known by the alarmingly descriptive name *al-kawi*, meaning "hot iron"; see Doreen Ingrams, *Survey*, 17.

4 The waters of the Gulf of Aden are literally luminous: for the nocturnal phenomenon described in the sailing manuals as "luminosity of the sea," see *Red Sea and Gulf of Aden Pilot*, 63–64. The phosphorescence may be connected with the biological richness of the local waters.

5 *Sailing Directions for the Red Sea* (1976), 4. In the Aden area, the gulf closes to about 120 miles wide.

6 TS24.64/IB.56/III.10, lines 30–35, details the deployment from Aden of "mariners" (*baḥḥārīn*), who dived and salvaged half of the iron cargo of a ship that had foundered near the straits (Goitein, *Letters*, 189). This document hints at a system of recruitment of salvage crews in Aden and suggests that such crews were deployed from the city on demand.

7 *Sailing Directions for the Red Sea* (1952), 28. An earlier handbook for mariners contrasts the navigation of the Red Sea, fraught as it is with a variety of maritime dangers, with the relatively easy and smooth sailing of the Gulf of Aden (*Red Sea and Gulf of Aden Pilot*, 472).

8 Sailing books caution against a year-round set of strong onshore currents in the general vicinity of Aden as well as against a dangerous local northerly current just east of the port (*Sailing Directions for the Red Sea* [1952], 29). Knowledge of seasonal variations in both winds and currents was codified by the late 9th/15th century but had certainly been a part of oral navigational tradition much earlier (Tibbetts, *Arab Navigation*, esp. 204–5). On the oral and written navigational traditions see Tibbetts, *Arab Navigation*, 1–7; George Faldo Hourani, *Arab Seafaring*, 107–8. See also Tibbetts, "Milāḥa." Yemeni almanacs record sailing seasons with respect to ship arrival and departure times to and from

Aden, which thus emerges not only as a reference point but also as a hub of navigational information and a center of production of navigational knowledge; see Varisco, *Medieval Agriculture and Islamic Science*, 215–31.

9 Goitein, *Mediterranean Society*, 1:319, 482 nn. 43, 44.

10 See, e.g., Pryor, *Geography, Technology, and War*; Udovitch, "Time, the Sea, and Society."

11 Chaudhuri, *Trade and Civilization*, esp. 22–24.

12 Varisco, *Medieval Agriculture and Islamic Science*, 225–31.

13 Tibbetts, *Arab Navigation*, 360. Tibbetts notes that to Ibn Mājid and the other great Arab navigator, Sulayman al-Maḥrī, "the term mawsim (meaning generally a fixed time in the year) meant the actual date for sailing from a port in order to reach another."

14 Tibbetts, *Arab Navigation*, 225–42, 360–78; for Ibn Mājid's data on the windows of time for departure and arrival at Aden, see 225–42.

15 TS20.137/IB.29/II.23, lines 23–24: *wa-kānat al-baḍā'iʿ kāsida wa-lam yuṭlab al-filfil wa-lā biḍāʿa bi-dirham ilā qabl al-safar bi-usbūʿ*; lines 26–28: *fa-ṣabartu ʿalayhim al-ʿushūr ilā yawm al-safar ḥattā waṣalū al-nās min kull mawḍ*[*iʿ*]. This passage will also be discussed in chapter 4, the section on the port's customs office and Maḍmūn's role in the city and its trade; in the same letter, Maḍmūn relates the dramatic story of the siege of Aden, which will be examined in chapters 2 and 3.

16 On the usage of the term "*safar*" to denote the designated or customary departure time of fleets from a certain port for a specific destination, see Varisco, *Medieval Agriculture and Islamic Science*, 225.

17 TS12.235/IB.54/III.9, line 18: *baʿd safar al-marākib*. The letter was sent by Joseph b. Abraham of Aden to Ben Yijū, who had left India and was spending time in Zabīd, a significant trading center on the Red Sea coast of Yemen. Shaked, *Tentative Bibliography*, 55, claims that the letter was sent to Ben Yijū in India, but Goitein later corrects that assessment in his unpublished notes to the India Book; the clue of the recipient's whereabouts lies in lines 1 and 2 of the verso, where the writer specifically mentions Zabīd in connection with a dispatch to Ben Yijū. The letter was probably written around 544/1149–50.

18 Goitein, *Mediterranean Society*, 1:320, 482 n. 50. The expression, thought to have been uttered by ʿUmar in his refutation of Muʿāwiya's maritime proposition, is "*Dūdī ʿalā ʿūdī*" and appears in a Hebrew poem by Samuel ha-Nagid.

19 On the "closing of the sea" in the Mediterranean, see Goitein, *Mediter-*

ranean Society, 1:316–18; Udovitch, "Time, the Sea, and Society," 530–33; Casson, *Ships and Seamanship*, 270–73.

20 For general conditions, including the difficulties of the southwestern summer monsoon, see *Sailing Directions for the Red Sea* (1952), 16–19. Ibn Mājid talks about the closing of the West India coast in June and July (Tibbetts, *Arab Navigation*, 226, 367–68). See also Varisco, *Medieval Agriculture and Islamic Science*, 222–25. The Rasulid almanacs give a possible departure date from Aden to India in the late spring. As Tibbetts notes, eastward voyages in April and May were occasionally possible (*Arab Navigation*, 368). As far back as the beginning of the 4th/10th century, geographer Ibn Faqīh wrote that while the Persian Gulf was navigable year-round, the Indian Ocean ("the sea of India") was closed to sailing while bad weather lasted (*Mukhtaṣar kitāb al-buldān*, 8: *baḥr Fāris qad yurkabu fī kull awqāt al-sana fa-ammā baḥr al-Hind fa-lā yarkabuhu al-nās ʿinda hayjānihi li-ẓulmatihi wa-ṣuʿūbatihi*).

21 Tibbetts, *Arab Navigation*, 226–27, 364–68; Varisco, *Medieval Agriculture and Islamic Science*, 225–26, 230.

22 Casson, *Periplus*, 284–86; Tibbetts, *Arab Navigation*, 243–44, 370 n. 410; Varisco, *Medieval Agriculture and Islamic Science*, 228. According to al-Malik al-Ashraf's almanac, the first ships arrived at Aden from Egypt as early as late spring. On the northwesterlies blowing out of the Red Sea in July and August, see *Red Sea and Gulf of Aden Pilot*, 32.

23 Casson, *Periplus*, 284–86; Tibbetts, *Arab Navigation*, 368–69; Varisco, *Medieval Agriculture and Islamic Science*, 213–14. Tibbetts points out that thanks to the winter monsoon, "ships could travel from Malacca almost to Jidda on one wind." Varisco notes that the "along the Yemeni coast *azyab* refers to a wind from the south," and in al-Malik al-Ashraf's almanac, the wind is called *rīḥ al-janūb al-azyab* (Varisco, *Medieval Agriculture and Islamic Science*, 41, line 14). This is surprising because the *azyab* (the prevailing winter wind) is predominantly a northeasterly (Tibbetts, *Arab Navigation*, esp. 226–30, 368–69, 513), and modern sailing pilots note that it turns into a southerly only near the Bāb al-Mandab. Such emphasis on the southerly *azyab* perhaps reflects the intense Rasulid interest in the area between Aden and the southern Red Sea Yemeni coast rather than in ports further east along the southern Yemeni coast.

24 Ibn al-Mujāwir, *Ta'rīkh al-mustabṣir*, 1:138. As Serjeant suggests, the lookouts would have been awaiting the ships expected to appear in horizon ("Ports of Aden and Shihr," 215).

25 Ibn Khaldūn, for example, reports that the soil of the peninsula produces nothing and that the local diet consists of fish (Kay, *Yaman*, 123: *wa-lā tanabbata zarʿ wa-lā shajar wa-maʿāshuhum al-samak*). On the continued abundance of fish in local waters, see Hunter, *Account of the British Settlement*, 22–23; Lindley, "Fisheries Development."

26 For dugongs as part of Indian Ocean diets, see Whitehouse, "Excavations at Sīrāf: Sixth Interim Report," 2; Horton, *Shanga*, 386–88. Horton notes that dugongs seem to have been widely distributed in the Indian Ocean. Dugongs were evidently caught near Aden into the early 20th century, as attested by photographs of stuffed specimens in rather grotesque displays; a little later, the animal vanished from this part of the world (Bel, *Aden*, 89). Evidence for the processing of whale flesh for blubber comes from the excavations at Sīrāf, where the rib of a whale lay among the remains of an industrial complex featuring channels and catchment basins (Whitehouse, "Excavations at Sīrāf: Sixth Interim Report," 18). Modern-day fishermen along the coast of Oman and Yemen use shark oil as a conditioning and protective coat on the exterior surfaces of their wooden vessels.

27 Ibn al-Mujāwir claims that the inhabitants of the site built after the destruction of Ẓafar feed dried *ʿayd* fish (*al-samak al-yābis wa-huwa al-ʿayd*) to their animals and use the fish to fertilize their fields (*Taʾrīkh al-mustabṣir*, 2:265). Hunter lists *ʿayd* among the smaller fish routinely caught in the area in his time, describes them as resembling sardines, and adds that casting nets were used to catch them (*Account of the British Settlement*, 23). In 1995, Camelin described the fishing of *ʿayd* off the town of al-Shiḥr ("Les pêcheurs de Shihr").

28 The story appears in the remarkable collection of maritime lore and tales of marvels relating to India collected sometime in the 4th/10th century and ascribed to sea captain Buzurg b. Shahriyār of Rāmhurmūz, *Kitāb ʿajāʾib al-hind*, 96.

29 Ibn al-Mujāwir, *Taʾrīkh al-mustabṣir*, 1:148. The author describes the place as "*wa-huwa mawḍiʿ yujmadu fīhi al-milḥ wa-kāna mukhliṣan rajaʿa al-ān ʿalayhi ḍamān wa-yuqālu inna baʿḍahu ṣāra li'l-sulṭān*."

30 Curiously, salted fish (*al-samak al-mumallaḥ*) appears on Ibn al-Mujāwir's list of imports. He claims that whole salted fish imported from the Hadrami port of al-Shiḥr incurred a customs tax, whereas the headless equivalent did not (Ibn al-Mujāwir, *Taʾrīkh al-mustabṣir*, 1:143). Importation of certain varieties, however, does not preclude the possibility of local production and exports.

31 In an itinerary from Aden to Mafālīs, Ibn al-Mujāwir mentions al-Mimlāḥ after the village of al-Mabāh and the isthmus that connects the peninsula with the mainland (discussed later in the chapter), which would place the saltworks on the mainland rather than on the Aden peninsula itself. Abū Makhrama explicitly states that al-Mimlāḥ was located outside Aden but seems to think that the distance of a quarter *farsakh* given by Ibn al-Mujāwir refers to distance from the isthmus, not distance from Aden. Abū Makhrama then faithfully quotes Ibn al-Mujāwir concerning salt production (*Ta'rīkh thaghr ʿadan*, 1:19–20). Ibn al-Mujāwir also says that a spring had previously existed in the middle of Aden, flowing "from the sea to al-Mimlāḥ," thereby enabling the harvesting of salt at the latter location. As enigmatic as it is, the story reveals that al-Mimlāḥ was somewhere other than on the sea, the location of Aden proper.

32 Hunter, *Account of the British Settlement*, 82.

33 See Watt, "Salt in a Pinch," a popular article illustrated with dramatic shots of the extensive 20th-century salt pans and the adjacent mountains of harvested salt.

34 As early as the 3rd/9th century, Ibn Khurradādhbih mentions ambergris among Aden's exports (*Kitāb al-masālik wa-al-mamālik*, 61). Ibn Mājid includes *ʿanbar* among Socotra's *ishārāt*, or "signs"—that is, the characteristic features of a particular maritime area, the knowledge of which serves a mariner in determining his position along a maritime route. He stresses the presence of ambergris in the area of a long reef stretching from Socotra toward Madagascar, "for amber is not seen or found on any coast, except this place" (Tibbetts, *Arab Navigation*, 196–97). In addition, Ibn al-Mujāwir and Marco Polo include ambergris among Socotra's exports; see Ibn al-Mujāwir, *Ta'rīkh al-mustabṣir*, 2:266–68; Polo, *Travels*, 253–54.

35 Ibn al-Mujāwir, *Ta'rīkh al-mustabṣir*, 1:120–21. According to the author, the sale of a particularly impressive piece of ambergris (*qiṭʿat ʿanbar kabīra malīḥa*) funded the building of the city's congregational mosque. More plausibly, he also claims that fishermen caught the ambergris in their nets between the city and the Bāb al-Mandab and sold it to any passing ship or merchant. He adds the story of a particular fisherman who caught a piece of what turned out to be ambergris and took it home and burned it as fuel under his cooking pot when he was out of firewood—all in all, not a bad reconstruction of the discovery

of the aromatic properties of the stuff. The use of ambergris in dress and domestic customs apparently continued well into the 19th century (Hunter, *Account of the British Settlement*, 44).

36 Hunter, *Account of the British Settlement*, 1. Hunter writes that the causeway was constructed "for the convenience of the land traffic, and the passage of the Shaykh ʿUthmān aqueduct." The construction of the aqueduct, which brought water to the city from two wells in the village of Shaykh ʿUthmān, about seven miles away, took place in 1867 or shortly thereafter (10–11).

37 Ibn al-Mujāwir, *Ta'rīkh al-mustabṣir*, 1:115–16.

38 Ibid., 116: *wa-huwa qanṭara buniyat ʿalā sabʿ qawāʿid fa-ṣārat al-khalq taslukuhu ʿalā al-dawābb wa-ghayrihā*. See also Abū Makhrama's recension of the same description (*Ta'rīkh thaghr ʿadan*, 1:9, 19). For a modern evaluation of Aden's island history, see Prados, "Archaeological Investigation," 299.

39 In one instance, Ibn al-Mujāwir calls the bridge al-Maksar (*Ta'rīkh al-mustabṣir*, 1:116); in another instance, he mentions its renovation and calls it al-Mazaff (1:148). Abū Makhrama explicitly states that the structure bore both names (*Ta'rīkh thaghr ʿadan*, 1:19). Ibn al-Mujāwir indicates that "al-Maksar" also applied to the land across from the isthmus on the mainland when he states that little boats unloaded people and merchandise onto camels and other beasts of burden at al-Maksar. For colonial times, see Hunter, *Account of the British Settlement*, 1, 142. According to Hunter, the district was known as Khor (Khawr) Maksar (Maksar Creek) and extended two miles north of the British defensive lines on the isthmus.

40 Ibn al-Mujāwir, *Ta'rīkh al-mustabṣir*, 1:148. Abū Makhrama, *Ta'rīkh thaghr ʿadan*, 2:117, lists ʿAbdallāh al-Tilimsānī's names but instead of a biography gives a single sentence on the man, mentioning Ibn al-Mujāwir's information about the restoration of the bridge.

41 For a discussion of the al-Mabāh's precise location, see the section on Aden's hinterland later in this chapter.

42 Abū Makhrama, *Ta'rīkh thaghr ʿadan*, 1:23. The 922/1516 expedition was a joint Mamluk-Ottoman venture that failed. Aden finally fell to the Ottomans only through treachery. In 1538, Suleyman Pasha tricked the rulers and notables of Aden into coming on board his ship for a feast, had them hanged, and took the city (Inalcik and Quataert, *Economic and Social History*, 321–22, 326).

43 See Hunter, *Account of the British Settlement*, 142. In this case, the harbor defended was the western bay, by then serving as the main anchorage. British troops were stationed elsewhere as well.

44 Ibn al-Mujāwir, *Ta'rīkh al-mustabṣir*, 1:106. The highest peak on the peninsula reaches 1,811 feet (*Sailing Directions for the Red Sea* [1976], 260); it belongs to the mountain range known today as Jabal Shamshān. Löfgren identifies the Medieval Jabal ʿUrr with Jabal Shamshān ("ʿAdan"). Ibn al-Mujāwir's comments on the castles built on the other two peaks, Jabal al-Akhḍar and "*al-jabal alladhī buniya ʿalā dhurwatihi ḥiṣn al-taʿkar*," have led me to conclude that they were part of the same volcanic range and were located immediately south and north of the Crater, respectively. Thus, ʿUrr referred to the central part of the mountain, west of the Crater, and the two others were its side segments. See also the discussion of urban topography in chapter 3.

45 Al-Hamdānī, *Ṣifat jazīrat al-ʿarab*, 70: *wa-hiya sāḥil yuḥīṭu bihi jabal*. Ibn al-Mujāwir, however, talks of a wadi surrounded by the sea (*Ta'rīkh al-mustabṣir*, 1:130: *binā' al-balad fī wādī al-baḥr mustadīr ḥawlahu*).

46 Prados, "Archaeological Investigation," 297, 299. For a description of the Crater and its relationship to the other parts of the settlement in the 19th and early 20th centuries, see Hunter, *Account of the British Settlement*, 7–9; *Sailing Directions for the Red Sea* (1952), 265. The town, which was rebuilt when the British took over, is said to have comprised some two thousand whitewashed houses, many two-storied. For pictures and information on the old town and its architecture both in the 19th century and more recently, see Bel, *Aden*.

47 Ibn al-Mujāwir, *Ta'rīkh al-mustabṣir*, 1:121; Abū Makhrama, *Ta'rīkh thaghr ʿadan*, 2:76. The gate was associated with the fort al-Taʿkar, seat of one of Aden's two governors. See the section on fortifications in chapter 3. Abū Makhrama refers to the pass as *bāb al-barr* (landward gate), probably to distinguish it from the gates built into the Ayyubid city wall.

48 For 19th- and 20th-century representations of the Main Pass, see Bel, *Aden*, 8 (a stamp), 33 (an 1861 drawing), and 74 (1880s and 1950s photographs). Ibn al-Mujāwir relates that the followers of Shaddād b. ʿĀd scouted the area of the Jabal ʿUrr and located a wadi, presumably the Crater; their leader then ordered the opening of a passage to that spot (*amara an yunqara lahu bāb fī ṣadr al-wādī*) (*Ta'rīkh al-mustabṣir*, 1:107–8); Abū Makhrama faithfully repeats the story (*Ta'rīkh thaghr ʿadan*, 1:15).

49 Al-Muqaddasī, *Kitāb aḥsan al-taqāsīm fī maʿrifat al-aqālīm*, 85: *wa-qad shuqqa fīhi ṭarīq fī-al-ṣakhr ʿajīb wa-juʿila ʿalayhi bāb ḥadīd.*

50 *Periplus Maris Erythraei*, 26:8.24. The anonymous author, himself probably an India merchant, notes that Eudaimôn Arabia boasts "*hormous epitedeious*" (suitable anchorages) (Casson, *Periplus*, 64–65). The U.S. Hydrographic Office's *Sailing Directions* reassures the sailor that the small bays along the peninsula's rocky southern shore "afford shelter for small craft during offshore winds" (*Sailing Directions for the Red Sea* [1976], 260).

51 The view that at the old harbor lay on the eastern side of the peninsula, contiguous with the city, prevails today (see, e.g., Löfgren, "ʿAdan"), and I have found it to be accurate despite Goitein's interpretation of the two different words, "*bandar*" and "*mukallā*," that appear in the Geniza in connection with Aden's anchorage space as referring respectively to the peninsula's western and eastern anchorages (Goitein, *Mediterranean Society*, 5:523 nn. 98, 101). I believe that a closer reading of the relevant documents and an examination of other written sources and Aden topography reveal that Goitein's statement is a misunderstanding; the two words in fact refer to different parts of the eastern anchorage. Another possibility is that the medieval harbor lay in the deeper eastern Ḥuqqāt/Holkat Bay; that hypothesis, however, does not agree with the testimony of the primary sources. See the following section in this chapter as well as chapter 2.

52 On the *azyab* wind and its equation with the winter northeastern monsoon, see Tibbetts, *Arab Navigation*, esp. 226–30, 368–69, 513.

53 Colonial coffers, a well-armed modern military, advanced engineering, and modern equipment allowed the fortification of the entire Aden peninsula and the paving of roads into the peninsula's hitherto forbidding mountainous core; see Playfair, *History of Arabia Felix*, 13; see also Hunter, *Account of the British Settlement*, 142–45.

54 For an older description of the geology of the Aden peninsula, see Hunter, *Account of the British Settlement*, 2–3.

55 Ibn al-Mujāwir, *Taʾrīkh al-mustabṣir*, 1:126; Abū Makhrama, *Taʾrīkh thaghr ʿadan*, 1:9, 2:151–52. Abū Makhrama's biography of Abū al-Ḥasan revolves entirely around his pioneering stone quarrying and the resulting boom in building construction in Aden. As a labor force in the quarry, Abū al-Ḥasan apparently employed African slaves.

56 Al-Muqaddasī, *Kitāb aḥsan al-taqāsīm fī maʿrifat al-aqālīm*, 85: *innahā yābisa ʿābisa lā zarʿ wa-lā ḍarʿ wa-lā shajar wa-lā thamar wa-lā māʾ wa-lā*

kala'; Ibn Baṭṭūṭa, *Riḥlat Ibn Baṭṭūṭa*, 194: *wa-hiya madīna kabīra wa-lā zarʿ bihā wa-lā shajar wa-lā mā'*.

57 Averaging between 1.54 and 8.69 inches and usually closer to the lower end of that spectrum, Aden's annual total rainfall is low even compared to a "poorly watered" port in the Mediterranean such as Malta, which gets an average of about 20 inches a year; for Aden, see *Sailing Directions for the Red Sea* (1952), 356; *Sailing Directions for the Red Sea* (1976), 22, 343; Hunter, *Account of the British Settlement*, 14 (which records an exceptional annual rainfall of more than 4 inches in 1872–73). For Malta, see *Sailing Directions (Planning Guide)*, 96. By comparison, Genoa's adequate water supplies during the Middle Ages depended on 51–55 inches a year (Epstein, *Genoa*, 10; *Sailing Directions [Planning Guide]*, 74).

58 Abū Makhrama, *Ta'rīkh thaghr ʿadan*, 1:9. Abū Makhrama describes the peninsula as inhabited by fisherfolk who lived near the water; the higher ground was covered with thorny trees that gave the place the appellation *jarām al-shawk* (field of thorns) (*al-jarām*, he explains, is an Indian term that denotes a piece of land: *qiṭʿa min al-arḍ bi-lughat al-hind*). In his "Botanical Notes," Hunter remarks on the prevalence of thorny species among the peninsula's flora (*Account of the British Settlement*, 6–7).

59 Shihāb, *ʿAdan furḍat al-Yaman*, 148.

60 The *Periplus* claims that in ancient times, Aden had sweeter water than other ports of call (*Periplus Maris Erythraei*, 26:8.24–25: *hydreumata glykitera*; Casson, *Periplus*, 64–65, 159). Casson believes that the sources to which the *Periplus* refers "must have been reservoirs for storing rain water such as Aden has had to use throughout the centuries." Similarly, on the eve of the British capture of Aden, Captain S. B. Haines assures his readers that good water was available at the port but does not specify the provenance ("Memoir," 139). This water too may have been cistern water. Finally, the British administration also resorted to a combination of different water sources yet still had to ration water, with allocations depending primarily on the individual's position in the colonial hierarchy (Hunter, *Account of the British Settlement*, 9–21).

61 Ibn al-Mujāwir, *Ta'rīkh al-mustabṣir*, 1:131–34.

62 Ibid., 1:131, 133.

63 This may be the same person as "our *nagid* David," who appears in a Geniza letter to India written in the second half of the 6th/12th century (TS Misc. Box 28, f. 187/IB.213/II.65); if so, he is probably the grand-

son of Maḍmūn b. Japheth and father of the second Maḍmūn, who was *nagid* during the short but oppressive rule of al-Malik al-Muʿizz Ismāʿīl. On this Ayyubid ruler and his interactions with Aden's Jews, see Goitein, *Letters*, 212–20; see also chapters 3 and 4 of this volume.

64 Ibn al-Mujāwir reports that during the time of the Zurayid rulers Saba' b. Abī al-Suʿūd and Muḥammad b. Abī al-Ghārāt, a riot broke out "on account of water and firewood" (*Ta'rīkh al-mustabṣir*, 1:124: *wa-kāna yajrī bayna al-qawm fitna ʿaẓīma li-ajl al-mā' wa-al-ḥaṭab*).

65 Ibid., 130: *mā'uhā min al-ābār wa shay' yujlabu min masīrat farsakhayn.* In colonial times, the best wells were located in or near the village of Shaykh ʿUthmān, opposite the western bay of Aden and at the time under the jurisdiction of the sultan of Laḥj; see Hunter, *Account of the British Settlement*, 10–11.

66 According to Ibn al-Mujāwir, the mythical Shaddād b. ʿĀd ordered wells to be dug at Laḥj; the chronicler adds that these wells provided the people of Aden with water to his day (Ibn al-Mujāwir, *Ta'rīkh al-mustabṣir*, 108). In the 4th/10th century, al-Hamdānī mentions a place named al-Ḥayq as the watering hole of Aden but adds that the town also had its own wells (*Ṣifat jazīrat al-ʿarab*, 70). Muḥayriz notes that the place-name "al-Ḥayq" is often associated with shallow coastal aquifers (*al-aḥsiya*, sing. *al-ḥaswa*) (*Al-ʿaqaba*, 105).

67 Ibn al-Mujāwir, *Ta'rīkh al-mustabṣir*, 1:117.

68 Ibn Baṭṭūṭa, *Riḥlat Ibn Baṭṭūṭa*, 194–95: *wa-al-mā' ʿalā buʿd minhā fa-rubbamā manaʿathu al-ʿarab wa-ḥallū bayna ahl al-madīna wa-baynahu ḥattā yuṣāniʿūhum bi-al-māl wa-al-thiyāb.*

69 Muḥayriz, *Ṣahārīj ʿadan*, esp. 5–7. Victorian efforts to restore the cisterns took place from 1856 onward; see Hunter, *Account of the British Settlement*, 11–13. The problems with these restorations were noted as early as the 1950s by British archaeologist C. H. Inge. A current research project on the cisterns and Aden's ancient water supply is sponsored by the United Nations and UNESCO; see Young, "Aden's Pipe Dreams."

70 Muḥayriz, *Ṣahārīj ʿadan*, 7, 61, provides a photograph of one of the British-built barrages. On the 19th-century understanding of the cisterns, their restoration, and subsequent use for Aden's water supply, see Hunter, *Account of the British Settlement*, 12–14.

71 It is no surprise that the "restored" tanks had only filled up twice between 1857 and 1877 when Hunter wrote his report: the neglect of the mountain channels and the blockage of the water courses meant that

the runoff was not tapped efficiently and that some of the water was absorbed behind the barriers. See Hunter, *Account of the British Settlement*, 14; Muḥayriz, *Ṣahārīj ʿadan*, 6–7.

72 Al-Muqaddasī, *Kitāb aḥsan al-taqāsīm fī maʿrifat al-aqālīm*, 85: *wa-lahum ābār māliḥa wa-ḥiyāḍ ʿidda*; Ibn Baṭṭūṭa, *Riḥlat Ibn Baṭṭūṭa*, 194: *wa-bihā ṣahārīj yajtamiʿu fīhā al-māʾ ayyām al-maṭar wa-al-māʾ ʿalā buʿd minhā*. For the *maṭarāt* and the special officials responsible for their upkeep and management, see Smith, "Rasulid Administration," 17 n. 73, 23. Smith offers Dozy's definition for "*maṭarāt*" as large water containers made of wood or leather, but given the connection with rainwater and the Adeni context, it is not implausible that the term here refers specifically to the Adeni *ṣahārīj*.

73 Harold Ingrams estimates the cisterns' total capacity in the vicinity of 20,000,000 gallons (*Arabia and the Isles*, 89). Hunter states that the thirteen cisterns that had been restored in his time could hold 7,718,630 gallons of water (*Account of the British Settlement*, 12). In his commentary on Marco Polo's description of Aden, Yule includes Ibn Baṭṭūṭa's discussion of the cisterns and quotes a total capacity of 30,000,000 gallons of water (*Book of Ser Marco Polo*, 375–76).

74 Ibn Baṭṭūṭa, *Riḥlat Ibn Baṭṭūṭa*, 194.

75 Pesce, *Jiddah*, 16–17, 19, 137. Pesce quotes al-Muqaddasī and Ibn al-Mujāwir; the latter's testimony reveals that cisterns were built both inside and outside the city, thus trapping enough rainwater to ensure that the city reservoirs constantly remained full.

76 See Hunter, *Account of the British Settlement*, 12. The account is attributed to traveler Henry Salt, who saw the cisterns before 1809.

77 Ibn al-Mujāwir, *Taʾrīkh al-mustabṣir*, 1:117.

78 *Quḍaḍ or qaḍaḍ* is made by pulverizing a kind of volcanic stone, mixing the powder with lime, and then adding water. Traditionally used for waterproofing the surfaces of all hydraulic installations, it also took on an ornamental function, especially in Tahirid architecture. For an expansive treatment of the material, its use, and its history, see al-Radi, *ʿAmiriya in Radaʿ*, 133–36, 191–95. See also Bel, *Yémen*, 164, 206; Porter, "Architecture," 106 (which notes the remains of *qaḍaḍ*-lined cisterns at the Tahirid capital, al-Miqrāna, and the presence of *qaḍaḍ* among the waterproofing materials at the Ma'rib dam).

79 Ibn al-Mujāwir, *Taʾrīkh al-mustabṣir*, 1:117. It is unclear here whether Ibn al-Mujāwir refers to the memory of Sasanian or later Iranian migrations to Yemen. On the Sasanians in Aden, see al-Marzūqī, *Al-azmina*

wa'l-amkina, 164. On Sasanian trade in the Indian Ocean, see Whitehouse and Williamson, "Sasanian Maritime Trade."

80 Löfgren, "ʿAdan." In the 1890s, British traveler Walter Harris described an example of Himyarite tanks located near the city of Dhamār (*Journey*, 256–57). His account reveals that despite the different terrain at the two places, the construction of the cisterns of Dhamār and Aden bears close similarities.

81 Smith, "Rasulid Administration," 17 n. 73; Serjeant, "Ports of Aden and Shihr," 211.

82 Abū Makhrama, *Taʾrīkh thaghr ʿadan*, 1:21; see section on Rubāk later in this chapter.

83 TS NS J1/IB.199/II.24, lines 3–4: *wa-bi-yad Bamma . . . shirāʾ māʾ wa-ḥawāʾij bilīj dīnār.*

84 In the first half of the 20th century, Harold Ingrams saw two realms in the general area of the Crater, the realm of men and the realm of mountains (*Arabia and the Isles*, 89). As noted earlier, al-Hamdānī describes Aden as "surrounded by mountains."

85 Cornu's geographical work, *Atlas du monde Arabo-Islamique*, features only Abyan and Laḥj—perhaps rightly so, since places such as al-Mabāh, Rubāk, and Lakhaba do not appear in any of the works by classical geographers. The archaeological study of Aden's hinterland by King and Tonghini, *Survey*, identifies Lakhaba. Finally, the seminal works of Sprenger (*Post- und Reisenrouten des Oriens*) and Grohmann (*Südarabien als Wirtschaftsgebiet*) mention the place-names in question as parts of itineraries extracted from medieval works but, because the authors are more interested in routes than in individual way stations and recognize the limitations of the sources, do not place these locales on a map. Sprenger's work represents an attempt to reconstruct travel and postal routes of the entire Middle East, whereas Grohmann's effort, which borrows from Sprenger, focuses on southern Arabian trade routes. Sprenger studies the case of Yemen in general and Aden in particular through the works of Ibn Khurradādhbih, ʿUmāra, and especially Ibn al-Mujāwir; Grohmann adds material from al-Hamdānī.

86 Ibn al-Mujāwir, *Taʾrīkh al-mustabṣir*, 1:148–49, 133–34. In his section on sweet-water wells behind or in the hinterland of Aden (*al-ābār al-ḥulwa bi-ẓahir ʿadan*), Ibn al-Mujāwir mentions wells on the road to Lakhaba, on the road to al-Mafālīs, and on the road to Abyan.

87 Ibid., 1:91: *min zabīd ilā ʿadan ʿalā ṭarīq al-sāḥil.* Evidence of this route also exists for Rasulid times, but it does not appear on a colonial map

of caravan routes included in Hunter's account of the colony; see al-Shamrookh, *Commerce and Trade*, 216; Hunter, *Account of the British Settlement*, 86–87 (map).

88 Ibn al-Mujāwir's "from Aden to al-Mafālīs": al-Mabāh (.25 *farsakh*), al-Mazaff (1 *farsakh*), al-Mimlāḥ (.25 *farsakh*), al-Maghdālī (.25 *farsakh*), al-Lakhaba (.25 *farsakh*), Ḥajr al-ʿUrr (1 *farsakh*), Bi'r al-Rajaʿ (2 *farsakhs*), Nuwayʿim (2 *farsakhs*), and al-Mafālīs (2 *farsakhs*). Nuwayʿim is reportedly a wadi, which, like Wadi Marḥab, is located the border between the plains and the mountains (*wa-humā ākhir al-waṭā'a wa-awwal al-jibāl*) (Ibn al-Mujāwir, *Ta'rīkh al-mustabṣir*, 1:148–49). Al-Mafālīs, however, is firmly located along the mountain trail and is described as a *qaṣba mukhtaṣara* (a simple fortified citadel) (Löfgren, *Arabische Texte*, 1:70 n. 16).

89 For the route between Aden and Shibām, see Sprenger, *Post- und Reisenrouten*, 142;. For the coastal route between Aden and the Dhofari ports, see Sprenger, *Post- und Reisenrouten*, 144; Grohmann, *Südarabien als Wirtschaftsgebiet*, 127. The coastal route remained in use during the Rasulid period, when caravans found it safer than other routes to the Ḥaḍramawt (al-Shamrookh, *Commerce and Trade*, 218).

90 See Sprenger, *Post- und Reisenrouten*, 149–50; Grohmann, *Südarabien als Wirtschaftsgebiet*, 129. For the connection to coastal caravan routes between Oman and Mecca, see Sprenger, *Post- und Reisenrouten*, 141.

91 On the Najd road from Sanaa to Mecca and the coastal road from Yemen to Mecca, which Ibn al-Mujāwir describes in considerable detail, see Sprenger, *Post- und Reisenrouten*, 125, 131–32. Grohmann shows that one of the two routes between Sanaa and Aden described by al-Hamdānī and later by ʿUmāra should be compared with what the British traveler Harris explains as a branch of the great pilgrim road leading from Aden via the mountain fortress town of Ibb to Mecca (*Südarabien als Wirtschaftsgebiet*, 129; see also Harris, *Journey*, 18).

92 Abū Makhrama, *Ta'rīkh thaghr ʿadan*, 2:60.

93 Hunter, *Account of the British Settlement*, 88.

94 Ibn al-Mujāwir includes al-Mabāh in his itineraries from al-ʿĀra to Aden and from Aden to al-Mafālīs and consistently gives the distance between Aden and al-Mabāh as .25 *farsakh*—that is, about 1.5 kilometers. He also tells a story that confirms the position of village very close to the city (*Ta'rīkh al-mustabṣir*, 1:106, 133, 148): four men he interviewed during his visit told him about a sweet-water spring located behind the Jabal ʿUrr in a wadi by the sea. Adenis could not take advan-

tage of that precious source, they told him, because the place was completely inaccessible by land. When asked how they knew of the spring, the men replied that on one occasion when the city was in upheaval and its gates were locked, they were stranded in al-Mabāh: while trying to find an alternative way into Aden, they chanced upon this well. Abū al-Makhrama describes al-Mabāh as a small village (*qarya ṣaghīra*), located *taḥt ʿadan* (opposite Aden) and .25 *farsakh* from Jabal al-Ḥadīd, the mountain height that extends from the sides of the crater north to the western side of the isthmus (*Ta'rīkh thaghr ʿadan*, 1:18). When threatened by the advancing Ottomans, the Adenis stationed troops at the harbor and at al-Mabāh. Finally, describing a battle that took place in Rasulid times, the same author relates that the force attacking Aden, initially stationed at Lakhaba on the mainland, made for al-Mabāh, while the defenders emerged from the city and routed the invaders to Jabal al-Ḥadīd (*Ta'rīkh thaghr ʿadan*, 2:144). The narrative, therefore, suggests that al-Mabāh stood guard on the immediate landward approach to the town through the Main Pass, at a location that more or less agrees with the estimates of distance of .25 *farsakh* from both Jabal al-Ḥadīd and from Aden town, coinciding with the site known today as al-Maʿalla'.

95 After reaching this conclusion independently, I discovered that my identification of medieval al-Mabāh with modern al-Maʿalla' agrees with the work of Muḥayriz, *Al-ʿaqaba*, 48–49.

96 In the latter part of the 19th century, Hunter describes al-Maʿalla' as a village with mostly Somali inhabitants. A customshouse was already located there, heralding the village's later incorporation into Greater Aden (*Account of the British Settlement*, 8–9).

97 For Abū Makhrama's account of al-Mabāh, see *Ta'rīkh thaghr ʿadan*, 1:18–19.

98 A parallel movement resulting from deliberate policy rather than organic development can be observed in the early British colonial period: in an effort to purge Aden of its poorest inhabitants, Captain S. B. Haines, conqueror and first governor of Aden, moved twenty-nine hundred Somalis to al-Maʿalla' (Bel, *Aden*, 27).

99 The only exception is Ibn Baṭṭūṭa's general statement that the population of Aden consisted of merchants, porters, and fishermen (*Riḥlat Ibn Baṭṭūṭa*, 195: *wa-ahl ʿadan mā bayna tujjār wa-ḥammālīn wa-ṣayyādīn al-samak*). Ibn Baṭṭūṭa probably saw these workers frequenting the harbor and the market; that porters worked in the city and fishermen sold their

fish there does not preclude the possibility that either or both groups lived elsewhere.

100 *Nūra* is traditionally used in shipbuilding and maintenance all along the Arabian littoral (Serjeant, "Maritime Customary Law," 204) and more rarely is used as a lining for drainage pipes in some parts of Yemen (Bel, *Yémen*, 204). See also *Oman*, 162.

101 Bel states on the authority of early-19th-century accounts of Aden that "until the British arrived, Aden was no more than a large native village, nestling in its volcano, with the presence of another village al-Maʿalla', made up of African peoples, dhowbuilders, fishermen, and caravaneers lying just outside the Crater" (*Aden*, 27). As late as the mid–20th century, the British colonial annual report on Aden published a photograph of sail makers working at "dhow building yards" on al-Maʿalla' beach (Colonial Office, *Annual Report*, 38–39).

102 Ibn al-Mujāwir, *Ta'rīkh al-mustabṣir*, 92. Jāzim, *Nūr al-maʿārif*, 132, notes that the substance was used in the manufacture of soap.

103 See Löfgren, *Arabische Texte*, 1:18, 2:29; Hunter, *Account of the British Settlement*, 82.

104 Hunter, *Account of the British Settlement*, 81. Hunter includes lime burning among Aden's native industries. The local term for lime was apparently "*chunam*," and the fifteen operational kilns of his days used "lumps of coral, found on the opposite coast of the [western] harbor."

105 This particular derivative from the root *ḥ-l-j* (to card or separate the fiber from seeds, etc.) does not appear in the standard medieval lexica (see Ibn Manẓūr, *Lisān al-ʿarab*; al-Zabīdī, *Tāj al-ʿarūs*), but its designation in Abū Makhrama's text is obvious, especially in view of later usage. Löfgren refers to Grohmann's explanation of the term in describing the contemporary textile industry in Yemen, including factories in the town of Laḥj and its surroundings, in the vicinity of Aden (*Texte*, 2:30; see also Piamenta, *Dictionary*).

106 The Rasulid material is surveyed by al-Shamrookh, *Commerce and Trade*, 137–42 (on the textile industry), 190–93 (on the textile trade). See also Baldry, *Textiles in Yemen*, 21–23.

107 Baldry, *Textiles in Yemen*, 21.

108 Al-Shamrookh, *Commerce and Trade*, 140–41; Serjeant, *Islamic Textiles*, 131. Serjeant is probably quoting Ibn al-Mujāwir's list of import taxes. Ibn al-Mujāwir indicates that most merchandise meant for reexport was not taxable (*Ta'rīkh al-mustabṣir*, 1:140–43). See also Smith, "Have You Anything to Declare?," 132–33, 137.

109 Al-Shamrookh, *Commerce and Trade*, 139–41.

110 Mosseri A55/IB.166/VII.22, line 11: *wa-burd aḥmar ʿamal al-balad*. The document is a *tadhkira* (memorandum or inventory), listing goods belonging to the deceased merchant, Isaac. The deceased is probably Isaac b. Nafūsī; in his unpublished notes to the text, Goitein observes that the writer of the inventory, Abraham b. Ismāʿīl al-Maghribī, is one of the signatories of document TS20.63/IB.82/VI.26, written in Aden and dated 527/1133; see also Shaked, *Tentative Bibliography*, 241, 73.

111 Baldry, *Textiles in Yemen*, 23; see also Varisco, *Medieval Agriculture and Islamic Science*, 201–2.

112 Ibn al-Mujāwir, *Ta'rīkh al-mustabṣir*, 1:105.

113 Abū Makhrama does not say that ships anchored at the village, only that on their way westward they *headed* there to get water (*Ta'rīkh thaghr ʿadan*, 1:20–21: *wa-qad taqṣiduhā al-marākib al-mā'rra ilā al-shām wa-zaylaʿ li'l-istisqā' minhā*). This probably happened when Aden itself was short on water, and it is conceivable that these ships anchored at a distance from shore and sent out supply parties on lighters to fetch the water from the village.

114 See Whitcomb, "Islamic Archaeology," 176, map 2.

115 Ibid., 191. Whitcomb regrets the fact that Bi'r Rubāk as well as other sites in the area have not been fully described. I have not been able to locate any mention of Bi'r Rubāk in archaeological reports postdating Whitcomb's report.

116 Abū Makhrama, *Ta'rīkh thaghr ʿadan*, 1:20; Ibn al-Mujāwir, *Ta'rīkh al-mustabṣir*, 1:105.

117 Hunter, *Account of the British Settlement*, 10.

118 Abū Makhrama, *Ta'rīkh thaghr ʿadan*, 1:20, 2:173; al-Hijji, *Art of Dhow Building*, 39. The medieval terms for the tree are "*al-shakī*" and "*al-barkī*"; the modern Kuwaiti term as recorded by al-Hijji is "*fanaṣ*."

119 Ibn al-Mujāwir, *Ta'rīkh al-mustabṣir*, 1:148. For Ibn al-Mujāwir's statements concerning this man's role in the building of new walls and the customshouse, see the sections in chapter 3 on the fortifications and the customshouse.

120 Abū Makhrama, *Ta'rīkh thaghr ʿadan*, 1:21.

121 Goitein first identified the Lakhaba mentioned in the Geniza documents with the place appearing in Ibn al-Mujāwir's narrative, though Goitein does not point out the chronological discrepancy between what the literary texts claim and what the Geniza text proves; see Goitein, *Letters*, 189 n. 13; Goitein, "Portrait," 458 n. 42.

122 Ibn al-Mujāwir, *Ta'rīkh al-mustabṣir*, 1:148 (*wa-minhā yunqalu al-ājurr wa-al-zujjāj*); Abū Makhrama, *Ta'rīkh thaghr ʿadan*, 1:21.

123 For Lakhabī glass, see ULC Or1081 J3/IB.61/II.26, line 7. Lakhabī glass is included in an account sent by Maḍmūn b. Japheth of Aden to Ben Yijū in India. Glass purchased in Aden for the same man on two other occasions appears in two other documents (TS24.64/IB.56/III.10, lines 41–45; TS20.137/IB.29/II.23, lines 44–45) and may well be Lakhabī glass. As Goitein observes in his publication of the first of these two documents, the low price of the particular consignments signals that the glass involved was a local, ordinary product rather than the finer, more costly wares imported from Egypt (*Letters*, 189 n. 13).

124 Kawd Amsayla was investigated first by Arthur Lane and Serjeant, "Pottery and Glass Fragments," and subsequently by the director of antiquities at Aden, Brian Doe, in "Pottery Sites." Serjeant first expressed the opinion that the place should be identified with the Lakhaba described in Ibn al-Mujāwir and Abū Makhrama; see King and Tonghini, *Survey*, 18, 20, 22; see also Doe, *Southern Arabia*, 134–37. Monod, "Sur une site à bracelets de verre," further studied the glass of the site, while the pottery was included in Whitcomb, "Islamic Archaeology," 188–92, a study of Islamic ceramic assemblages from Aden and Abyan. Whitcomb dated the material to his Middle Islamic period (1150–1500), mostly from the 7th/13th century onward. Further field research conducted at the site in 1993 by a French team located material dating mostly to after the 8th/14th century (Hardy-Guilbert and Rougeulle, "Archaeological Research," 36). The fact that most of the ceramic finds date slightly later than the period covered by this book does not necessarily preclude an earlier date for the site: archaeologists have already observed that the 5th/11th and 6th/12th centuries are very difficult to identify in the material record of the region and may easily be confused with earlier or later finds (Hardy-Guilbert and Rougeulle, "Archaeological Research," 35; Whitcomb, "Islamic Archaeology," 186). Muḥayriz also notes that this place conforms to the medieval description of Lakhaba's wells, glass, and pottery but cautions that other sites also fit these parameters (*al-ʿAqaba*, 101).

125 Ibn al-Mujāwir, *Ta'rīkh al-mustabṣir*, 1:148.

126 Abū Makhrama, *Ta'rīkh thaghr ʿadan*, 1:22. Sesame oil presses, known as *maʿṣara* or *ṭāḥūn*, consist of a big wooden mortar and pestle worked by a blindfolded camel walking in circles around the mortar; for a description, see Stone, *Studies on the Tihāmah*, 131, plate 8.9.

127 Ibn al-Mujāwir, *Ta'rīkh al-mustabṣir*, 1:134.

128 Abū Makhrama, *Ta'rīkh thaghr ʿadan*, 1:21.

129 This wonderful document appears in the article that constitutes Goitein's last contribution to the study of the documentary Geniza; it was published after his death. Through this and two other letters, Goitein traces the career of an India trader, ʿAllān b. Hassūn, and thus exposes what must have been a common trajectory for the men who took the plunge into the India trade. This letter was written when ʿAllān was at the beginning of his career. See Goitein, "Portrait."

130 TS10J16, f. 1/IB.143/VI.11, line 11: *wa-lā tas'āl mā faʿala maʿī Yūsuf*. See also Goitein, "Portrait," 455 (original), 457 (translation).

131 TS10J16, f. 1/IB.143/VI.11, postscript: *wa-qad jalasa Yūsuf fī Lakhaba maʿ al-zonot wa-al-ṣuḥba wa-aḥad amrad yus*[*qīhim*]. See also Goitein, "Portrait," 455 (original), 458 (translation). Here I give a modified version of Goitein's translation. Goitein identifies Lakhaba and points out ʿAllān's effort to denigrate his cousin Joseph.

132 On the use of the term "*zonot*," see Goitein, "Portrait," 458, n. 43. Goitein convincingly argues that "the word 'whores' was written in Hebrew so that it would not be understood by everyone."

133 This was a celebration at a Jewish merchant's house, the coincidence of which with a Muslim holiday seems to have led to an explosive outcome; see Goitein's discussion of the incident in *Mediterranean Society*, 5:40, 516 n. 150, 223, 568 n. 19. The other two reported cases of drinking in town do not seem to have ended disastrously. Around 1204, a long-absent India trader writing to his wife in Egypt, apparently from Aden, admits he has been drinking but assures her of his continued loyalty and piety (ENA 2739, f. 16/IB.176/VII.60; see Goitein, *Letters*, 223–24). About seventy years earlier, Maḍmūn b. Japheth accuses Ben Yijū's Indian slave/agent, Bamma, of drunkenness and general unruliness (TS20.137/IB.29/II.23; see Gosh, "Slave of MS. H. 6," 188–89).

134 Ibn al-Mujāwir recounts the tale of Bilāl b. Jarīr's triumph during the Zurayid power struggle (*Ta'rīkh al-mustabṣir*, 45): *wa-bayna ʿadan wa-bayna laḥj masīrat layla*. Smith gives a distance of about twenty-five kilometers between Aden and Laḥj ("Laḥdj").

135 For a summary of the geographical sources written before the 7th/13th century, see Cornu, *Atlas*, 78; on Laḥj, see maps VII and VIII.

136 Smith, "Laḥdj."

137 See King and Tonghini, *Survey*, 19, 23–25. Al-Ḥabīl, a site northwest of Laḥj, has yielded, among other Islamic finds, imitations of imported

Chinese pottery dating to the 13th to 15th centuries (King and Tonghini, *Survey*, 18, a report on field research by Serjeant). See also Whitcomb, "Islamic Archaeology," 191, which mentions the study of the irrigation systems near al-Ḥabīl.

138 Ibn al-Mujāwir, *Ta'rīkh al-mustabṣir*, 1:106, 108.

139 Laḥj features in both routes connecting Aden to Sanaa as described by al-Hamdānī; see Grohmann, *Südarabien als Wirtschaftsgebiet*, 128–29. In addition, Ibn al-Mujāwir includes the town in his itineraries from Aden to Shibām and from the region of Dhofar through the ports of Mukallā and al-Shiḥr and then inland to Aden (Grohmann, *Südarabien als Wirtschaftsgebiet*, 127; Sprenger, *Post- und Reisenrouten*, esp. 144).

140 Varisco, *Medieval Agriculture and Islamic Science*, 37, 69, 161–62, 167–68, 184. Melons are also mentioned both at Laḥj and at Aden. According to Hunter, in the 19th century the land surrounding Laḥj produced grains such as sorghum (a variety designated by the term "*jowari*"), vegetables, sesame, cotton, and dates and wild almonds (*Account of the British Settlement*, 63–69, 155).

141 Abū Makhrama, *Ta'rīkh thaghr ʿadan*, 1:19: *wa-awqafa ʿalā ʿimāratihi mustaghallāt arāḍ muzdaraʿa bi-laḥj*; Ibn al-Mujāwir, *Ta'rīkh al-mustabṣir*, 1:148: *wa-awqafa ʿalā ʿimāratihi mustaghallāt bi-ʿadan*. Abū Makhrama elaborates on Ibn al-Mujāwir's account.

142 The literary sources often refer to Aden-Abyan as a town in its own right or an independent territory. Ibn Khaldūn, for example, says that Aden-Abyan is "a well-built city in the neighborhood of al-Shiḥr." Kay, *Yaman*, xxi, remarks on the misleading view that "Aden Abyan and the well-known seaport of Aden were two different places." See Cornu, *Atlas*, 69.

143 See Whitcomb, "Islamic Archaeology," esp. 181, 188; King and Tonghini, *Survey*, 19–20, 27–31.

144 See Sprenger, *Post- und Reisenrouten*, 142, 144; Grohmann, *Südarabien als Wirtschaftsgebiet*, 127.

145 Whitcomb, "Islamic Archaeology," 187–88, dates most of the material, local and imported, to between the 12th and 13th centuries, while Hardy-Guilbert and Rougeulle, "Archaeological Research," 33–36, report Chinese imports datable to the 13th and 14th centuries. In his *Al-nisba ilā al-mawāḍiʿ wa-al-buldān*, Abū Makhrama, conversely, mentions Khanfar and al-Mahall as Abyan's famous towns (*mudunuha al-mashhūra*), probably referring to his own time (Serjeant, "Two Sixteenth-Century Arabian Geographical Works," 260).

146 Ibn al-Mujāwir, *Ta'rīkh al-mustabṣir*, 1:117: *wa-nuqila ṭīn al-binā' min nawāḥī abyan*; 126: *wa-kāna yujlabu al-ḥajr ilā ʿadan min aʿmāl abyan li-ajl al-ʿimāra*.

147 Ibn al-Mujāwir, *Ta'rīkh al-mustabṣir*, 1:130: *wa-al-aṣaḥḥ inna mā ʿamirat illā baʿd kharāb furḍat abyan wa-hiram*. See also Abū Makhrama's entry on Abyan in his *Al-nisba ilā al-mawāḍiʿ wa-al-buldān* (Serjeant, "Two Sixteenth-Century Arabian Geographical Works," 260: *wa-kāna fīhā min qadīm qurā wa-mudun kharibat wa-baqiyat bi-lā sākin*).

148 For madder, *Rubia tinctorum* (Ar. *fuwwa*), see Löfgren, *Arabische Texte*, 2:51. Ibn al-Mujāwir includes madder among the taxable imports into Aden (*Ta'rīkh al-mustabṣir*, 1:141–42). Abū Makhrama gives the biography of a *faqīh* living in the Highlands and taking the Mafālīs road to Aden to sell madder from his estate (*Ta'rīkh thaghr ʿadan*, 2:125). For the possible use of madder in a local cloth-making industry, see the section on al-Mabāh earlier in this chapter. Sesame occurs in Ibn al-Mujāwir's lists of nontaxable imports from India (*Ta'rīkh al-mustabṣir*, 1:142–43) yet is a traditional crop of the Yemeni highlands and the Red Sea Tihāmah coast (Stone, *Studies on the Tihāmah*, 131). As discussed earlier in this chapter, Abū Makhrama states that Lakhaba featured presses (*maʿāṣir*), probably sesame oil presses of the type that remains common in Yemen today.

149 JTS Geniza Misc. 8/IB.235/II.51, lines 7–9: *ṭara'a fī al-balad ʿindana wa-fī jamīʿ al-yaman ghalā' ʿaẓīm wa-qaḥṭ*.

150 Ibid., lines 9–11: *balagha al-dukhn wa-al-burr ʿindana 3 makāyyal bi-dīnār wa-dūn dhālika wa-jamīʿ al-mā'kulāt ghālīya min awwalihā ilā akhīrihā*. The term "*dukhn*" means "millet"; on the cultivation and varieties of millet in Yemen, see Varisco, *Medieval Agriculture and Islamic Science*, 165, 167; Varisco, "Agriculture in Rasulid Zabīd," 331–32. For *burr* (also the usual word for "wheat" in the Rasulid almanacs, which record a number of varieties), see Varisco, *Medieval Agriculture and Islamic Science*, 175–79. In the Tihāmah, for example, millet (*Pennisetum typoides*), still known as *dukhn*, *dukhn mahallī*, or *dukhn tihāmah*, is one of the major cereal crops (Stone, *Studies on the Tihāmah*, 17).

151 JTS Geniza Misc. 8/IB.235/II.51, lines 12–19. See also the discussion in chapter 3 of the city's forts and the leadership struggle of the middle of the 6th/12th century.

152 Ibn al-Mujāwir, *Ta'rīkh al-mustabṣir*, 1:142.

153 TS18J2, f. 7/IB.24/II.14, lines 25–26: *wa-qad ishtarā bazz miṣrī wa-ṭalaʿa ilā al-jabal*. For the full text of the letter, see Goitein, "From Aden to

India," 47, 52, 55. As Goitein notes, *al-jabal* can only refer to the "Highlands of Yemen."

Chapter Two

1 For example, according to its modern excavators, the harbor of Caesaria Maritima in Roman Palestine "can serve as a paradigm of Roman imperial culture and maritime technology" (Oleson et al., "Caesaria Ancient Harbor Project," 285). See also Hadjidaki, "Harbour Studies," 188.

2 See Blackman's seminal two-part article, "Ancient Harbours." See also Hadjidaki, "Harbour Studies," 189; Shaw's illustrated survey, "Greek and Roman Harborworks."

3 Important new work, including excavation and postexcavation analysis, is currently being carried out on the port of Quṣayr al-Qadīm; see the interim excavation reports in Peacock et al., *Myos Hormos*. For a very good case study of the development of a port and its transition from the Late Antique to the early Islamic period, including attention to the physical space of the harbor, see Mayerson, "Port of Clysma." For a short account of the Muslim town at Caesarea Maritima that offers glimpses of the postclassical harbor and includes references to a seawall and an extraordinary jetty made of column spolia, see Holum et al., *King Herod's Dream*, 201–14, 231–33. Petersen's important account of the Palestinian littoral under Muslim rule indicates that coastal sites that might yield important archaeological evidence for harbor development have not been fully explored (*Towns of Palestine*, 79–80, 83–89).

4 See, e.g., Soucek, "Mīnā'," the *Encyclopaedia of Islam* entry on ports.

5 For transformations at Caesarea, see Holum et al., *King Herod's Dream*, 202, 231–32.

6 Contraction of coastal settlement does not exclusively signify lack of interest and concerted official investment in coastal affairs as a whole, and evidence exists for such investment, especially for naval purposes, in Abbasid and Fatimid times; see El'ad, "Coastal Cities," esp. 146, 151–55; Petersen, *Towns of Palestine*, 79–80.

7 Mayerson, "Port of Clysma," 126.

8 Soucek, "Mīnā'."

9 On Sīrāf and its roadstead arrangements, see Bosworth, "Sīrāf"; Whitehouse, "Excavations at Sīrāf: First Interim Report," 3. On the possible coexistence at Ṣuḥār of relatively open roadstead and inlet moorings, see Williamson, "Harvard Archaeological Survey," 82, 88–90.

10 For built structures in the ports of the Lamu Archipelago, see Chittick, *Manda*, 21, 36, 41.

11 On Kish/Qays, its open roadstead, and rock-cut galleries that may have served as loading bays for boats, see Whitehouse, "Kīsh," 147.

12 See Bel, *Aden*, 18, 20, 26, 34, 78, 80, 84. Bel misattributes some of the illustrations; see Graham, review. The earliest known engravings of Aden city views are based on an account by Ludovico di Varthema, an Italian traveler who wrote an account of his visit and imprisonment in Yemen in the first decade of the 16th century. The best example is the late-16th-century rendition that appears in Braun and Hogenberg's celebrated collection of city views, *Civitates orbis terrarum*, 1:53.

13 Abū Makhrama, *Ta'rīkh thaghr ʿadan*, 1:12–13, 16. Abū Makhrama relates that the harbor's breakwater, or *shiṣna* (discussed later in the chapter), was virtually dismantled and its stones scavenged, with catastrophic results, for the purposes of the building of the Dār al-Bandar. Ibn al-Mujāwir does not mention the space or the building. According to Abū Makhrama, the Portuguese (*al-faranj*), whom he blames for the destruction of the edifice, used it as a shooting station in their attack on Aden; this enigmatic statement may indicate that the space was located on the northern or southern side of the Crater or even on the island of Ṣīra, outside the city wall.

14 A glimpse of the same predilection for maritime vistas and promenades by the sea is offered by a perusal of the rules (*takkanot*) of the Jewish community of Candia, Crete, from the 13th to the 16th centuries: members of the congregation were forbidden to "go to the ships" during the holidays. Arbel points out that it appears that people sometimes skipped the Sabbath prayer at the synagogue to "go to the ships," a phrase that he takes to denote promenading along the seashore and watching the ships at the harbor (*Trading Nations*, 182 n. 53).

15 TS28.22/IB.14/I.14, line 10: *wa-tafaḍḍalta wa-nazalta shayyaʿ tanī fī al-baḥr*. On *sh-y-ʿ*, see Kazimirsky, *Dictionnaire*, "reconduire quelqu'un et lui faire ses adieux." The verbal construction supplied here, *sh-yy-ʿ fī al-baḥr*, conveys the special meaning of seeing someone off as he or she is boarding a vessel and going back out to sea.

16 Goitein, *Mediterranean Society*, 1:314, 480 n. 6. The day before sailing, the prospective travelers were probably busy with preparations, which probably kept them at the harbor all day. The Geniza documents even provide evidence for special terms such as the participle "*muqliʿ*" and the phrase "*laylat al-mabīt*" that respectively describe the states of get-

ting ready to set sail and of spending the night on board at the harbor; see also the section in chapter 3 on transient merchants' accommodations.

17 TS20.137/IB.29/II.23; TS18J5, f. 5/IB.149/II.46. These two letters have been partially published in Goitein, "Two Eyewitness Reports."

18 Ibn al-Mujāwir, *Ta'rīkh al-mustabṣir*, 1:115. Ibn al-Mujāwir records a purportedly local tradition according to which the temperature of the channel's water provides a weather forecast for the entire year. The information is repeated in Abū Makhrama, *Ta'rīkh thaghr ʿadan*, 1:17. The British colonial maps from the first half of the 20th century record the name of the straits as Ma'qilein, a term that must be related to (a corruption of) *al-maʿjalayn*; see Colonial Office, *Annual Report*, map at end.

19 The first modern scholar to identify Ṣīra Bay with the medieval harbor was George Percy Badger, editor of the Hakluyt Society's 1863 publication of Ludovico di Varthema's account of his travels translated by John Winters Jones (Ludovico di Varthema, *Travels*, 59). Ludovico's account of the anchorage of ships is suggestive of the relationship between Ṣīra, city, and anchorage: "At a stone's cast from this city there is a mountain, upon which stands a castle, and at the foot of this mountain the ships cast anchor."

20 Ibn al-Mujāwir claims that seventy to eighty ships put into port every year (*Ta'rīkh al-mustabṣir*, 1:144). The basis for this estimate is unclear. Descriptions of the various Portuguese sieges of Aden in the early 10th/16th century mention eighteen, twenty, twenty-four, and thirty ships putting into the harbor each time; see Serjeant, *Portuguese off the South Arabian Coast*, 48, 50, 169; see also Varisco, *Medieval Agriculture and Islamic Science*, 218.

21 On the geomorphology of the bay and its transformations, see Prados, "Archaeological Investigation," 299–301.

22 Ibid., 300–302. The date of the structure's construction is uncertain. The first iconographic evidence of its existence appears in 19th-century engravings, although Hogenberg's engraving of the city features a tall minaret flanked by two shorter structures just behind the seawall. Prados points to structural and stylistic characteristics that resemble Seljuk architectural features and suggests a possible 5th/11th century date. Harold Ingrams, conversely, dates it to "the days of Suleyman the Magnificent"—that is, the first Ottoman occupation of Yemen in the 10th/16th century—and regards it as a proper minaret that served a

mosque that has since disappeared (*Arabia and the Isles*, 88). Bel, who worked on the restoration of the nearby Rimbaud House, agrees and posits that the mosque must have been razed in the 19th century (*Yémen*, 163). Prados's identification of the "Aden Minaret" as a light- or signal house rests on the structure's location as well as on its general configuration: small windows located near its top are suitable for flashing lights to observation points in the surrounding mountain peaks and out to sea, while the position of the internal platform, apparently at the same level as the windows, renders it unsuitable for a person to stand on and call for prayer. He also finds no evidence that the structure was ever used as a minaret ("Archaeological Investigation," 301–2).

23 *Sailing Directions for the Red Sea* (1976), 260.

24 Concrete evidence shows that such was the case in at least one year. The combined testimony of the two Geniza letters recounting a naval siege (discussed later in this chapter) shows that in that year, Aden's harbor was devoid of ships from early November until two months later, when two ships arrived together at the port.

25 Abū Makhrama, *Ta'rīkh thaghr ʿadan*, 1:15: *mabnīya binā' muḥkaman*; location: *bi-aʿlā al-bandar khalfa marsā al-marākib min jihat al-baḥr*.

26 Ibid., 15–16: *li-maṣlaḥat al-bandar wa-dhālika anna al-mawj yaqwā fī ayyām al-azyab fa-idhā jā'at al-mawja al-ʿaẓīma inkasara hiddatuhā ʿalā hādhā al-binā' fa-lā taṣilu ilā al-bandar wa-maḥall al-marākib illā wa-qad fāshat wa-hānat*.

27 See Prados, "Archaeological Investigation," 302. See also Braun and Hogenberg, *Civitates orbis terrarum*, 1:53.

28 Prados, "Archaeological Investigation," 302. Prados's account is valuable because to my knowledge, it provides the only testimony to both the visible and the underwater remains of the mole. He also notes the existence of a chart by the British conqueror of Aden, Captain Haines, that shows the mole with ships anchored to its lee.

29 Blackman, "Ancient Harbours," 79.

30 For a history of the island and a detailed analysis of the variant spellings of its name, see Streck, "Ḳais." See also Wilson, *Persian Gulf*, 98–100; Whitehouse, "Kīsh"; Goitein, "Two Eyewitness Reports," 247–48.

31 In the later part of the 6th/12th century, Jewish traveler Benjamin of Tudela, *Itinerary*, 62–63, reports on both the island's market and the local Jewish community of five hundred. Ibn al-Mujāwir, *Ta'rīkh al-mustabṣir*, 2:287–300, devotes a lengthy section to the island state's history and geography as well as the local rulers' exploits on the high

seas. In his geographical dictionary of the early 7th/13th century, Yāqūt, *Muʿjam al-buldān*, 4:215–16, attributes Qaysi influence overseas to ships and shipping.

32 Goitein, "Two Eyewitness Reports," 250.

33 Ibn al-Mujāwir, *Ta'rīkh al-mustabṣir*, 1:124. On the two forts and their significance in the city's administration and the control of its international trade, see chapter 3. In his article analyzing the incident as portrayed in the two Geniza letters, Goitein states that Saba''s coruler during the siege was ʿAlī b. Abī al-Ghārāt ("Two Eyewitness Reports," 250). Ibn al-Mujāwir, however, makes it clear that the siege took place in the days of Muḥammad b. Abī al-Ghārāt. Abū Makhrama informs us that Muḥammad was ʿAlī's brother and that ʿAlī succeeded Muḥammad in the leadership of the city (*Ta'rīkh thaghr ʿadan*, 2:76). The confusion in Goitein's account stems from the fact that Saba' b. Abī al-Suʿūd ruled with both brothers successively: he faced the besieging force from Qays with Muḥammad, and while rivalries seem to have existed all along, his conflict with ʿAlī led to a full-blown crisis. As in the case of the siege, two Geniza letters supplement Ibn al-Mujāwir's account of these later events, from which Saba' emerged victorious.

34 Ibn al-Mujāwir, *Ta'rīkh al-mustabṣir*, 1:122, 123. Ibn al-Mujāwir places Saba''s death in 545/1150, but his chronology is consistently low; he places the death of Bilāl b. Jarīr in 577/1182, well into the Ayyubid period. Cf. ʿUmāra's account of the same events in Kay, *Yaman*, 54 (Arabic), 72 (English); Abū Makhrama's biography of Saba' b. Abī al-Suʿūd in *Ta'rīkh thaghr ʿadan*, 2:89, both of which set Saba''s death in 532/1137 or 533/1138 and Bilāl's death in 546/1151.

35 The besiegers arrived sometime in early November, and the siege lasted for two months; since the letters were written after the siege had been lifted and since they must have gone out sometime in the early months of 1135, the siege can be dated to November and December 1134. See Goitein, "Two Eyewitness Reports," 250; his chronology hinges on the reference in one of the two letters to a prominent Cairo merchant, Ḥalfon b. Nethanel, who was apparently in Egypt when the letter was written. Other, dated letters show that Ḥalfon had been in Aden in the spring of 528/1134 and was traveling west in the Mediterranean in 531/1136. Goitein's calculations constitute a great example of the potential to use internal Geniza evidence to solve problems of more general historical interest.

36 TS20.137/IB.29/II.23, line 13–14: *wa-qaʿadū fī mukallā ʿadan yantaẓirū*

al-marākib. See also Goitein, "Two Eyewitness Reports," 254–55 (text transcribed in Arabic script), 256 (translation).

37 On the port of the Ḥaḍramawt al-Mukallā, which derives its name from the same root, see van Donzel, "al-Mukallā."

38 TS20.137/IB.29/II.23, line 9: *wa-kāna hādhihi al-sana awwal al-waqt*. See also Goitein, "Two Eyewitness Reports," 254, 256.

39 Tibbetts, *Arab Navigation*, 228.

40 Varisco, *Medieval Agriculture and Islamic Science*, 25, 43, 229. Data on the "Qaysi" season include departures for Qays from Aden and arrivals from Qays to Aden. The date of the earliest Qaysi arrivals to Aden given in the Rasulid almanac is the sixth day of Tishrīn al-Thānī, which coincides with November.

41 TS20.137/IB.29/II.23, lines 15–16: *fa-lam yunṣirhum allāh wa-lam yuwaffiqhum wa-qutila minhum khalq kathīr wa-julikhat marākibuhum wa-mātū ʿaṭshan wa-juʿan*. See also Goitein, "Two Eyewitness Reports," 254, 256.

42 Rāmisht was a wealthy and well-known shipowner (*nākhudhā*), probably of Persian origin, who appears repeatedly in the letters of the India trade merchants and is also known from literary and epigraphical sources; see Goitein, "From Aden to India," 63; Goitein, *Letters*, 193 n. 1; Stern, "Rāmisht of Sīrāf." On Rāmisht, the title "*nākhudhā*," and shipping in general, see chapter 5.

43 TS20.137/IB.29/II.23, lines 18–20: *fa-lamman dakhalū al-markabayn ilā al-bandar aṭlaʿū fīhim al-dīwān al-kathīr fa-inṭaradū min al-bandar wa-ṣārū yudūrū fī al-baḥr*. Goitein translates the term "*dīwān*" as "regular troops," quoting a personal communication with Serjeant, who had found the term "*dīwānī*" used in the sense of "professional soldier" in Yemeni manuscripts (Goitein, "Two Eyewitness Reports," 254).

44 As discussed in chapter 1, n. 51, Goitein mistook the text's distinction between *al-bandar* and *al-mukallā* as evidence that medieval Aden was served by two separate harbors, with the two terms corresponding to the western and eastern bay, respectively. I think that a closer reading of Maḍmūn's letter leaves no doubt that *al-mukallā* was but a part of *al-bandar* and that both were located in the eastern, or Front Bay, closely associated with the town.

45 TS18J5, f. 5/IB.149/II.46, lines 3–29. Khalaf's description is more than twice the length of that by Maḍmūn, even though Khalaf calls it just a summary and tells his correspondent that were he to put in writing the various events in detail, ten pieces of paper would not suffice: "*wa-*

ammā akhbārunā wa-mā ṭarā ʿalaynā baʿd safarikum fa-huwa shay yaṭūlu sharḥuhu wa-law ajraytu ʿashara waraqāt ḥattā aṣifu bihi baʿḍ mā ṭarā ʿalaynā lā yakfī dhālika." See also Goitein, "Two Eyewitness Reports," 255–56.

46 TS18J5, f. 5/IB.149/II.46. Throughout his narrative, Khalaf emphasizes the positions taken by defenders and invaders: lines 9–11: *hum fī al-baḥr wa-naḥnu fī al-barr wa-lam yabqā fī al-balad kabīr wa-lā saghīr illā fī al-ḥuṣūn wa-taḥt al-ḥuṣūn illā buyūt fārigha*"; lines 15–16: *wa-al-ʿadūw fī al-mukallā wa-al-nās qad haribū min buyūtihim.*

47 For Ibn al-Mujāwir's report of both a light stone wall and a subsequent latticework substitute, see the section in chapter 3 on the city's fortifications and seawall.

48 TS18J5, f. 5/IB.149/II.46, lines 19–20: *li'annahum kānū qad malakū ṣ[īr]a wa-nazalū bihā qāṭinīn layl wa-nahār.* Goitein translates this as "they stayed one day and one night," but I think it is more reasonable to assume that they had conquered Ṣīra early on, when their arrival had terrorized the strongly fortified but thinly manned town, and that they had been using it as a land base where the troops could find a respite from the cramped quarters on board the ships. See also Goitein, "Two Eyewitness Reports," 255, 256–57.

49 TS18J5, f. 5/IB.149/II.46, lines 17–19: *wa-nazaʿa al-baḥr wa-hum fī ṣīra maʿa al-ṣabāḥ wa-iqtatalū hum wa-ahl al-balad wa-qutila maʿa diyārihim jamāʿa wa-huzzat rū'usuhum wa-nuhiba mā kāna qad nuzzila lahum bi-ṣīra.* That there was plundering of what the enemy "had off-loaded on Ṣīra" indicates a camp or at least enough of a setup for its plundering to be worth mentioning. The reference reinforces the idea that the enemy remained on Ṣīra for some time.

50 TS18J5, f. 5/IB.149/II.46, lines 22–24: *ḥattā waṣala markabay rāmisht wa-kharajū lahum yurīdū ya'khudhūhum wa-kāna al-rīḥ ṭayyib fa-tashattatū fī al-baḥr yamīn wa-yasār wa-dakhalā al-markabayn bi-al-salāma.* See also Goitein, "Two Eyewitness Reports," 255–56. Khalaf says that the wind "was good," meaning, I believe, both that it was beneficial for the purposes of the defenders and that it was quite literally a good—that is, strong—wind.

51 Lateen sails were the typical and ubiquitous rigging on western Indian Ocean ships from antiquity to the end of the sail era in the twentieth century. For a history of the lateen sail in the region, see George Faldo Hourani, *Arab Seafaring*, 100–105. While lateen sails can perform a proper tack (slight change of direction that involves bringing the bow

of the ship across the wind) in extreme emergencies, the safer and most commonly followed procedure when a direction change is required to keep the vessel on the desired course is to wear around—that is, to bring the stern up to the wind and then across it. For the difficulties of tacking with a lateen sail, see Villiers, *Sons of Sinbad*, 48–49, 257–58; Bowen, "Arab Dhows," 125–29; George Faldo Hourani, *Arab Seafaring*, 109.

52 TS18J5, f. 5/IB.149/II.46, lines 24–26: *wa-dakhala ilayhim al-ʿaskar wa-lam ʿāda yabqā lahum ḥīla lā fī al-muka*[*llā*] *wa-lā fī al-balad fa-rajaʿū rāḥū khalfa al-jabal ilā an ṭāba lahum al-rīḥ wa-sāfarū.*

53 So called by Abū Makhrama and Ibn al-Mujāwir but never by the Geniza writers. See Abū Makhrama, *Ta'rīkh thaghr ʿadan*, esp. 1:17: *huwa jabal shāmiḥ fī al-baḥr*; Ibn al-Mujāwir, *Ta'rīkh al-mustabṣir*, 1:111, 112, 114, 124, 144. Ibn al-Mujāwir refers to anchoring *taḥt jabal ṣīra*, a phrase that appears to be symmetrical with Khalaf's *khalfa al-jabal*, "in front of" and "behind the mountain (ṣīra)."

54 In his 1954 article on the two letters examined here, Goitein takes the phrase to mean "behind Ṣīra" and apparently identifies medieval Ṣīra as a mountain connected to the main mass of the peninsula, different from the islet in the harbor ("Two Eyewitness Reports," 257, 251 n. 1). By the time he completed the fifth volume of *Mediterranean Society*, he appears to have changed his mind and to have recognized medieval Ṣīra as the islet in front of Aden's old town (Goitein, *Mediterranean Society*, 5:523 nn. 98, 101).

55 Goitein points to the differences in style and emphasis between the eyewitness reports on the one hand and Ibn Mujāwir's text on the other. While the former are largely unmediated accounts, the latter is a stylized historical construct ("Two Eyewitness Reports," 251). However, Ibn al-Mujāwir visited Aden less than a century after the events, which must surely have been fresh in the city's collective memory and oral tradition.

56 Ibn al-Mujāwir, *Ta'rīkh al-mustabṣir*, 1:124: *fa-lammā waṣalat al-dawānīj arsaū taḥt jabal ṣīra*; 125: *fa-lammā arsat al-jāshū marsā ʿadan.* The author again demonstrates this connection between *al-marsā* and Ṣīra in his account of the number of ships that put into the harbor each year, for he describes the incoming ships as "anchoring by Ṣīra" (Ibn al-Mujāwir, *Ta'rīkh al-mustabṣir*, 1:144: *wa-kāna yursī fī kull ʿām taḥt jabal ṣīra 70–80 markab zā'id nāqiṣ*).

57 Abū Makhrama, *Ta'rīkh thaghr ʿadan*, 1:15: *bi-aʿlā al-bandar khalfa marsā al-marākib min jihat al-baḥr.*

58 Ibn al-Mujāwir, *Ta'rīkh al-mustabṣir*, 1:138–39: *fa-idhā qaruba al-markab rakiba al-mubashshirūn al-ṣanābīq li-liqā' al-markab fa-idhā qarubū min al-markab ṣaʿadū wa-sallamū ilā al-nākhūdha . . . fa-idhā waṣala al-markab al-marsā wa-arsā taqaddama ilayhi nā'ib al-sulṭān*. In recent times, the term "*ṣanbūq*" (*ṣanābīq*) has generally come to refer to medium- or large-sized square-transom seagoing vessels, mostly of the Red Sea (Bowen, "Primitive Watercraft," 212; Hornell, "Tentative Classification," 17–18). Until recently, however, some isolated coastal communities in Yemen and in Oman used the term "*ṣanbūq*" to describe their small sewn boats, which are widely thought to be relics of the indigenous Indian Ocean boatbuilding tradition. Ibn al-Mujāwir and Abū Makhrama make it clear that at least in the former's time, *ṣanābīq* were small boats (Ibn al-Mujāwir, *Ta'rīkh al-mustabṣir*, 1:116; Abū Makhrama, *Ta'rīkh thaghr ʿadan*, 1:9, 19). In the specific context discussed here, it should be understood as a lighter—that is, a small harbor workboat ferrying passengers and merchandise between shore and ships' berths.

59 Ibn al-Mujāwir, *Ta'rīkh al-mustabṣir*, 1:124: *fa-lammā samiʿa al-qawm hādhihi al-maqāla nazalū min al-dawānīj wa-al-burmāt ilā al-sawāḥil.*

60 Ibid., 125–26.

61 Braun and Hogenberg, *Civitates orbis terrarum*, 1:53.

Chapter Three

1 Ibn al-Mujāwir, *Ta'rīkh al-mustabṣir*, 127–28; Abū Makhrama, *Ta'rīkh thaghr ʿadan*, 1:13. Ibn al-Mujāwir does not explicitly date the foundation of the wall, but his references to the ruler at the time as a *dāʿī* (a "missionary" of the Ismāʿīlī movement; the Zurayids claimed the *daʿwa* when Sulayhid power was waning and Sulayhid leaders had invested in the leadership of the dispossessed son of al-ʿAmir, al-Ṭayyib; the result of divided loyalties was a schism in the Ismāʿīlī *daʿwa* of Yemen [see the introduction to this volume; Bates, "Chapter"]) and to the succeeding regime, renovators of the wall, as the Ayyubids suggest strongly that the story is set in the Zurayid period. Abū Makhrama states clearly that these events happened "*fī ayyām āl zurayʿ*."

2 Abū Makhrama does not use the term "shipmaster" but refers to the man only as a merchant, "*al-tājir*." Ibn al-Mujāwir's "*nākhūdha*" is certainly a broad enough term to include someone who owned or managed a boat as well as part or all of its commercial cargo. For a dis-

cussion of this variably spelled term and its variable meaning in Aden's maritime society, see chapter 5.

3 Abū Makhrama again elaborates: he tells us that the foreigner took the house to be a fellow merchant's residence, implying that this conclusion encouraged him to knock on the door (*Ta'rīkh thaghr ʿadan*, 1:13: *fa-ẓanna annahā dār baʿḍ al-tujjār fa-daqqa*).

4 Ibn al-Mujāwir, *Ta'rīkh al-mustabṣir*, 1:127: *khawfan min al-dāʿī*. Slightly more explicitly, Abū Makhrama has the man justify his actions by saying that he was wary of the injustice of the ruler (*Ta'rīkh thaghr ʿadan*, 1:13: *akhshā min jawr al-dāʿī*).

5 Abū Makhrama states that the merchandise smuggled into town included low-volume, high-price items, presumably those that would have been most heavily taxed (*Ta'rīkh thaghr ʿadan*, 1:13: *fa-bāta al-tājir yanqulu min al-markab ilā tilka al-dār mā khaffa ḥamluhu wa-kathurat qīmatuhu ilā an naqala mā arāda*).

6 Ibn al-Mujāwir, *Ta'rīkh al-mustabṣir*, 1:127–28: *khiftu min al-maṭar, waqaʿtu taḥta al-mīzāb*.

7 Ibid., 128: *li-dukhūlika ʿalaynā al-bāriḥa manzilanā fī niṣf al-layl*.

8 ʿUmāra and Ibn al-Mujāwir give multiple figures to express the magnitude of revenues from customs at Aden; see chapter 4.

9 Al-Muqaddasī, *Kitāb aḥsan al-taqāsīm fī maʿrifat al-aqālīm*, 85: *wa-maddū min naḥū al-baḥr ḥa'iṭan min al-jabal ilā al-jabal fīhi khams abwāb*.

10 See the introduction and the discussion of the naval siege in chapter 2.

11 Ibn al-Mujāwir, *Ta'rīkh al-mustabṣir*, 1:121.

12 Ibid., 128.

13 Abū Makhrama consistently refers to the fort as Ḥiṣn al-Khadrā' (*Ta'rīkh thaghr ʿadan*, 1:14).

14 Ibn al-Mujāwir, *Ta'rīkh al-mustabṣir*, 1:121: *wa-jaʿala maqarr al-ʿabbās taʿkar ʿadan wa-huwa yaḥūzu al-barr wa-al-bāb wa-jaʿala li-masʿūd ḥiṣn al-khaḍrā' wa-huwa yaḥūzu al-sāḥil wa-al-marākib*.

15 Kay, *Yaman*, 54: *fa-dakhala madīnat ʿadan wa-lam yuqim bihā illā sabʿat ashhur kamā qadamnāhu wa-dufina bihā fī safḥ al-taʿkar min dākhil al-balad*.

16 Ibn al-Mujāwir, *Ta'rīkh al-mustabṣir*, 1:138. The passage provides significant information for the organization of the harbor and will be further discussed in chapter 4. For a partial translation and general analysis, see Smith, "Have You Anything to Declare?," 127–40.

17 Ibn al-Mujāwir, *Ta'rīkh al-mustabṣir*, 1:123.

18 JTS Geniza Misc. 8/IB. 235/II.51, lines 7–12. In a different letter, Khalaf speaks more broadly of the conflict that arose "between the two sultans" (*waqaʿa al-khulf bayna al-sulṭanayn*) and the effects on the city and its traders; see TS Misc. Box 28, f. 256/IB.207/II.48, lines 10–12. See also the section in chapter 1 on farther hinterland.

19 Ibid., lines 12–15: *wa-ʿāda al-bilād ilā al-sāʿa mukhīfa ʿindanā min al-sulṭān ʿalī b. al-[ghārā]t li'anna al-sulṭān Saba' kāna ḥāribuhu wa-akha[dha . . .] wa-hadama al-khaḍrā' allatī kānat ḥiṣnuhu*. Further in the letter, Khalaf reports Saba''s death shortly after his victory.

20 Ibn al-Mujāwir, *Ta'rīkh al-mustabṣir*, 1:128: *wa-ūdīra sūr ḍaʿīf wa-irtadama baʿḍuhu ʿalā baʿḍ wa-ihtudama li-dawām al-mawj ʿalayhi*. This destruction occurred despite the fact that the Zurayid wall may have been built with newly quarried stone at a time when, according to Ibn al-Mujāwir, stone construction became more prevalent in Aden.

21 Ibn al-Mujāwir, *Ta'rīkh al-mustabṣir*, 1:128: *fa-lammā khariba ūdīra ʿalayhi sūr thāni min al-qaṣab shubbak*. This could be an instance of the use of *barasti* construction, prevalent in both Yemen and the Persian Gulf region to this day.

22 For Sīrāf, see Whitehouse, "Excavations at Sīrāf: First Interim Report," 5, 10; Whitehouse, "Excavations at Sīrāf: Fourth Interim Report," 10. The wall was massive and featured buttresses. See also the excavator's report of a "curtain wall" built between waterfront buildings, presumably to face off a sudden attack by sea sometime in the late 4th/10th century (Whitehouse, "Excavations at Sīrāf: Sixth Interim Report," 18–21). "Seawalls" dating to the 4th–5th/10th–11th centuries were also uncovered at the medieval African port of Manda, in the Lamu archipelago (Chittick, *Manda*, 17–35).

23 Ibn al-Mujāwir, *Ta'rīkh al-mustabṣir*, 128; Abū Makhrama, *Ta'rīkh thaghr ʿadan*, 1:14–15. For a biography of al-Zanjabīlī (or al-Zanjīlī), see Abū Makhrama, *Ta'rīkh thaghr ʿadan*, 2:131–32. On the foundation of Lakhaba, see chapter 1; on the building of the customshouse, see chapter 4.

24 Ibn al-Mujāwir, *Ta'rīkh al-mustabṣir*, 1:128; according to his account, the wall along the shore stretched from a site known as al-Ṣināʿa or al-Ṣibāgha (the corrupt state of the manuscript and ambiguous nature of the script render both readings possible) to Jabal Ḥuqqāt. A waterfront wall must have extended along the entire length of the beach to be effective, and since Jabal Ḥuqqāt is at the southern end of Aden's

waterfront, the other end of the wall must have stood at the northern end of the beach. Abū Makhrama, *Ta'rīkh thaghr ʿadan*, 1:14, gives slightly different coordinates for the waterfront wall—the foot of the Jabal al-Khadrā' to Jabal Ḥuqqāt. Both accounts presumably are talking about the same thing; if so, the Ṣināʿa/Ṣibāgha site must have been located on the foot of the Jabal al-Khadrā'. The issue, however, is complicated by a statement in the *Ta'rīkh al-mustabṣir* that Jabal al-Manẓar had a commanding view of al-Ṣināʿa. Jabal al-Manẓar appears to have stood near Jabal Ḥuqqāt and opposite Ṣīra. Therefore, either this statement must be completely discarded, or the texts must be referring to two different buildings. The term "*al-ṣināʿa*" can refer to an arsenal in the sense of a boatbuilding facility (Dozy, *Supplément*) or to "port structures or buildings" (Löfgren, *Arabische Texte*, 2:35 n. 18), but in Fusṭāṭ, *al-ṣināʿa*, translated by Goitein as "the arsenal," appears to have served as a customshouse (*Mediterranean Society*, 4:27, 355). A *ṣibāgha*, conversely, is a tannery; if located in town at all, such a site could only have stood as far from the center of urban activities as possible, whence its foul emissions would least harm the town. The northern end of the beach, then, could have served the purpose, while any site closer to town, such as one close to Jabal al-Manẓar, would have been entirely inappropriate. Thus, it seems plausible that the waterfront wall ran from a tannery at the extreme northern end of the beach to the southern end at Jabal Ḥuqqāt.

25 According to both Ibn al-Mujāwir and Abū Makhrama, a building known as Dār al-Manẓar or al-Manẓar al-Sulṭānī stood on Jabal Ḥuqqāt (Ibn al-Mujāwir, *Ta'rīkh al-mustabṣir*, 1:111, 127; Abū Makhrama, *Ta'rīkh thaghr ʿadan*, 1:12, 17, 2:20). Ibn al-Mujāwir also speaks of a Qaṣr al-Manẓar built on the slopes of Jabal Ṣīra (*Ta'rīkh al-mustabṣir*, 1:115). This statement further complicates the issue of the exact location of Jabal al-Manẓar. However, Ibn al-Mujāwir explicitly states that Jabal al-Manẓar was opposite Ṣīra, adding that the island was considered a (broken-off) piece of that hill (*Ta'rīkh al-mustabṣir*, 1:111; see also Abū Makhrama, *Ta'rīkh thaghr ʿadan*, 1:17).

26 Ibn al-Mujāwir, *Ta'rīkh al-mustabṣir*, 1:127: *wa-baʿdahum malakū al-ghuzz al-bilād wa-banū al-manẓar ʿalā jabal huqqāt baʿd rujūʿ Shams al-Dawla Tūrānshāh b. Ayyūb min al-yaman ilā miṣr*. See also Abū Makhrama, *Ta'rīkh thaghr ʿadan*, 2:19–20.

27 Mosseri L12/IB.348/II.66 (IV.7). See also Goitein, *Letters*, 213 n. 6. Goitein translates "*al-manẓar*" literally, as audience hall, and explains

that in Yemeni architecture, it designates "a room on the upper floor, open to the fresh air"; however, given its association with the ruler and the literary evidence, al-Manẓar in the context of Adeni topography must mean the ruler's residence. For the use of the term to denote a "palace" in Yemeni Arabic, see Piamenta, *Dictionary*. The continued use of al-Manẓar as a royal residence a hundred years after al-Muʿizz, well into Rasulid times, finds confirmation in the biography of Abū al-Faḍl al-Sharīf al-ʿAbbāsī. According to al-Janādī and al-Ahdal, when the Rasulid ruler al-Muẓaffar (d. 694/1294) asked to consult with the *sharīf*, the latter's host ran to al-Manẓar to convey the holy man's response to the sultan (Abū Makhrama, *Ta'rīkh thaghr ʿadan*, 2:254).

28 Ibn al-Mujāwir, *Ta'rīkh al-mustabṣir*, 1:115. As noted earlier, Jabal al-Manẓar must have been opposite Ṣīra, which Ibn al-Mujāwir describes as a (broken-off) piece of Jabal al-Manẓar (*Ta'rīkh al-mustabṣir*, 1:111; see also Abū Makhrama, *Ta'rīkh thaghr ʿadan*, 1:17).

29 The term "*furḍa*" has a semantic history (with at least two major shifts in meaning) similar to that of the term "*thaghr*," which went from denoting an opening or mouth through the notion of borderland to the general meaning of port town. The entry for "*furḍa*" in Edward Lane, *Lexicon*, shows that its meaning shifted from the general notion of an opening or gap, including a gap in the banks of a river or stream where water or boats could be drawn up to the land, to the generalized notion of an anchorage and a seaport. Kazimirski, *Dictionnaire*, gives a similar sequence. Dozy, *Supplément*, reports that in the dialects of Egypt and the Ḥijāz, the term had the meaning of customs revenue (*le revenu de la douane*), and the term appears with the same definition in Stace, *English-Arabic Vocabulary*, based on the Yemeni and more specifically the Adeni colloquial. Its usage in the Geniza clearly illustrates that the semantic shift from the notion of anchorage and seaport to that of customs' clearinghouse had already occurred by the 6th/12th century, perhaps initially only at Aden.

30 Al-Muqaddasī, *Kitāb aḥsan al-taqāsīm fī maʿrifat al-aqālīm*, 85.

31 Ibn al-Mujāwir uses the term in its general meaning once in reference to Aden, when he is reporting the various appellations by which the city is known, presumably to outsiders: "*wa-tusammā furḍat al-Yaman*" (*Ta'rīkh al-mustabṣir*, 1:110). In the next phrase, the term denotes the specific building to be discussed here. In several other instances, the term clearly refers to that building; in two cases, it is ambiguous and could refer to either the seaport or the customshouse as an institution,

but it most likely is intended in the former, more general sense. One of these references occurs in the simile that compares a man's return from the sea with his emergence from the grave on judgment day and proceeds to say that the *furḍa* is like the place of congregation on that day (Ibn al-Mujāwir, *Ta'rīkh al-mustabṣir*, 1:129); the other refers to the destruction of the *furḍa* of Abyan (Ibn al-Mujāwir, *Ta'rīkh al-mustabṣir*, 1:128, 130). See also Löfgren's glossary entry in *Arabische Texte*, 2:50, which claims that the meaning of "harbor" does not fit any of the occurrences of the term "*furḍa*" in Ibn al-Mujāwir.

32 Ibn al-Mujāwir, *Ta'rīkh al-mustabṣir*, 1:139: *wa-baʿd thalāthat ayyām tunzalu al-aqmisha wa-al-baḍā'iʿ ilā al-furḍa tuḥallu shaddatan shaddatan wa-tuʿaddu thawban thawban*. See also chapter 4.

33 For weighing goods at the customshouse, see TS20.137/IB. 29/II.23, line 40. This letter from Maḍmūn b. Japheth to Ben Yijū in India was mentioned earlier for its account of the naval siege of 529/1134–35. The main part of the letter, which includes the reference to the customshouse, has not been published. Maḍmūn's records show that two sacks of cardamom were weighed at al-Furḍa before being weighed again and sold at a different place; see the discussion of the Dār al-Saʿāda later in this chapter; see also chapters 4, 6. For merchandise kept at the customshouse, see TS AS148, f. 9/IB. 363/II.49, verso, line 8: [*lā fī*] *al-furḍa aw al-makhzan ʿamal*. This fragmentary letter from Khalaf b. Isaac b. Bundār to someone in India, probably Ben Yijū, appears to be reporting, among other things, no activity "either in the Furḍa or in the storerooms." It is probably referring to a slow period when merchandise is either not arriving or is being delayed from sale.

34 Ibn al-Mujāwir, *Ta'rīkh al-mustabṣir*, 1:128: *wa-banā al-furḍa wa-jaʿala lahā bābayn*. For the foundation of Lakhaba, see chapter 1.

35 Ibn al-Mujāwir, *Ta'rīkh al-mustabṣir*, 1:128: *wa-bāb al-furḍa wa-minhu tudkhalu al-baḍā'iʿ wa-tukhraju*. In the list of the six gates of the seafront wall, the *bāb al-furḍa* comes fourth, so if the order in which Ibn al-Mujāwir lists the gates reflects their relative position on the wall, then the Furḍa Gate would been located toward the center.

36 See Um, "Red Sea Society," 35, 108.

37 Ibn al-Mujāwir simply speaks of two doors (*Ta'rīkh al-mustabṣir*, 1:128): *wa-banā al-furḍa wa-jaʿala lahā bābayn*. Abū Makhrama explains their function (*Ta'rīkh thaghr ʿadan*, 1:14): *wa-jaʿala lahā bābayn bāb ilā al-sāḥil tudkhalu minhu al-baḍā'iʿ allatī tuʿashsharu wa-bāb ilā al-madīna tukhraju minhu al-baḍā'iʿ baʿd an tuʿashsharu*.

38 Ibn al-Mujāwir, *Taʾrīkh al-mustabṣir*, 1:110: *wa-tusammā ʿinda al-sūqa dār al-saʿāda bi-dār banāhu Sayf al-Islām Ṭughtakīn muqābila al-furḍa*.

39 Abū Makhrama, *Taʾrīkh thaghr ʿadan*, 1:10–11.

40 Ibid., 10: *ʿalā al-baḥr aw mushrifan ʿalā al-baḥr*.

41 Ibid., 10–11. The position of port superintendent was in Rasulid times known as "*naẓar*," and according to the author, some of the Banū Khaṭba "were in charge of the *naẓar* of Aden" (*waliya naẓar ʿadan*). The author attempts to reconcile the stories: the Banū Khaṭba built the place; it then passed to Ṭughtakīn and was finally taken over by al-Ghassānī, who enlarged it by building a *mufarrash baḥrī*, presumably a kind of seashore pavilion.

42 TS13J25, f. 13/IB.31/VI.27, lines 19–21: *tanʿamu ḥaḍratuha al-sāmiya idhā kataba allāh salāmatahum an tāʾmura iḥdā ʿabīdihā an yatasallamahā wa-tubāʿa fī al-dār al-saʿīda*. It is hard to imagine that the *dār al-saʿāda* and *al-dār al-saʿīda* are not the same. The letter, sent by Isḥaq b. Makhlūf al-Nafūsī from India, preserves only the internal address to a *nagid* at Aden, but Goitein identified the recipient more specifically with Maḍmūn b. Japheth, who held the title at the time; see Shaked, *Tentative Bibliography*, 135.

43 This letter has already been examined for its report on the siege of Aden and its reference to the Furḍa; the latter is mentioned in connection with the same consignment of cardamom that ended up in *al-dār* (TS20.137/IB.29/II.23, lines 30–32: *wa-min al-hayl . . . ṣaḥḥa al-wajn ʿinda al-bayʿ bi-al-dār baḥār wa-miʾatayn 22 raṭl*). See also chapter 4.

44 This rendering of *dār al-saʿāda* is Goitein's and appears in his unpublished notes to the India Book. The title fits the context much better than "happiness," "bliss," or "good fortune."

45 Goitein, *Mediterranean Society*, 4:27–28, 351 n. 63.

46 Goitein briefly refers to this *dār* in his passage about the near-homonymous establishment in Fusṭāṭ. The Dār al-Mubāraka appears in a letter by Mūsā b. Abī al-Ḥayy written in Alexandria around 1050. The writer mentions it in connection with the arrival of a fellow merchant, who is said to have "merchandise with him, which he should drop at the *dār al-mubāraka* and ask me [to sell them?]." The place clearly was at least a depot and probably was also a marketplace for wholesale trade (TS8J21, f. 29, lines 8–9: *wa-lahu maʿahu baḍāʾiʿ yanziluha fī al-dār al-mubāraka wa-yasāluni al-*[*bayʿ*]).

47 A perusal of the entries for *dār* in Goitein's "Cumulative Indices," *Mediterranean Society*, 6:26, produces eleven such houses mentioned in

the Geniza papers: Dār al-Aruzz (House of Rice), Dār al-Ḥarīr (House of Silk), Dār al-Jawhar (House of Jewels), Dār al-Kattān (House of Flax), Dār al-Khall (House of Vinegar), Dār al-Lawz (House of Almonds), Dār al-Mat (House of Carpets), Dār al-Sukkar (House of Sugar), Dār al-Zabīb (House of Raisins), Dār al-Zaʿfarān (House of Saffron), and Dār al-Zayt (House of Oil).

48 Goitein, *Mediterranean Society*, 1:194–95; for the connection between illustrious Jewish merchant Joseph b. ʿAwkal (active ca. 990–1030) and the Dār al-Jawhar, where he appears to have held office, see 4:26–27.

49 Ibn al-Mujāwir, *Ta'rīkh al-mustabṣir*, 1:130: *wa-banā Ibn al-Zanjabīlī qayṣārīya al-ʿaṭīqa wa-al-aswāq wa-al-dakākīn . . . wa-banā al-malik al-muʿizz [Ismāʿīl b.] Ṭughtakīn b. Ayyūb bināya jamiʿahā dakākīn bi-al-bāb wa-al-qufl li'l-ʿaṭṭārīn qayṣārīya jadīda.*

50 Streck, "Ḳayṣāriyya."

51 Abū Makhrama, *Ta'rīkh thaghr ʿadan*, 1:11. Abū Makhrama relates the eventual replacement of al-Dār al-Ṭawīla with a building named Dār Ṣalāḥ, after its owner, a trader who fled the oppressive al-Nāṣir al-Ghassānī. The house apparently was confiscated following his flight and was turned into a *matjar* in the days of the Tahirids, who expanded it to include "large storerooms."

52 Ibn al-Mujāwir, *Ta'rīkh al-mustabṣir*, 1:111: *wa-tusammā dār al-ṭawīla bi-dār banāhā Ibn al-Khā'in ʿalā muḥādhāt al-furḍa.* The name of the founder in the extant manuscripts reads Ibn al-Khā'in.

53 For the equation of *matjar* with a state-operated "commercial office" in Rasulid times, see Smith, "More on the Port Practices," 214–15, section on *al-matjar al-sulṭānī*. Smith notes that the *Mulakhkhaṣ* "mentions the commercial office in the context of the *nā'ib al-diwān* and its clerks . . . selecting the best livestock of the imported animals housed in a special pen . . . beneath the customs house in Aden and choosing the best as the share . . . of the *dīwān*."

54 Abū Makhrama, *Ta'rīkh thaghr ʿadan*, 1:11: *wa-ʿalā bābihā dikkatān masqūfatān yajlisu ʿalayhimā kuttāb al-furḍa.*

55 Whitehouse, "Excavations at Sīrāf: Fourth Interim Report," 10–12.

56 Whitehouse, "Excavations at Sīrāf: First Interim Report," 12–14; Whitehouse, "Excavations at Sīrāf: Fourth Interim Report," 12–15.

57 Ibn al-Mujāwir, *Ta'rīkh al-mustabṣir*, 1:127, tells us that the *dāʿī* directed the aspiring smuggler to hide his merchandise in *al-dār al-fulānīya*. Abū Makhrama, *Ta'rīkh thaghr ʿadan*, 1:13, relates that the ruler prepared a house expressly for the purpose: *fa-hayyā' lahu dāran*

wa-amarahu bi-naql mā arāda ilā tilka al-dār. Both authors report that this house was later presented to the foreigner.

58 TS24.64/IB.56/III.10, lines 33–37: *wa-katabtu kitābī hādhā wa-hum yukhalliṣūhu min al-furḍa jamīʿhu ilā dār al-shaykh al-ajall mawlāya Maḍmūn b. al-Ḥasan*. See also Goitein, *Letters*, 185–92, which interprets the word "*dār*" as "storeroom." Because the term "*makhzan*" appears so frequently in the Geniza documents, I think that the term "*dār*" denotes something other than a regular storeroom.

59 JTS Geniza Misc. 8/IB.235/ II.51/ lines 16–17: [*lā*] *kharaja minhā illā baʿd ṣuʿūba ʿaẓīma wa-ḥarīq buyūt wa-nahb makhāzin*; TS Misc. Box 28, f. 256/IB.207/II.48, lines 11–12: *wa-ṣāra al-sirqa wa-al-nahb fī al-balad*.

60 On the fate of archaeological layers during the colonial period, see Serjeant, "Ports of Aden and Shihr," 210.

61 Abū Makhrama, *Ta'rīkh thaghr ʿadan*, 1:13: *fa-ẓanna annahā dār baʿḍ al-tujjār fa-daqqa*; see also the section on fortifications in this chapter.

62 Ibn al-Mujāwir, *Ta'rīkh al-mustabṣir*, 1:137: *wa-binā' dūrihim murabbaʿa kull dār waḥduhu ṭabaqatayn al-asfal minhumā makhāzin wa-al-aʿalā minhumā majālis bi-al-ḥajr wa-al-jaṣṣ*.

63 Al-Iṣṭakhrī, *Kitāb al-masālik wa'l-mamālik*, 127–28.

64 For residential remains at Sīrāf, see Whitehouse, "Excavations at Sīrāf: First Interim Report," 11; Whitehouse, "Excavations at Sīrāf: Third Interim Report," 9–15; Whitehouse, "Excavations at Sīrāf: Fourth Interim Report," 5–10; Whitehouse, "Excavations at Sīrāf: Sixth Interim Report," 9–12.

65 Evidence for witnessing in a private home appears in a Geniza letter referring to a transaction that took place before Maḍmūn b. Japheth in his "noble *majlis*" (TS13J25, f. 13/IB.31/VI.27). See also Shaked, *Tentative Bibliography*, 135. For further discussion of this document, see chapter 6.

66 Apart from some storage, al-Mukhā's customshouse served primarily for assessing taxes. Because all merchants had to go through that process, the building emerged as the "single common room for overseas trade in the city" (Um, "Spatial Negotiations," 181–83). See also Um, "Red Sea Society," esp. 108–18.

67 Abū Makhrama, *Ta'rīkh thaghr ʿadan*, 1:9: *fa-lā yaqdiru ʿalā binā' al-ḥajr illā ahl al-qūwa wa-al-tharwa*.

68 Ibid.: *wa-kāna ghālib binā' buyūtihā al-khūṣṣ li-ʿizzat al-ḥajr*. Palm fronds and reed-and-mat structures, lumped under the generic name "*barasti*," are used in traditional architecture around the Arabian coast

to this day; see Stone, *Studies on the Tihāmah*, 84–88. From Aden itself, Hunter reports that in the 19th century, part of the population lived in reed-and-mat houses, using light, easy-to-transport materials available in Aden's immediate hinterland (*Account of the British Settlement*, 80).

69 Ibn al-Mujāwir, *Ta'rīkh al-mustabṣir*, 1:117. Ibn al-Mujāwir calls these structures *ṣarā'if* (sing. *ṣarīfa*).

70 Kay, *Yaman*, 116: *wa-akthar binā'ihim bi-al-akhṣāṣ wa-lidhālika yaṭruquhā al-ḥarīq kathīran*.

71 Ben Yijū's slave/agent, Bamma, for example, spent no less than four months in town on one visit; his expenditures (*nafaqa*) during this stay amounted to eight dinars, as recorded by Maḍmūn and charged to Ben Yijū's account; see TS20.137/IB.29/II.23, lines 41–42. See also Gosh, "Slave of MS. H. 6," 188–89.

72 Um, "Red Sea Society," 110–18.

73 Goitein, *Mediterranean Society*, 1:350, 4:91–97. According to Goitein, wealthy merchants might also own houses in the different places where they traveled; the poor generally lived in rented property. In 18th-century al-Mukhā, too, nonnative merchants kept houses in town (Um, "Spatial Negotiations," 183–86).

74 The relevant document, TS10J14, f. 2/IB.71/III.33, is a letter from Yeshūʿā Kohen b. Jacob, a native of Dhū Jibla, to Ben Yijū in Aden. From Ben Yijū's correspondence and other Geniza letters mentioning his affairs, we know that at the time he had permanently left his longtime residence in India and had stopped off in Yemen before continuing on to Egypt, his final destination. Two more letters sent to Ben Yijū relate to his stay in Dhū Jibla. In ENA 1822, f.75/IB.240/III.31, apparently written before his arrival and residence in town, Yeshūʿā inquires about Ben Yijū's prospective stay. In Bodl. MS Heb. d66, f. 61/IB.70/III.32, conversely, a correspondent from Aden reports to Ben Yijū in Dhū Jibla that political turmoil in Aden has died down and the place is again safe for his return. While Ben Yijū visited Dhū Jibla primarily to conduct business, this letter indicates an additional reason why he may have chosen to stay away from Aden for a considerable length of time.

75 TS10J14, f. 2/IB.71/III.33, lines 17–24. A *maṭḥan* and a *marḥa* are said to form part of the house rented on behalf of Ben Yijū. Given the location of Dhū Jibla in the Yemeni Highlands, surrounded by agricultural, grain-producing land, the *maṭḥan* could be either a mill for the production of flour or a press for the extraction of sesame oil. The term for a

traditional sesame seed oil press in Yemen today is *maʿṣara* or, significantly, *ṭaḥūn* (Stone, *Studies on the Tihāmah*, 131, plate 8.9).

76 Bodl. MS Heb. b11, f. 21/IB.20/I.33: *mūna fī ʿadan wa-ujra makhzan wa-ghayruhu wa-bilīj wa-mā yushbiḥu dhālika 30 dīnār*. Living expenses, the rent of a storeroom, the *bilīj*, and related payments—all of which are clearly expenditures in the city—amount to the substantial sum of thirty dinars. The document is an accounting of expenditures in India, Aden, five Red Sea ports, and Fusṭāṭ made by Abū al-Barakāt b. Joseph Lebdī for merchant Isḥāq al-Nafūsī and deposited at court during litigation between the two partners. The deposition is dated to 7 Shebat 1443/26 January 1132 (verso, bottom part, lines 11–12; Shaked, *Tentative Bibliography*, gives a different, incorrect date). On the meaning and provenance of the word *bilīj*, see Goitein, *Mediterranean Society*, 1:481 n. 15.

77 Goitein, *Mediterranean Society*, 1:314, 480 n. 6.

78 Accommodation of crews on board while away from the home port is a diachronic, cross-cultural phenomenon of maritime life. Crews sleeping, cooking, eating, and generally spending the day on board can be seen nowadays on Arabian Gulf booms in the port of Dubay and Sharja, and they are historically attested. For an example of living on board an early-20th-century Yemeni merchantman, see Villiers, *Sons of Sinbad*, 23.

79 Al-Muqaddasī, *Kitāb aḥsan al-taqāsīm fī maʿrifat al-aqālīm*, 85 (*wa-al-jāmiʿ nāʾ ʿan al-aswāq*); Ibn al-Mujāwir, *Taʾrikh al-mustabṣir*, 1:120 (*fa-banū bi-thamanihi jāmiʿ ʿadan fī ṭaraf al-balad*); Whitehouse, *Sīrāf III*, 1–3.

80 Ibn al-Mujāwir, *Taʾrīkh al-mustabṣir*, 1:120: *wa-kāna al-sabab fī bināʾhu annahum wajadū fī zamānihim qiṭʿat ʿanbar kabīra malīḥa*.

81 Ibid.: *fa-lastu aʾrā dirhaman aḥall min hādhā al-dirham wa-lā yukhraju fī wajh aḥaqq min hādhā al-wajh*.

Chapter Four

1 Kay, *Yaman*, 66 (English), 49 (Arabic).

2 Ibn al-Mujāwir, *Taʾrīkh al-mustabṣir*, 1:144–45. The author specifies that this tribute was no longer in effect in his time. The change must have coincided with the rise of the Rasulids, a line of generals who arrived in Yemen with the Ayyubids and later took over the government of the land.

3 Smith, "More on Port Practices," 212, 218 n. 25; see also Smith, "Rasulid Administration," 15.

4 Smith, "Have You Anything to Declare?"; Smith, "More on the Port Practices"; al-Shamrookh, *Commerce and Trade*, 259–81, 315–36 (tables).

5 Ibn al-Mujāwir, *Ta'rīkh al-mustabṣir*, 1:138–43. See also Smith's rendering of Ibn al-Mujāwir's information in "Have You Anything to Declare?"

6 See esp. the Muẓaffar register, Jāzim, *Nūr al-ma'ārif*, 409–60. See also al-Shamrookh, *Commerce and Trade*, 316–36.

7 As mentioned earlier, the tax information from these two sources receives full attention in al-Shamrookh's *Commerce and Trade* and in Smith's important article, "More on the Port Practices." Smith's new edition and translation of *Mulakhkhaṣ al-fiṭan* will appear shortly in the Hakluyt Society series. Important information on taxation also appears in Smith, "Rasulid Administration."

8 Goitein, *Mediterranean Society*, vol. 1, esp. 440–46; Cahen, "Douanes et commerce." Cahen supplements al-Makhzūmī's information with insights from the more theoretical work of Ibn al-Mammatī. See also Cahen, "al-Makhzūmī." Commercial taxation is also discussed in general works on taxation in Egypt; see esp. Rabie, *Financial System*.

9 Goitein, *Mediterranean Society*, vol. 1, esp. 62, 341–46.

10 Cahen, "Douanes et commerce," 262; Goitein, *Mediterranean Society*, 1:343–44.

11 Cahen, "Douanes et commerce," 262–65. Given the severe impositions on exports relative to those on imports, Cahen concludes that "*la politique du gouvernement égyptien consiste a decourager l'exportation, ou en tous cas a ne la considerer comme utile que pour autant qu'elle encourage d'abord l'importation*" and explains this phenomenon by positing that "*la puissance de l'État n'est pas liée à ce qu'il vend, mais à ce qu'il acquiert.*"

12 Goitein, *Mediterranean Society*, 1:343–44. An average of 5 percent was charged on both exports and imports.

13 Cahen, "Douanes et commerce," 267–71. Cahen refers his readers to Heffening, *Das islamische Fremdenrecht*, which argues that a system of excess imposts levied on the commerce of *dhimmīs* and foreigners was in place until the time of the Crusades. Cahen then suggests that neither the Geniza documents nor the evidence in al-Makhzūmī support such a statement. See also Goitein, *Mediterranean Society*, 1:61–62, 344–45, which points out that had a double customs duty been imposed on

non-Muslim merchants, at least some of the Geniza documents relating to trade would have alluded to the practice. The only reference to additional customs duties imposed on denominational grounds occurs in the letter of an India trader who instructs his brother in Alexandria to entrust his goods to a Muslim traveling companion and thus avoid the extra dues; this letter dates from the rule of Saladin (TS13J28, f. 15v/IB.291/VI.42, line 16). Soon thereafter, Saladin repealed this anti-commercial measure; see Goitein, "New Sources," 152–53.

14 Goitein, *Mediterranean Society*, 1:344–45.

15 Cahen, "Douanes et commerce," 250–51; Goitein, *Mediterranean Society*, 1:343–44.

16 ULC Or1080 J180/IB.244/V.5, margin: *wa-al-asʿār bi-yad allāh taʿālā*. The formulation appears in a letter written by Abū Zikrī in Fusṭāṭ to Yaḥyā b. Sulaymān in ʿAydhāb in which the author informs the recipients about prices of merchandise in Cairo and urges them to buy certain commodities if available.

17 Cahen, "Douanes et commerce," 252.

18 Deferral of customs payments until after the sale was the norm at the port of al-Mukhā as late as the 17th century, a parallel that highlights the economic merit of the practice; see Brouwer, *Al-Mukhā*, 268.

19 See the discussion of the customshouse in chapter 3.

20 Ibn al-Mujāwir, *Ta'rīkh al-mustabṣir*, 1:128: *wa-bāb al-furḍa wa-minhu tudkhalu al-baḍā'iʿ wa-tukhraju*.

21 Ibid., 138. The term "*nāẓir*" is later applied to a very different office, that of superintendent of the port, a fact that highlights the danger in assuming universal continuity in the port's practices and customs.

22 Ibn al-Mujāwir, *Ta'rīkh al-mustabṣir*, 1:138.

23 Ibid., 139.

24 Ibid., 144. See also chapter 2.

25 Al-Shamrookh, *Commerce and Trade*, 262–63; Smith, "More on the Port Practices," 210.

26 TS 12.235/IB.54/III.9, lines 14–15: *al-filfil wa-baʿḍ al-ḥad*[*īd* . . .] *muḥayyar fī al-furḍa*. For the association of the root *ḥ-y-r* with the meaning "delayed," see Stace, *English-Arabic Vocabulary*.

27 According to Ibn al-Mujāwir, the *nāẓir* cried, "*Hīriyan*." The word must be related to the modern term "*hūrī*," used in southern Arabia (both Yemen and Oman) to denote a small craft, most often but not always a single-log dugout canoe; for modified dugouts featuring sheer

strakes, keels, posts, and thwarts, and even fiberglass boats designated by the term "*hūrī*," see Prados, "Contemporary Wooden Fishing Craft." See also Stone, *Studies on the Tihāmah*, 125, for the use of the term "*hūrī*" to denote the "common open-hulled, rib-and-plank type of fishing vessel" on the Tihāmah. In the medieval Arabic colloquial, the meaning of the term was perhaps as fluid as the ethnographically attested usage.

28 Ibn al-Mujāwir, *Ta'rīkh al-mustabṣir*, 1:138: *wa-in kāna mā dhakarahu ṣaḥīḥan yuʿṭā lahu min kull markab dīnār malikī wa-in kāna kādhiban yuḍrabu ʿasharat ʿuṣīyin*. On the *malikī* dinar, the local gold coin, or *naqd al-balad*, going at 4.5 to the Egyptian dinar, see Ibn al-Mujāwir, *Ta'rīkh al-mustabṣir*, 1:144; Goitein, *Letters*, 182 n. 5.

29 Smith, "More on the Port Practices," 210.

30 See Smith, "Rasulid Administration," 16–18. Smith lists the titles of all Aden port officials, including those involved with the customshouse, culled from the *Mulakhkhaṣ*.

31 See the section later in this chapter on Maḍmūn b. Japheth and his function as a high customshouse official.

32 Ludovico di Varthema, *Travels*, 60.

33 See Smith, "More on the Port Practices," 211. The *Mulakhkhaṣ* describes a hierarchy of officials—*wālī* (governor), *nāẓir* (overseer), and *kuttāb* (scribes)—and lists other official titles such as *ʿāmil* (comptroller) and *mushārif* (supervisor); see Smith, "Rasulid Administration," 16–18.

34 Ibn al-Mujāwir, *Ta'rīkh al-mustabṣir*, 1:139. For ship's scribe, Ibn al-Mujāwir uses the Indian term "*al-karānī*"; see Löfgren, *Arabische Texte*, 2:55; see also Smith, "Have You Anything to Declare?," 135 n. 12. For the use of the term in later Mughal contexts, see Conermann, "Müslimische Seefahrt," 155.

35 Goitein points out that in the Geniza documents, the term refers both to the register and to registration charges, a set fee paid to the ship's captain for entering merchandise into his list ("From Aden to India," 65). For the appearance of the same term in Rasulid sources, including the plural form, "*satāmī*," see Smith, "More on the Port Practices," 211, 218 n. 17. Quoting Serjeant and Piamenta, Smith posits that the word is of Gujerati origin. See also chapter 5.

36 Ibn al-Mujāwir, *Ta'rīkh al-mustabṣir*, 1:139.

37 Ibid.: *wa-baʿd thalāthat ayyām tunzalu al-aqmisha wa-al-baḍā'iʿ ilā al-furḍa tuḥallu shaddatan shaddatan wa-tuʿaddu thawban thawban wa-in*

kāna min baḍā'iʿ al-bahār yūzanu bi-al-qubbān. To emphasize the thoroughness of the inspection, Ibn al-Mujāwir specifies that merchandise was unpacked "bundle by bundle" and counted "robe by robe."

38 Abū Makhrama, *Ta'rīkh thaghr ʿadan*, 1:11. See also the discussion of the customshouse in chapter 3.

39 Ibn al-Mujāwir, *Ta'rīkh al-mustabṣir*, 1:140. See also the epigraph to this chapter.

40 See Goitein, *Letters*, 14.

41 This is the same legal paper trail that led Goitein to his lifelong engagement with the Geniza material of the India trade world. See the introduction to this volume. For the earliest account of the Lebdī affair published by Goitein, see Goitein, "From the Mediterranean to India," 189, 191–95.

42 TS28.22/IB.14/I.14, lines 48–50, and margin: *wa-anā ujaddid al-su'āl li-mawlāya al-shaykh . . . an yuḥaqqiq lī mā ṣaḥḥa fī kull ḥāja min hādhihi al-ḥawā'ij . . . bi-awzānihim wa-asʿārihim wa-athmānihim baʿd ikhrāj mā rasamtahu ʿalayhi min maks*. Here "*maks*" appears as the generic term for "tax."

43 Bodl. MS Heb. d66, f. 66 v/IB.13/I.13, line 4. See Goitein, *Letters*, 179.

44 On the dating of this letter, see Goitein, "Two Eyewitness Reports," 250; chapter 2 in this volume.

45 TS20.137/IB.29/II.23, lines 25–29: *wa-waṣalat akhbār diyār miṣr muqāriba wa-kānat al-baḍā'iʿ kāsida wa-lam yuṭlab lā filfil wa-lā biḍāʿa bi-dirham ilā qabl yawm al-safar bi-usbūʿ fa-law ṭālabtu aṣḥāb al-filfil bi-al-ʿushūr la-bāʿūhu bi-dīnār al-ʿishrīn fa-ṣabartu ʿalayhim bi-al-ʿushūr ilā yawm al-safar ḥattā waṣala al-nās min kull mawḍ[iʿ] wa-inqasaʿa siʿr al-filfil 23 dīnār al-bahār*. The part where Maḍmūn postulates what would have happened had he demanded the import tax at the time when the market was still down is not entirely clear to me. The formulation "*la-bāʿūhu bi-dīnār al-ʿishrīn*" must either mean that they would have given the pepper away for a mere dinar instead of twenty for each *bahār* or that they would have sold twenty *bahārs* for one dinar. The latter seems too extreme to be right, so I have preferred the former interpretation. The final price is still very low. As table 2 shows, the usual price for pepper ranged between thirty and thirty-seven dinars.

46 Goitein, *Mediterranean Society*, 1:201, 218. Goitein notes that the practice was legal and acknowledged in both Islamic and Jewish law. It seems, at first, that such a measure would go against the interests of

the customshouse, especially since imports were taxed ad valorem, so higher market prices would fetch higher customs revenues. If, however, the merchants who came later found themselves in the position of having to sell at much lower prices—that is, if the demand was bound to drop dramatically after the early arrivals sold their goods—then the customshouse would lose on the later transactions. Moreover, the state had a vested interest in regulating the market to render it attractive to as many merchants as possible.

47 See, e.g., Bodl. MS Heb. a3, f. 19/IB.32/II.32, a letter to prominent Cairene merchant Abū Zikrī Kohen b. Joseph in which Maḍmūn relates his partnership with the "illustrious *shaykh* Bilāl"; see commentary and translation in Goitein, *Letters*, 181–85, esp. 183.

48 Ibn al-Mujāwir, *Ta'rīkh al-mustabṣir*, 1:139.

49 Ibn Jubayr, *Travels*, 39–40. The difference between both Ibn al-Mujāwir's and Ibn Jubayr's laments and the dry and cool description of customs procedure in al-Makhzūmī's manual highlights the issue of the positionality of these sources.

50 Bodl. MS Heb. d66, f. 108/IB.131/V.8, lines 15–19. This letter from Samuel al-Majjānī to Abū Zikrī will be examined in detail in the section on maritime policing and enforcement in chapter 5.

51 Mosseri L288/IB.292/VI.28, lines 24–26: *wa-sāfara ilā al-tīz fa-waṣalanā khabaruhu bi-anna ṣāḥib al-tīz ẓalamahu wa-akhadha min udumihi laʿlla //thulthahu// bi-lā shay*. The letter was written by Joseph b. Abraham to his brother-in-law, Abū Zikrī ha-Kohen.

52 TS10J29, f. 3/IB.262/VII.45, lines 9–10: *wa-kharaja min yadayya min al-mukūs wa-al-mu'ūn shay kathīr*. In his unpublished summaries of India Book documents, Goitein tentatively identifies the hand of this letter with Abraham b. Ismāʿīl al-Maghribī. It is possible that the expenses and taxes that so burdened the author were partly incurred at Aden itself and that this thus constitutes one complaint about the Adeni customshouse.

53 Goitein characterizes this Ayyubid prince as "eccentric." Abū Makhrama's biography clearly depicts al-Muʿizz as an unusual and troubled man. After a falling out with his father, Ṭughtakīn, al-Muʿizz was practically ousted from power. When Ṭughtakīn died, however, al-Muʿizz managed to reinstate himself in Yemen. Abū Makhrama disapproves of al-Muʿizz's Ismaʿīlī leanings and categorically describes his disturbed mental state (*ḥūliṭa ʿaqluhu*) (*Ta'rīkh thaghr ʿadan*, 2:19–20). On the

role of this ruler in the arguments of Maimonides' "Epistle to Yemen" and the conflation by some scholars of the forcible conversion of the Jews during his reign with events under the reign of the Mahdid ʿAbd al-Nabī, see the introduction to this volume.

54 Mosseri L12/IB.348/II.66. This letter dates to 594/1198; see Goitein, *Letters*, 212–14. Goitein interprets the passage discussing the plight of foreigners as referring specifically to nonresident Jews, but the term used, "*al-ghurabā*'" (line 19), is ambiguous and might in fact refer to all non-Muslim foreigners, presumably including Indian merchants and ship crews.

55 TS28.11/IB.154/II.67. This letter dates to 598/1202; see Goitein, *Letters*, 217. Abū Makhrama details the conspiracy that led to the murder of al-Muʿizz (*Ta'rīkh thaghr ʿadan*, 2:19).

56 Ibn al-Mujāwir, *Ta'rīkh al-mustabṣir*, 1:143.

57 *Dilāla*, *wakāla*, and *zaka'a* taxes feature in Ibn al-Mujāwir's example of tax payment in Aden. According to this story, ʿUthmān b. ʿUmar al-Amīdī, a *nākhudhā* coming from Egypt, was charged with the following customs taxes on aloes wood (*ʿud*) worth six dinars (Ibn al-Mujāwir, *Ta'rīkh al-mustabṣir*, 1:144; Smith, "Have You Anything to Declare," 134; Smith, "More on the Port Practices," 209): .5 dinars for *ʿashūr*, .75 dinars for *shawānī*, 8 dinars and 2 measures of the imported goods for *wakāla*, 1.25 dinars for *zaka'a*, and .5 dinars for *dilāla*. Ibn al-Mujāwir adds up the total at 15 dinars. Something is clearly wrong with these numbers: the man ends up owing nine dinars on merchandise that is supposed to bring him at least some profit. It is unclear if the value Ibn al-Mujāwir quotes is the purchase price or the sale price in the place of destination, and if it is the former, the ultimate profit margin remains unclear. In any case, Ibn al-Mujāwir intends to show that Adeni customs officials and the government of the city in general took rapacious advantage of merchants trading in the city, and the story becomes symbolic of the extortion. Various kinds of *ʿud* incurring various tax rates per ten *mann* appear in the Muẓaffari register, but without knowing the ultimate sale value, it is difficult to draw any conclusions about the tax burden; see Jāzim, *Nūr al-maʿārif*, 441–43.

58 See discussion of *ḥalqa* sales, by which foreigners sold their goods in the Egyptian markets, in Cahen, "Douanes et Commerce," 241; Goitein, *Mediterranean Society* 1:192–93.

59 See, e.g., Jāzim, *Nūr al-maʿārif*, 409, where *ibrīsim* silk from Qays/Kish and India incur a *shawānī* tax but *ibrīsim* from Mecca incurs no *sha-*

wānī tax. This pattern is not consistent throughout, however. See also al-Shamrookh, *Commerce and Trade*, 264–69.

60 See TS24.37/IB.91/IV.12, margin: a letter from Khalaf b. Isaac of Aden to Ḥalfon b. Nethanel noting *dilāla* costs in the Indian port of al-Qaṣṣ, which together with the fees of guards (for the merchandise) amount to one-third dinar; TS Box J1, f. 53/IB.81/IV.1, line 29: another letter from Khalaf to Ḥalfon, this time quoting the amount of two dinars charged for *dilāla* on pepper; TS18J5, f. 1/IB.60/III.11, line 31: a third letter from Khalaf, this time to Ben Yijū in India, speaking of "taking on the cost of the *dilāla* for me" (*wa-qad ḥamaltanī al-dilāla ʿalā tafaḍḍulika*).

61 The *dallāl* acted as an official certifier of prices both in al-Makhzūmī's Egypt and in Rasulid Yemen; see al-Shamrookh, *Commerce and Trade*, 268. Serjeant reported a similar system in place in Qalansiyyah, the main port of Socotra, in the 20th century (Smith, "More on the Port Practices," 212–13).

62 Ibn al-Mujāwir, *Ta'rīkh al-mustabṣir*, 1:140–41; Smith presents some of this information in "Have You Anything to Declare?," 132–33, table 1.

63 Ibn al-Mujāwir, *Ta'rīkh al-mustabṣir*, 140–41: *khurūjihi min/ʿalā al-furḍa*, or *fī khurūjihi ilā al-baḥr*, or *idhā kharaja min al-bāb*. Smith does not include these quotes in his tabulation of taxes listed by Ibn al-Mujāwir ("Have You Anything to Declare?," 132–33), but elsewhere he states that "Ibn al-Mujāwir . . . speaks almost exclusively of imports, although he does mention exports" ("More on the Port Practices" 211).

64 On Ibn al-Mujāwir's use of the peculiar form *ʿashūr/ʿashūrāt* versus the more commonly encountered *ʿushr/ʿushūr*, which is the form used in Geniza documents, see Smith, "Have You Anything to Declare?," 131.

65 Al-Shamrookh, *Commerce and Trade*, 265.

66 Cahen, "Douanes et commerce," 256. Cahen also argues that a similarly complex system of tax assessment existed in the port of Acre.

67 See, e.g., TS13J25, f. 13/IB.31/VI.27, line 23: general reference to "*al-ʿushūr wa-al-mu'ūn*," which had been charged to the recipient's account and extracted from the total proceeds of the sale of his goods (table 3, item 7); Bodl. MS Heb. d66, f. 64/IB.6r/I.6, line 7: similar case of extraction from proceeds of "*mukūs wa-ʿishār wa-mu'ūn*."

68 The term "*mūna*" designates living expenses, victuals, or provisions but in these documents can also have the more general meaning of "expenses." For examples, see table 2, item 2, and table 3, items 7, 10, and 12.

69 Goitein, *Mediterranean Society*, 1:343–44. Goitein's examples include an

import tax of less than 7 percent levied on a large shipment of Egyptian flax in Sicily, an export toll of around 4 percent charged for a consignment of silk in Alexandria in 1143, and another export toll of 50 percent incurred on a shipment of madder from Alexandria around 1100.

70 TS24.66/IB.26/II.16, lines 3–12, 33–38. See table 3, items 10 and 11.

71 TS20.137/IB.29/II.23, lines 8, 28–30, 38–39, 31–41. See table 3, item 5.

72 However, very little is known about Ibn al-Mujāwir or the real itinerary of the travels that resulted in the writing of his *Ta'rīkh al-mustabṣir*; see Smith, "Ibn al-Mujāwir's 7th/13th Century Guide to Arabia." It is reasonable to assume, however, that the customs imposts he reports simply represent the going rates at the time of his visit.

73 An accounting drafted by Abū al-Barakāt b. Joseph al-Lebdī in 526/1132 records the highest exit toll attested, a tax of 16 dinars on a shipment of brazilwood, cinnamon, and rhubarb bought for 144 dinars—that is, roughly 11 percent of the goods' total value (see table 2, item 3). Yet, as will be discussed in the section on exemptions, it is not clear whether the amount charged also includes an exit toll for a sizable consignment of lac, which Abū al-Barakāt sent to the same recipient in Egypt at the same time.

74 Jāzim, *Nūr al-maʿārif*, 409–60; al-Shamrookh, *Commerce and Trade*, 316–36.

75 Ibn al-Mujāwir, *Ta'rīkh al-mustabṣir*, 1:142–43. Smith presents the tax-free items on Ibn al-Mujāwir's list in a table titled "green channel" ("Have You Anything to Declare?," 133).

76 In Fatimid Egypt, commercial state offices administered the storage of staples, including wood, iron, and soap. While there is no evidence for a similar practice in Zurayid or Ayyubid Aden, the later Rasulid treatise *al-Mulakhkhaṣ* describes a similar organization known as *al-matjar*, which, however, appears to have been dedicated to the procurement of staples for the rulers; see Smith, "More on the Port Practices," 214–15.

77 For the evidence for local cloth manufacture, see the section on al-Mabāh in chapter 2. I have not been able to find other references to *dafwā'* wood (the term seems to designate a big, shady tree; see Smith "Have You Anything to Declare?," 136), but it may have served as firewood, boatbuilding or building construction timber, or an aromatic/fumigating substance.

78 Bodl. MS Heb. b11, f. 21/IB.20/I.33; this document was dated 7 Shebat 1443/26 January 1132.

79 Ibid., line 8: *wa-kharj maks al-lakk* 80 *dīnār malikīya*; line 13: *ʿubbiya al-lakk bi-ʿadan* 8 *aʿdāl.*

80 Ibn al-Mujāwir, *Taʾrīkh al-mustabṣir*, 1:142; Smith, "Have You Anything to Declare?," 133.

81 TS24.66/IB.26/II.16, lines 11–13, an account by Maḍmūn for Ben Yijū dated to the mid-530s/1140s. See also Goitein, "From Aden to India," 48–49, 61, 64; table 3, item 8. The amount charged works out to about 1 percent of the total value of the pepper.

82 See Gil, *History of Palestine*, 250–51.

83 Goitein, "From Aden to India," 64.

84 See Cahen, "Douanes et commerce," 245–50.

85 The particular shipment from Ben Yijū for which Maḍmūn recorded the *ḥaqq al-qabḍ* comprised 11 *bahār* of pepper; in addition, Ben Yijū's account included a separate shipment of about 14 *bahār* of iron, which may have cleared customs at the same time; perhaps the *ḥaqq al-qabḍ* was levied for both of these bulky shipments.

86 Ibn al-Mujāwir, *Taʾrīkh al-mustabṣir*, 1:141–42.

87 Ibid., 141: *fa-akhraja al-shawānī ilā al-hind fa-kānat al-shawānī taqifu ʿalā raʾs al-manādikh yaḥfaẓūn marākib al-tujjār min saṭwat al-surrāq.*

88 Ibid., 1:141: *lam yakūnū mulūk banī zurayʿ yaʿrifūn al-shawānī.*

89 See Jāzim, "Nūr al-Dīn et al-Muẓaffar," 78–79. Al-Muẓaffar's naval activities are detailed in Ibn Ḥātim, *Kitāb al-Simṭ al-ghālī*, 509–10.

90 TS20.137/IB.29/II.23, line 12.

91 Goitein, "Two Eyewitness Reports," 253; Goitein, *Mediterranean Society*, 5:67, 523 n. 97.

92 See Goitein, "Two Eyewitness Reports," 253, quoting Dozy and Fraenkel. See also Kindermann, *"Schiff" im Arabischen*, 45–46, which attests to the occurrence of the term in Ṭabarī and al-Muqaddasī to describe boats of the Tigris but also to the meaning "royal barge" and "half-galley" in 17th- and 18th-century India.

93 Goitein, "Two Eyewitness Reports," 253. The early Arabic lexica attest to the meaning "knife" but do not make the association with a type of ship; see Ibn Manẓūr, *Lisān al-ʿarab*; al-Zabīdī, *Tāj al-ʿarūs*.

94 E.g., TS18J4, f. 18/IB.58/III.12, lines 11–13. In this letter from Khalaf b. Isaac to Ben Yijū, written around 1146, Khalaf mentions pepper and ginger sent *fī al-shaffāra*.

95 A *shaffāra* was the accompanying ship of the ship *Gazelle*, which belonged to the *nākhudhā* Bashīr: TS18J2, f. 14/IB.62/III.22, lines 2, 6,

9. Two ships belonging Fatān Swamī and sailing in convoy from India to Aden until disaster struck are referred to as *al-markab al-ṣaghīr* (the one that escaped) and *al-markab al-kabīr* (the one that foundered).

96 In one incident in which a ship was taken by pirates, its secondary boat that fled to tell the tale is referred to as *jalbat al-markab* and is explicitly said to have carried soldiers (*muqāṭilā*): Bodl. MS Heb. b11, f. 22/IB.133/II.55, lines 10–12. The ship is called not *shaffāra* but *jalba*. More on ships and nomenclature appears in chapter 5.

97 E.g., TS18J4, f. 18/IB.58/III.12, lines 11, 16.

98 See the section on maritime protection in chapter 5.

Chapter Five

1 Löfgren, *Arabische Texte*, 2:255. The tale was transmitted by Rasulid functionary and *muḥtasib* of Aden Muḥammad b. Yaʿqūb al-Janadī (d. 732/1332) and 19th-century Yemeni scholar ʿAbd al-Raḥmān b. Sulaymān al-Ahdal (d. 1250/1830). On the biographies of persons related to Aden from the works of al-Janadī and al-Ahdal, see Löfgren, *Arabische Texte*, 1:21–22. The text uses the term "*nākhūdha*" (with this spelling) to refer both to the man in charge of the boat on the high seas and to Kāfūr in his capacity as a shipowner. I have attempted to bypass the ambiguity by translating the term as "shipmaster" in the first instance and as "shipowner" in the second case. A full discussion of the term appears later in this chapter.

2 The only other miracle mentioned in the *sharīf's* biography consists of his foretelling the outcome of al-Muẓaffar's project to take the stronghold of al-Dumlūwa. Locked in a power struggle with his brother over succession after the death of their father, Nūr al-Dīn, al-Muẓaffar first secured Aden and only then turned to the full conquest of the Yemeni hinterland, where Dumlūwa was a vital strategic and symbolic possession. Aden was important to any leader aspiring to rule over Yemen; see Löfgren, *Arabische Texte*, 2:254–55. On al-Muẓaffar and the consolidation of his power in the late 13th century, see Jāzim, "Nūr al-Dīn et al-Muẓaffar," 73–77.

3 The invocation "*kataba allāh salāmatahu*" accompanies many a notice of merchandise dispatches and ship departures. See, e.g., a letter written by Maḍmūn b. Japheth to his colleague, Ben Yijū, in India, TS20.130/IB.28/II.20, lines 28–30: *wa-anfadhtu lahu yaday al-shaykh Abū Saʿīd*

b. Maḥfūẓ fī al-markab al-mubārak ilā manjarūr kataba allāh salāmatahu.

4 In his important work on trading diasporas and cross-cultural trade, Curtin writes about both the importance of the variety of activity that qualifies a trading settlement as a city and the hierarchy of cities on the basis of that variety, which he dubs "multifunctionality" (*Cross-Cultural Trade*, 6–11).

5 See Guo, *Commerce, Culture, and Community*, 153–56; Guo, "Arabic Documents, Part 1," 181–85, text 3. In this fragment of a letter, the author speaks of being stranded at "al-Qaṣr al-Yamānī," a hitherto unknown place, probably on the Arabian coast of the Red Sea. Wind and weather appear to have been the main causes of their plight but affected only the men's ability to sail to their destination, not communications with Quṣayr al-Qadīm, which clearly remained open. Guo even speaks of a possible "maritime shuttle service" between Quṣayr and other Red Sea ports. The situation, including the urgent appeal for relief, makes sense if the sailors took refuge from foul weather in a small, undeveloped haven and in light of regional weather patterns: northerlies blowing in the southern part of the Red Sea would prevent sailors from sailing south but would not hinder sailing in the northern segment.

6 Scholars agree that medieval traders used the Persian title to describe both shipowners and captains. Kazimirski, *Dictionnaire*, and Dozy, *Supplément*, translate "*nākhudhā*" as "*patron de la barque, capitaine d'un vaisseau*"—that is, both as "boat owner" and as "captain." Similarly, Löfgren, *Arabische Texte*, 2:58–59, offers "*shiffsherr*," "*reeder*," and later "*kapitain*," in the final instance providing the Arabic synonyms "*rubbān*" and "*ra'īs*." Diem, *Dictionary*, records only the meaning "shipowner," reflecting what Goitein believed was the most common usage of the word in Geniza documents. Goitein was also well aware that the term could take on a different meaning and notes such an instance in TS24.64/IB.56/III.10, where in his opinion the *nākhudhā*, clearly not a shipowner, is "the man in command of the finances and other matters related to the passengers, i.e., the purser" (*Letters*, 191). Little sufficient evidence exists for the presence of a purser on board Indian Ocean ships before the 7th/13th century, however, and the phrase "*satmī al-rubbān*" to designate the bill of lading suggests that the main economic responsibilities on board and the functions of a purser fell to the captain.

7 TS24.64/IB.56/III.10, verso lines 1–2. This is a letter from Khalaf b.

Bundār, who notifies Ben Yijū of a dispatch of glassware sent "*ṣuḥbat al-nākhudhā Aḥmad nākhudhat markab al-Fidiyār*." See also Goitein, *Letters*, 191.

8 See TS20.63/IB.82/VI.26, line 3. Maḍmūn b. Japheth appears with a wide range of honorifics attached to his name but is hailed as *nākhudhā* only in this one instance.

9 TS12.320/IB.51/III.1, verso lines 9–16. Joseph b. Abraham informs Ben Yijū that Aḥmad *al-rubbān* is in charge of a dispatch; given the people involved and the provenance and destination of the shipment, Aḥmad may well be "*al-nākhudhā Aḥmad nākhudhat markab al-Fidiyār*" mentioned in n. 7. In TS24.66/IB.26/II.16, verso line 10, Maḍmūn informs Ben Yijū that Abū al-Ghālib *rubbān al-markab* had been entrusted with a dispatch of twenty dinars. There are also "Bakhtiyār *al-rubbān*" (TS20.137/IB.29/II.23, line 43) and "Masʿūd al-Ḥabashī *al-rubbān*" (TS24.64/IB.56/III.10, lines 59, 65). Jewish traders' letters refer to the ship's bill of lading as "*satmī al-rubbān*."

10 Identifying a ship by the name of its skipper/captain—that is, the person responsible on board and on the high seas—made sense in many different maritime cultural contexts. See, e.g., Hadziiosif, "Social Values and Business Strategies," 135–36.

11 Chakravarti, "Nakhudhas and Nauvittakas," 37, 41–42, 56.

12 Ibn al-Athīr, *Kitāb kāmil al-ta'wārīkh*, 43.

13 Stern, "Rāmisht of Sīrāf," 10–13.

14 The grave monument itself has never been found, but its legend survives in a compilation of funerary inscriptions of Mecca by al-Shaybī. The full text of that inscription appears in the *Répertoire chronologique d'épigraphie arabe* (3099): "This is the tomb of the martyred elder, the refuge of the two sanctuaries, the shipowner (*nā-khudhā*) Abū'l-Qāsim Rāmisht, son of al-Ḥusayn, son of Shīrawayhi, son of al-Ḥusayn, son of Jaʿfar, of the province of Fārs. He died in the month of Shaʿbān, in the year 534" (Stern, "Rāmisht of Sīrāf," 11).

15 Maḥrūz appears with the title *nākhudhā* at least twice (TS12.235/IB.54/III.9, lines 22–23; TS NS J10/IB.200/III.23, lines 9–15) and once alludes to his own ships, urging his brother-in-law that it is better to travel "with me" than on the ships of "other people [*marākib al-nās*]" (Bodl. MS Heb. b11, f. 22/IB.133/II.55, lines 29–31; cf. translation in Goitein, *Letters*, 64).

16 Goitein identifies Joseph b. Abraham with "*Yūsuf al-nākhudhā*" in TS24.64/IB.56/III.10, line 17; see Goitein, *Letters*, 188.

17 This man appears frequently in these letters as a *nākhudhā*. Later, when one of his ships apparently foundered (Bodl. MS Heb. b11, f. 22/IB.133/II.55), he ran into grave trouble with his colleagues; see the section on enforcement later in this chapter. Earlier on, Maḍmūn entrusted this man with business in India (TS NS J1/IB.199/II.24, lines 1, verso, lines 2–21), and he accompanied a consignment of pepper to Aden on the boat of someone named Buda (ENA 3616, f. 19/IB.30/II.25, lines 8–10).

18 Goitein, *Mediterranean Society*, 1:311. As this chapter will subsequently discuss, the crucial difference is that in the Mediterranean, most of these merchants are identified as Muslims.

19 Goitein, *Mediterranean Society*, 1:310.

20 Al-Shamrookh, *Commerce and Trade*, 159–61.

21 Goitein, *Studies*, 349–50.

22 Goitein, *Letters*, 188 n. 8; Goitein, *Studies*, 349. Goitein explains that the name *f-t-n s-w-m-y* that occurs in one Geniza text must be identified with the Hindi *pattana svami*—literally, "lord of the mart," the head of a large merchant guild who served as a kind of mayor.

23 For the office and title of *al-muqaddam*, see Goitein, *Mediterranean Society*, 2:68–75.

24 TS Misc. Box 25, f. 103/IB.208/III.15, line 19–21. TS Misc. Box 28, f. 256/IB.207/II.48, line 24, also may allude to a sultan's ship, but only the word for sultan has been preserved. Both are letters written by Khalaf b. Isaac, one to Ben Yijū in 1147 and one to Egypt about seven years earlier. In the 1147 letter, Khalaf mentions a dispatch to Ben Yijū "*fī al-markab al-jarbatānī markab al-sulṭān*" in India and alludes to a disaster that prevented his shipment from reaching its destination.

25 Bodl. MS Heb. a3, f. 19/IB.32/II.32, lines 21–27; TS18J5, f. 1/IB.60/III.11, lines 25–31. See also Goitein, *Letters*, 181–85.

26 Udovitch, "Merchants and Amīrs," 62–64. See also the section on interdenominational business collaboration later in this chapter.

27 TS28.22/IB.14/I.14, line 9: *li-markab al-Qummī wa-li-markab Bihzād*. This letter from Joseph al-Lebdī to Ḥasan b. Bundār mentions in passing the two ships, in which Ḥasan sent two separate consignments of merchandise.

28 Tinbū appears in Bodl. MS Heb. b11, f. 22/IB.133/II.55, which will be examined later in this chapter; see Goitein, *Letters*, 64. Buda's ship appears in ENA 3616, f. 19/IB.30/II.25, line 11, an 1134 letter from Maḍmūn to Ben Yijū. The ship belonging to Fatan Swamī appears in a let-

ter from Khalaf b. Isaac to Ben Yijū, TS24.64/IB.56/III.10, dating to around 1139 or later (Goitein, *Letters*, 185–92).

29 TS24.64/IB.56/III.10, lines 59, 65. See also Goitein, *Letters*, 185–92.

30 Goitein notes this ambiguity in his treatment of the Mediterranean material (*Mediterranean Society*, 1:311).

31 For Hindu shipowners, see Chakravarti, "Nakhudhas and Nauvittakas." Christian presence in the Indian Ocean trade is barely visible in the period covered by this volume. ʿAbd al-Masīḥ the deacon (*al-shammās*) appears once in these documents as an agent for two Jews (TS18J2, f. 7/IB.24/II.14, line 11; see also Goitein, "From Aden to India," 52, 54 n. 11).

32 Among the long-term residents of the Indian Ocean region visible in Cairo Geniza documents, only Ḥasan b. Bundār, Ben Yijū, and Khalaf b. Bundār are nowhere mentioned as owning ships. Given the nature, production, and mostly erratic pattern of preservation of the documents, this absence of evidence does not conclusively prove that these men had nothing to do with ships other than shipping goods on them. However, Ben Yijū's apparent abstinence from the field may be ascribed to the fact that in addition to his trading interests he, unlike any other known Jewish trader, had his hands full running a bronze factory in India; for a document illuminating the workings of his plant, see Goitein, *Letters*, 192–97.

33 Both Abū al-Ḥasan b. Abī al-Katā'ib and Abū ʿAbdallāh bear the title *nākhudhā*; Abū al-Ḥasan's ships are mentioned in a number of letters between Ben Yijū and his Adeni contacts, notably Maḍmūn b. Ḥasan and his cousin, Khalaf: TS24.66/IB.26/II.16, lines 16–20 (where it is clear that ʿAbū ʿAbdallāh delivered iron to Maḍmūn in Aden); TS10J12, f. 5/IB.53/III.4, lines 20–21; TS NS J1/IB.199/II.24, line 32; TS18J5, f. 1/IB.60/III.11, lines 10–12; TS24.64/IB.56/III.10, lines 13–16 (where the father delivers iron to Khalaf in Aden). See the section on family businesses later in this chapter.

34 On Tāna and other ports of the Konkan coast, see Chakravarti, "Nakhudhas and Nauvittakas," 39, 51; see also Goitein, *Letters*, 64.

35 For the location of the port of Fandarayna, south of Cannanore on the Malabar coast, and shipments from there, see Goitein, *Letters*, 188 n. 7.

36 See, e.g., TS12.320/IB.51/III.1, a letter from Joseph in Aden to Ben Yijū in India that reveals Joseph's interest in trading bronze vessels; see also Goitein, *Letters*, 192–97.

37 TS AS148, f. 9/IB.363/II.49, verso, line 2, a letter from Khalaf mention-

ing that Maḥrūz received letters sent to him from India; Bodl. MS Heb. b11, f. 22/IB.133/II.55, lines 29–31, a letter from Maḥrūz telling of his intention to return to Aden in his own vessel at the end of the sailing season (see also Goitein, *Letters*, 62–65).

38 TS28.20/IB.280/II.61, a letter by Maḍmūn b. Japheth's two sons to Abū Zikrī's son, Sulaymān, offering condolences on his father's death. The two men inform their Cairene colleague that the widow of his maternal uncle, Maḥrūz, is doing fine in Aden.

39 Stern, "Rāmisht of Sīrāf," 10. The anonymous author of the epitome of Ibn Ḥawqal's work includes Rāmisht among the inhabitants of Sīrāf and describes him as very wealthy. By the 6th/12th century, however, Sīrāf was no longer the great entrepôt it had been in earlier times. Its harbor had silted up, a major earthquake had destroyed much of the city, and the island of Kish/Qays had wrested away most of its trade. A Sīrāfī himself, the abridger understandably claimed the great man, who probably did not live at his place of origin, however.

40 TS NS J1/IB.199/II.24, line 31: *fī markab Rāmisht wa-markab waladayhi wa-ṣahrayhi.*

41 PER H161/IB.36/II.71, lines 48–62; see also the section on shipwreck, rescue, and salvage later in this chapter.

42 For delivery by Abū al-Ḥasan, see TS24.64/IB.56/III.10, lines 13–16; see also Goitein, *Letters*, 188.

43 A shipment of iron from India is reportedly sent on the father's ship, *markab al-nākhudā Abū al-Ḥasan b. Abū al-Katā'ib*, but the son, *al-nākhudā Abū ʿAbdallāh waladuhu*, delivers it to Aden (TS24.66/IB.26/II.16, lines 16–20; for the text and a translation, see Goitein, "From Aden to India," 48, 61).

44 ULC Or1080 J95v, a/IB.66/III.21a, lines 1–12: payments made or money owed to Abū ʿAbdallāh by Ben Yijū for goods transferred from India to Aden; ULC Or1080 J95v, b/IB.67/III.21b, lines 1–3, 26–31: goods delivered and freight owed or paid to Abū ʿAbdallāh or owed by him on behalf of his father ("*min qabl wālidihi*").

45 TS Misc. Box 25, f. 103/IB.208/III.15, lines 15–28. This letter mentions two incidents at sea, but it is unclear whether either of them is a full-fledged shipwreck. Khalaf seems sure that Ben Yijū had been informed about Abū ʿAbdallāh and the ship he was on (lines 20–21): *wa-qad ʿalima mawlāya alladhī jarā ʿalayhi*. Jettison of parts of the cargo in a storm may have resulted in the loss of the letter.

46 TS20.130/IB.28/II.20, lines 24–27.

47 TS20.137/IB.29/II.23, line 43.

48 See Tibbetts, *Arab Navigation*, 60–61. Again the lack of consistency even within single authors and certainly within and across time periods is confusing. In his *Fawā'id*, Ibn Mājid distinguishes among the *nākhoda* (owner; thus transliterated by Tibbetts), *muʿallim* (captain/navigator), and *rubbān* (coasting pilot), although he uses the last term more broadly in other works. In modern usage, the hierarchy seems to have been reversed: in Tibbetts's experience, the *rubbān* is considered the more knowledgeable and important captain of a large vessel, whereas the *nākhudhā* sails smaller boats. The term "*rubbān*" is similarly associated with seniority and leadership among the fishermen of al-Shiḥr; see Camelin, "Les pêcheurs de Shihr."

49 TS24.64/IB.56/III.10, line 65; see also Goitein, *Letters*, 190.

50 TS20.130/IB.28/II.20, lines 44–45: *fī hādhihi al-sana lam yaṣil jilāb min zabīd illā inna sāfarat al-marākib*.

51 JTS Geniza Misc. 10/IB.237/II.31, lines 16–19: *waṣala jawniyatayn laṭāf min ʿaydhāb wa-fīhim ṣurra min al-ṣufr wa-dhakarū an khalfahum 4 marākib min ʿaydhāb fīhim al-tujjār al-kathīr wa-al-baḍā'īʿ*. The phrase "*jawniyatayn laṭāf*" must refer to vessels of a light construction, speedier than the vessels whose news they were conveying. The origin of the term "*jawniya*" is uncertain. Kazimirski, *Dictionnaire*, enters the root *j-w-n* with the meaning of a small bag or sack used by perfume merchants; in his recent ethnographic work among sea captains and shipwrights in the Gulf and Oman, Agius records the term "*jūniyye/yūnya*" with the meaning of "sack of rice or sometimes another food product" used by the older generation specifically for a unit of ship cargoes (*In the Wake of the Dhow*, 137).

52 TS20.137/IB.29/II.23, lines 25–29. The day was saved when *waṣala al-nās min kull mawḍiʿ wa-inqasaʿa siʿr al-filfil 23 dīnār al-bahār*. "From every place" must refer to the various Red Sea ports, including Zabīd and ʿAydhāb. See chapter 4.

53 For the ships of al-Dibājī, see Bodl. MS Heb. d66, f. 108/IB.131/V.8, line 11 (a voyage to Dahlak, perhaps from ʿAydhāb); BM Or5566 d, f. 6/IB.152/VI.39, lines 6–7; ENA 4020, f. 8/IB.153/VI.38, line 9 (a voyage from ʿAydhāb to Aden); ULC Or1080 J180/IB.244/V.5, margin (a voyage to ʿAydhāb that apparently ended in shipwreck and salvage). For the ships of al-Sharīf, see Bodl. MS Heb. d66, f. 108/IB.131/V.8, line 16, in which they are sailing in convoy with the ships of al-Dibājī; Westmin. Frag. Cairens. Misc. 13/IB.96/VI.32, lines 9–19, and margins, mention-

ing two vessels belonging to al-Sharīf, a large one and a small one, and a shipwreck between Suwākin and Dahlak.

54 Labib, "Kārim." See also Fischel, "Spice Trade." The etymology of the term remains uncertain, and none of the hypotheses proposed is entirely satisfactory; for a summary and full bibliography, see Labib, "Kārim." In the latest attempt at etymological interpretation, Wansbrough tentatively proposed an intriguing if fraught connection with the Akkadian term "*kārum*" ("Medieval Kārim").

55 As Wansbrough wrote, the extant record is "just the tip of the iceberg, and it is appropriate to guess that random mention of persons is nothing more than arbitrary and discrete witness to the general phenomenon" ("Medieval Kārim," 300). In his extensive and influential early work on the *kārim*, Fischel refutes both the rash early notion that the *kārim* were exclusively Jewish and the more measured later assessments of the group's mixed ethnic composition ("Spice Trade," 166). In the same volume of the *Journal of Economic and Social History of the Orient*, however, Goitein shows that Jewish merchants of the 6th/12th and 7th/13th centuries participated in the *kārim* as convoys of ships, concluding that they "carried both Jewish passengers and goods, and there is no reason why the same should not apply to the members of any other denomination" and deferring on the question of whether that was true in subsequent periods ("New Light," 183).

56 Goitein collected these references in stages; see "New Light," 177–80, 184; *Studies*, 353–57; *Letters*, 214, 226, 250.

57 TS16.345/IB.134/II.56; BM Or5542, f. 17/IB.135/II.57 (copies of the same letter, from Maḥrūz to someone in Cairo, mentioning goods forwarded in the *kārim*; see Goitein, "New Light," 177; Goitein, *Studies*, 353); TS NS J23/IB.214/VII.56 (a letter from an India trader to his wife in Cairo; see Goitein, "New Light," 179; Goitein, *Studies*, 355); ENA2739, f. 16/IB.176/VII.60 (a letter from a trader in Maʿbar, on the Coromandel coast of India, to his wife in Cairo; see Goitein, "New Light," 180; Goitein, *Studies*, 357; Goitein, *Letters*, 226 n. 30); TS NS J182 (a late fragment of a letter from Aden referring to goods sent with "*al-kārim al-mubārak*"; see Goitein, *Studies*, 357).

58 BM Or5549, III, fol. 5/IB. 221a/V.4 (a letter from Abū Zikrī in Egypt possibly to a partner in Aden; see Goitein, "New Light," 177–78; Goitein, *Studies*, 354); JTS Geniza Misc. 4/IB.227/VI.36 (a letter from Joseph b. Abraham in Aden to addressee traveling with the *kārim* in ʿAydhāb; see Goitein, "New Light," 184; Goitein, *Studies*, 356); ULC

Or1080 J180/IB.244/V.5 (a letter from Abū Zikrī from Cairo to ʿAydhāb; see Goitein, *Studies*, 356–57); TS13 J21, f.26 (a fragmented reference to the contents of the *kārim*; see Goitein, *Letters*, 250).

59 TS Misc. Box 28, f. 33/IB.215/VI.44 (a letter from Alexandria possibly to Aden; see Goitein, "New Light," 184; Goitein, *Studies*, 356).

60 Mosseri L12/IB.348/II.66; see Goitein, *Letters*, 214 n. 9.

61 Goitein argues that the *kārim* visited Aden only every other year ("New Light," 177–78; *Studies*, 354). He bases his claim on his interpretation of a single letter in which the writer in Egypt informs the addressee somewhere in the Indian Ocean, presumably Aden, about the total cargo and Jewish travelers on the *kārim* that had just arrived at the Red Sea port of Suwākin (BM Or5549, III, fol. 5/IB. 221a/V.4; see Goitein, "New Light," 178). Goitein assumes that the addressee was in Aden at the time and concludes that the *kārim* had skipped Aden that year, on the basis that the addressee would not otherwise have needed the information. While not implausible, this interpretation is far from secure, and many other possible scenarios exist: for example, the *kārim* could have stopped at other ports between Aden and Suwākin, so the writer's information would have been new to anyone who been present at the *kārim*'s departure from Aden, or the letter meant to inform the addressee in Aden not who had been on board at the time when the fleet left Aden but who was getting ready to return to Aden in it. The letter might also have traveled on a faster ship on a more direct route, so the information would have been new to the addressee.

62 Al-Shamrookh, *Commerce and Trade*, 244, 247. That the Muẓaffar register mentions "*al-baḍāʾiʿ al-kārimīya al-musaffara ilā al-hind*" may support the pattern of the earlier period, in which the *kārim* brought to Yemen merchandise to be picked up by other shippers in charge of the eastward routes. I intend to pursue the issue of the *kārim* in a subsequent project on the formation of merchants' networks.

63 Al-Shamrookh, *Commerce and Trade*, 246–47.

64 See Abu Lughod, *Before European Hegemony*.

65 PER H161/IB.36/II.71, recto, margin, lines 1–4: *waṣalū al-safr fī hādhayn al-sanatayn fī al-marākib min kull baḥr min sāʾir bilād al-hind wa-aʿmālihā wa-min bilād al-zanj wa-aʿmālihā wa-min barr barbara wa-al-ḥabash wa-aʿmālihā wa-min al-ashḥār wa-al-qamr wa-aʿmāliha al-kull*. The remarkable designation "*al-ashḥār wa-al-qamr*" must refer to the area of the Ḥaḍramawt port of al-Shiḥr and the adjacent region of al-Qamr mountain near the promontory of Ra's Fartak in Dhofar, espe-

cially since the formulation "*abyan wa-al-shiḥr wa-balad al-qamr*" in the same letter, verso, line 17, further reinforces the geographical association between the three toponyms.

66 Nineteenth- and 20th-century vessels of the western Indian Ocean are known collectively as "dhows," a Western name that derives from the Swahili term for a native double-ended boat (Steere, *Handbook*). The issue of variety in post-1500 boatbuilding is complex, because Westerners—that is, Ottomans, Portuguese, and their successors—brought with them a completely different tradition of shipbuilding that influenced regional and local styles. See Hornell, "Tentative Classification"; Hornell, "Sailing Craft." For the distinct East African seagoing craft, see Hornell, "Sea-Going *Mtepe*"; Adams, "Construction and Qualitative Analysis."

67 Bodl. MS Heb. b11, f. 22/IB.133/II.55, line 10: *waṣalat baʿd dhālika jalbat al-markab*; this phrase coupled with the fact that this *jalba* was carrying soldiers suggests that it was a military escort boat; see also Goitein, *Letters*, 63 n. 5. Goitein's "lifeboat" is not accurate, as a lifeboat is a small skiff, carried on board, and used only in the event of an emergency.

68 See Agius, *In the Wake of the Dhow*, 93–95, whose earliest example of the use of the term to denote an Indian Ocean boat is by al-Nuwayrī al-Iskandānī (d. 775/1372). See also Kindermann, *"Schiff" im Arabischen*, 19–20.

69 Goitein, *Mediterranean Society*, 1:157.

70 In a letter from Maḥrūz to his brother-in-law, Abū Zikrī, mentioned earlier with connection to the ship type/term *jalba* and discussed at length later in this chapter, a note specifies that it is to be delivered "in trust," presumably without payment: Bodl. MS Heb. b11, f. 22/IB.133/II.55, verso, address; see also Goitein, *Letters*, 65.

71 TS20.130/IB.28/II.20, line 27: *wa-qad sāmaḥūnī bi-al-nawl*. This formulation clearly demonstrates that the exemption was granted to Maḍmūn personally. For an example of *nawl* charges, see TS24.66/IB.26/II.16, lines 49–50: 3 *aṣira al-nawl ʿalayhā 4 danānīr* (four dinars' *nawl* for three bags of copper sent by Maḍmūn to Ben Yijū in India). See also Goitein, "From Aden to India," 49, 59, 62.

72 Bodl. MS Heb. a3, f. 19/IB.32/II.32, lines 21–27. In this letter, Maḍmūn says specifically that he built a ship in Aden and outfitted it for travel to Ceylon (Sri Lanka) in partnership with Bilāl (*anshāʾ markab fī ʿadan wa-jahaztuhu bi-shirkat al-shaykh al-ajall ilā saylān*); see also Goitein, *Letters*, 181–85.

73 TS20.130/IB.28/II.20, verso, lines 1–3: *wa-baʿd hādhā dafaʿa lī fī al-markab alfayn wa-miʾa dīnār thaman* [. . .] *qaṭṭ*. This intriguing passage is too broken to reconstruct the circumstances with any certainly, but Maḍmūn seems to have received the sum for building or outfitting a ship, and the amount was not enough. In his unpublished notes, Goitein reconstructs the broken phrase "*thaman . . . qaṭṭ*" as "unheard of price," and the gist of the letter shows the assessment to be in a negative tone.

74 TS18J5, f. 1/IB.60/III.11, lines 25–31. In the end, Khalaf was apparently promised some of the glass, probably thanks to his family ties to Maḍmūn; Khalaf promised to send whatever he acquired to Ben Yijū.

75 As Goitein notes, the presence of these craftsmen on the trading venture to Ceylon "is remarkable and not without interest for the history of minor arts" (*Letters*, 182, 183–84 nn. 13, 14).

76 For the apparent "reticence" to form partnerships in shipbuilding in the Mediterranean, see Goitein, *Mediterranean Society*, 1:309; Goitein, *Letters*, 253. More work on this topic is required for the Indian Ocean case. The contrast with the Italian maritime republics, where fractional ship ownership appeared in the first decades of the 12th century and soon became a prevalent practice, is striking.

77 Udovitch, "Merchants and Amīrs," 64. See also the section on merchant shipowners earlier in this chapter.

78 In a fragment of a note written by Maḍmūn, this statement comes by way of explanation of why all available *darky* has been bought by Bilāl and why the author was at the time unable to acquire any for the recipient; see JTS Geniza Misc. 2r/IB.225/II.27, lines 6–7: *wa-laysa yaqdiru aḥad yaṭlubu shay yaṭlubuhu al-mālik Bilāl*.

79 Bodl. MS Heb. b11, f. 22/IB.133/II.5; see also Goitein, *Letters*, 62–65.

80 Goitein, *Letters*, 62–63; for the location of the port of Tāna, see 63 n. 4.

81 Ibid., lines 39–40: "*wa-baynī wa-baynahu mā lā yunfaṣalu min al-ṣadaqa wa-al-akhawīya*" is the touching way Maḥrūz describes his bond with Tinbū; translation by Goitein, *Letters*, 64.

82 See Constable, *Trade and Traders*, 57–59.

83 Bodl. MS Heb. b11, f. 22/IB.133/II.55, verso, lines 1–2; see also Goitein, *Letters*, 65. This practice reappears in a letter from Abū Zikrī ha-Kohen to an unknown correspondent; see TS NS J44/IB.242/V.7, right margin, lines 14–15: *kitābī hādhā nuskha . . . bi-ʿarabī wa -ʿibrānī*.

84 Epstein, *Genoa*, 61.

85 According to an account appended to the *Akhbār al-ṣīn wa-al-hind*, this

did happen in the 4th/10th century. Sailors and boatbuilders set out from Oman, landed in the Maldives or the Laccadives, and used local timber and coir to build boats, which they then sailed back to Oman loaded with cargoes of coconuts; see Abū Zayd Ḥasan al-Sīrāfī, *Supplement*, 130–31.

86 See discussion in the section on interdenominational collaboration.

87 TS20.130/IB.28/II.20, lines 29–30, verso lines 4–5. Maḍmūn informs Ben Yijū that he is sending money care of Abū Saʿīd in *al-markab al-mubārak*. Then on the verso, he mentions the outfitting of a ship as well as another dispatch care of Abū Saʿīd.

88 TS20.130/IB.28/II.20, lines 42–44: *wa-ammā mā dhakarahu min sabab shirā'* [*sā'ir al-*] *tafārīq fa-mawlāya yaʿlamu al-ishghāl allatī ʿalaya* [. . .] *al-marākib wa-hādhā shay yurīd farja*.

89 ULC Or1080 J171/IB.243/V.9, right and top margins: *Jāshujiyāt* [. . .] *Maḍmūn fī jihāzihim wa-ja*[*mīʿ*] *mā yaḥtāju ilayhi*; after eight lines, the text continues: *wa-ammā al-shaykh al-ajl mawlāya maḍmūn* [*fa-jahaza*] *4 al-jāshujiyāt ilā zabīd*. The ship term is related to *jāshū*, a term associated with mariners and the Persian Gulf that appears in Ibn al-Mujāwir's description of the naval siege; see Goitein, "Two Eyewitness Reports," 251 n. 3, 252. See also the section on maritime policing and enforcement in this chapter.

90 Ibn al-Mujāwir, *Ta'rīkh al-mustabṣir*, 1:116; Abū Makhrama, *Ta'rīkh thaghr ʿadan*, 1:9. The terms "*ṣanbūq*" and "*zarūka*" are currently used to describe medium-sized Red Sea boats and small laced vessels, respectively.

91 TS18J2, f. 7/IB.24/II.14. A partial edited and annotated translation of this document appears in Goitein, "From Aden to India," 46–47, 50–56.

92 TS18J2, f. 7/IB.24/II.14, verso, lines 13–14: *wa-idhā ḥaṣala jihāzahum fī ʿadan wa-arādū minnī al-shirka shāraktuhum*. Goitein, "From Aden to India," 53, gives this passage in translation only.

93 TS NS J1/IB.199/II.24, lines 19–24; Maḍmūn receives betel nuts and "two boards" (*lawḥayn/alwaḥ*), presumably of teak, from India. Ibn al-Mujāwir lists teak boards (*alwāḥ al-sāj*) among commodities in the Aden market (*Ta'rīkh al-mustabṣir*, 1:145). For the contemporary use of teak and its appellation by the term "*al-sāj*," see al-Hijji, *Art of Dhow Building*, 38.

94 Literary sources that attest to the prevalence of this tradition in the Indian Ocean from at least as early as the 1st century A.D. include the

anonymous merchant's work *Periplus of the Erythraean Sea*, Procopius, Abū Zayd Ḥasan, Ibn Jubayr, Christian missionaries such as Jordanus, Odoric of Ponderone, and John of Monte Corvino, Marco Polo, and Ibn Baṭṭūṭa. Impressive iconographic evidence appears in some of the illuminations of al-Ḥarīrī's thirty-ninth *maqāma* that show a ocean-going vessel with obvious stitches or lacings between its planks. For a good summary and references, see George Faldo Hourani, *Arab Seafaring*, 87–97. The dominance of this method of building ships came to an end with the arrival of the Portuguese in the Indian Ocean in the beginning of the 10th/16th century; see Moreland, "Ships of the Arabian Sea." Boatbuilders in parts of Arabia, Africa, and India continued to lace smaller vessels, with modern examples; see, e.g., *Oman, a Seafaring Nation*; Hornell, "Sea-Going *Mtepe*"; Adams, "Construction and Qualitative Analysis."

95 See the section on al-Mabāh in chapter 1.

96 Ibn al-Mujāwir, *Ta'rīkh al-mustabṣir*, 1:137. Entries in biographical dictionaries and lexica associate the *nisba qunbārī* with the word that they explain as coconut husk twine used in laced boatbuilding and discuss its imputed association with a location in Aden where such twine was produced. See, e.g., Ibn Ḥajar al-ʿAsqalānī, *Tahdhīb al-tahdhīb*: *al-qunbār ḥibāl tuftalu min layf shajar al-nārjīl*. In his entry on Mūsa b. ʿAbd al-ʿAzzīz al-Yamanī al-ʿAdanī al-Qunbārī, al-ʿAsqalānī mentions but disputes the association of the man's *nisba* and the term "*qunbār*" with a place in Aden.

97 As noted earlier, Ibn al-Mujāwir mentions teak boards (*alwāḥ al-sāj*), and they are implied in a Geniza reference. For ethnographic data on the importation and use of teak in Arabia, see al-Hijji, *Art of Dhow Building*, 38.

98 According to Abū Makhrama's story, jackfruit trees (*al-shakī* or *al-barkī*) grew in Rubāk, where they had been initially imported from India by a *nākhudhā* in 625/1228 (*Ta'rīkh thaghr ʿadan*, 1:20, 2:173). For the use of jackfruit-tree timber, known as "*fanaṣ*" in Kuwait today, to make ribs and tackle and sometimes even planking and keels, see al-Hijji, *Art of Dhow Building*, 39; al-Hijji, "Shipbuilding Timber," 15.

99 PER H161/IB.36/II.71, lines 60–63. The document provides a remarkable account of a shipwreck in the time of Maḍmūn's son, Ḥalfon, who has already been mentioned as inheriting his father's shipping business and who will appear in chapter 6 as succeeding his father in the community's leadership. The document was edited in the late 1930s by Eliahu

Strauss (Ashtor); see Strauss, "Voyage to India." Here, I propose some revisions to that edition. See also the section on shipwreck, rescue, and salvage in this chapter.

100 PER H161/IB.36/II.71, lines 62–63: *wa-mā kāna markab jadīd wa-ʿudaduhu judud siwā al-markab al-kūlamī fī marākib tīk(!) al-sana.*

101 See the section on the topography of Aden's harbor in chapter 2.

102 In his treatment of the *kārim* fleet, Goitein hints at the possibility that the lapses in that fleet's stops at the port of Aden could reflect periods of political upheaval at port, yet he concludes that these lapses in fact resulted from a set schedule that entailed stopping at port one year and bypassing it the next (*Studies*, 358). In view of the lack of evidence for such a regular pattern and the difficulties with assuming that the early *kārim* sailed all the way to India, however, it is safer to assume that political instability or fear of it occasionally led ships to touch down but not call in at a port; for a possible such instance, see TS NS J44/IB.242/V.7, verso, right margin, lines 4–6: *wa-ammā akhbār ʿadan . . . jāʾū ilā balad wa-lam yunzilū fīhā liʾanna kāna fī-al-balad ʿaskar wa-kānū qalaq.*

103 TS20.137/IB.29/II.23, lines 11–13; Ibn al-Mujāwir, *Taʾrīkh al-mustabṣir*, 1:124. See also Goitein, "Eyewitness Accounts," 252–53. On the problem with identifying the *shaffāra* as a longship or galley, see the section on the galley tax in chapter 4. The correspondence with the term "*dawānīj*" does not definitively solve the problem; see Kindermann, *"Schiff" im Arabischen*, 28–30.

104 I have only two points to raise with regard to Goitein's otherwise successful effort to determine the vessel types involved in the blockade in "Two Eyewitness Accounts," 252–53. First, in addition to the correspondence of the term "*burma*" with the literal meaning of the word "pot" and the sense of round shape, there is the possibility of a connection with the name of the most well-known contemporary traditional Arab trading vessel type, the *būm*. Second, I must disagree with Goitein's tentative effort to link the *burma* of the texts in question with the single dugout hulls (*meshidi*) that according to Idrīsī took up to fifty men and featured in the fleets of both Qays and the Indian maritime states. For structural reasons, a long and narrow dugout hull would have been good for attacking ships near the shore but entirely incapable of long voyages on the high seas, such as the jaunt from Kish/Qays to Aden would have required.

105 Weapons carried on board ships have been discovered in premodern

shipwreck sites. For the remarkable insights on the armament of medieval ships offered by the excavation of an 11th-century Mediterranean shipwreck, see Schwarzer, "Weapons," esp. 384–96.

106 Piracy on the Red Sea, along the South Arabian coast, and on the Indian seaboard plagued Roman trade with India and is mentioned in the *Periplus*; see Casson, *Periplus*, esp. 146. The history of piracy in the Indian Ocean remains to be written.

107 See the section on the galley tax in chapter 4.

108 ULC Or1080 J171/IB.243/V.9, right margin, lines 1–3: *jāshujiyāt* [. . .] *Maḍmūn fī jihāzihim wa-ja*[*mīʿ*] *mā yaḥtājū ilayhi*.

109 Ibid., top margin: *wa-ammā al-shaykh al-ajall mawlāya Maḍmūn yu*[*nfidhu*] *4 jāshujiyāt ilā zabīd wa-tawaṣṣā ra*[*yyīsah*]*ā bi-al-ḥirṣ ʿalā qabḍ al-Fawfalī aw ʿalā t*[. . .] *jilābihi wa-aʿdālihi liʾannahu maʿawwil ʿalā* [. . .] *diyār Miṣr*.

110 Bodl. MS Heb. d66, f. 108/IB.131/V.8, lines 11–19. The place name al-Qaṣṣ, which apparently refers to a port town on the Indian littoral and should not be confused with the Egyptian entrepôt of Qūṣ, is mentioned again in TS10J29, f. 3/IB.262/VII.45, line 12, a letter in which the writer states that he is planning to set out from Aden for al-Qaṣṣ and Nahrawāra, a north Indian port. Qaṣṣī textiles are also mentioned in the Geniza documents; see Goitein, *Letters*, 183–84, 200.

111 Bodl. MS Heb. d66, f. 108/IB.131/V.8, line 13: *wa-rubbamā yatūhū* [*or: yatawwahū*] *fī dahlak fa-innahum mā laḥaqūnā*. This line is stricken through. The verb is either *t-y-h* (to wander, stray) or *t-w-h* (to moor). Either case conveys a sense of lingering at the island.

112 For examples of merchandise sold in Dahlak, see ULC Add. 3421v, b/IB.4/I.4, verso, lines 7–9 (textiles); Bodl. MS Heb. d66, f. 64r/IB.6/I.6, lines 4–6 (storax). Both are documents from the litigation between Jekuthiel and al-Lebdī and date to 491/1098.

113 Bodl. MS Heb. d66, f. 64r/IB.6/I.6, lines 4–5: *bi-arbaʿīn nuqar Dahlak yakūn thamanuhā ʿasharat dīnār miṣrīya*. For "*nuqra*" as a numismatic term denoting pure silver coinage, see Goitein, *Mediterranean Society*, 1:369; Diem and Radenberg, *Dictionary*, 215.

114 One letter of uncertain date mentions the case of a man considered lost "in the sea of ʿAydhāb" who later turned up in Dahlak along with his travel companions and most of his shipwrecked goods (TS NS J426/IB.305/VII.54, lines 8–13). Around 564–65/1169–70, David Maimonides wrote to his brother, Moses, from the Indian Ocean, mentioning shipwrecked traders who ended up similarly on the island of

Dahlak with some of their goods (ULC Or1081 J1/IB.178/VI.4; translated in Goitein, *Letters*, 209–12). Very often the outcome of a shipwreck was much grimmer than in these two cases; nevertheless, Dahlak functioned as an information terminal, and news of shipwrecks in the Red Sea reached there first and were then disseminated to any interested parties, as in Westmin. Frag. Cairens. Misc. 13/IB.96/VI.32, right and top margins, where it is reported that one of al-Sharīf's two ships perished on its way from Suwākin.

115 The instance of bribery appears in the records of the al-Lebdī affair in the last decade of the 5th/11th century. In one instance, Joseph al-Lebdī declares that at Dahlak, he was charged a customs tax of six dinars after he paid a bribe of one dinar (*baʿd mā barṭaltu dīnār*); see Bodl. MS Heb. d66, f. 65/IB.7/I.7, lines 4–5.

116 Bodl. MS Heb. d66, f. 108/IB.131/V.8, top right margin upside down: *karamatan lahu akramnā b. al-Yatīm wa-saraqnā lahu al-marjān min al-maks*.

117 Ibid., lines 17–18: *wa-ṣādaranā wa-akhadha baʿḍ amwālinā fa-kunnā minhu mukhriṭīn*.

118 Ibid., line 18.

119 For the legal and political framework within which merchants in the Mediterranean (12th–15th centuries) disputed and demanded restitution for attacks suffered on the high seas, see Tai, "Marking Water."

120 PER H161/IB.36/II.71, lines 48–65; see Strauss, "Voyage to India," 217–31. Given here is my partial translation.

121 PER H161/IB.36/II.71, recto margin, verso lines 1–4, 18–20. This passage was also quoted as evidence for the segmentation of shipping lines in the western Indian Ocean.

122 Ibid., verso line 8.

123 Ibid., margin and verso lines 24–26: *li-shiddat al-baḥr wa-dufʿat al-sāḥil wa-kithrat al-asmāk*.

124 The port of Balipattana is first mentioned on a Sanskrit document dating to 1008 C.E. The affinity of the two spellings provides, I think, adequate indication that the place-name mentioned in the Geniza document can refer to none other than the Konkani port. For the rise of Balipattana as a major port on the Konkan coast and the role of Konkan ports in general, see Chakravarti, "Nakhudhas and Nauvittakas," 39–41.

125 PER H161/IB.36/II.71, lines 58–59: *ṭarā hādhā al-ṭārī ʿalā al-Kūlamī wa-dhālika min qabl dukhūlihim al-maṣabb*.

126 All the secondary lexical sources give the sense of confluence of waters:

Edward Lane, *Lexicon*, "a place where water or the line pours out or forth from a river into another river or into the sea; Kazimirski, *Dictionnaire*, "*embouchure, d'une fleuve, d'une rivière*"; Dozy, *Supplément*, "*source, l'endroit d'ou l'eau sort, l'endroit ou coule une rivière, canal de derivation*"; Piamenta, *Dictionary*, "funnel."

127 In the 4th/10th century, al-Muqaddasī testifies to the knowledge of seamen of all description, including merchants, concerning the limits and topography of the Indian Ocean (*al-Aqālīm*, 11). Ibn Mājid speaks specifically of the tradition of navigational authors (but not necessarily writers) going back to much earlier times; he emphasizes the difference between armchair theoreticians who had never actually practiced navigation and seasoned experts whose lives were spent at sea (Tibbetts, *Arab Navigation*, 5–7).

128 TS13J8, f. 17/IB.35/II.70, line 9: "The ship was wrecked and he drowned in the port of Aden; his body floated out at the port." This document is written in Hebrew; for an edition, see Assaf, "Relations," 118–19. I thank Orit Bashkin for helping me identify and translate this crucial line.

129 TS24.64/IB.56/III.10, lines 30–35; translated by Goitein, *Letters*, 185–92.

130 TS10J18, f. 8, lines 6–7: *wa-aqāmū al-ghaṭṭāsīn yawmayn ilā an ṭalaʿū al-ʿidl wa-al-ḥamdu li-llāh*. The term for divers in this case is not "*baḥḥārīn*" but "*ghaṭṭāsīn*."

131 The distance between Bāb al-Mandab and Aden is about ninety-five nautical miles; according to Casson, the distance that a square-rigged vessel would sail in a day is fifty miles; a day-and-night run is one hundred miles (*Periplus*, 278–79).

132 TS24.64/IB.56/III.10, lines 35–37: *fa-mahmā taḥaṣṣala minhu akhrajū jamīʿ mā nābahu min ghūṣ wa-kirāʾ wa-al-bāqī yaqtasimūhu bi-al-ḥiṣṣa ya'khudh kullunā ḥaṣṣatahu*; translation from Goitein, *Letters*, 189. The merchants clearly paid for both the salvage operations and the transportation of the salvaged goods to port, as Islamic law permits; see Khalilieh, *Islamic Maritime Law*, 109–10.

133 Bodl. MS Heb. b11, f. 22/IB.133/II.55, lines 29–31: *wa-kawnika tusāfiru min manjarūr ṣuḥbati . . . afḍal min mā tusāfiru fī marākib al-nās*. Maḥrūz's words must have had particular resonance for Abū Zikrī after his adventure on a ship that would qualify as one of those "other people's ships." See also Goitein, *Letters*, 64; Goitein translates this passage as "the ships of foreign people."

134 TS18J4, f. 18/IB.58/III.12, lines 25–26: *kunta tashtarī mā qasaṭa allāh taʿālā min al-filfil wa-ghayrihi wa-tunfidhhu lī bi-baʿḍ al-marākib al-mutakhalliṣa awwal al-zamān*. This statement comes after Khalaf has complained about his losses as a result of water damage and jettison and contribution.

Chapter Six

1 Even bigger ships will be operating in the future; see Holusha, "Making Way."

2 Data on medieval ship size are very scarce. In his seminal article, "Ships of the Arabian Sea," Moreland suggests one hundred tons, of sixty cubic feet per ton, as the capacity of a large trader. The *Sohar*, a reconstruction of a medieval Arab trader that sailed from Muscat to Canton, had an overall length of eighty feet and a waterline length of sixty-three feet; its beam (maximum width) was twenty feet, four inches, its draft (depth) was six feet, and it attained an average speed of two knots (Severin, *Sindbad Voyage*, 235–38). Severin does not give tonnage, but my research on and reconstruction of a vessel of approximately that size gave an estimated displacement of 125 tons, a figure that corresponds to Moreland's estimate.

3 See Casson's excellent analysis of the timing of the round trip from Egypt to India in the time of the Periplus (*Periplus*, 284–90). The combination of seasonal sailing and unpredictable markets easily led to excessively long absences from home; it is not a surprise that after a while, some India traders' wives wished for divorce, as is revealed by a sentimental letter from an India trader to his wife in Egypt (ENA 2739, f. 16/IB.176/VII.60; see Goitein, *Letters*, 220–26).

4 PER H161/IB.36/II.71; see chapter 5.

5 For a map illustrating the segmentation of the Indian Ocean into intersecting sailing units with major port cities at the overlaps, see Chaudhuri, *Trade and Civilization*, 41, map 9.

6 Goitein, *Mediterranean Society*, 1:186–92; Goitein, *Studies*, 345–46.

7 Goitein, *Mediterranean Society*, 1:187.

8 Ibid., 187–88. Goitein argues that a proper *wakīl* had to have a *dār wakāla* and refers to the occurrence of the title *ṣāḥib dār al-wakāla*. He also insists on the official nature of the place and of the transactions taking place in it; see the discussion of the *dār (al-)wakāla* later in this chapter.

9 Ibid., 188–89. The notion of officialdom at least partly informs Goitein's suggestion that the position was likely a precursor of the *shāh bandar* (provost of the merchants) and that it might be connected with the institution of the consulate in the Italian merchant colonies of the Levant (*Mediterranean Society*, 1:192). On the *shāh bandar*, see Raymond, "Shāh Bandar." The question of any connection of the *wakīl al-tujjār* with the institution of Italian consulates is complex: while a parallel exists between the general mission of both the *wakīl al-tujjār* and the Italian consul—that is, their commitment to the business welfare of foreign merchants—important differences also exist. The crucial point here is that the Italian consul was clearly a government employee and served only citizens of his own state. The Venetian consul, for example, was elected by the Maggior Consiglio in Venice; moreover, he had formal ties to two governments—his own and, at least in Mamluk times, that of the host state, which, significantly, paid his salary (Howard, *Venice and the East*, 32–33). On Italian consulates, see also Prawer, "Roots of Medieval Colonialism"; Jacoby, "Italiens en Egypte," 76–89, 102–7.

10 Goitein, *Studies*, 348.

11 See, e.g., Gil, *History of Palestine*, 248–49. Gil presents the *wakīl al-tujjār* as a government official, a formally appointed mercantile representative, and a mediator between merchants and the state.

12 Udovitch, "Merchants and Amīrs," 65. Following Goitein and Udovitch, Constable states that the *wakīl al-tujjār* "occupied a rank between that of government officer and private partner" (*Trade and Traders*, 118).

13 Clearly with Maḍmūn in mind, Goitein states, "In a maritime city a *wakīl tujjār* could simultaneously serve as *nāẓir*, or superintendent of the port, and as tax-farmer of customs and other dues" (*Mediterranean Society*, 1:189).

14 Ibid., 188. Goitein claims that the semiofficial character of the *dār (al-) wakāla* "is underlined by the titles borne by two Jewish representatives of merchants, one living in Fatimid and another in Ayyubid times, which designate them as persons serving the government." The men in question are Amīn al-Dawla, who appears in an unspecified document dating to 1140, and Amīn al-Dawla "*ṣāḥib dār al-wakāla*," appearing in Bodl. MS Heb. c28, f. 54, in 1203; in addition, a "*dār wakalāt al-shaykh al-ʿAmīd b. Kushik*" appears in TS20.80v/IB.273/IV.58, lines 20–24; see Goitein, *Mediterranean Society*, 2:376, 609 n. 8.

15 Goitein, *Mediterranean Society*, 1:191. Goitein posits that "the *wakīls* must also have differed widely with regard to the power and influence they wielded," contrasting judges and superintendents of harbors (clearly having Maḍmūn in mind) with "newcomers."

16 Entries in Maqrīzī's *Al-khiṭaṭ*, for example, include casual references to the subject's role as a *wakīl al-tujjār*—for example, Abū al-Ḥasan al-Qarqūbī, "*wakīl al-tujjār* in Miṣr in the year 415."

17 Cahen notes the importance of the Geniza documents in providing glimpses of the *wakīl al-tujjār*, which, as is implicit in his analysis, do not appear in the *Minhāj* (review, 217).

18 Ibn al-Mujāwir, *Ta'rīkh al-mustabṣir*, 1:143.

19 See al-Shamrookh, *Commerce and Trade*, 268–69 (which notes that Ibn al-Mujāwir only mentions the *wakāla* tax and that its nature is unclear); Jāzim, *Nūr al-maʿārif*; Jāzim "Nūr al-Dīn et al-Muẓaffar," esp. 75–76. In his summary of the Muẓaffar register, Jāzim makes no mention of a *wakīl al-tujjār*. Smith, "Rasulid Administration," does not indicate that al-Ḥusaynī mentions this tax or the institution.

20 The same is true of mercantile representation in Cairo, where there is no solid evidence of a license and where more than one sedentary merchant might represent a traveling colleague. A letter from Mukhtār, a Cairene merchant writing from Aden, to a business friend in Cairo provides a good example. Three representatives of the sender appear in this letter. One is the recipient, who is asked to receive a consignment of clover and odoriferous wood and forward it to Jekuthiel Abū Yaʿqūb al-Ḥakīm and to deal with a dispatch of good silk on behalf of the sender. Second comes Abū Yaʿqūb, who appeared in the al-Lebdī affair as *peqīd ha-soḥarim* (Bodl. MS Heb. d66, f. 66r/IB.12/I.12, line 5; see Goitein, *Mediterranean Society*, 1: 447 n. 23) and whom Mukhtār empowered to receive and presumably sell the consignment. Finally, there is Ḥasan b. Bundār, at whose Aden address the sender receives letters from Cairo and who writes to the Egyptian capital concerning Mukhtār's affairs, presumably while he is traveling in India (TS8J15, f. 24/IB.22/II.1, lines 6–9, 12–14 [the recipient as a representative]; lines 8–10 [Abū Yaʿqūb as a formally empowered agent]; lines 4–5, 14–16 [Ḥasan b. Bundār as a recipient of letters to Mukhtār]).

21 Three letters discussed later in this chapter show both Joseph and Khalaf dealing with Ben Yijū's business affairs in Aden. This correspondence relates to a dispute between these three Jewish merchants and an official of an Indian port referred to as the *kārdār* (TS18J4, f. 18/IB.58/III.12;

TS12.320/IB.51/III.1 [Goitein, *Letters*, 192–97]; TS12.235/IB.54/III.9). TS18J5, f. 1/IB.60/III.11, lines 25–31 (a letter from Khalaf former to Ben Yijū that was examined in chapter 5 as testimony of Maḍmūn's powerful shipping collaboration with Bilāl) shows Khalaf in Aden working for Ben Yijū in India. In TS24.64/IB.56/III.10 (Goitein, *Letters*, 187–92), both Khalaf and Maḍmūn act as Ben Yijū's representatives. Joseph b. Abraham sends items that Ben Yijū had ordered in Zabīd, noting that almonds were not available (lines 13–18). Joseph b. Meshullām corresponds with Ben Yijū during his stay in Jibla (Bodl. MS Heb. d66, f. 61/IB.70/III.32), while Yeshūʿā b. Jacob looks after Ben Yijū's affairs in Jibla before and after his stay (ENA1822, f. 75/IB.240/III.31 and TS10J14, f. 2/IB.71/III.33).

22 TS Box J1, f. 53/IB.81/IV.1; a fully preserved account written by Khalaf in Aden for the well-known merchant Abū Saʿīd Ḥalfon b. Nathanel. Ḥalfon was in India at the time but had sent textiles, pepper, and other Indian merchandise ahead to Aden. Khalaf received these goods and took all the necessary actions on Ḥalfon's behalf, paying import taxes and selling, airing, and brushing textiles before storing them, as discussed later in this chapter.

23 E.g., TS NS J402/IB.298/II.42, a letter from Joseph to an unnamed merchant in India that mentions actions taken by both him and Khalaf with regard to the delivery and sale of merchandise that the addressee had sent from India to Aden.

24 Bodl. MS Heb. a2, f. 16/IB.150/II.53, line 31: *fa-qad ghamaranī baḥr ifḍālihā* (as quoted in the epigraph to this chapter); this letter was written by well-known court clerk Ḥalfon b. Manasse in Fusṭāṭ to Khalaf b. Isaac; see Shaked, *Tentative Bibliography*, 203; Mann, *Jews in Egypt*, 2:337–38, which confuses sender and recipient. ENA 3363, fs. 1–2/IB.209/II.54 are two drafts of letters, mostly in rhymed prose; according to Goitein's unpublished summaries of India Book documents, they are addressed to Khalaf and to Joseph. Shaked, *Tentative Bibliography*, 196, misidentifies the recipient as Ḥalfon b. Manasse.

25 Nor, for that matter, does a *wakīl al-tujjār* appear in the literary sources that deal with Aden in the period covered by this book.

26 Goitein first presented Joseph al-Lebdī's adventures on the route to India in "From the Mediterranean to India," 191–95. See also Goitein, *Letters*, 177–81. Three surviving court documents refer to Ḥasan as *al-wakīl*: ULC Add. 3418/IB.1/I.1, verso line 14; Bodl. MS Heb. d66, f. 65/IB.7/I.7, lines 18–20; and Bodl. MS Heb. d66, f. 66r/IB.12/I.12,

lines 9–10. Goitein, *Letters*, 179 n. 2, appears to generalize from the title *al-wakīl*, characterizing Ḥasan as the "trustee of the merchants."

27 See Udovitch, "Formalism and Informalism," esp. 74. Udovitch discusses "personal guarantee" and shows that the ratio of informal to formal business arrangements in a total of known business transactions can be as lopsided as nineteen to one.

28 See Goitein, *Mediterranean Society*, 1:192.

29 Goitein, *Studies*, 191–92; Goitein, *Mediterranean Society*, 1:192. See also Curtin, *Cross-Cultural Trade*, 113–15. Curtin specifically notes that the ideal person for the position of *wakīl* was a foreign merchant who had established himself overseas and speculates that the institution of the *wakīl al-tujjār* "may represent a remnant of a trade diaspora that worked its way out of business." He compares the "office" with that of the English commission agent of later times. Curtin puts excessive emphasis on the foreign origin of trading groups, appearing to imply that Maḍmūn and the Aden's Jewish traders constituted a "foreign" group, an "Egyptian community overseas."

30 For a concise but well-informed survey of the history of Adeni Jews, see Goitein, "Aden." On the connection between the Bundārs' family name and their Iranian origins, see Goitein, *Letters*, 14.

31 Jekuthiel is hailed *peqīd ha-soḥarīm* in one of the court records from his lawsuit against al-Lebdī in 491/1098 (Bodl. MS Heb, d.66, f. 66r/IB.12/I.12, line 5). On Jekuthiel's appearances on communal lists of charitable contributors, see Goitein, *Mediterranean Society*, 2:477–79.

32 Goitein, *Mediterranean Society*, 1:191.

33 Goitein, *Letters*, 179.

34 Goitein, *Mediterranean Society* 1:189.

35 Bodl. MS Heb. d66, f. 66v/IB.13/I.13, lines 2–4, a letter in which Joseph al-Lebdī writes to Ḥasan b. Bundār, "May God preserve the life of my lord, the illustrious shaykh Abū ʿAlī our master and teacher Japheth . . . Prince of the Congregations [*sar ha-qehillot*]." See also Goitein, *Letters*, 179. Ḥasan's name appears here in its Hebrew form, Japheth; see Goitein, *Letters*, 178. For the use of the Hebrew title "*sar*," meaning "prince" or "notable," see Goitein, *Mediterranean Society*, 1:75–77; Cohen, *Jewish Self-Government*, 124. Ḥasan's son, Bundār, and his brothers, Abraham and Isaac, also bore the title (ENA 2728, f. 2v/II.11b, a short note of just these titles by court clerk Ḥalfon b. Manasse).

36 JNUL H15.4577/IB.39/II.36, lines 11–12; trustee: *ne'eman*.

37 Ḥalfon/Khalaf, the son of the first Maḍmūn, is referred as "our *nagid*"

in the letter, discussed in chapter 5, that was drafted by the rabbinical court of Aden concerning the estate of the shipwrecked Egyptian merchant Hiba b. Abī Saʿd (PER H161/IB.36/II.71, verso margin). The second Maḍmūn's father, David, was probably a son of this Ḥalfon/Khalaf and must be the person referred to as "our *nagid* David" in TS Misc. Box 28, f. 187/IB.213/II.65, line 35. His son (and the first Maḍmūn's great-grandson) was Maḍmūn/Shemarya b. David, referred to as "*nagid* of the Land of Yemen" (TS NS J242/IB.311/II.73, lines 12–13: *Shemarya nagid arḍ teman*; TS6J2, f. 10/IB.310/II.68, lines 3–4). See also Goitein's identification of this Maḍmūn in *Letters*, 216 n. 2. As chapters 3 and 4 showed, Maḍmūn b. David was forced to convert in 594/1198; in 598/1202, however, the tyrant was murdered, and circumstances returned to normal. The two relevant Geniza letters appear in translation in Goitein, *Letters*, 212–20. A diagram of the main Bundār family line and their titles appears in Goitein, *Yemenites*, 82.

38 Goitein, *Yemenites*, 79–80; Goitein, "Jews of Yemen."

39 Goitein explores the incident based on the testimony of six documents included in the India Book corpus; see Goitein, "Jews of Yemen"; Goitein, *Yemenites*, 53–74. For the invocation of both authorities in India, see Goitein, *Mediterranean Society*, 2:20–21.

40 For example, in TS13J25, f. 13/IB.31/VI.27, lines 28–31 and margin, lines 1–4, the sender, whom Goitein identifies as Isḥaq b. Makhlūf (see Shaked, *Tentative Bibliography*, 135) after discussing a consignment of textiles that the recipient (probably Maḍmūn, who is addressed as "our *nagid*") is supposed to receive and sell, talks about a different consignment of pepper to be handled by Khalaf b. Isaac; Khalaf b. Isaac holds an official document, a *wakāla tāma*, in which the sender has empowered him to deal with the pepper. When Nahray b. Nissīm, who also offers services of a *wakīl tujjār* to a number of merchants, similarly receives an official legal power of attorney to represent someone in court, Goitein argues that Nissīm "was clearly no full-fledged, officially recognized" *wakīl tujjār*; otherwise, he would not have needed a *wakāla* document (see *Mediterranean Society*, 1:189 n. 11). If, however, no one had official recognition by license and the relationship was informal, a more relevant question focuses on which functions required a power of attorney and which did not.

41 See Goitein, *Letters*, 177–79.

42 Bodl. MS Heb. d66, f. 65/IB.7/I.7, lines 18–19. See also n. 26.

43 Bodl. MS Heb. d66v, f. 67/IB.13/I.13, folio 67, verso lines 10–12; TS28/22/IB.14/I.14, line 5. See also Goitein, *Letters*, 179, 181.

44 ULC Add. 3421r and v, a/IB.2/I.2, recto, lines 11–13. The same advance (*salaf*) is discussed in Bodl. MS Heb. d66, f. 65/IB.7/I.7, lines 14–15; Bodl. MS Heb. d66, f. 67/IB.13/I.13, lines 4–6.

45 Bodl. MS Heb. 66, f. 67/IB.13/I.13, lines 15–17; see also Goitein, *Letters*, 179–81; "assembly of the elders": *mahḍar ha-zeqenim*. TS28.22/IB.14/I.14, line 55 also mentions ratification of Ḥasan's papers and appointment by the Adeni court of an empowered representative who would accompany them to serve as evidence in Egypt.

46 Goitein has assembled a series of eight letters that lay out the details of this interesting affair. They form the first part of the second chapter of the India Book (II.2–II.9). The first three letters were sent by Amram b. Joseph, Nissīm's brother-in-law, who pleads the case on behalf of the family in Alexandria, to Nahray b. Nissīm, who is asked to intervene. Amram explicitly mentions Mevorakh's involvement and Ḥasan's eventual release and dispatch of the goods in a letter to a contact in Cairo who is to arrange for the sale or transfer to Alexandria (DK 230 h–j/IB.217/II.6, esp. lines 11–18, verso lines 6–8). In the first of the three letters, the writer stresses that it is wrong and a sin on the part of Ḥasan to take possession of the camphor's price as security against possible claims (TS13J23, f. 10/IB.45/II.2, verso lines 14–24).

47 TS13J23, f. 10/IB.45/II.2, verso lines 14–24, esp. 21–22: *wa-lā awjaba ta'khīruhu . . . ʿaqlulu ʿindahu mā [samaḥa allāh] dhālika*; detention or sequestration: *ʿaql*.

48 On Mevorakh and the transformations, influence, and power of the office of *nagid* in his days, see Cohen, *Jewish Self-Government*, esp. 232–50. See also the discussion of the relationship between the *wakīl tujjār* and the courts of law later in this chapter.

49 ULC Or1080 J171/IB.243/V.9, top margin. See the detailed discussion of the episode in chapter 5.

50 JNUL H15.4577/IB.39/II.36. I am indebted to Mark R. Cohen and Orit Bashkin for translating crucial segments of this document.

51 Mosseri L296–2/IB.38/II.35. Unfortunately no date is preserved on either this or the subsequent legal document pertaining to this affair.

52 Ibid., lines 30–31: *raddū ʿalayhi jawāb bihi kalām kathīr mimmā yuḍayyaqu bihi ṣadr sayyidinā Maḍmūn wa-mimmā yughayyiḍuhu*. The document refers to Maḍmūn as "*moraynu wa-rabaynu*," "*sar ha-sarim*," and "*rosh ha-qehillot*" (lines 17–18).

53 JNUL H15.4577/IB.39/II.36; for the fine to be paid to Maḍmūn by each of the brothers, see line 13; for the evils of slander (*leshon hara*ᶜ) on the authority of Rabbi Eliezer b. Perata, see lines 27–30. I am indebted to Mark R. Cohen for the interpretation of this passage.

54 Goitein, *Mediterranean Society*, 1:191.

55 Ibid.

56 TS Box J1, f. 53/IB.81/IV.1.

57 Ibid., lines 1–17. The account begins with a header, "*ḥisāb mawlāya al-shaykh abū sa*ᶜ*īd ḥalfon b. nathanel*." Each subsequent line begins with the indication of credit, "*wa lahu qīma*." Line 17 gives the total, "*al-jumla*."

58 Ibid., lines 18 (pepper), 19 (some textiles: *maqṣūr*, *maḥābis*, and *khām*), 20–21 (musk).

59 Ibid., lines 22 (silver), 23 (Egyptian *mithqāl*), 24–25 (coral).

60 Ibid., line 26: *wa-kirā' makhzan dīnār wa-niṣf wa-furush li'l-makhzan rub*ᶜ *dīnār*.

61 Ibid., line 27: *wa-dinarayn* ᶜ*an sirqat al-abrād wa-dīnār* ᶜ*an sirqat al-fuwaṭ*. *Fūṭa* and *barad* cloth appear in the credits section, lines 9–10, but not in the list of import taxes.

62 TS NS J285/IB.297/II.29, verso, line 2: *lam takun fusḥa li-ḥall wa-*ᶜ*iba'*.

63 TS10J9, f. 24/IB.55/III.3, lines 3–4: *wa-ammā jiḥlat al-laymūn wa-al-*ᶜ*inabā' fa-waṣa*[*lat wa*]*-hiya tālifat jīfa ramaynā bihā*.

64 TS24.66/IB.26/II.16, lines 44–49; Maḍmūn's report of his dispatch of copper to Ben Yijū in India notes that the goods had been packed in three bags (*āṣira*) of equal weight, each containing twenty-three pieces of copper and each sent on a different ship. See also Goitein's edition and translation in "From Aden to India," 49, 61.

65 Goitein, *Mediterranean Society*, 1:332–39. Goitein explains that "in view of the long duration of a journey, the imperfect means of transport, and the ever-present danger of damage by seawater, adequate packing was of utmost importance" (332).

66 TS10J29, f. 3/IB.262/VII.45, lines 8–9: *wa-ammā al-qumqum al-mā' ward sāla jamī*ᶜ*uhu wa-al-sillat al-zujjāj inkasarat*.

67 TS20.137/IB.29/II.23, a letter from Maḍmūn to Ben Yijū. Baskets are *shutūt* (sing. *shatt*); see Goitein, *Yemenites*, 90 n. 604. The arrangement of the glass in these small baskets is said to be *maḥkam* (orderly), or as Goitein writes in an unpublished note to this text, "firmly set."

68 TS18J5, f. 5/IB.149/II.46, lines 46–47: *qafaṣayn jayyidayn qawīyayn*. Crates are *aqfāṣ* (sing. *qafaṣ*). This is Khalaf's letter to Egypt describing the siege of the port by the ruler of Qays/Kish; see chapter 2.

69 TS24.66/IB.26/II.16, line 45. Skins (*julūd*) were apparently used to pack Yijū's three batches of copper.

70 TS18J2, f. 7/IB.24/II.14, lines 11–14: *shiddat ḥiṣar barbarī al-ʿadad sittat ḥiṣr wa-qad khayyashnā ʿalayhi khīsha*. The rough canvas packaging material was *khīsha*. See Goitein, "From Aden to India," 47.

71 E.g., TS24.66/IB.26/II.16, line 45: *qīmat julūd wa-ʿabāʾ dīnār wa-niṣf*. The packer is more commonly known as "*ḥazzām*" and sometimes as "*shaddād*" or "*mukawwir*" (Goitein, *Mediterranean Society*, 1: 486 nn. 21, 25). Goitein notes another term for the profession, "*muqāṭ*," that occurs in TS13J22, f. 33/IB.84/IV.3, line 15.

72 Labeling is mentioned in both letters from Maḍmūn to Ben Yijū. Maḍmūn notifies Ben Yijū about his dispatches of mats from Berbera, sent care of ʿAbd al-Masīḥ, a deacon (significantly, a Christian included in the circle of trust), and packed and labeled appropriately (TS18J2, f. 7/IB.24/II.14, lines 13–14: *wa-maktūb ʿalayhi ismuka ʿarabī wa-ʿibrānī*). See also Goitein's edition and translation in "From Aden to India," 47, 52; for TS24.66/IB.26/II.16, verso lines 5–7, see 49, 62.

73 TS10J29, f. 3/IB.262/VII.45, lines 10–12: *thumma ayḍan kassartu fī al-marjān shay akbar li-annanī lam altaqī bi-al-rajul wa-ḥamalnāhu ʿalā al-sūq bi-aswāq*.

74 Abū Yaʿqūb relates in a court statement that he had instructed Joseph al-Lebdī to send, upon his arrival at Aden, "half of these consignments in the hand of Ḥasan b. Bundār to Minibār, the land of pepper, to buy me pepper with it and to take the other half with you to Nahrawara to buy me lac" (ULC Add. 3418/IB.1/I.1, lines 5–8).

75 On the multifunctionality of merchants' houses in the port of al-Mukhā in the 18th century, see Um, "Red Sea Society," 108–18.

76 See, e.g., Goitein, *Mediterranean Society*, 1: 187–89 and notes. Detailed evidence about the financing, construction, and running of a *dār (al-) wakāla* comes from later contexts. An excellent example emerges from Hanna's study of the life and times of Abū Taqiyya, a Cairene merchant of the turn of the 17th century (*Making Big Money*, esp. 66–68, 128). Merchants of Abū Taqiyya's standing shouldered the enormous investment necessary for the building of a *dār (al-)wakāla*. The place could then generate profit and prestige, but the reality of the initial investment is important. Could merchants in Fatimid and Ayyubid times, either in Cairo or in Aden, generally afford to open such facilities?

77 The connection between sale and the *dār al-saʿīda/saʿāda* is made in TS13J25, f. 13/IB.31/VI.27, line 20–21: *an taʾmura iḥdā ʿabīdihā an yata-*

sallamahā wa-tubāʿa fī al-dār al-saʿīda. This letter, presumably from Isaac b. Makhlūf al-Nafūsī from India to Maḍmūn, was mentioned earlier in connection with Khalaf b. Isaac as a representative of merchants; see Shaked, *Tentative Bibliography*, 135.

78 Ibid., right margin: *wa-huwa mā salamahu li'l-shaykh Abū Saʿīd Ḥalfon ha-Levī bar Shemarya bayna yadayhā fī majlisihā al-karīm wa-huwa mi'atayn dīnāran malikīya*. The term "*majlis*" appears in a similar context in a letter referring to Maḍmūn' s great-grandson, Maḍmūn b. David; see the section on settlement of estates after shipwreck later in this chapter.

79 The literal meaning of the word is, of course, sitting room, but as Goitein points out, its functions are better conveyed by "living room" (*Mediterranean Society*, 4:48, 64). Goitein provides evidence for the existence of very large such rooms, with a capacity for four hundred guests (*Mediterranean Society*, 4:65). "*Majlis*" could also signify a meetinghouse or communal common room, as in "*majlis sūq al-yahūd*" (Goitein, *Mediterranean Society*, 2:165–66). Given the particularly deferential reference to the specific *majlis*, however, it is uncertain whether the writer is referring to Maḍmūn's house or to the local rabbinical court of law over which Maḍmūn presided as a *nagid* of Yemen and India.

80 See Cohen, *Jewish Self-Government*, 165 n. 19. For the *majlis* of the head of the Jews during the time of Maimonides and his successors, Cohen refers to Goitein, "Letter to Maimonides," 243.

81 TS24.64/IB.56/III.10, lines 33–35. In his translation of this letter, *Letters*, 197, Goitein translates the word "*dār*" as "storehouse." See also Khalaf's reference to transactions at "*al-bayt*" in the much damaged TS AS148, f. 9/IB.363/II.49, lines 7, 10.

82 TS20.137/IB.29/II.23, line 31: *ṣaḥḥa al-wazn ʿinda al-bayʿ bi-al-dār bahār*. This is a strange case in which Maḍmūn reports to Ben Yijū two different weights for the same cardamom consignment, one weight at the assessment of dues at the customshouse and a higher number at its sale at the *dār*.

83 Pellat, *Life and Works of Jāḥiẓ*, 272.

84 Goitein, *Mediterranean Society*, 1:188 n. 6.

85 ENA 4020, f. 26/IB.196/VII.25, lines 1–3 and 15; for the customary practice, see lines 2–3: *al-ʿāda bi-miṣr bayna al-tujjār fī al-shirka*.

86 Ibid., lines 3–4: *immā li-dār wakāla aw li-makhzan tujjār*.

87 Ibid., line 3: *idhā dakhalū minhum jamāʿa*.

88 Ibid., line 7: *fī daftar al-wakīl aw al-tujjār*.

89 Ibid., line 9: *fī tarīq lā fī dār wakāla wa-lā fī makhzan*; lines 12–14: *wa-ishtarahā ba'd dhālika wa-lam yakun ma'ahu aḥad lā fī wazn wa-lā 'inda salam al-shirā'*.

90 For optimal sailing up the Red Sea from the winter through early April, see Brouwer, *al-Mukhā*, 124, 347; Casson, *Periplus*, 285–86; Tibbetts, *Arab Navigation*, 230–31.

91 TS NS J285/IB.297/II.29, lines 8–11.

92 One example appears in the letter from Isaac b. Makhlūf to Maḍmūn mentioned earlier (TS13J25, f. 13/IB.31/VI.27, lines 25–28). The writer explains that he is sending six bales of textiles belonging to himself and a partner and asks the recipient to sell the entire consignment unless it seems preferable to split the goods in half. Maḍmūn presumably is to gauge the market and decide how much can be sold profitably at that moment. If splitting the consignment is deemed best, Makhlūf adds, the partner would prefer that his half be stored in Maḍmūn's storeroom, presumably for sale at an unspecified future time.

93 Joseph al-Lebdī, for example, proceeded to India after storing the remainder of the textile consignment he was handling for Jekuthiel as well as some personal effects, including a turban (Bodl. MS Heb. d66, f. 64v/IB.5/I.5, line 18: *al-bāqī bi-'adan fīhi 'imāmat lī malfūfa*).

94 TS Box J1, f. 53/IB.81/IV.1, line 26 (from the account in the hand of Khalaf b. Isaac): *wa-kirā' makhzan dīnār wa-nisf wa-furush li'l-makhzan rub' dīnār*.

95 An indignant Ben Yijū writes to a correspondent in Aden that what he had stored for him or for their partnership in a storage space in Aden was mere bric-a-brac (*dabash*) with no value at all. With more than a hint of sarcasm, he invites the addressee to have someone sell the bric-a-brac if he thinks it has any value (TS8J21, f. 10/IB.189/III.39, lines 10–15).

96 TS10J27, f. 4/IB.9/I.9, verso, lines 10–11, a court record from the litigation between the two men, dated 8 Tammūz 1409/10 June 1098. Jekuthiel pressed Joseph, and the latter apparently backpedaled and tried to cut a deal. No evidence indicates that he ever produced the missing ledger.

97 JTS Geniza Misc. 8/IB.235/II.51, line 17: *ḥarīq al-buyūt wa-nahab makhāzin*; TS Misc. Box 28, f. 256/IB.207/II.48, lines 11–12: *wa-ṣāra al-sirqa wa-al-nahb fī al-balad*.

98 Goitein, *Mediterranean Society*, 1:164–69; Udovitch, "Formalism and Informalism." As mentioned earlier, Udovitch shows that the ratio of

informal to formal business arrangements in a total of known business transactions can be as lopsided as nineteen to one.

99 On normative Islamic legal theory and practice of partnership contracts, see Udovitch, *Partnership and Profit*, 196–203. As an example of how legal discussions provide evidence for the use of contracts, Udovitch quotes the discussion of the case of a man holding written evidence of his *commenda* investment with a man who had since died. Udovitch also points to general similarities between Islamic legal formularies of partnership contracts with the nature of contracts as they emerge from Geniza letters and contracts. The Geniza documents show that death of a partner holding assets of an investor constitutes the circumstance that most frequently results in recourse to written proof of a debt or investment.

100 Thus, Maḍmūn notifies Ben Yijū in India that ʿAlī al-Fawfalī is his official, empowered agent for selling merchandise sent from Aden (*wakaltu al-nākhudhā ʿAlī al-Fawfalī ʿalā bayʿ al-shiddāt*) and for taking possession (*wakīl ʿalā qabḍihi*) of goods belonging to Maḍmūn and held by various merchants or stored in a storehouse in Mangalore or Fandarayna (TS NS J1/IB.199/II.24, verso, lines 13–22). In another case, Joseph b. Abraham provides a witnessed *kitāb al-wakāla* to a man who is to appear in a Cairo court and claim on Joseph's behalf items entrusted to the deceased merchant *shaykh* Tamīm (JTS Geniza Misc. 4/IB.227/VI.36, lines 33–37 and margin).

101 TS20.130/IB.28/II.20, line 41: *mawlāya ghalaṭa wa-huwa mutawahhim.*

102 Mosseri L296-2/IB.38/II.35; for the deposit, see line 21: *wadīʿa mithl muʿmala wa-hiya maktūba fī* [*dafātirihi*]; for Yaʿqūb's trip to Aden, see lines 22–25: *nuzūl wālidihim min baʿd hulk ḥayy sayyidinā Bundār . . . ilā ḥaḍrat sayyidinā akhīhi Maḍmūn*; for looking into the books, see lines 23–25: *wa-in al-shaykh Yaʿqūb ha-kohen fattasha al-dafātir al-ladhī li-ḥayy sayyidinā Bundār . . . fa-wajada lahu alladhī dhakara*; for Maḍmūn offering a writ, see line 25: *wa-in sayyiduna Maḍmūn kataba lahu khaṭṭ bi-dhālika wa-ashhada lahu ʿalā nafsihi.*

103 Mosseri L296-2/IB.38/II.35, line 28–29: *yaqūl lahum idhā kāna maʿahum ʿalayhi //khaṭṭ// wa-shahāda kāna yaṣilu aḥaduhum bi-dhālika al-khaṭṭ wa-al-shahāda wa-aḥkamahu ʿinda yisrael.*

104 My ideas on the question of merchants' archiving practices owe much to conversations with Mark R. Cohen.

105 On these two merchants and the voluminous remains of their written

records, see Goitein, *Mediterranean Society*, 1:153–56, 158–59. On Ibn ʿAwkal, see also Stillman, "Eleventh-Century Merchant House."

106 For the final publication of this material, see Guo, *Commerce, Culture, and Community*; Guo, "Arabic Documents, Part 1"; Guo, "Arabic Documents, Part 2." For the structure in which the documents were discovered, see report by excavators Whitcomb and Johnson, "1982 Season," 25. On the dating of the fragments, see Guo, *Commerce, Culture, and Community*, 3–4.

107 Guo, *Commerce, Culture, and Community*, xi.

108 Ibid., 1–11.

109 Guo, "Arabic Documents, Part 1," 162; Guo, *Commerce, Culture, and Community*, xii.

110 Guo, *Commerce, Culture, and Community*, xii.

111 Ibid., 104.

112 Goitein, *Mediterranean Society*, 1:187.

113 TS24.64/IB.56/III.10, translated in Goitein, *Letters*, 187–92. See also the section on shipwreck, rescue, and salvage in chapter 5.

114 TS13J8, f. 17/IB.35/II.70. See also Assaf, "Relations," 118–19; Shaked, *Tentative Bibliography*, 118. I am indebted to Orit Bashkin for the translation of crucial passages of this document.

115 PER H161/IB.36/II.71; Strauss, "Voyage to India," 217–31. In his unpublished summaries of India Book documents by chapter, Goitein notes that the document was drafted by Adeni court clerk Saʿīd b. Marḥab, whose signed documents include TS12.216/IB.264a/VI.51, TS NS Box 264, f. 1/IB.264b/VI.52, and ENA 2741, f. 4/IB.264c/VI.53.

116 PER H161/IB.36/II.71, verso, margin line 1.

117 Ibid., verso, margin, lines 2–3: *wa-al-makhlaf qabaḍa minhu al-mulk jamīʿahu bet din*. Goitein apparently reads line 2 as *wa-al-makhlaf qabaḍa ʿalayhi al-malik jamiʿahu*. My interpretation rests on reading differently only two letters of the most poorly visible word, "*minhu*" (which Goitein reads as "*ʿalayhi*") and including the first two words of the following line into the sentence. According to my understanding, Goitein reads the rest of the phrase—that is, the part that reads "*bayt dīn*"—as a separate clause, indicating the body that signed the report.

118 TS12.527/IB.218/II.72, lines 8–9. The widow, "*armalat Hiba b. Abū Saʿd*" (line 3), declares that she has received the sum from Abū al-Surūr ha-Levi.

119 TS NS J242/IB.311/II.73. The case had further developments, as is re-

vealed by a later document in which the brother of Petaḥya (Futūḥ) claims a share of the estate as promised by his brother during a drinking bout just before his departure (TS10J17, f. 4/IB.37/II.74, edited by Goitein in "Chief Justice Hananel b. Samuel," 377–78). Goitein briefly mentions the affair in *Mediterranean Society*, 5:333, 516 n. 147, 582 n. 80, 598 n. 5.

120 TS8Ja1, f. 3/IB.183/II.75, lines 6–12; the proceedings at the Egyptian court are mentioned in lines 2–5. Significantly, the term "*majlis*" appears earlier with reference to Maḍmūn's great-grandfather and the delivery of a sum from one merchant to another (see TS13J25, f. 13/IB.31/VI.27 and discussion of commercial business spaces earlier in this chapter). On Abraham Maimonides, see Goitein, *Mediterranean Society*, 5:476–77.

121 Cohen, *Jewish Self-Government*, 248–50.

122 ENA 3616, f. 19/IB.30/II.25, lines 12–14. The text is very broken, but Makhlūf's nickname (*ʿayn sārra*), his demands (*ṭalabihi*), and the Islamic legal document (*ḥujja*) can be read clearly. On Makhlūf's nickname, see Goitein, *Mediterranean Society*, 5:575 n. 136.

123 See ULC Or1081 J3/IB.61/II.26, margin; TS NS J1/IB.199/II.24, lines 2–3. Both are letters from Maḍmūn to Ben Yijū that mention the sum of three hundred dinars that Ben Yijū was obliged to pay. In the second letter, Maḍmūn describes Makhlūf as a senile, foolish, and ignorant man. Goitein mentions this affair and refers to the relevant documents in *Mediterranean Society*, 5:247, 575 nn. 141, 142.

124 TS Misc. Box 28, f. 187/IB.213/II.65, lines 10–42.

125 See Goitein, *Letters*, 193; Gosh, "Slave of MS. H. 6," 206–8.

126 See Goitein, "Portrait," 460–61. In this well-known letter by Allān b. Hassūn, a different *kārdār* appears as one of the three officials who boarded a vessel that had remained without a captain for days at sea but had finally safely reached port. While the role of the *kārdār* in returning the ship to its rightful owner may indeed indicate that he was a port official, his presence could also be explained through a purely commercial connection to the merchants and/or cargo on board. See also Goitein, *Letters*, 193 n. 4.

127 Gosh, "Slave of MS. H. 6," 206–8.

128 TS12.320/IB.51/III.1, lines 13–15: *dhakara mawlāya al-kārdāl wa-mawlāya yatalaṭṭaf bihi wa-yastakhliṣu lanā minhu wa-law tahadhdharahu mawlāya bi-an naḥnu nashmatu fī ʿadan kull man lanā shay wa-lā yuwaffīnā*. See also Goitein, *Letters*, 193; Gosh, "Slave of MS. H. 6," 207

n. 233, where Gosh modifies Goitein's translation of the term based on the root *sh-m-t*, as discussed later in the chapter.

129 TS18J4, f. 18/IB.58/III.12, lines 26–31.

130 On Ben Yijū's liaison with Ashū, an Indian slave whom he manumitted in Mangalore, see Goitein, *Letters*, 202; Goitein, *Mediterranean Society*, 2:20. Gosh argues that this woman may have been somehow related to the *kārdār*, and a family tie indeed would have played a role in his connection with the Jewish merchants ("Slave of MS. H. 6," 208).

131 Goitein notes the Talmudic sanction for a "ban as punishment for defaulting debtors" (*Letters*, 193). Gosh reads the term used in the documents, *sh-m-t*, as "the metathesized form of sh-t-m and modifies Goitein's translation from 'excommunication' to 'disgrace' and 'censure'" ("Slave of MS. H. 6," 207 n. 233).

Conclusion

1 Ludovico di Varthema, *Travels*, 59–60.

2 Abu Lughod, *Before European Hegemony*, 353, posits that although it was "uneven," the world system that culminated in the first decades of the 1300s "had newly integrated an impressive set of interlinked subsystems in Europe, the Middle East (including the northern portion of Africa), and Asia (coastal and steppe zones)."

3 On the importance of these embassies to the Rasulid sultans, see al-Shamrookh, *Commerce and Trade*, 77, 164–66.

4 Um, "Spatial Negotiations," 181–83; Um, "Red Sea Society," esp. 108–18.

5 Jāzim, "Nūr al-Dīn et al-Muẓaffar," 76, 78.

6 Al-Shamrookh, *Commerce and Trade*, 246–47.

7 Acknowledging that the integration of medieval economies was partial, Abu Lughod, *Before European Hegemony*, 353, points to the interconnectedness of the "archipelago of 'world cities' elevated above a sea of relatively isolated rural areas and open stretches."

8 Al-Shamrookh, *Commerce and Trade*, 165; Jāzim, "Nūr al-Dīn et al-Muẓaffar," 76 n. 65, 83.

Bibliography

Geniza Documents

Texts are arranged alphabetically by library. Where applicable, shelf marks are followed by India Book designations. The first of these includes the initials "IB" for India Book and a serial number corresponding to Goitein's original seriation. New designations reflect Goitein's final chapter arrangement and document seriation within each chapter. Asterisks denote documents with partly or fully published text.

Ethan Nathan Adler Collection, Jewish Theological Seminary, New York

ENA 1822, f. 75/IB.240/III.31
ENA 2728, f. 2v/II.11b
ENA 2739, f. 16/IB.176/VII.60*
ENA 2741 f. 4/IB.264c/VI.53
ENA 3363, fs. 1–2/IB.209/II.54
ENA 3616, f. 19/IB.30/II.25
ENA 4020, f. 8/IB.153/VI.38
ENA 4020, f. 26/IB.196/VII.25
JTS Geniza Misc. 2r/IB.225/II.27
JTS Geniza Misc. 4/IB.227/VI.36
JTS Geniza Misc. 8/IB.235/II.51
JTS Geniza Misc. 10/IB.237/II.31

Bodleian Library, Oxford

Bodl. MS Heb. a2, f. 16/IB.150/II.53
Bodl. MS Heb. a2, f. 16/IB.298/II.42
Bodl. MS Heb. a3, f. 19/IB.32/II.32*
Bodl. MS Heb. b3, f. 26/IB.193/VII.36
Bodl. MS Heb. b11, f. 21/IB.20/I.33
Bodl. MS Heb. b11, f. 22/IB.133/II.55*
Bodl. MS Heb. c28, f. 54
Bodl. MS Heb. d66, f. 21/IB.177/VII.58*
Bodl. MS Heb. d66, f. 61/IB.70/III.32

Bodl. MS Heb. d66, f. 64v/IB.5/I.5
Bodl. MS Heb. d66, f. 64r/IB.6/I.6
Bodl. MS Heb. d66, f. 65/IB.7/I.7
Bodl. MS Heb. d66, f. 66r/IB.12/I.12
Bodl. MS Heb. d66, fs. 66v, 67/IB.13/I.13*
Bodl. MS Heb. d66, f. 108/IB.131/V.8
Bodl. MS Heb. f103, f. 39/IB.194/VII.63

British Museum, London
BM Or5542, f. 17/IB.135/II.57
BM Or5549, III, fol. 5/IB. 221a/V.4
BM Or5566 d, f. 6/IB.152/VI.39

Dropsie College, Philadelphia
Dropsie 384/IB.184/VII.46

Jerusalem National University Library
JNUL H15.4577/IB.39/II.36

David Kaufmann Collection, Budapest
DK 230h–j/IB. 217/II.6

Mosseri Collection, Paris
Mosseri A55/IB.166/VII.22
Mosseri L12/IB.348/II.66*
Mosseri L288/IB.292/VI.28
Mosseri L296-2/IB.38/II.35

Papyrus Ehrzog Reiner Collection, State Library, Vienna
PER H161/IB.36/II.71*

Taylor Schechter Collection, Cambridge
TS6J2, f. 10/IB.310/II.68
TS8Ja1, f. 3/IB.183/II.75
TS8J15, f. 24/IB.22/II.1
TS8J21, f. 10/IB.189/III.39
TS8J21, f. 29
TS10J9, f. 24/IB.55/III.3
TS10J12, f. 5/IB.53/III.4
TS10J14, f. 2/IB.71/III.33
TS10J16, f. 1/IB.143/VI.11
TS10J17, f. 4/IB.37/II.74*

TS10J18, f. 8
TS10J27, f. 4/IB.9/I.9
TS10J29, f. 3/IB.262/VII.45
TS12.216/IB.264a/VI.51
TS12.224
TS12.235/IB.54/III.9
TS12.320/IB.51/III.1*
TS12.527/IB.218/II.72
TS13J8, f. 17/IB.35/II.70*
TS13J21, f.26*
TS13J22, f. 33/IB.84/IV.3
TS13J23, f. 10/IB.45/II.2
TS13J25, f. 13/IB.31/VI.27
TS13J28, f. 15/IB.291/VI.44*
TS13J28, f. 15v/IB.291/VI.42
TS16.345/IB.134/II.56
TS18J2, f. 7/IB.24/II.14*
TS18J2, f. 14/IB.62/III.22
TS18J4, f. 18/IB.58/III.12
TS18J5, f. 1/IB.60/III.11
TS18J5, f. 5/IB.149/II.46*
TS20.63/IB.82/VI.26
TS20.80v/IB.273/IV.58
TS20.130/IB.28/II.20
TS20.137/IB.29/II.23*
TS20.137v/IB.64/III.18
TS24.37/IB.91/IV.12
TS24.64/IB.56/III.10*
TS24.66/IB.26/II.16*
TS28.11/IB.154/II.67*
TS28.20/IB.280/II.61
TS28.22/IB.14/I.14
TS AS148, f. 9/IB.363/II.49
TS AS156.237
TS AS156.238
TS Box J1, f. 53/IB.81/IV.1
TS Misc. Box 25, f. 103/IB.208/III.15
TS Misc. Box 28, f. 33/IB.215/VI.44
TS Misc. Box 28, f. 187/IB.213/II.65

TS Misc. Box 28, f. 256/IB.207/II.48
TS NS Box 264, f. 1/IB.264b/VI.52
TS NS J1/IB.199/II.24
TS NS J10/IB.200/III.23
TS NS J23/IB.214/VII.56
TS NS J44/IB.242/V.7
TS NS J182
TS NS J241/IB.296/II.21
TS NS J242/IB.311/II.73
TS NS J285/IB.297/II.29
TS NS J300*
TS NS J402/IB.298/II.42
TS NS J426/IB.305/VII.54

University Library Collection, Cambridge
ULC Or1080 J95v, a/IB.66/III.21a
ULC Or1080 J95v, b/IB.67/III.21b
ULC Or1080 J171/IB.243/V.9
ULC Or1080 J180/IB.244/V.5
ULC Or1081 J1/IB.178/VI.4*
ULC Or1081 J3/IB.61/II.26
ULC Add. 3418/IB.1/I.1
ULC Add. 3421r and v, a/IB.2/I.2
ULC Add. 3421v, b/IB.4/I.4

Westminster College, Cambridge
Westmin. Frag. Cairens. Misc. 13/IB.96/VI.32

Printed Primary Sources

Abū Makhrama, Abū Muḥammad ʿAbdallāh. *Taʾrīkh thaghr ʿAden*. 2 vols. In *Arabische Texte zur Kenntnis der Stadt Aden im Mittelalter*, edited by L. Oscar Löfgren. Leiden: Brill, 1936–50.

Abū Zayd Ḥasan al-Sīrāfī. *Supplement to Akhbār aṣ-ṣīn wa'l-hind*. In *Relations des voyages faits par les Arabes et les Persans à l'Inde et à la Chine dans le IX siècle Chrétienne*. Edited by L. M. Langlès and Joseph Toussaint Reinaud. Paris: Imprimerie Royale, 1845.

Benjamin of Tudela. *The Itinerary of Benjamin of Tudela*. Edited and translated by Marcus Nathan Adler. London: Frowde, 1907.

Buzurg b. Shahriyār al-Rāmhurmuzī. *Kitāb ʿajāʾib al-hind*. Edited by Pieter

Antonie Van der Lith. French translation by L. Marcel Devic. Leiden: Brill, 1883–86.
Casson, Lionel, ed. and trans. *The Periplus Maris Erythraei*. Princeton: Princeton University Press, 1989.
al-Hamdānī, al-Ḥasan b. Aḥmad. *Ṣifat jazīrat al-ʿarab*. 2 vols. Edited by David Heinrich Müller. Leiden: Brill, 1884–91.
Ibn al-Athīr, Abū al-Ḥasan ʿAlī. *Kitāb kāmil al-taʾwārīkh*. Vol. 6. Edited by Carl Johan Tornberg. Leiden: Brill, 1851.
Ibn al-Faqīh al-Hamadhānī, Aḥmad b. Muḥammad. *Mukhtaṣar kitāb al-buldān*. Edited by Michael Jan de Goeje. Bibliotheca geographorum Arabicorum 5. Leiden: Brill, 1969.
Ibn al-Mujāwir, Abū Bakr b. Muḥammad. *Taʾrīkh al-Mustabṣir*. 2 vols. Edited by Oscar Löfgren. Leiden: Brill, 1951–54.
Ibn Baṭṭūṭa, Muḥammad b. ʿAbdallāh. *Riḥlat Ibn Baṭṭūṭa*. Beirut: Dār Ṣādir, 1960.
Ibn Ḥajar al-ʿAsqalānī, Aḥmad b. ʿAlī. *Tahdhīb al-tahdhīb*. Beirut: Dār Iḥyāʾ al-Turāth al-ʿArabī, 1993.
Ibn Ḥātim, Muḥammad. *Kitāb al-simṭ al-ghālī al-thaman fī akhbār al-mulūk min al-ghuzz biʾl-yaman*. 2 vols. Edited by G. Rex Smith. E. J. W. Gibb Memorial Series 26. London: Luzac, 1974–78.
Ibn Ḥawqal, Abū al-Qāsim. *Kitāb ṣurat al-arḍ*. Edited by Johannes Hendrik Kramers. Bibliotheca geographorum Arabicorum 2. Leiden: Brill, 1967.
Ibn Jubayr, Muḥammad b. Aḥmad. *The Travels of Ibn Jubayr*. Edited by William Wright and Michael Jan de Goeje. E. J. W. Gibb Memorial Series 5. Leiden: Brill, 1907.
Ibn Khallikān. *Wafayāt al-aʿyān wa-anbāʾ abnāʾ al-zamān*. Vol. 3. Beirut: Dār al-Thaqāfa, 1968.
Ibn Khurradādhbih, ʿUbayd Allāh. *Al-masālik waʾl-mamālik*. Edited by Michael Jan de Goeje. Bibliotheca geographorum Arabicorum 6. Leiden: Brill, 1967.
al-Iṣṭakhrī, Ibrāhīm b. Muḥammad. *Kitāb al-masālik waʾl-mamālik*. Edited by Michael Jan de Goeje. Bibliotheca geographorum Arabicorum 1. Leiden: Brill, 1967.
Jāzim, Muḥammad ʿAbd al-Raḥīm, ed. *Nūr al-maʿārif fī nuẓum wa-qawānīn wa-aʿʿrāf al-yaman fī al-ʿahd al-muẓaffarī al-wārif*. Sanaa: Centre Français d'Archéologie et de Sciences Sociales de Sanaa, 2003.
Kay, Henry Cassels, ed. *Yaman, Its Early Medieval History by Najm al-Dīn ʿOmārah al-Ḥakamī*. London: Arnold, 1892.

Ludovico di Varthema. *The Travels of Ludovico di Varthema in Egypt, Syria, Arabia Deserta, and Arabia Felix, in Persia, India, and Ethiopia, A.D. 1503 to 1508*. Edited by George Percy Badger. Translated by John Winter Jones. Works issued by the Hakluyt Society 32. New York: Franklin, 1963.

al-Maqrīzī, Aḥmad b. ʿAlī. *Al-mawāʿiz waʾl-iʿtibār bi-dhikr al-khiṭaṭ waʾl-āthār*. Bulaq: Dār al-Ṭibāʿa al-Miṣrīya, 1853–54.

al-Marzūqī, Aḥmad b. Muḥammad. *Al-azmina waʾl-amkina*. Hyderabad: Maṭbaʿat Majlis Dāʾirat al-Maʿārif, 1913.

al-Muqaddasī, Muḥammad b. Aḥmad. *Kitāb aḥsan al-taqāsīm fī maʿrifat al-aqālīm*. Edited by Michael Jan de Goeje. Bibliotheca geographorum Arabicorum 3. Leiden: Brill, 1967.

Polo, Marco. *The Travels of Marco Polo*. Translated by Ronald Latham. London: Penguin Books, 1988.

ʿUmāra, Ibn ʿAlī al-Ḥakamī. *Taʾrīkh al-yaman*. In *Yaman, Its Early Medieval History by Najm al-Dīn ʿOmārah al-Ḥakamī*, edited by Henry Cassels Kay. London: Arnold, 1892.

Yāqūt b. ʿAbdallāh al-Ḥamawī. *Muʿjam al-buldān*. Edited by Ferdinand Wüstenfeld. Leipzig: Brockhaus, 1869.

Yule, Henry, ed. *The Book of Ser Marco Polo Concerning the Kingdoms and Marvels of the East*. London: Murray, 1871.

Dictionaries and Lexical Aids

Diem, Werner, and Hans-Peter Radenberg. *A Dictionary of the Arabic Material of S. D. Goitein's "A Mediterranean Society."* Wiesbaden: Harrassowitz, 1994.

Dozy, Reinhart Pieter Anne. *Supplément aux dictionnaires arabes*. 2 vols. Leiden: Brill, 1967.

Ibn Manẓūr, Muḥammad b. Mukarram. *Lisān al-ʿarab*. Beirut: Dār Ṣādir, 1955.

Kazimirski, Albert. *Dictionnaire arabe-français contenant toutes les racines de la langue arabe*. 2 vols. Paris: Maisonneuve, 1960.

Landberg, Carlo. *Ḥaḍramout*. Vol. 1 of *Études sur les dialectes de l'Arabie méridionale*. Leiden: Brill, 1901.

Lane, Edward W. *An Arabic-English Lexicon*. 8 vols. London and Edinburgh: Williams and Norgate, 1863–93.

Piamenta, Moshe. *Dictionary of Post-Classical Yemeni Arabic*. 2 vols. Leiden: Brill, 1990–91.

Rossi, Ettore. *L'Arabo parlato a Sanʿa: Grammatica, testi, lessico.* Rome: Istituto per l'Oriente, 1939.
al-Selwi, Ibrahim. *Jemenitische Wörter in den Werken von al-Hamdānī und Nashwān und ihre Parallelen in den Semitischen Sprachen.* Marburger Studien Zur Afrika- und Asienkunde. Serie B: Asien, Band 10. Berlin: Reimer, 1987.
Stace, E. V. *An English-Arabic Vocabulary.* London: Quaritch, 1893.
Steere, Edward. *A Handbook of the Swahili Language, as Spoken at Zanzibar.* London: Society for Promoting Christian Knowledge, 1908.
al-Zabīdī, Muḥammad b. Muḥammad. *Tāj al-ʿarūs min jawāhir al-qāmūs.* 10 vols. Cairo: Kharṭiya, 1888–90.

Secondary Materials

Abu Lughod, Janet. *Before European Hegemony: The World System, A.D. 1250–1350.* New York: Oxford University Press, 1989.
———. "The Islamic City: Historic Myth, Islamic Essence, and Contemporary Relevance." *International Journal of Middle Eastern Studies* 19 (1987): 155–76.
Adams, Robert Marshall. "Construction and Qualitative Analysis of a Sewn Boat of the Western Indian Ocean." Master's thesis, Texas A & M University, 1985.
Adler, Elkan Nathan. *Von Ghetto Zu Ghetto: Reisen und Beobachtungen.* Stuttgart: Strecker und Schröder, 1909.
Agius, Dionisius A. *In the Wake of the Dhow: The Arabian Gulf and Oman.* Reading, Eng.: Ithaca Press, 2002.
Ahroni, Reuben. *The Jews of the British Crown Colony of Aden: History, Culture, and Ethnic Relations.* Series in Jewish Studies 12. Leiden: Brill, 1994.
Arbel, Benjamin. *Trading Nations: Jews and Venetians in the Early Modern Eastern Mediterranean.* Series in Jewish Studies 14. Leiden: Brill, 1995.
Ashtor, Eliahu. *Histoire des prix et des salaires dans l'Orient médiéval.* Paris: S.E.V.P.E.N., 1969.
Assaf, Simha. "The Relations between the Jews of Egypt and Aden in the 12th Century" [in Hebrew]. *Bulletin of the Jewish Palestine Exploration Society* 12 (1946): 116–19.
———. *Texts and Studies in Jewish History* [in Hebrew]. Jerusalem: Mosad ha-Rav Kuk, 1946.

Attal, Robert. *A Bibliography of the Writings of Professor Shelomo Dov Goitein*. Jerusalem: Ben Zvi Institute, 1975.

Aubin, Jean. "La ruine de Siraf et les routes du Golfe Persique aux XI et XII siècles." *Cahiers de Civilisation Médiévale* 2 (1959): 295–301.

Baldry, John. *Textiles in Yemen: Historical References to Trade and Commerce in Textiles in Yemen from Antiquity to Modern Times*. British Museum Occasional Paper 27. London: British Museum, 1982.

Balog, D. *Coinage of the Ayyūbids*. Special Publication 12. London: Royal Numismatic Society, 1980.

Bass, George, Sheila D. Matthews, J. Richard Steffy, and Frederick H. van Doorninck Jr., eds. *Serçe Limani: An Eleventh-Century Shipwreck*. Vol. 1, *The Ship and Its Anchorage, Crew, and Passengers*. College Station: Texas A & M University Press, 2004.

Bates, M. L. "The Chapter on the Fatimid Dāʿīs in Yemen in the Ta'rīkh of ʿUmāra al-Ḥakamī (d. 569/1174): An Interpolation." In *Studies in the History of Arabia*, vol. 1, *Sources for the History of Arabia*, 2: 51–57. Riyadh: University of Riyadh Press, 1979.

Bel, Jose-Marie. *Aden: Port mythique du Yémen*. Brussels: Amyris, 1998.

———. *Yémen: L'art des batisseurs, architecture, et vie quotidienne*. Paris: Amyris, 1997.

Ben-Sasson, Menahem. *The Cairo Genizah: A Mosaic of Life*. Jerusalem: Israel Museum, 1997.

Ben Zvi, Itzak. "Jewish Tombstones from Persia and Aden." *Tarbiz* 22 (1951): 196–201.

Blackman, David J. "Ancient Harbours in the Mediterranean." *International Journal of Nautical Archaeology and Underwater Exploration* 11 (1982): 79–104, 185–211.

Bosworth, Clifford Edmund. "Sīrāf." In *The Encyclopaedia of Islam*, new ed., 9:667–68. Leiden: Brill, 1997.

Bowen, Richard Le Baron. "Arab Dhows of Eastern Arabia." *American Neptune* 20 (1949): 87–132.

———. "Primitive Watercraft of Arabia." *American Neptune* 22 (1952): 186–221.

Braslavsky, Joseph. "Jewish Trade between the Mediterranean and India in the Twelfth Century" [in Hebrew]. *Zion* 7 (1941–42): 135–39.

Braudel, Fernand. *The Mediterranean and the Mediterranean World in the Age of Phillip II*. Translated by S. Reynolds. Vol. 1. New York: Harper and Row, 1976.

Braun, Georg, and Franz Hogenberg. *Civitates orbis terrarum, 1572–1618*. Basel: Bärenreiter, 1965.

Brouwer, C. G. *Al-Mukhā: Profile of a Yemeni Seaport as Sketched by Servants of the Dutch East India Company (VOC), 1614–1640*. Amsterdam: D'Fluyte Rarob, 1997.

Cahen, Claude. "Douanes et commerce dans les ports méditerranéens de l'Egypte d'après le Minhādj d'al-Makhzūmī." *Journal of Economic and Social History of the Orient* 7 (1964): 217–314.

———. "al-Makhzūmī." In *The Encyclopaedia of Islam*, new ed., 6:140–41. Leiden: Brill, 1991.

———. Review of *A Mediterranean Society*, vol. 1, by S. D. Goitein. *Journal of Economic and Social History of the Orient* 12 (1969): 217.

Cahen, Claude, and Robert Bertram Serjeant. "A Fiscal Survey of the Medieval Yemen: Notes Preparatory to a Critical Edition of the *Mulakhkhaṣ al-fiṭan* of al-Ḥasan b. ʿAlī al-Sharīf al-Ḥusaynī." *Arabica* IV (1957): 23–33.

Camelin, Sylvaine. "Les pêcheurs de Shihr: Transmission de savoir et identité sociale." *Chroniques Yéménites* 5 (1995), <http://cy.revues.org/document80.html>. 15 February 2006.

Casson, Lionel. *Ships and Seamanship in the Ancient World*. Princeton: Princeton University Press, 1971.

Chakravarti, Ranabir. "Nakhudas and Nauvittakas: Ship-Owning Merchants in the West Coast of India (c. A.D. 1000–1500)." *Journal of Economic and Social History of the Orient* 43 (2000): 34–64.

Chaudhuri, K. N. *Trade and Civilization in the Indian Ocean: An Economic History from the Rise of Islam to 1750*. Cambridge: Cambridge University Press, 1985.

Chittick, Neville. *Kilwa: An Islamic Trading City on the East African Coast*. 2 vols. Nairobi: British Institute in Eastern Africa, 1974.

———. *Manda: Excavations at an Island Port on the Kenya Coast*. Nairobi: British Institute in Eastern Africa, 1984.

Cohen, M. R. "Geniza for Islamicists, Islamic Geniza, and the 'New Cairo Geniza.'" *Harvard Middle Eastern and Islamic Review* 7 (2006): in press.

———. "Goitein, the Geniza, and Muslim History." *Middle Eastern Lectures* 4 (2001), <http://www.dayan.org/mel/cohen.htm>. 17 January 2005.

———. "Jewish and Muslim Life in the Middle Ages: Through the Window of the Cairo Geniza." Forthcoming.

———. *Jewish Self-Government in Medieval Egypt: The Origins of the Office of Head of the Jews, ca. 1065–1126*. Princeton: Princeton University Press, 1980.
———. *Poverty and Charity in the Jewish Community of Medieval Egypt*. Princeton: Princeton University Press, 2005.
———. *Under Crescent and Cross: The Jews in the Middle Ages*. Princeton: Princeton University Press, 1994.
Colonial Office. *Annual Report on Aden and Aden Protectorate for the Year 1946*. London: His Majesty's Stationery Office, 1948.
———. *Report on Aden, 1955–1956*. London: His Majesty's Stationery Office, 1958.
Conermann, Stephan. "Muslimische Seefahrt auf dem Indischen Ozean vom 14. Bis zum 16. Jahrhundert." In *Der Indische Ozean in historischer Perspektive*, vol. 1 of *Asien und Afrika*, edited by Stephan Conermann, 143–80. Hamburg: Eb, 2001.
Constable, Olivia Remie. *Housing the Stranger in the Mediterranean World: Lodging, Trade, and Travel in Late Antiquity and the Middle Ages*. Cambridge: Cambridge University Press, 2003.
———. *Trade and Traders in Muslim Spain: The Commercial Realignment of the Iberian Peninsula, 900–1500*. Cambridge: Cambridge University Press, 1994.
Cornu, Georgette. *Atlas du monde Arabo-Islamique à l'époque classique: IX–Xe siècles*. Leiden: Brill, 1985.
Costa, Paolo Maria. "La Moschea Grande di Sana." *Annali Istituto Orientale di Napoli* 34 (1974): 505–6.
Costa, Paolo Maria, and Tony James Wilkinson. "The Hinterland of Sohar: Archaeological Surveys and Excavations within the Region of an Omani Seafaring City." *Journal of Oman Studies* 9 (1987): 1–238.
Cronon, William. *Nature's Metropolis: Chicago and the Great West*. New York: Norton, 1991.
Curtin, P. D. *Cross-Cultural Trade in World History*. Cambridge: Cambridge University Press, 1984.
Dallal, Aḥmad. "On Muslim Curiosity and the Historiography of the Jews of Yemen." *Bulletin of the Royal Institute of Interfaith Studies* 1 (1999): 77–112.
Doe, Brian. "Pottery Sites near Aden." *Journal of the Royal Asiatic Society* 63 (1963): 150–62.
———. *Southern Arabia*. London: Thames and Hudson, 1971.

Dresch, Paul. *A History of Modern Yemen*. Cambridge: Cambridge University Press, 2000.
Eickelman, Dale. "Is There an Islamic City?" *International Journal of Middle Eastern Studies* 5 (1974): 274–94.
Elʿad, Amikam. "The Coastal Cities of Palestine during the Early Middle Ages." In *The Jerusalem Cathedra: Studies in the History, Archaeology, Geography, and Ethnography of the Land of Israel*, edited by Lee I. Levine, 2:146–67. Jerusalem: Ben Zvi Institute, 1982.
Epstein, Steven A. *Genoa and the Genoese, 958–1528*. Chapel Hill: University of North Carolina Press, 1996.
Ferrand, Gabriel. *Relations de voyages et textes géographiques arabes, persans, et turcs relatifs à l'extrême Orient*. Paris: Leroux, 1913–14.
Fischel, Walter J. *Jews in the Economic and Political Life of Mediaeval Islam*. London: Royal Asiatic Society, 1937.
———. "The Spice Trade in Mamluk Egypt." *Journal of Economic and Social History of the Orient* 1 (1958): 157–74.
Frantz, Douglas. "Giving Proper Burial to Holy Books." *New York Times*, 29 September 2001, A4.
Freedman, Paul, and Gabrielle Spiegel. "Medievalisms Old and New: The Rediscovery of Alterity in North American Medieval Studies." *American Historical Review* 103 (1998): 677–704.
Frenkel, Miriam. "The Jewish Community of Alexandria under the Fatimids and the Ayyubids: Portrait of a Leading Elite" [in Hebrew]. Ph.D. diss., Hebrew University, 2001.
Friedman, Mordechai A. "Abraham b. Yijū, a Jewish Trader in India" [in Hebrew with English summary]. In *Teʿuda: A Century of Geniza Research*, edited by Mordechai Friedman, 259–92. Tel Aviv: Tel Aviv University, 1999.
Gavin, R. J. *Aden under British Rule, 1839–1967*. London: Hurst, 1975.
Gil, Moshe. *A History of Palestine, 634–1099*. Cambridge: Cambridge University Press, 1992.
———. *In the Kingdom of Ishmael* [in Hebrew]. Tel Aviv: Tel Aviv University, 1997.
Goitein, S. D. "Aden." In *Encyclopaedia Judaica*, 2:260–64. Jerusalem: Encyclopaedia Judaica, 1971.
———. "The Age of the Hebrew Tombstones from Aden." *Journal of Semitic Studies* 7 (1962): 81–84.
———. "Chief Justice Hananel B. Samuel" [in Hebrew]. *Tarbiz* 50 (1981–82): 371–95.

———. "The Contributions of the Jews of Yemen to the Maintenance of the Babylonian and Palestinian Yeshivot and of Maimonides' School" [in Hebrew with English summary]. *Tarbiz* 31 (1962): 357–70.
———. "From Aden to India: Specimens of the Correspondence of India Traders of the Twelfth Century." *Journal of Economic and Social History of the Orient* 23 (1980): 43–66.
———. *From the Land of Sheba: Tales of the Jews of Yemen*. New York: Schocken, 1949.
———. "From the Mediterranean to India: Documents on the Trade to India, South Arabia, and East Africa from the Eleventh and Twelfth Centuries." *Speculum* 29 (1954): 181–97.
———. *Jemenica: Sprichtwörter und Redensarten aus Zentral Yemen*. Leipzig: Harrassowitz, 1934.
———. "The Jews of Yemen: Between Babylon and Egypt" [in Hebrew]. *Sinai* 16 (1953): 225–37.
———. "A Letter to Maimonides and New Sources Regarding the Negidim of his Family" [in Hebrew]. *Tarbiz* 34 (1964–65): 232–56.
———. *Letters of Medieval Jewish Traders*. Princeton: Princeton University Press, 1973.
———. *A Mediterranean Society: The Jewish Communities of the Arab World as Portrayed in the Documents of the Cairo Geniza*. 6 vols. Berkeley: University of California Press, 1967–93.
———. "New Light on the Beginnings of the Kārim Merchants." *Journal of Economic and Social History of the Orient* 1 (1958): 175–84.
———. "New Sources on Eretz-Israel in Crusader Days" [in Hebrew]. *Eretz-Israel* 4 (1956): 147–56.
———. "Portrait of a Medieval India Trader: Three Letters from the Cairo Geniza." *Bulletin of the School of Oriental and African Studies* 50 (1987): 449–64.
———. *Studies in Islamic Social History and Institutions*. Leiden: Brill, 1968.
———. "Two Eyewitness Reports on an Expedition of the King of Kish (Qais) against Aden." *Bulletin of the School of Oriental and African Studies* 16 (1954): 247–57.
———. *The Yemenites: History, Communal Organization, Spiritual Life* [in Hebrew]. Jerusalem: Ben Zvi Institute, 1983.
Gosh, A. *In an Antique Land: History in the Guise of a Traveler's Tale*. New York: Vintage, 1994.
———. "The Slave of MS. H. 6." *Subaltern Studies* 3 (1994): 159–219.

Graham, Murray. Review of *Aden: Port Mythique du Yemen*, by Jose-Marie Bel. <http://www.al-bab.com/bys/books/bel.htm>. 1 February 2006.
Grohmann, Adolf. *Südarabien als Wirtschaftsgebiet*. Vienna: Forschungsinstitut fur Osten und Orient, 1922–33.
Guo, Li. "Arabic Documents from the Red Sea Port of Quseir in the 7th/13th Century, Part 1: Business Letters." *Journal of Near Eastern Studies* 58 (1999): 161–90.
———. "Arabic Documents from the Red Sea Port of Quseir in the 7th/13th Century, Part 2: Shipping Notes and Account Records." *Journal of Near Eastern Studies* 60 (2001): 81–117.
———. *Commerce, Culture, and Community in a Red Sea Port in the Thirteenth Century: The Arabic Documents from Quseir*. Leiden: Brill, 2004.
Hadjidaki, Elpida. "Harbour Studies." In *Encyclopaedia of Underwater and Maritime Archaeology*, edited by James P. Delgado, 187–89. London: British Museum Press, 1997.
Hadziiosif, Christos. "Social Values and Business Strategies in the Naming of Ships in Greece, Eighteenth–Twentieth Centuries." In *The Greeks and the Sea*, edited by Spyros Vryonis, 135–51. New Rochelle, N.Y.: Caratzas, 1993.
Haines, S. B. "Memoir to Accompany a Chart of the South Coast of Arabia." *Journal of the Royal Geographical Society of London* 9 (1839): 125–56.
Halkin, Abraham S. "The Judeo-Islamic Age." In *Great Ages and Ideas of the Jewish People*, edited by Leo Walder Schwarz, 215–63. New York: Random House, 1956.
Haneda, Masashi, and Toru Miura, eds. *Islamic Urban Studies: Historical Review and Perspectives*. London: Kegan Paul International, 1994.
Hanna, Nelly. *Making Big Money in 1600: The Life and Times of Abū Taqiyya, Egyptian Merchant*. Syracuse, N.Y.: Syracuse University Press, 1998.
Hansman, John. *Julfar, an Arabian Port: Its Settlement and Far Eastern Ceramic Trade from the 14th to the 18th Centuries*. Prize Publication Fund 22. London: Royal Asiatic Society of Great Britain and Ireland, 1985.
Hardy-Guilbert, Claire. "The Harbour of al-Shiḥr, Ḥaḍramawt, Yemen: Sources and Archaeological Data on Trade." *Proceedings of the Seminar for Arabian Studies* 35 (2005): 71–85.
Hardy-Guilbert, Claire, and Axelle Rougeulle. "Archaeological Research

into the Islamic Period in Yemen: Preliminary Notes on the French Expedition." *Proceedings of the Seminar for Arabian Studies* 25 (1995): 29–44.
———. "Ports islamiques du Yémen: Prospections archéologiques sur les côtes Yéménites, 1993–1995." *Archéologie Islamique* 7 (1997): 147–96.
———. "Al-Shihr and the Southern Coast of Yemen: Preliminary Notes on the French Archaeological Expedition, 1995." *Proceedings of the Seminar for Arabian Studies* 27 (1997): 129–40.
Harris, Walter. *A Journey through the Yemen and Some General Remarks upon That Country*. London: Blackwood, 1893.
Heyd, Wilhelm. *Histoire du commerce du Levant au moyen âge*. 2 vols. Leipzig: Harrassowitz, 1885–86.
al-Hijji, Yusuf. *The Art of Dhow Building in Kuwait*. Kuwait: Centre for Research and Studies on Kuwait, 2001.
———. "Shipbuilding Timber in Kuwait." In *Navigation in the Red Sea, the Arabian Gulf, and the Indian Ocean*, vol. 2 of *Sailing Ships of the Mediterranean Sea and the Arabian Gulf*, edited by Christos G. Makrypoulias, 13–18. Athens: Kuwait-F.A.S., 2000.
Hinz, Walther. "Farsakh." In *The Encyclopaedia of Islam*, new ed., 2:812–13. Leiden: Brill, 1965.
———. *Islamische Mässe und Gewichte*. Leiden: Brill, 1955.
Hodgson, Marshall. *The Venture of Islam: Conscience and History in a World Civilization*. 3 vols. Chicago: University of Chicago Press, 1974.
Holum, Kenneth G., Robert L. Hohlfelder, R. J. Bull, and Avner Raban. *King Herod's Dream: Caesaria on the Sea*. New York: Norton, 1988.
Holusha, John. "Making Way for Bigger Ships." *New York Times*, 5 August 2001, 11:1.
Hornell, James. "The Sailing Craft of Western India." *Mariner's Mirror* 32 (1946): 195–217.
———. "The Sea-Going *Mtepe* and *Dau* of the Lamu Archipelago." *Mariner's Mirror* 27 (1941): 54–68.
———. "A Tentative Classification of Arab Sea-Craft." *Mariner's Mirror* 28 (1942): 11–40.
Horton, Mark C. *Shanga: The Archaeology of a Muslim Trading Community*. London: British Institute in Eastern Africa, 1996.
Hourani, Albert. *A History of the Arab Peoples*. New York: Warner, 1991.
Hourani, George Faldo. *Arab Seafaring in the Indian Ocean in Ancient and Early Medieval Times*. Rev. and exp. ed. by John Carswell. Princeton: Princeton University Press, 1995.

Howard, Deborah. *Venice and the East: The Impact of the Islamic World on Venetian Architecture, 1100–1500*. New Haven: Yale University Press, 2000.

Humphreys, R. Stephen. *Islamic History: A Framework for Inquiry*. Princeton: Princeton University Press, 1991.

Hunter, Frederick Mercer. *An Account of the British Settlement of Aden in Arabia*. London: Trübner, 1877.

Inalcik, Halil, and Donald Quataert, eds. *An Economic and Social History of the Ottoman Empire, 1300–1914*. Vol. 1, *The Classical Period*. Cambridge: Cambridge University Press, 1994.

Ingrams, Doreen. *A Survey of the Social and Economic Conditions in the Aden Protectorate*. Asmara: Government Printer, 1949.

Ingrams, Harold W. *Arabia and the Isles*. London: Murray, 1942.

Jacoby, David. "Les Italiens en Egypte au XIIe et XIIIe siècles: Du comptoir a la colonie?" In *Coloniser au Moyen Âge*, edited by Michel Balard and Alain Ducellier, 76–107. Paris: Colin, 1995.

Jāzim, Muḥammad ʿAbd al-Rahim. "Nūr al-Dīn et al-Muẓaffar: La construction de l'état Rasoulide au Yemen." *Chroniques Yemenites* 6 (1997): 68–91.

Kervran, Monik. "Archaeological Research at Suhār, 1980–1986." *Journal of Oman Studies* 13 (2004): 263–381.

Khalilieh, Hassan. *Islamic Maritime Law: An Introduction*. Leiden: Brill, 1998.

Kindermann, Hans. *"Schiff" im Arabischen: Untersuchung über Vorkommen und Bedeutung der Termini*. Zwickau: Friedrich-Wilhelms Rhein University, 1934.

King, Geoffrey, and Cristina Tonghini. *A Survey of the Islamic Sites near Aden and in the Abyan District of Yemen*. London: School of Oriental and African Studies, 1996.

Labib, Subhi Y. "Kārimī." In *The Encyclopaedia of Islam*, new ed., 4:640–43. Leiden: Brill, 1978.

Lane, Arthur, and Robert Bertram Serjeant. "Pottery and Glass Fragments from the Aden Littoral, with Historical Notes." *Journal of the Royal Asiatic Society* (1948): 108–33.

Lapidus, Ira P. "Traditional Muslim Cities: Structure and Change." In *From Madina to Metropolis: Heritage and Change in the Near Eastern City*, edited by L. Carl Brown, 51–69. Princeton: Darwin, 1973.

Lewis, Bernard. "The Fatimids and the Route to India." *Revue de la Faculté des Sciences Economiques de l'Université d'Istanbul* 2 (1953): 50–54.

———. *The Jews of Islam*. Princeton: Princeton University Press, 1984.
Lindley, R. "Fisheries Development in Yemen." *Port of Aden Annual* (1994): 39–42.
Löfgren, Oscar. "Abyan." In *The Encyclopaedia of Islam*, new ed., 1:169. Leiden: Brill, 1960.
———. "ʿAdan." *The Encyclopaedia of Islam*, new ed., 1:180–82. Leiden: Brill, 1960.
———. "Makhrama." *The Encyclopaedia of Islam*, new ed., 6:132–33. Leiden: Brill, 1991.
———, ed. *Arabische Texte zur Kenntnis der Stadt Aden im Mittelalter*. 2 vols. Leiden: Brill, 1936, 1950.
Lundin, A. G. "The Jewish Communities in Yemen during the 4th–6th Centuries (According to Epigraphic Material)." In *Judeo-Yemenite Studies: Proceedings of the Second International Congress 1999*, edited by Yosef Tobi and Efraim Itzak, 17–25. Princeton: Princeton University Press, 1999.
Lunt, James D. *The Barren Rocks of Aden*. London: Jenkins, 1966.
Mann, Jacob. *The Jews in Egypt and Palestine under the Fatimid Caliphs*. 2 vols. New York: Ktav, 1970.
Mayerson, Philip. "The Port of Clysma (Suez) in Transition from Roman to Arab Rule." *Journal of Near Eastern Studies* 55 (1996): 119–26.
Monod, Theodore. "Sur un site à bracelets de verre des environs d'Aden." *Raydan* 1 (1978): 111–12.
Moreland, W. H. "The Ships of the Arabian Sea about A.D. 1500." *Journal of the Royal Asiatic Society* (1939): 63–74, 173–92.
Muḥayriz, ʿAbdallāh Aḥmad. *Al-ʿaqaba*. Aden: Mu'assasa 14 Uktūbir Li'l-Ṣaḥāfa Wa'l-Ṭibāʿa Wa'l-Nashr, n.d.
———. *Ṣahārīj ʿadan*. Aden: Dār al-Hamdānī, 1987.
Norris, H. T., and F. W. Penhey. *An Archaeological and Historical Survey of the Aden Tanks*. Aden: n.p., 1935.
Oleson, John P., Robert L. Hohlfelder, Avner Raban, and Robert L. Vann. "The Caesaria Ancient Harbor Excavation Project (C.A.H.E.P.): Preliminary Report on the 1980–1983 Seasons." *Journal of Field Archaeology* 11 (1984): 281–305.
Oman, a Seafaring Nation. Muscat: Ministry of Information and Culture, Sultanate of Oman, 1991.
Peacock, David, Lucy Blue, Nick Bradford, and Stephanie Moser. *Myos Hormos—Quseir al-Qadim: A Roman and Islamic Port on the Red Sea Coast of Egypt*. <http://www.arch.soton.ac.uk/Projects>. 15 June 2006.

Pellat, Charles. *The Life and Works of Jāḥiẓ*. Berkeley: University of California Press, 1969.
Pesce, A. *Jiddah: Portrait of an Arabian City*. Cambridge: Falcon, 1974.
Petersen, Andrew. *The Towns of Palestine under Muslim Rule, 600–1600*. B.A.R. International Series 1381. Oxford: Archaeopress, 2005.
Piacentini, Valeria. "Merchants-Merchandise and Military Power in the Persian Gulf (Suriyanj/Shahriyaj-Siraf)." *Atti della Accademia Nazionale dei Lincei, Memorie* 9 (1992): 105–89.
Playfair, Robert Lambert. *A History of Arabia Felix or Yemen from the Commencement of the Christian Era to the Present Time, Including an Account of the British Settlement of Aden*. Salisbury, N.C.: Documentary Publications, 1978.
Porter, Venetia. "The Architecture of the Tahirid Dynasty of the Yemen." *Proceedings for the Seminar of Arabian Studies* 19 (1989): 105–20.
———. "The Ports of Yemen and the Indian Ocean Trade during the Tahirid Period (1454–1517)." In *Studies on Arabia in Honour of Professor G. Rex Smith*, edited by John F. Healey and Venetia Porter, 171–89. Journal of Semitic Studies Supplement 14. Oxford: Oxford University Press, 2002.
Prados, Edward. "An Archaeological Investigation of Sira Bay, Aden, Republic of Yemen." *International Journal of Nautical Archaeology* 23 (1994): 297–307.
———. "Contemporary Wooden Fishing Craft of Yemen." *Yemen Update* 40 (1998), <http://www.aiys.org/webdate/prados.html>. 10 February 2006.
Prawer, Joshua. "The Roots of Medieval Colonialism." In *The Meeting of Two Worlds: Cultural Exchange between East and West during the Period of the Crusades*, edited by Vladimir P. Goss and Christine V. Bornstein, 23–38. Kalamazoo, Mich.: Medieval Institute, 1986.
Pryor, John H. *Geography, Technology, and War: Studies in the Maritime History of the Mediterranean, 649–1571*. Cambridge: Cambridge University Press, 1988.
Rabie, Hassanein. *The Financial System of Egypt, A.H. 564–741/A.D. 1169–1341*. London: Oxford University Press, 1972.
al-Radi, Selma. *The ʿAmiriya in Radaʿ: The History and Restoration of a Sixteenth-Century Madrasa in the Yemen*. Oxford: Oxford University Press, 1997.
Raymond, A. "Shāh Bandar." In *The Encyclopaedia of Islam*, new ed., 9:193–94. Leiden: Brill, 1997.

Red Sea and Gulf of Aden Pilot. Washington, D.C.: U.S. Hydrographic Office, 1922.
Reif, Stefan C. *A Jewish Archive from Old Cairo: The History of Cambridge University's Geniza Collection*. Surrey, Eng.: Curzon, 2000.
Rimbaud, Arthur. *Complete Works*. Edited and translated by P. Schmidt. New York: HarperCollins, 1975.
Rougeulle, Axelle. "Les importations de céramiques chinoises dans le Golfe arabo-persique (8–11èmes s.)." *Archéologie Islamique* 2 (1991): 5–46.
———. "Notes on the Pre- and Early Islamic Harbours of the Ḥaḍramawt (Yemen)." *Proceedings of the Seminar for Arabian Studies* 31 (2001): 1–11.
———. "The Sharma Horizon: Sgraffiato Wares and Other Glazed Ceramics of the Indian Ocean Trade (ca. 980–1150)." *Proceedings of the Seminar for Arabian Studies* 35 (2005): 223–46.
———. "Le Yemen entre Orient et Afrique: Sharma, un entrepôt du commerce médiéval sur la côte sud de l'Arabie." *Annales Islamologiques* 38 (2004): 201–53.
Sadan, J. "Geniza and Geniza-Like Practices in Islamic and Jewish Traditions." *Bibliotheca Orientalis* 43 (1986): 36–58.
Sailing Directions for the Red Sea and the Gulf of Aden. Hydrographic Office Publication 157. Washington, D.C.: U.S. Naval Oceanographic Office, 1952.
Sailing Directions for the Red Sea and the Gulf of Aden. Hydrographic Office Publication 61. Rev. ed. Washington, D.C.: U.S. Naval Oceanographic Office, 1976.
Sailing Directions (Planning Guide) for the Mediterranean. U.S. Naval Oceanographic Office Publication 130. Washington, D.C.: U.S. Naval Oceanographic Office, 1971.
Schwarzer, Joseph K. "The Weapons." In *Serçe Limani: An Eleventh-Century Shipwreck*, vol. 1, *The Ship and Its Anchorage, Crew, and Passengers*, edited by George F. Bass, Sheila D. Matthews, J. Richard Steffy, and Frederick H. van Doorninck Jr., 362–98. College Station: Texas A & M University Press, 2004.
Serjeant, Robert Bertram. "Early Islamic and Medieval Trade and Commerce in the Yemen." In *Yemen: 3000 Years of Art and Civilization in Arabia Felix*, edited by Werner Daum, 163–66. Innsbruck: Pinguin, 1987.
———. *Islamic Textiles: Materials for a History up to the Mongol Conquest*. Beirut: Librairie du Liban, 1972.

———. “Maritime Customary Law off the Arabian Coasts.” In *Sociétés et compagnies de commerce en Orient et dans l’Ocean Indien: Actes du VIIIième Colloque International Maritime (Beyrouth 5–10 Septembre 1966)*, edited by Michel Mollat, 195–207. Paris: S.E.V.P.E.N., 1970.
———. “Materials for South Arabian History.” *Bulletin of the School of Oriental and African Studies* 13 (1950): 281–307, 581–601.
———. “The Ports of Aden and Shihr (Medieval Period).” *Les Grandes Escales, Receuils de la Société Jean Bodin* 34 (1974): 207–24.
———. *The Portuguese off the South Arabian Coast: Ḥaḍramī Chronicles*. Oxford: Clarendon, 1963.
———. “Two Sixteenth-Century Arabian Geographical Works.” *Bulletin of the School for Oriental and African Studies* 21 (1958): 254–75.
———. “Yemeni Merchants and Trade in Yemen, 13th–16th Centuries.” In *Marchands et hommes d’affaires asiatiques dans l’Ocean Indien et la mer de Chine, 13e–20e siècles*, edited by Denys Lombard and Jean Aubin, 61–82. Paris: Éditions de l’École des Hautes Études en Sciences Sociales, 1988.
Severin, Timothy. *The Sindbad Voyage*. London: Hutchinson, 1982.
Shaked, Shaul. *A Tentative Bibliography of Geniza Documents*. The Hague: Mouton, 1964.
al-Shamrookh, Nayef ʿAbdallāh. *The Commerce and Trade of the Rasulids in the Yemen, 630–858/1231–1454*. Kuwait: al-Shamrookh, 1996.
Shaw, Joseph W. “Greek and Roman Harbourworks.” In *A History of Seafaring Based on Underwater Archaeology*, edited by George Fletcher Bass, 90–112. London: Thames and Hudson, 1972.
Shihāb, Ḥasan Ṣāliḥ. *ʿAdan furḍat al-yaman*. Sanaa: Markaz al-Dirāsāt Wa’l-Buḥūth al-Yamanī, 1990.
Smith, G. Rex. “Have You Anything to Declare? Maritime Trade and Commerce in Ayyubid Aden: Practices and Taxes.” *Proceedings of the Seminar for Arabian Studies* 25 (1995): 127–40.
———. “Ibn al-Mujāwir on Dhofar and Socotra.” *Proceedings of the Seminar for Arabian Studies* 15 (1985): 79–92.
———. “Ibn al-Mujāwir’s 7th/13th Century Guide to Arabia: The Eastern Connection.” *Occasional Papers of the School of Abbasid Studies* (1990): 71–89.
———. “Ibn al-Mujāwir’s Ta’rīkh al-Mustabṣir: A Source for the Historical Geography and of the Economic and Social History of Medieval Yemen.” Paper presented at the MESA 29th Annual Meeting, Washington, D.C., 6–10 December 1995.

———. "Laḥdj." In *The Encyclopaedia of Islam*, new ed., 5:601–2. Leiden: Brill, 1986.
———. "More on the Port Practices and Taxes of Medieval Aden." *Arabian Studies* 3 (1996): 208–18.
———. "The Rasulid Administration in Ninth/Fifteenth Century Yemen—Some Government Departments and Officials." In *Studia Semitica 50th Jubilee Issue*, 223–47. Journal of Semitic Studies Supplement Series 16. Manchester, Eng.: Manchester University Press.
———. "Rasūlids." In *The Encyclopaedia of Islam*, new ed., 8:455–57. Leiden: Brill, 1995.
———. "Ṣuhayḥids." In *The Encyclopaedia of Islam*, new ed., 9:815–17. Leiden: Brill, 1997.
———. "Zurayʿids." In *The Encyclopaedia of Islam*, new ed., 11:572. Leiden: Brill, 2002.
Smoor, P. "ʿUmāra al-Yamanī." In *The Encyclopaedia of Islam*, new ed., 10:836. Leiden: Brill, 2000.
Soucek, S. "Mīnā'." In *The Encyclopaedia of Islam*, new ed., 7:66–72. Leiden: Brill, 1993.
Sprenger, Aloys. *Die Post- und Reisenrouten des Oriens*. Leipzig: Deutschen Morgenländischen, 1864.
Stein, Aurel. *Archaeological Reconnaissances in North-Western India and South-Eastern Iran*. London: Macmillan, 1937.
Stern, Samuel Miklos. "Rāmisht of Sīrāf, a Merchant Millionaire of the Twelfth Century." *Journal of the Royal Asiatic Society* (1967): 9–14.
———. "The Succession to the Fatimid Imam al-Amir, the Claims of the Later Fatimids to the Imamate, and the Rise of Tayyibi Ismailism." *Oriens* 4 (1951): 193–255.
Stillman, Norman A. "The 11th-Century Merchant House of Ibn Awkal (a Geniza Study)." *Journal of Economic and Social History of the Orient* 16 (1973): 15–88.
———. *The Jews of Arab Lands: A History and Sourcebook*. Philadelphia: Jewish Publication Society of America, 1979.
Stone, Francine, ed. *Studies on the Tihāmah: The Report on the Tihāmah Expedition 1982 and Related Papers*. Harlow, Eng.: Longman 1985.
Strauss/Ashtor, Eliahu. "Documents for the Economic and Social History of the Jews in the Near East" [in Hebrew]. *Zion* 7 (1942): 140–55.
———. "Voyage to India: A Letter from Aden to Egypt, A.D. 1153" [in Hebrew]. *Zion* 4 (1939): 217–36.

Streck, M. "Ḳais." In *The Encyclopaedia of Islam*, 1st ed., 2:649–51. Leiden: Brill, 1913–36.

———. "Ḳayṣāriyya." In *The Encyclopaedia of Islam*, new ed., 4:840–41. Leiden: Brill, 1978.

Subar, Eli. "Medieval Jewish Tombstones from Aden." *Jewish Quarterly Review* 49 (1959): 301–9.

Tai, Emily Sohmer. "Marking Water: Piracy and Property in the Pre-Modern West." Paper presented at Seascapes, Littoral Cultures, and Trans-Oceanic Exchanges, Library of Congress, Washington, D.C., 12–15 February 2003. <http://www.historycoooperative.org/proceedings/seascapes/tai.html>. 12 June 2006.

Taminian, Lucine. "Rimbaud's House in Aden, Yemen: Giving Voice(s) to the Silent Poet." *Cultural Anthropology* 13 (1998): 464–90.

Tampoe, Moira. *Maritime Trade between China and the West: An Archaeological Study of the Ceramics from Siraf (Persian Gulf) 8th–15th Century A.D. British Archaeology International Series* 555. Oxford: B.A.R., 1989.

Tibbetts, G. R. *Arab Navigation in the Indian Ocean before the Coming of the Portuguese*. London: Royal Asiatic Society of Great Britain and Ireland, 1971.

———. "Milāḥa." In *The Encyclopaedia of Islam*, new ed., 7:50–53. Leiden: Brill, 1993.

Tobi, Yosef. *The Jews of Yemen: Studies in their History and Culture*. Leiden: Brill, 1999.

Trooper Bluegum. "The Home-Sick Anzac." In *The Old Country: A Book of Love and Praise of England*, edited by Ernest Rhys, 296. London: Dent, 1917.

Udovitch, Abraham L. "An Eleventh-Century Islamic Treatise on the Law of the Sea." *Annales Islamologiques* 27 (1993): 37–54.

———. "Fals." In *The Encyclopaedia of Islam*, new ed., 2:768–69. Leiden: Brill, 1965.

———. "Foreword." In *The Individual*. Vol. 5 of *A Mediterranean Society: The Jewish Communities of the Arab World as Portrayed in the Documents of the Cairo Geniza*, ix–xviii. Berkeley: University of California Press, 1988.

———. "Formalism and Informalism in the Social and Economic Institutions of the Medieval Islamic World." In *Individualism and Conformity in Classical Islam*, edited by Amin Banani and Spyros Vryonis Jr., 61–71. Wiesbaden: Harrassowitz, 1977.

———. "Medieval Alexandria: Some Evidence from the Cairo Genizah Documents." In *Alexandria and Alexandrianism: Papers Delivered at a Symposium Organized by the J. Paul Getty Museum and the Getty Center for History of Art and the Humanities and Held at the Museum, April 22–25, 1993*, 273–83. Malibu, Calif.: Getty Museum, 1996.

———. "Merchants and Amīrs: Government and Trade in Eleventh-Century Egypt." *Asian and African Studies* 22 (1988): 53–72.

———. *Partnership and Profit in Medieval Islam*. Princeton: Princeton University Press, 1970.

———. "A Tale of Two Cities." In *The Medieval City*, edited by David Herlihy, Harry A. Miskimin, and A. L. Udovitch, 144–48. New Haven: Yale University Press, 1977.

———. "Time, the Sea, and Society: Duration of Commercial Voyages on the Southern Mediterranean during the High Middle Ages." In *La Navigazione Mediterranea nell'alto Medioevo*, 503–63. Settimane di Studio del Centro Italiano di Studi sull'Alto Medioevo 25. Spoleto: Presso la Sede del Centro, 1978.

Um, Nancy Ajung. "A Red Sea Society in Yemen: Architecture, Urban Form, and Cultural Dynamics in the Eighteenth-Century Port City of al-Mukhā." Ph.D. diss., University of California, Los Angeles, 2001.

———. "Spatial Negotiations in a Commercial City: The Red Sea Port of Mocha, Yemen, during the First Half of the Eighteenth Century." *Journal of the Society of Architectural Historians* 62 (2003): 178–90.

Van Donzel, E. "al-Mukallā." In *The Encyclopaedia of Islam*, new ed., 7:496–97. Leiden: Brill, 1993.

Varisco, Daniel Martin. "Agriculture in Rasulid Zabīd." In *Studies on Arabia in Honour of G. Rex Smith*, edited by John F. Healey and Venetia Porter, 323–51. Journal of Semitic Studies Supplement 14. Oxford: Oxford University Press, 2002.

———. *Medieval Agriculture and Islamic Science: The Almanac of a Yemeni Sultan*. University of Washington Publications on the Near East 6. Seattle: University of Washington Press, 1994.

———. "The Study of 'Medieval Yemen': Recent Work and Future Prospects." *Yemen Update* 32 (1993): 10–13, 34.

Varisco, Daniel Martin, and G. Rex Smith. *The Manuscript of al-Malik al-Afḍal: A Medieval Arabic Anthology from the Yemen*. Warminster, Eng.: Aris and Phillips, 1998.

Villiers, Alan. *Sons of Sinbad*. New York: Scribner's, 1969.

Von Bothmer, Hans-Casper Graf. "Masterworks of Islamic Book Art: Koranic Calligraphy and Illumination in the Manuscripts found in the Great Mosque in Sanaa." In *Yemen: 3000 Years of Art and Civilization in Arabia Felix*, edited by Werner Daum, 178–81. Innsbruck: Pinguin, 1987.

———. "Spätantike Voraussetzungen der frühislamischen Koran-Handschriften in Sanaa." *Eothen* 2–3 (1994): 7–12.

Von Grunebaum, Gustave. "Eastern Jewry under Islam." *Viator* 2 (1971): 365–72.

———. "The Structure of the Muslim Town." In *Islam: Essays in the Nature and Growth of a Cultural Tradition*, 141–58. Anthropological Association Memoir 81. Menasha, Wis.: American Anthropological Association, 1955.

Wansbrough, John. "The Medieval Kārim: An Ancient Near Eastern Paradigm?" *Studies in Islamic and Middle Eastern Texts in Memory of Norman Calder*, 301–4. Journal of Semitic Studies Supplement 12. Oxford: Oxford University Press, 2000.

Watt, N. "Salt in a Pinch." *Port of Aden Annual* (1961–62): 49–51.

Whitcomb, Donald S. *Ayla: Art and Industry in the Islamic Port of Aqaba*. Chicago: Oriental Institute of the University of Chicago, 1994.

———. "Islamic Archaeology in Aden and the Hadhramaut." In *Araby the Blest: Studies in Arabian Archaeology*, edited by Daniel T. Potts, 176–263. Copenhagen: Niebuhr Institute, 1988.

Whitcomb, Donald S., and Janet Johnson. "1982 Season of Excavation at Qusayr al-Qadim." *American Research Center in Egypt Newsletter* 120 (1982): 24–30.

Whitehouse, David. "Excavations at Sīrāf: First Interim Report." *Iran* 6 (1968): 1–22.

———. "Excavations at Sīrāf: Second Interim Report." *Iran* 7 (1969): 36–62.

———. "Excavations at Sīrāf: Third Interim Report." *Iran* 8 (1970): 1–18.

———. "Excavations at Sīrāf: Fourth Interim Report." *Iran* 9 (1971): 1–67.

———. "Excavations at Sīrāf: Fifth Interim Report." *Iran* 10 (1972): 63–87.

———. "Excavations at Sīrāf: Sixth Interim Report." *Iran* 12 (1974): 1–30.

———. "Kīsh." *Iran* 14 (1976): 146–47.

———. "Sīrāf: A Medieval Port on the Persian Gulf." *World Archaeology* 2 (1970): 141–58.

———. *Sīrāf III: The Congregational Mosque and Other Mosques from the Ninth to the Twelfth Centuries*. London: British Institute of Persian Studies, 1980.

Whitehouse, D., and A. Williamson. "Sasanian Maritime Trade." *Iran* 11 (1973): 29–49.

Wilkinson, T. J. "Agricultural Decline in the Siraf Region, Iran." *Paléorient* 2 (1974): 123–32.

———. "The Definition of Ancient Manured Zones by Means of Extensive Sherd-Sampling Techniques." *Journal of Field Archaeology* 9 (1982): 323–33.

Williamson, A. "Harvard Archaeological Survey in Oman, 1973: Sohar and the Sea Trade of Oman in the 10th-Century A.D." *Proceedings of the Seminar for Arabian Studies* 4 (1974): 78–96.

———. *Sohar and Omani Seafaring in the Indian Ocean*. Muscat: Petroleum Development (Oman), 1973.

Wilson, Arnold Talbot. *The Persian Gulf: A Historical Sketch from the Earliest Times to the Beginning of the 20th Century*. Oxford: Clarendon, 1928.

Young, Penny. "Aden's Pipe Dreams." *History Today*, May 1997, 30.

Zettersteen, Karl Vilhelm. "Abnā'." In *The Encyclopaedia of Islam*, new ed., 1:102. Leiden: Brill, 1960.

Index

Judeo-Arabic personal names in this index and in the text appear as they are most frequently rendered in Geniza scholarship, especially in the work of S. D. Goitein.

ʿAbd al-Masīḥ (merchant), 278 (n. 31), 299 (n. 72)
Abū ʿAbdallāh (shipowner, captain), 147, 149, 278 (n. 33). *See also* Ibn Abī al-Katāʾib, Abū al-Ḥasan
Abū al-Barakāt b. Joseph al-Lebdī (merchant), 103–4, 135–36
Abū al-Ḥasan ʿAlī b. al-Daḥḥāk al-Kūfī (merchant), 47, 147
Abū ʿAmr ʿUthmān b. ʿAlī al-Zanjabīlī (Ayyubid governor), 61, 91, 95–96, 256 (n. 23)
Abu Lughod, Janet, 9, 26, 153, 208, 211, 213, 216 (nn. 10, 11, 15), 224 (n. 80), 305 (nn. 2, 7)
Abū Makhrama, Abū Muḥammad al-Ṭayyib b. ʿAbdallāh (Adeni historian), 22, 23; on Aden's environment, 44, 47, 48, 234 (n. 58); on water, 52; on Aden's environs, 56–57, 58, 59, 61, 62, 64, 230 (n. 31), 239 (n. 94), 244 (n. 145); on harbor topography, 71, 72, 75–76, 83, 84; on city topography, 92–93, 97, 99, 102, 103, 119, 255 (nn. 3–5), 257 (nn. 24, 25), 261 (n. 51); on boats, 159; on al-Muʿizz, 269 (n. 53), 270 (n. 55)
Abū Mufarrij (merchant), 198
Abū Yaʿqūb. *See* Jekuthiel Abū Yaʿqūb al-Ḥakīm
Abū Zikrī Judah ha-Kohen (merchant), 145, 148; and India adventure, 157–58, 175, 283 (n. 70), 290 (n. 133); correspondence of, 159, 165, 166, 266 (n. 16), 269 (nn. 47, 51), 281 (n. 58), 284 (n. 83); death of, 279 (n. 45). *See also* Cairo: merchants of
Abyan, 59, 61, 64–65, 237 (n. 85), 259 (n. 31); as source of raw materials, 47, 51, 57, 245 (n. 146); shipwrecks near, 162, 170–72, 212, 244 (nn. 142, 145), 245 (n. 147)
Aden, port of, 2, 207, 211; location of, 2, 34; history and historiography of, 6, 7, 10, 11, 17, 22–23, 27–29; naval blockade of, 19, 76–77, 91; Aden peninsula, 34, 35, 43–44, 46, 47, 56, 65, 81, 85, 102, 229 (n. 25), 232 (n. 44), 233 (nn. 50, 51, 53); climate of, 34, 226 (n. 3); Gulf of Aden, 35–37, 38, 154, 159, 226 (nn. 3, 4, 7); medieval harbor of Aden, 46–47, 72–85 passim, 233 (n. 51),

248 (nn. 19–21), 249 (n. 24), 253 (n. 54); as shipbuilding center, 158–62. *See also* Indian Ocean; Ports; Ṣīra Bay
Aden balsam, 57
Aden minaret, 74
Africa: east coast of, 7, 9, 10, 49, 51, 101, 151, 212; ships of, 115, 153–54, 283 (n. 66), 286 (n. 94); circumnavigation of, 161, 189. *See also* Ports
Africans, 102, 233 (n. 55), 240 (101). *See also* Al-Ḥabash; Al-Ḥabashī; Zanj
Aḥmad b. Bakhtiyār (shipowner or captain) 150, 155. See also *Nākhudhā*
Alexandria, 38, 98, 177, 186, 203, 260 (n. 46); study of, 6, 215 (n. 6); taxation practices, 112, 113, 123, 125, 266 (n. 13), 272 (n. 69); merchants of, 146, 177, 185–86, 202, 297 (n. 46)
ʿAlī al-Dibājī (shipowner), 151–52, 166–67, 280 (n. 53). See also *Nākhudhā*
ʿAlī al-Fawfalī (shipowner), 145, 147–48, 151, 165, 168–69, 186, 277 (n. 17), 302 (n. 100). See also *Nākhudhā*
ʿAlī b. Abī al-Ghārāt (Zurayid ruler of Aden), 28, 77, 90, 250 (n. 33). *See also* Zurayids
Almanacs, 38, 40, 78, 228 (n. 20), 245 (n. 150). *See also* Rasulids
Ambergris (*ʿanbar*), 42–43, 105, 160, 230 (nn. 34, 35), 264 (n. 80)
Anchorage: types of, 9, 69–70, 216 (n. 13); in Aden, 71–75, 77, 79–80, 82, 84, 232 (n. 43), 233 (nn. 50, 51). *See also* Ḥuqqāt Bay; Ṣīra Bay
Al-ʿĀra (Yemen), 53
Arabia, 22, 154, 161; coasts of, 42, 49, 58, 240 (n. 100)
Arabian Peninsula, 2, 55
Arabian Sea, 35, 41
Arabic language and script, 16, 18, 21–22, 158, 284 (n. 83)
Aramaic language, 22, 139
Archaeology: contributions of, 7, 9–12 passim, 215 (n. 6), 216 (nn. 7–9, 13, 14), 217 (nn. 23, 24), 242 (n. 124); and Aden topography, 67, 69–70, 74, 76, 91, 101; and ships, 154, 171–73
Arwā (Sulayhid queen), 28, 110
Al-Ashraf b. al-Afḍal (Rasulid sultan), 97
Al-Ashraf ʿUmar b. Yūsuf (Rasulid sultan and author), 24, 78, 228 (nn. 22, 23)
Asthor, Eliahu, 15
ʿAydhāb, port of, 136, 151–52, 166, 266 (n. 16), 280 (nn. 51–53), 281–82 (n. 58), 288 (n. 114)
Ayla/Aqaba, port of, 7, 216 (n. 8)
Ayyubids, 24, 28, 29; and urban development of Aden, 2, 26, 42, 44, 61, 91–99 passim; and taxation practices, 95, 100, 112, 113–14, 118, 125; and maritime patrols, 138, 164, 208, 210
Azyab (northeastern winter monsoon wind), 40, 46, 75, 83, 228 (n. 23), 233 (n. 52). *See also* Aden, port of: medieval harbor of Aden; Monsoons; Sailing times

Bāb al-barr (landward pass or "gate"), 45, 89, 92, 232 (nn. 47, 48), 255 (n. 14), 271 (n. 63). *See also* Main Pass
Bāb al-Mandab, straits of, 34, 35–37, 53, 145, 228 (n. 23), 230 (n. 35), 290 (n. 131); and navigational hazards, 37, 166–67, 173–74, 193, 226 (n. 6)
Back Bay, 46, 47. *See also* Aden, port of: medieval harbor of Aden
Baḍiʿ, port of, 136
Bakhtiyār (captain), 150, 276 (n. 9)
Bamma (slave agent), 15, 52, 191, 243 (n. 133), 263 (n. 71). *See also* Ben Yijū, Abraham; Gosh, Amitav
Banū Maʿn (rulers of Aden), 28
Barasti (reed-and-mat construction), 256 (n. 21), 262–63 (n. 68)
Barībatān (Ballipattana), port of, 169–71, 289 (n. 124)
Behzād (shipowner), 146. See also *Nākhudhā*
Ben Ezra Synagogue, 18, 20. *See also* Cairo Geniza
Ben Yijū, Abraham (merchant), 67, 148; and Maḍmūn b. Japheth, 52, 67, 77, 121, 132, 242 (n. 123); and shipwreck, 100, 149, 173–74; in Yemen, 103, 116, 227 (n. 17), 263 (nn. 71, 74, 75); and Adeni mercantile representatives, 203–5 passim; and Indian woman, 205, 305 (n. 130); correspondence with Adeni merchants, 243 (n. 133), 259 (n. 33), 271 (n. 60), 273 (nn. 85, 94), 274 (n. 3), 276 (n. 9), 277 (n. 24), 278 (n. 28)
Berbera, port of, 153, 173, 299 (n. 72); product of (*barbarī*), 282 (n. 65), 299 (n. 70)
Bilāl b. Jarīr (Zurayid governor), 17, 90, 243 (n. 134), 250 (n. 34); partnership with Maḍmūn b. Japheth, 17, 122, 146, 155–57, 159, 187, 269 (n. 47), 283 (n. 72), 284 (n. 78), 294 (n. 21). *See also* Maḍmūn b. Japheth b. Bundār
Bilīj (hut, shipboard shelter), 103–4, 166, 264 (n. 76)
Boats: types of, 46, 56, 117, 159, 231 (n. 39), 254 (n. 58), 266–67 (n. 27), 285 (n. 90). *See also* Fishing and fishermen; Shipbuilding; Ships
Bombay, 147
Braudel, Fernand, 11, 35
Braun, Georg, 85, 247 (n. 12)
Bremen (Germany), 117
British colonial period, 43, 44–45, 59, 71, 73, 215 (n. 3), 225 (n. 90), 234 (n. 60); and medieval material record, 50–51, 101, 235 (nn. 69–71), 262 (n. 60)
Broach, port of, 157
Brokerage (*dilāla/dalāla*), 124–25, 180, 271 (nn. 61, 62). *See also* Customs taxes
Bronze factory, 278 (nn. 32, 36). *See also* Ben Yijū, Abraham
Buda (shipowner), 146, 277 (nn. 17, 28). See also *Nākhudhā*

Caesarea Maritima, port of, 246 (nn. 1, 3, 5)
Cahen, Claude, 112–13, 132, 137, 265 (n. 13), 271 (n. 66), 293 (n. 17)

Cairo, 7, 17, 18, 20, 25, 29, 102, 148, 159; merchants of, 79, 120, 145, 166, 184, 250 (n. 35), 269 (n. 47); taxation practices in, 113, 122; courts of, 120, 185, 199
Cairo Geniza, 12–13, 15, 18–22, 221 (nn. 55, 59). *See also* Goitein, Shlomo Dov; Judeo-Arabic
Candia (Crete), 247 (n. 14)
Cape Asir (Cape Guardafui), 35
Central place theory, 3, 215 (n. 2)
Ceylon, 155–56, 159, 283 (n. 72), 284 (n. 75)
Chakravarti, Ranabir, 15, 144
Chaudhuri, K. N., 6–7, 11
China, 27, 151, 153, 209; ceramics of, 65, 67, 243 (n. 137)
Christian merchants, 113, 146–47, 152. *See also* ʿAbd al-Masīḥ
Christians, of Najran, 16
Clysma (Kulzum), port of, 70. *See also* Suez
Cohen, Mark, 13, 15, 203, 217 (n. 27), 218 (nn. 29, 32), 220 (nn. 48, 49, 51)
Constable, Remie, 15
Crater (Aden), 44–45, 46, 48, 50–51, 53, 71, 72, 74, 217 (n. 22), 232 (n. 46), 237 (n. 84)
Customshouse, 61, 94–96, 115, 205, 239 (n. 96), 258 (nn. 29, 31), 260 (n. 43); revenues of, 77, 88, 110, 255 (n. 8); procedures of, 111, 114–19; study of practices of, 111–14; officials of, 117, 119–22
Customs taxes, 113–14, 122–26; on imports, 67, 133–34, 135, 229 (n. 30); on exports, 134, 135–36; galley tax, 138–40. *See also* Ships
Al-Daftar al-Muẓaffarī. *See* Muẓaffar register; Rasulids
Dahlak, island port of, 123, 136, 152, 165–68, 211–12, 280–81 (n. 53), 288 (nn. 111–14), 289 (n. 115); customshouse of, 123, 167
Damietta, port of, 112
Dār al-Bandar (Aden), 71, 75, 247 (n. 13)
Dār al-Manẓar (Aden), 92–94, 124, 257 (nn. 25–27)
Dār al-Saʿāda (Aden), 96–98, 99, 192, 259 (n. 33), 260 (nn. 42, 44), 299 (n. 77)
Dār al-Ṭawīla (Aden), 96, 97, 99, 119, 261 (nn. 51, 52)
Dār (al-)wakāla (agency house), 124, 179, 180, 192–94. See also *Wakīl al-tujjār*
David b. Maḍmūn (merchant and communal leader), 183, 202, 204
Dhamār (Yemen), 237 (n. 80). See also *Ṣahārīj*
Dhimmī system, 13, 210, 218 (n. 39), 265 (n. 13)
Dhofar, 61, 63, 65, 244 (n. 139), 282 (n. 65). *See also* Ports
Dhū Jibla (Yemen), 16, 103, 180, 187, 197, 218–19 (n. 41), 263 (nn. 74, 75), 294 (n. 21)
Al-Dibājī. *See* ʿAlī al-Dibājī
Diem, Werner, 15, 218 (n. 30)
Dilāla (*dalāla*). *See* Brokerage; Customs taxes
Dugong, 42, 229 (n. 26)

Egypt, 27–29 passim, 58, 62, 67, 72, 135, 158, 165, 173, 177, 209; taxation practices in, 112–14, 122, 132;

and *kārim*, 152–53; items sent to, 121, 136, 155; courts of, 183, 199, 202, 264 (n. 76)
Egyptian merchants, 57, 97, 153
Elizabeth, N.J., 177
Embeddedness, 13, 15, 182
Epstein, Steven, 68, 158
Ethiopia/Eritrea, 154, 207

Fandarayna, port of, 145, 148, 200, 278 (n. 35), 302 (n. 100)
Fatan Swamī (shipowner), 145, 146, 200,(n. 273–74 (n. 95), 277 (nn. 22, 28). See also *Nākhudhā*
Fatimids, 27, 28, 112–13, 152–53, 225 (n. 87), 246 (n. 6), 272 (n. 76), 292 (n. 14), 299 (n. 76)
Al-Fawfalī (shipowner). *See* ʿAlī al-Fawfalī
Al-Fidiyār (shipowner), 144–46 passim, 275–76 (n. 7). See also *Nākhudhā*
Fish, 41–42, 135, 170, 229 (nn. 25, 27, 30)
Fishing and fishermen, 46, 56, 159, 160, 229 (n. 26), 230 (n. 35), 234 (n. 58), 239 (n. 99), 266–67 (n. 27), 280 (n. 48)
Food crisis, 66–67, 90, 245 (n. 151). *See also* Grains
Food supply. *See* Fish; Grains
Fortifications, 87–94
Friedman, Mordechai, 222 (n. 59)
Funduq, 103–4
Al-Furḍa. *See* Customshouse
Fusṭāṭ (Old Cairo), 18, 202, 256–57 (n. 24), 260 (n. 46), 264 (n. 76), 266 (n. 16), 294 (n. 24)
Geniza, 13, 18, 198–99, 217 (n. 27), 220 (n. 49). *See also* Goitein, Shlomo Dov
Geniza. *See* Cairo Geniza
Genoa, 7, 68, 69, 158
Al-Ghassānī. *See* Al-Mujāhid al-Ghassānī
Glass: production of, 49, 58, 61, 65, 242 (nn. 123, 124); as merchandise, 156–57, 190, 242 (nn. 123, 124), 275–76 (n. 7), 298 (n. 67). *See also* Lakhaba
Goitein, Shlomo Dov, 19–20, 221 (n. 55), 243 (n. 129); and study of navigation and shipping, 38, 145, 152–53, 155, 282 (n. 61); and study of commercial taxation, 112, 122, 137; and study of mercantile representation, 178–79, 296 (n. 40); research archive (S. D. Goitein Laboratory for Geniza Research, Princeton University), 221–22 (n. 59); and Aden, 250 (nn. 33, 35), 252 (nn. 43, 44), 253 (n. 54)
Gosh, Amitav, 15, 304 (n. 128), 305 (nn. 130, 131)
Grains, 63–67 passim, 245 (nn. 150, 151)
Gujarat, 40, 267 (n. 35)
Guo, Li, 198

Al-Ḥabash, 153, 282 (n. 65)
Al-Ḥabashī, Masʿūd (captain), 146, 279 (n. 9). See also *Al-rubbān*
Ḥaḍramawt, region of, 7, 54, 61, 63, 135, 238 (n. 89), 251 (n. 37), 282 (n. 65). *See also* Ports

Ḥalfon b. Maḍmūn (merchant and communal leader), 162, 169, 177, 183, 201–2, 219 (n. 44), 286 (n. 99)
Ḥalfon b. Nathanel (merchant), 66, 90, 189, 195, 250 (n. 35), 271 (n. 60), 294 (n. 22)
Al-Hamdānī, al-Ḥasan b. Aḥmad (historian and geographer), 44, 60, 235 (n. 66), 238 (n. 91), 244 (n. 139)
Harbors. *See* Aden, port of; Anchorage; Ports
Ḥasan b. Bundār (merchant and communal leader), 72; and customshouse, 120; as mercantile representative, 183, 184–86, 197, 277 (n. 27), 278 (n. 32), 293 (n. 20)
Hebrew language and script, 16, 18, 21–22, 62, 243 (n. 132), 284 (n. 83)
Hindu merchants, 147, 160
Ḥuqqāt Bay (Holkat Bay), 46, 73, 233 (n. 51). *See also* Aden, port of; Ports
Al-Ḥusayn b. Salāma (Ziyadid regent), 55
Al-Ḥusaynī, al-Ḥasan b. ʿAlī al-Sharīf, 25. See also *Mulakhkhaṣ al-fiṭan*

Ibn Abī al-Katā'ib, Abū al-Ḥasan (shipowner), 147, 149, 151, 181. See also *Nākhudhā*
Ibn ʿAwkal, Joseph (merchant), 198, 261 (n. 48), 302–3 (n. 105)
Ibn Baṭṭūṭa (traveler), 48, 49, 51, 239 (n. 99)
Ibn Faqīh (geographer), 228 (n. 20)
Ibn Jubayr (traveler), 123, 126
Ibn Khaldūn (historian), 102, 225 (n. 87), 229 (n. 25), 244 (n. 142)
Ibn Mājid (navigational theorist), 39, 40, 43, 78, 227 (n. 13), 228 (n. 20), 230 (n. 34), 280 (n. 48), 290 (n. 127)
Ibn al-Mujāwir (traveler), 2, 19, 22–23, 27, 82, 222 (nn. 64, 65), 250 (nn. 33, 34); on Aden's environment and environs, 34, 42–65 passim, 159; on taxation practices, 41, 110–12 passim, 114–19, 122–38 passim, 173; on Aden's harbor topography, 72–73, 76–77, 81–83; on Aden's urban topography, 88–100 passim, 102, 103, 104–5
India: maritime connections of, 39–41, 115, 165, 177; Geniza merchants' commerce in, 120–21, 135; merchants of, 157–58, 160
India Book, 18–22, 221–22 (n. 59). *See also* Goitein, Shlomo Dov
Indian Ocean: study of, 9, 11, 12, 15, 91; seasons of, 38–41; harbors of, 70; boatbuilding tradition of, 154, 161, 254 (n. 58), 285–86 (n. 94)
India trade, 2, 13, 21, 38, 215 (n. 1)
Islamic cities, 8, 216 (nn. 9–12)

Jabal al-Akhḍar (Aden peak), 44, 115. *See also* Al-Khaḍrā'
Jabal al-Manẓar (Aden peak), 92–93, 256 (n. 24), 257 (n. 25)
Jabal Ḥuqqāt (Aden peak), 89, 92–93, 256 (n. 24), 257 (n. 25)
Jabal ʿUrr (Aden peak), 44, 92, 232 (n. 44), 238 (n. 94)

Jackfruit tree (shipbuilding timber), 59–60, 241 (n. 118), 286 (n. 98)
Al-Jāḥiẓ (writer), 193
Jeddah, port of, 38, 51, 110, 236 (n. 75)
Jekuthiel Abū Yaʿqūb al-Ḥakīm (merchant), 19, 120, 182, 184–85, 191, 196, 288 (n. 112), 293 (n. 20), 295 (n. 31), 299 (n. 74), 301 (n. 93). *See also* Joseph al-Lebdī
Jewish merchants, 13, 19, 22, 113; and commercial disputes, 184–88, 196–97, 203–5
Joseph al-Lebdī (merchant), 19, 72, 120, 184–86, 196, 197. *See also* Ḥasan b. Bundār
Joseph b. Abraham b. Bundār (Adeni shipowner), 145, 147, 148, 276 (n. 16); letters of, 116, 159, 165, 227 (n. 17); as mercantile representative, 180, 188, 191, 276 (n. 9), 278 (n. 36), 302 (n. 100); and dispute, 204–5
Judeo-Arabic, 13–15, 21–22. *See also* Cairo Geniza; Cohen, Mark; Goitein, Shlomo Dov
Julfār, port of, 7

Kāfūr (shipowner), 142, 143. See also *Nākhudhā*
Kārdār (Indian merchant and/or official), 204–5, 304 (n. 126), 305 (n. 130). *See also* Ben Yijū, Abraham
Kārim, 152–53, 281 (nn. 54, 55), 282 (nn. 61, 62), 287 (n. 102)
Kawd Amsayla (Aden environs), 61, 242 (n. 124)
Al-Khaḍrā' (Aden fort and mountain), 28, 77, 83, 89–90, 92, 94, 115
Khalaf b. Isaac (Isḥāq) (merchant), 66, 149, 156; and naval blockade, 79–81, 83; on Adeni politics, 90–91, 100, 196; and salvage operation, 173–75, 193; as mercantile representative, 180, 188–89, 191, 195, 200; and *kārdār*, 204–5
Khalilieh, Hassan, 15
Kilwa, 7, 10, 215–16 (n. 7)
Kish (Persian/Arabian Gulf island). *See* Qays
Konkan coast (India), 157, 171, 289 (n. 124)
Kūlam, port of, 169–71

Laḥj, 49, 57, 59, 63–64, 235 (n. 66), 237 (n. 85), 240 (n. 105), 243 (n. 137), 244 (nn. 139, 140)
Lakhaba (Aden environs), 60–63, 91, 237 (nn. 85, 86), 238 (n. 88), 239 (n. 94), 241 (n. 121), 245 (n. 148). *See also* Glass; Kawd Amsayla
Lamu Archipelago, 7, 70, 91, 247 (n. 10), 256 (n. 22). *See also* Manda, port of; Ports; Shanga, port of
Lateen sails, 81, 252–53 (n. 51)
Al-Lebdī. *See* Joseph al-Lebdī
Lighterage, 69, 254 (n. 58). *See also* Boats; *Ṣanbūq*
Ludovico di Varthema, 87, 117, 207, 247 (n. 12), 248 (n. 19)

Al-Maʿalla' (Aden environs), 47, 56, 57, 239 (nn. 95, 96, 98), 240 (n. 101)

Al-Mabāh (Aden environs), 44, 56–58, 161, 230 (n. 31), 238 (nn. 88, 94), 239 (n. 95)
Maḍmūn b. David (communal leader), 93
Maḍmūn b. Japheth (Ḥasan) b. Bundār (merchant and communal leader), 39, 183–84; family of, 17, 219 (n. 44); and customs administration, 97, 112, 120–22; and ships and shipbuilding, 144–50 passim, 155–57, 159, 162; as *wakīl al-tujjār*, 179, 180, 187–93 passim, 197, 200–201, 203
Al-Mafālīs (Yemen), 54, 55, 238 (nn. 88, 94)
Maḥrūz b. Jacob (shipowner), 145, 147, 148, 175, 276 (n. 15), 281 (n. 57), 283 (n. 70); and Tinbū, 157–58, 284 (n. 81). See also *Nākhudhā*
Maimonides, Abraham, 202, 300 (n. 80)
Maimonides, David, 14, 288 (n. 14)
Maimonides, Moses, 14, 219 (n. 42), 269–70 (n. 53), 288 (n. 14), 300 (n. 80)
Main Pass (landward pass or "gate"), 45, 89, 92, 102, 232 (n. 48), 239 (n. 94). See also *Bāb al-barr*; Crater
Al-Maʿjalayn (Aden channel), 73, 248 (n. 18)
Al-Makhzūmī, Abū al-Ḥasan ʿAlī b. ʿUthmān (administrative writer), 112–13, 125, 137, 180
Al-Maksar (Aden land bridge, isthmus), 43–44, 53, 56, 58, 59, 89, 159, 231 (n. 39)
Malabar, 40, 121, 185
Manda, port of, 7, 9, 70, 91, 216 (nn. 7, 13, 14), 247 (n. 10), 256 (n. 22)
Mangalore, port of, 157, 160, 302 (n. 100), 305 (n. 130)
Al-Manẓar. *See* Dār al-Manẓar
Mawāsim, 38–39, 41. *See also* Monsoons; Sailing times
Al-Mazaff. *See* Al-Maksar
Mecca, 55, 144, 148, 207, 238 (nn. 90, 91), 276 (n. 14)
Mediterranean, 2, 95; study of, 6, 19, 20, 69–70; and sailing seasons, 38, 39–40; and taxation practices, 113–14, 121–22, 132–33; and shipping practices, 145, 155, 156, 158, 174
Merchants' residences, 10–11, 100–102, 192–93, 209, 262 (n. 64), 300 (n. 79)
Mevorakh (*nagid*), 185–86, 188, 297 (nn. 46, 48)
Miḥlaja (cotton gin), 57–58. *See also* Textiles
Al-Mimlāḥ (saltworks, Aden environs), 42, 230 (n. 31), 238 (n. 88)
Monsoons, 38–41, 75, 78, 81, 228 (nn. 20, 22, 23). See also *Azyab*; *Mawāsim*; Sailing times
Muḥammad b. Abī al-Ghārāt (Zurayid ruler), 77, 235 (n. 64), 250 (n. 33)
Muḥayriz, ʿAbdallāh b. Aḥmad, 50, 215 (n. 3), 217 (n. 23), 235 (nn. 66, 70), 239 (n. 95)
Al-Muʿizz Ismāʿīl (Ayyubid ruler), 93, 124, 153, 219 (n. 42), 258 (n. 27), 269 (n. 53)

Al-Mujāhid al-Ghassānī (Rasulid sultan), 97, 260 (n. 41)
Al-mukallā. *See* Aden, port of
Al-Mukallā, port of, 55, 244 (n. 139), 251 (n. 37)
Al-Mukhā, 9, 10–11, 96, 102, 103, 198, 209, 262 (n. 66), 263 (n. 73), 299 (n. 75)
Mulakhkhaṣ al-fiṭan (Rasulid administrative document), 25, 110, 111, 117, 223 (n. 73), 261 (n. 53), 265 (n. 7), 267 (n. 33). *See also* Rasulids
Al-Muqaddasī (geographer), 27, 45, 48, 51, 88, 94, 104, 236 (n. 75), 290 (n. 127)
Muslim merchants, 21, 22, 113–14, 134, 277 (n. 18)
Al-Muẓaffar, Yūsuf b. ʿUmar b. ʿAlī b. Rasūl (Rasulid sultan), 24, 142, 257–58 (n. 27), 273 (n. 89), 274 (n. 2)
Muẓaffar register (Rasulid administrative document), 24, 57, 111, 116, 134, 223 (n. 68), 270 (n. 57), 282 (n. 62), 293 (n. 19). *See also* Rasulids

Nagid (head of Jews), 183–88, 192–93, 200, 201, 234–35 (n. 63), 260 (n. 42), 295–96 (n. 37), 297 (n. 48). *See also* Maḍmūn b. Japheth b. Bundār; Mevorakh
Nahray b. Nissīm, 146, 156, 198, 296 (n. 40), 297 (n. 46)
Nākhudhā (master of ship), 143–45, 150, 251 (n. 42), 254–55 (n. 2), 274 (n. 1), 275 (n. 6), 276 (nn. 8, 14), 280 (n. 48)
Naval blockade, 19, 76–83, 91, 121, 163, 249 (n. 24), 259 (n. 33), 285 (n. 89), 287 (n. 104)
Navigational works, 39, 226 (nn. 7, 8), 227 (n. 13), 228 (n. 23). *See also* Ibn Mājid
Nizāla, African port of, 136. *See* Ports: East African
Nūra (fat-and-lime compound), 56–57, 161, 240 (n. 100)
Nūr al-maʿārif. *See* Muẓaffar register

Oman, 10, 55, 285 (n. 85); Gulf of Oman, 35
Ottomans, 23, 24, 56, 59, 164, 238–39 (n. 94), 283 (n. 66); and India trade, 215 (n. 1); capture of Aden, 231 (n. 42), 248 (n. 22)

Packing, 136, 178, 189–90, 194, 298 (nn. 64, 67, 68), 299 (nn. 69–72)
Peqid ha-soharim. See *Wakīl al-tujjār*
Periplus Maris Erythraei (Greek merchant's manual), 27, 40, 46, 164, 224 (n. 82), 233 (n. 50), 234 (n. 60)
Persian/Arabian Gulf (*baḥr fāris*), 7, 19, 70, 77, 78, 226 (n. 3), 228 (n. 20), 256 (n. 21), 285 (n. 89). *See also* Qays
Persians: as early settlers at Aden, 27, 43, 49, 105; as merchants and shipowners, 144, 146. *See also* Bakhtiyār; Al-Qummī; Rāmisht
Piracy and pirates, 35, 37, 138–39, 142, 157, 164, 168, 274 (n. 96), 288 (n. 106), 289 (n. 119)
Ports: study of, 6–11, 69–70, 158, 211–12; East African, 7, 9, 10, 135;

Red Sea, 10, 38, 123, 151; Arabian, 51, 69, 94; Hadrami, 54, 212, 216 (n. 9), 229 (n. 30); Dhofari, 54, 238 (n. 89); and harbors, 69–70; Egyptian, 125; Indian, 288 (n. 110). *See also* Indian Ocean
Portuguese, 23, 25, 56, 161, 164, 189, 283 (n. 66), 285–86 (n. 94); and sieges of Aden, 87, 247 (n. 13), 248 (n. 20)
Prados, Edward, 74, 76, 78, 83, 217 (n. 23), 248 (n. 22), 249 (n. 28)

Al-Qamr, 153–54, 282–83 (n. 65)
Al-Qaṣṣ, port of, 166–67, 288 (n. 110)
Qays (Persian/Arabian Gulf island), 70, 77, 165, 247 (n. 11), 249 (n. 30), 270 (n. 59), 279 (n. 39); and naval siege, 76–83, 91, 139, 163, 164, 287 (n. 104)
Qayṣarīya (closed market), 98–99
Quḍaḍ (waterproofing compound), 51, 236 (n. 78). See also *Ṣahārīj*
Quillon. *See* Kūlam, port of
Al-Qummī (shipowner), 146, 277 (n. 27). See also *Nākhudhā*
Qunbār (coconut husk twine), 160–61, 285 (n. 85), 286 (n. 96). *See also* Shipbuilding
Quṣayr al-Qadīm, 7, 21, 143, 198–99, 246 (n. 3), 275 (n. 5)

Rabie, Hassanein, 15
Rāmisht (shipowner): and naval siege, 79, 81, 140, 164; as merchant and shipper, 144–45, 146–51 passim, 155, 251 (n. 42), 279 (n. 39). See also *Nākhudhā*
Rasulids, 23–24, 26, 29, 208–9, 223 (n. 74), 264 (n. 2); and urban development of Aden, 52, 97, 99, 257–58 (n. 27); and taxation practices, 64, 112, 125, 126, 132; and naval power, 138, 210, 273 (n. 89); and commerce, 145, 153, 260 (n. 41), 261 (n. 53). See also *Mulakhkhaṣ al-fiṭan*; Muẓaffar register
Red Sea, 27, 35, 226 (n. 7); sailing times, 40, 195; shippers of, 115, 143, 151–53, 166–67. *See also* Ports
Rimbaud, Arthur, 34, 47, 225 (n. 2), 248–49 (n. 22)
Rubāk (Aden environs), 52, 58–60, 162, 237 (n. 85), 241 (n. 115), 286 (n. 98)
Al-rubbān (captain), 144, 146, 150, 280 (n. 48)

Saba' b. Abī al-Suʿūd (Zurayid ruler), 28, 77, 89–90, 92, 235 (n. 64), 250 (nn. 33, 34), 256 (n. 19)
Ṣahārīj (cisterns), 50–52, 217 (n. 23), 235 (nn. 69–71), 236 (nn. 72–76). *See also* Water
Sailing seasons. See *Mawāsim*; Monsoons
Sailing times (*al-safar*), 39, 227 (nn. 15–17)
Salt, 42, 229 (n. 29), 230 (n. 33)
Sanaa, 13, 16, 55, 217 (n. 27), 238 (n. 91), 244 (n. 139)
Ṣanbūq (small boat), 117, 159, 254 (n. 58)
Satmī (ship's register), 118, 275 (n. 6), 276 (n. 19)

Shaffāra. *See* Ships
Shanga, port of, 7, 10, 216 (nn. 8, 16), 229 (n. 26)
Sharma, port of, 9, 216 (nn. 9, 14)
Shawānī. *See* Customs taxes; Ships
Shaykh ʿUthmān, 42, 59, 231 (n. 36), 235 (n. 65)
Shibām (Ḥaḍramawt), 54, 64, 238 (n. 89), 244 (n. 139)
Al-Shiḥr, port of, 55, 110, 135, 153, 162, 170–71, 212, 229 (n. 30), 244 (n. 139), 282 (n. 65)
Shipbuilding, 56–58, 59–60, 153–54, 158–62, 254 (n. 58), 285–86 (n. 94). *See also* Jackfruit tree; *Nūra*; *Qunbār*; Teak
Ships: *shawānī*, 124, 138; *shaffārāt*, 139, 163–64, 273–74 (nn. 92–96), 287 (n. 103); types of, 153–54, 158, 159, 163; *jāshujīyāt*, 159, 163, 165, 285 (n. 89); *dawānīj*, 163, 287 (n. 103); *burmāt*, 163, 287 (n. 104). *See also* Boats
Shipwreck and salvage, 37, 169–75, 177, 200–203, 226 (n. 6), 280–81 (n. 53), 286–87 (n. 99), 287–88 (n. 105), 288–89 (n. 114)
Al-shiṣna (breakwater), 75–76, 78–79, 82, 83–84, 247 (n. 13), 249 (n. 28)
Shuqrā, port of, 55
Ṣīra Bay (Front Bay), 46, 57, 83–84; as Aden's main harbor, 46, 72–75, 248 (n. 19). *See also* Aden, port of: Aden peninsula; Anchorage; Prados, Edward
Sīrāf, port of, 7, 70, 91, 229 (n. 26), 246 (n. 9), 279 (n. 39); and water supply, 9, 51–52; topography of, 10, 99–100, 101, 104–5, 256 (n. 22)
Ṣīra Island, 46, 72–76 passim, 89, 247 (n. 13), 257 (nn. 24, 25); and breakwater, 76, 78, 79, 80; and naval siege, 80–83 passim, 252 (nn. 48, 49), 253 (nn. 54, 56)
Smith, G. Rex, 111, 136, 222 (n. 64), 223 (n. 73)
Socotra, 43, 230 (n. 34)
Spain, 13, 182
Sri Lanka. *See* Ceylon
Storerooms and storage, 100, 185, 189, 193, 194–96, 198
Suez, 70, 161
Ṣuḥār, port of, 7, 9, 10, 70, 215 (n. 7), 216 (nn. 13, 14, 16), 246 (n. 9)
Sulayhids, 16, 28–29, 89, 110, 254 (n. 1)
Suwākin, port of, 136, 152, 281 (n. 53), 282 (n. 61), 289 (n. 114)

Tahirids, 208, 236 (n. 78); and urban development of Aden, 71, 75, 261 (n. 51)
Taʿizz, 54, 55, 110
Al-Taʿkar (Aden fort), 28, 77, 83, 89, 92, 232 (n. 47), 255 (nn. 14, 15)
Tāna, Indian port of, 147, 157, 278 (n. 34), 284 (n. 80)
Taʾrīkh al-mustabṣir. *See* Ibn al-Mujāwir
Taʾrīkh thaghr ʿadan. *See* Abū Makhrama, Abū Muḥammad al-Ṭayyib b. ʿAbdallāh
Al-Tawāhī (Aden district), 47
Ṭawīla Tanks. See *Ṣahārīj*

Teak, 162, 285 (n. 93), 286 (n. 97). *See also* Shipbuilding
Teredo (marine borer), 161
Textiles, 57–58, 119, 240 (nn. 105, 106, 108), 241 (n. 110), 245 (n. 148), 267–68 (n. 37), 272 (n. 77)
Tihāma, 7, 54, 55, 245 (nn. 148, 150)
Al-Tilimsānī, ʿAbdallāh b. Yūsuf (Ayyubid official), 44, 64
Tinbū (shipowner), 146, 147, 157–58, 277 (n. 28). See also *Nākhudhā*
Al-Tīz, port of, 123, 269 (n. 51)
Tobi, Yosef, 16, 218 (n. 39)
Ṭughtakīn b. Ayyūb (Ayyubid ruler), 29, 93, 96, 138, 260 (nn. 38, 41)
Tūrānshāh Shams al-Dawla b. Ayyūb (Ayyubid ruler), 28, 29, 138, 225 (n. 86), 257 (n. 26)

Udovitch, Abraham, 15, 156, 179, 210, 215 (n. 6), 295 (n. 27), 302 (n. 99)
Um, Nancy, 10–11, 102, 217 (n. 19), 299 (n. 75)
ʿUmāra al-Ḥakamī (historian), 28, 89, 110, 218–19 (n. 41), 225 (nn. 87, 88), 237 (n. 85), 250 (n. 34)

Varisco, Daniel, 223 (nn. 74, 76)
Varthema. *See* Ludovico di Varthema
Venice, 7, 224 (n. 80)
Von Grunebaum, Gustave, 8, 216 (n. 11)

Wakāla tax, 124–25, 180, 192, 270 (n. 57). *See also* Customs taxes
Wakīl al-tujjār (representative of merchants): term and institution, 178–81, 210–11; in Aden, 181–88; services rendered by, 188–91, 194–98, 199; base of, 191–94
Water: scarcity of, 9, 34–35, 47–48; water supply, 49–53, 231 (n. 36), 241 (n. 113). See also *Ṣahārīj*; Wells
Wells, 48–49, 53, 59–63 passim, 235 (n. 66)
Women, 17, 205, 243 (n. 133), 305 (n. 130). *See also* Arwā

Yāqūt b. ʿAbdallāh al-Ḥamawī (geographer), 249–50 (n. 31)
Yemen, 2, 7, 27, 57, 94, 184, 237 (n. 85), 247 (n. 12); highlands of, 10; study of medieval period of, 13, 25; Jews of, 15–16, 19, 124, 182; and dynastic history, 24, 26, 28–29, 248 (n. 22); architecture of, 51–52, 101, 236 (n. 78), 237 (n. 85), 256 (n. 21), 257–58 (n. 27), 262–63 (n. 68)
Yeshūʿā b. Jacob (merchant), 180, 263 (n. 74), 293–94 (n. 21)

Zabīd (Yemen), 44, 53, 57, 59, 110, 219 (n. 17); Ben Yijū at, 116, 180, 294 (n. 21); Aden connection to ports of, 151, 165, 168, 227 (n. 17), 280 (n. 52)
Ẓafar, 110, 229 (n. 27). *See also* Dhofar
Zanj (East Africa), 153, 282 (n. 65)

Al-Zanjabīlī, Abū ʿAmr ʿUthmān b. ʿAlī, 61, 91–92, 95, 256 (n. 23)
Zarūka (small vessel), 159, 285 (n. 90). *See also* Boats
Zaylaʿ, port of, 49, 50, 51, 241 (n. 113)
Ziyadids. *See* Al-Ḥusayn b. Salāma
Zurayids, 2, 10, 27–29, 63, 77, 201; and urban development, 47, 65, 87–91, 92–93, 207, 254 (n. 1); and harbor development, 71; and taxation practices, 95, 110, 114, 118, 120, 122, 126; and galleys, 138–39, 163–64

Roxani Eleni Margariti, *Aden and the Indian Ocean Trade: 150 Years in the Life of a Medieval Arabian Port* (2007).

Sufia M. Uddin, *Constructing Bangladesh: Religion, Ethnicity, and Language in an Islamic Nation* (2006).

Omid Safi, *The Politics of Knowledge in Premodern Islam: Negotiating Ideology and Religious Inquiry* (2006).

Ebrahim Moosa, *Ghazālī and the Poetics of Imagination* (2005).

miriam cooke and Bruce B. Lawrence, eds., *Muslim Networks from Hajj to Hip Hop* (2005).

Carl W. Ernst, *Following Muhammad: Rethinking Islam in the Contemporary World* (2003).

www.ingramcontent.com/pod-product-compliance
Lightning Source LLC
Chambersburg PA
CBHW021340300426
44114CB00012B/1018
* 9 7 8 1 4 6 9 6 1 4 9 2 2 *